International Handbook on the Continuing Professional Development of Teachers

International Handbook on the Continuing Professional Development of Teachers

Edited by
Christopher Day and Judyth Sachs

Open University Press

Open University Press
McGraw-Hill Education
McGraw-Hill House
Shoppenhangers Road
Maidenhead
Berkshire
England
SL6 2QL

email: enquiries@openup.co.uk
world wide web: www.openup.co.uk

First published 2004

A catalogue record of this book is available from the British Library

ISBN 0 335 20974 2

Library of Congress Cataloging-in-Publication Data
CIP data has been applied for

Typeset by RefineCatch Limited, Bungay, Suffolk
Printed in the UK by Bell & Bain Ltd, Glasgow

Contents

The editors and contributors

Beatrice Avalos was until its conclusion in 2002 the National Coordinator for the Programme to Improve Initial Teacher Education of the Chilean Ministry of Education. Currently she teaches in master programmes on public policy in the University of Playa Ancha and Alberto Hurtado in Chile and works as an independent consultant. Previously she taught at the University of Wales, Cardiff, and the University of Papua New Guinea. She is the author of *Profesores para Chile: Historia de un Proyecto* (Santiago, Mineduc, 2002) and has contributed to a number of journals and books on issues related to teacher education.

Ray Bolam was Professor of Education in the School of Social Science at Cardiff University from 1994 to 2002, where he was Head of the School of Education (1996–99) and Director of the National Professional Qualification for Headteachers (NPQH) Centre for Wales. From 1992 to 1994 he was Professor of Education at the University of Swansea and, prior to that, Senior Research Fellow at the University of Bristol, where he was Director of the government-funded National Development Centre (NDC) for School Management Training from 1983 to 1990. His research and publications have focused on school leadership, professional development, school improvement and the management of change. He is currently co-directing a nationally funded study which is investigating how to create and sustain effective professional learning communities in schools. He has acted as consultant to UNESCO, the OECD, the British Council, the European Commission and to governments and national and international agencies in Africa, Asia, Australia, Europe and North America.

Pam Christie is an Associate Professor at the University of Queensland, Australia, and visiting professor at the University of the Witwatersrand, South Africa. Her current research interests are in the areas of leadership and school change, and globalization and education. She has worked extensively on education policy development and change in South Africa, and has published in the areas of sociology of education, education policy, comparative education and school desegregation.

Marion Dadds is Professor of Education at St Martin's College, Lancaster. She has engaged in practitioner research for over 20 years, pursuing her own and supporting the research of others. She has developed a particular interest in the emotional dimensions of doing practitioner research. Previous publications include *Passionate Enquiry and School Development* (Falmer Press 1995) and *Doing Practitioner Research Differently*, with Susan Hart (Routledge-Falmer 2001).

Christopher Day is Professor of Education and Co-director of the Centre for Research on Teacher and School Development at the School of Education, University of Nottingham. He has worked as a schoolteacher, teacher educator and local authority adviser. He has extensive research and consultancy experience in England, Europe, Australia, South East Asia and North America in the fields of teachers' continuing professional development, action research, leadership and change. He is editor of *Teachers and Teaching: Theory and Practice*, and co-editor of *Educational Action Research*. He is a board member of the International Council for Teacher Education (ICET). In addition to *Leading Schools in Times of Change* (Open University Press 2000), recent publications include *The Life and Work of Teachers: International Perspectives in Changing Times* (co-editor and contributor) (Falmer Press 2000), *Educational Research in Europe: Yearbook 2000* (co-editor) (Leuven-Apeldoorn Garant 2000), *Developing Teachers: Challenges of Lifelong Learning* (Falmer Press 1999) and *A Passion for Teaching* (Routledge-Falmer 2004).

John Elliott is Professor of Education at the Centre for Applied Research in Education, which he directed from 1996 to 1999. He is well known internationally for his role in developing the theory and practice of action research in the contexts of curriculum and teacher development, and has directed a number of funded collaborative classroom research projects with teachers and schools. These include the Ford Teaching Project (1972–74) and, more recently, the TTA-funded Norwich Area Schools Consortium (NASC) on the 'curriculum and pedagogical dimensions of student disaffection' (1997–2001). He is currently an Advisory Professor to the Hong Kong Institute of Education and a consultant to the Hong Kong government on the strategic development of its curriculum reform proposals. In 2000, he was appointed a local council member of the Norfolk Learning & Skills Council.

Susan Groundwater-Smith is the Co-director for the Centre for Practitioner Research, Faculty of Education and Social Work at the University of Sydney. She is also Adjunct Professor of Education at the University of Western Sydney. Since the 1970s she has been involved in practitioner inquiry, including sustained research into her own practice. She has worked extensively with individual teachers, whole schools and education systems to build valid and authentic processes to enhance learning for students, teachers and policy makers in education.

Shirley Grundy is Professor and Dean of the Faculty of Education at Deakin University in Victoria, Australia. She has held positions as a teacher-educator at Murdoch University in Western Australia and the University of New England in New South Wales. Maintaining partnerships with the schooling sector and with teachers has been a strong feature of her work. From 1994 to 1996 she was the Joint National Coordinator of the National Professional Development programme, Innovative Links. For the period 1998–2000 she held the position of District Director of Education in the Warren-Blackwood District in the rural south-west of Western Australia. She is widely published across the areas of curriculum studies, educational policy and administration and qualitative research methodology. Her work in the area of action research is internationally recognized.

Ken Harley is a Professor in the School of Education at the University of Natal, Pietermaritzburg, South Africa, where he has recently completed a cycle of headship. His research interests and publications are in the fields of curriculum, teacher development, research methods and evaluation. In the recent past he has conducted evaluations of donor-funded teacher development projects in East Africa and South Africa. He edits the *Journal of Education*.

Alma Harris is Professor of School Leadership and Director of the Leadership, Policy and Improvement Unit at the Institute of Education, University of Warwick. She has published extensively on the theme of leadership and school improvement and her latest books include *School Improvement: What's in it for Schools?* (Routledge-Falmer 2002), *Leading the Improving Department* (David Fulton 2002) and *School Effectiveness and School Improvement: Alternative Perspectives* (with Bennett, Cassell 2001). Her most recent research work has focused on effective leadership in schools facing challenging circumstances and the relationship between teacher leadership and school improvement. She is currently working with the National College for School Leadership in a research and development capacity.

Geert Kelchtermans is a Professor at the Centre of Educational Policy and Innovation, University of Leuven, Belgium. His key research interests are teachers' work lives and professional development, micro-politics in schools, educational policy and narrative-biographical research.

Geoff Lindsay is Professor of Special Educational Needs and Educational Psychology at the University of Warwick, where he is also Director of the Centre for Educational Development, Appraisal and Research (CEDAR). He was previously Principal Educational Psychologist for Sheffield LEA. He is currently undertaking several research projects, including the evaluation of electronic registration systems in secondary schools; the impact and evaluation of CPD; educational provision for children with specific speech and language difficulties; and underachievement in boys. Recent books include *Researching Children's Perspectives* (edited with Ann Lewis) (Open University Press 2000).

Agnes McMahon is a Senior Lecturer in the University of Bristol Graduate School of Education, specializing in the field of educational management and policy. Her research and publications focus on the continuing professional development of teachers, school improvement and school effectiveness. She has undertaken research projects with colleagues on management development for headteachers and senior staff, teacher appraisal, headteacher mentoring and effective school management. More recently she has researched secondary school teachers' perceptions of continuing professional development and is currently co-director of a nationally funded study which is investigating how to create and sustain effective professional learning communities in schools.

Daniel Muijs is a Research Fellow at CEDAR and a lecturer in quantitative research methods at Warwick University's Institute of Education. His research interests are school effectiveness and school improvement, teacher effectiveness, leadership and research methods.

Alan Penny was Senior Education Advisor for the UK Department for International Development (DIFD) in Eastern Africa (Uganda, Tanzania and Kenya). Prior to this he followed an academic career, and was Professor of Education at Rhodes University and the University of Natal (South Africa), and at King Alfred's University College (UK). He has worked in international development in West Africa, the Middle East (Palestine) and Asia. He is currently head of the European Commission's Education Programme Office in New Delhi, India. His primary research interest is in the area of teacher and whole-school development.

Judith Robison is a Senior Lecturer in the School of Education at Murdoch University where she lectures pre-service teachers in contemporary issues affecting the teaching profession and in the society and environment learning area. A focus for Judith's work has been her engagement in various professional development programmes for experienced teachers, beginning in 1994 with the Innovative Links project. Since then she has been the Project Director for federally funded projects in history, Asian studies and citizenship education and has been a principal consultant for projects involving the Department of Education, the Catholic Education Office and the Independent Schools Association in Western Australia.

Judyth Sachs is Professor of Education in the Faculty of Education and Social Work at the University of Sydney. She is a past President of the Australian Association for Research in Education and Fellow of the Australian College of Education. Her research interests lie in the areas of teacher professional development, teacher professionalism and women in leadership. Her most recent publication is *The Activist Teaching Profession* (2003), Open University Press.

Ciaran Sugrue is Director of Postgraduate Studies in Education at St Patrick's College, Dublin City University. He is general editor of the journal *Irish Educational Studies* and a member of the editorial boards of several international journals. His research interests include educational leadership, continuing professional development, educational change, teacher educational reform in developing countries, qualitative methods in educational research, curriculum reform and policy analysis. His more recent publications include (with Christopher Day) *Developing Teachers and Teaching Practice: International Research Perspectives* (Routledge-Falmer 2002) and (with Catherine Furlong) 'The cosmologies of Irish primary principals' identities: between the modern and the postmodern?', *International Journal of Leadership in Education*, 5(3): 189–210.

David Tripp is an Associate Professor at Murdoch University in Western Australia, and an Honorary Research Fellow at the University of Exeter. He specializes in action learning processes in learning organizations, programme evaluation and qualitative research methods. He has pioneered a journal-writing and critical incident approach to reflective practice, and his book on the method (Routledge 1993) is a widely used text. He has recently completed two years as a Senior Fellow in Policy and Management Studies at the National Institute of Education, Singapore, where he has been working mainly with school managers and various action research programmes including the Teachers' Network.

Judith Warren Little is Professor at the Graduate School of Education, University of California, Berkeley. Her research focuses on teachers' work and careers, the contexts of teaching, and policies and practices of professional development. Her earliest work established the importance of norms of collegiality and experimentation for schools' capacity for change. In subsequent research she has investigated teachers' professional community and its relationship to teacher development and school reform. She has co-edited two books and published numerous papers in the areas of teachers' work, school reform, teacher policy and leadership, and is a member of the National Academy of Education.

Foreword

Views of professional development for teachers vary widely. Some see it as everything that a learning experience should not be. It is brief and rarely sustained, deficit oriented, radically under-resourced, politically imposed rather than professionally owned, lacking in intellectual rigour or coherence, treated as an add-on rather than as part of a natural process and trapped in the constraints of a bureaucratic system that poses barriers to even modest levels of success. In short, it is an ill-designed, pedagogically naïve, demeaning exercise that often leaves participants more cynical and no more knowledgeable, skilled or committed than before.

Others, however, see professional development for teachers very differently. Although they recognize that what passes for professional development in many contexts may be naïve and uninspiring, in other contexts it is an essential intellectual and emotional endeavour that rests at the heart of dedicated efforts to improve the quality of education. In these contexts professional development for teachers uses our best knowledge about pedagogy, about professional renewal and growth, about individual commitment and about organizational life and change. It enhances the preparation of new teachers, renews the professional skills and enthusiasm of classroom veterans, even those who may feel disenchanted or disenfranchised, and improves the professional expertise, self-confidence and commitment of all. Amazingly, readers will find descriptions of professional development similar to both of these perspectives included in this handbook.

As editors, Christopher Day and Judyth Sachs have done a remarkable job of pulling together an outstanding collection of essays on professional development that reflect its stunning diversity in different regions around the world. They have done for readers what no one else has accomplished in nearly a quarter of a century: combined in a single volume a clear and concise description of professional development's past, present and projected future, internationally.

Readers are likely to have several reactions to these collected essays. Some will be discouraged by the many conflicts presented. Should professional development be about nurturing inquiry, self-reflection and individual professional identity, for example, or should it focus on compliance and conformity to specified reform agendas? Will improvements more likely arise from deepening teachers' understanding of how children learn or from clarifying expectations, defining standards, specifying practice and exercising sanctions?

Should professional development provide opportunities for individual, autonomous growth based upon where teachers are in their personal lives and professional careers, or should it focus on collaborative work, shared responsibilities and the development of cohesive learning communities? Can professional development of any form provide teachers with the time, skills, knowledge, commitment and emotional energy needed to do the complex planning and implement the new practices required of them as agents of change?

Other readers will be distressed by the complicated nature of the issues involved and the lack of consistency in the authors' responses to them. All the research described, for example, points to the complexity of teacher professional development, which mirrors the complexity of the purposes and practices of teaching. But the research different authors cite draws from different philosophical perspectives and different theoretical disciplines. As a result, it leads to different and sometimes competing understandings. Several authors argue that the purpose of professional development is to deepen teachers' knowledge, strengthen individual practice and build collective capacity for improvement of teaching and learning at the school level in order to build cultures of inquiry. Others suggest that professional development is a political process used by governments to align the curriculum in order to achieve broader political agendas, particularly with regard to standards implementation and external accountability. Huge differences in educational needs and agendas among the developed and underdeveloped countries of the world, the economic 'haves' and 'have nots', complicate matters still further.

In the midst of this controversy and conflict, however, readers will be deeply impressed by the keen insights of the authors, the diversity of perspectives on improvement and the creativity and breadth of the proposed solutions. They will see that professional development for teachers is not about particular forms of activity but rather about a range of activities – formal and informal – that meet the thinking, feeling, acting, context and change purposes of teachers over the span of their careers. They will recognize that teachers in different phases of their career and working in different contexts have professional development needs that may be distinctly different from those of teachers in other phases, in different contexts and at different times. And as Day and Sachs remind us, they will appreciate that 'it is not only the variety and range of activities, the promotion of schools as learning communities, or even the acknowledgement that teachers need time to learn over the whole course of their careers that will move professional development forward as a real and accepted part of every school and every teacher's learning and change agendas'. They will understand that to make significant progress, governments, policy makers, strategists, researchers, professional associates, teachers and parents all need to engage in an ongoing dialogue about what kind of teachers are needed as we progress in the twenty-first century.

This is not a book that can be read lightly. The ideas and arguments set forth are too provocative and too complex to be skimmed. They require thoughtful analysis and careful probing. Readers should come to it prepared to argue with the authors, to contest their interpretations and to suggest alternative perspectives. But they also must come with an open mind, ready to have their assumptions questioned, their ideas tested and their understandings challenged.

Yet regardless of what they bring to the book, it will affect readers in two important ways. First, they will see that there remains a considerable gap in our knowledge of the effects of professional development, in all its forms, on the thinking, planning and practices of individual teachers, on schools as learning organizations and on the learning outcomes of students. But second, the authors' commitment to informed and purposeful inquiry will undoubtedly renew efforts to improve. In today's world and in the foreseeable future, teachers will need to engage in high-quality professional development if they are to keep pace with and respond to changes in society and, at the same time, retain their energy, enthusiasm and commitment to high-quality teaching. Although the precise path we will take in this challenging endeavour remains uncertain, this book helps make our direction much clearer.

Thomas R. Guskey
Professor of Educational Policy
Studies and Evaluation
University of Kentucky

PART 1
A Critical Overview

1 Professionalism, performativity and empowerment: discourses in the politics, policies and purposes of continuing professional development

Christopher Day and Judyth Sachs

Continuing professional development (CPD) is a term used to describe all the activities in which teachers engage during the course of a career which are designed to enhance their work. Yet this is a deceptively simple description of a hugely complex intellectual and emotional endeavour which is at the heart of raising and maintaining standards of teaching, learning and achievement in a range of schools, each of which poses its own sets of special challenges. Moreover, because teachers, like the students they teach, think and feel, are influenced also by their biographies, social histories and working contexts, peer groups, teaching preferences, identities, phase of development and broader sociopolitical cultures, the purposes, design and processes of CPD will need to mirror these if it is to result in effective outcomes.

Introduction

The impact of the changing economic, social and knowledge contexts upon the education service as a whole has caused a move from the traditional post-war model of the autonomous professional in which decisions about the curriculum, teaching, learning and assessment are the business of teachers. Now what students learn, what they must achieve as the outcome of learning and what standards apply are explicitly the everyday business of the state. Concerned with the need to raise standards of achievement, and improve their positions in the world economic league tables, governments over the last 20 years have intervened more actively to improve the system of schooling. Higher expectations for higher quality teaching demands teachers who are well qualified, highly motivated, knowledgeable and skilful, not only at the point of entry into teaching but also throughout their careers.

Furthermore, CPD takes place in many countries within contexts of increasing governmental interventions for the purpose of 'accountability' and 'performativity'; and in some in contexts of raising standards of teaching where pre-service programmes are inadequate to produce a sufficient supply of competent novice teachers. These political purposes will be embedded both in CPD content – the targeting of resources towards particular programmes designed to support the implementation of government curricula, teaching or assessment agendas – and CPD forms. Both content and form will imply particular conceptions of 'professionalism'. Whereas in the past it was enough to describe professionals in a politically neutral way as 'restricted' or 'extended' (Hoyle 1980), in the twenty-first century, in which the struggle for the soul of professionalism is acute (Friedson 2001), professionals no longer have that choice. Indeed, it may be argued that the new agenda is concerned with being compliant or 'activist'. CPD is no longer an option but an expectation of all professionals.

In this chapter we are concerned with examining policies, practices and conceptions of CPD in various designated regions: Europe, North America, Australia, South America, Southern Africa and Singapore. In order to draw together the commonalities and differences of the provision of CPD in these various areas we use the following questions to interrogate the politics, practices and policies of CPD across a diverse range of contexts: what are the common drivers shaping the provision of CPD? What are the functions of CPD? What is its point of initiation? And finally, what are some of the strategies used to deliver CPD?

The pressures of globalization have universally shaped government policies for education provision in general and CPD in particular. The power of globalization is clearly defined by the Commission on Global Governance (1995: 42–3) as 'The shortening of distance, the multiplying of links, the deepening of interdependence: all these factors, and their interplay, have been transforming the world into a neighbourhood'. The imperatives for education systems to be able to deliver education programmes for both students and teachers that are efficient, effective and economical are common to all of the examples presented. The common drivers of education reform, with its increased emphasis on accountability through rituals of verification (Power 1997), audit cultures (Strathern 2000) and standards regimes (Sachs 2003) underscore the pervasiveness of these initiatives. However, it is clear as Christie *et al.* have pointed out in this book (see Chapter 7), that 'the stages of development are different in various developed and developing countries and that this needs to be understood in relation to broader issues of education, the state and development'. The factors shaping education provision in South America and Africa are more aligned because of the similarities in issues of economic growth and political stability, while Australia, Singapore, Europe and North America have considerably more in common than the South American or African examples.

Discourses of educational reform

Discourses offer particular kinds of subject positions and identity through which people come to view their relationships with different loci of power (Clarke and Newman 1997: 92). This is an important point given the emergence of two distinct but not entirely oppositional discourses that are dominating educational policies around teacher professionalism: democratic professionalism and managerial professionalism. These discourses set the limits of what can be said, thought and done with respect to debates and initiatives which are designed to enhance the political project of teacher professionalism nationally across various educational sectors.

Recent reforms particularly concerning devolution and marketization have encouraged the development of a set of paradoxes about the nature of teaching as a profession and about the professional identity and professional development of teachers. First is that the call for teacher professionalism related to a revisioning of occupational identity is occurring at a time when there is evidence that teachers are being deskilled and their work intensified. Externally imposed curriculum, management innovations and monitoring and assessment systems have often been poorly implemented and have resulted in periods of destabilization, increased workload, intensification of teachers' work (Day *et al.* 1996) and a crisis of professional identity for many teachers who perceive a loss of public confidence in their ability to provide a good service. The circumstances in which teachers work and the demands made upon them are changing as communication technologies erode the role of the teacher as exclusive holder of expert knowledge. As the social fabric of society becomes more fragmented, the educative role of schools becomes more complex. Second, while it is acknowledged that rethinking classroom practice is exceptionally demanding, *fewer* resources are being allocated to support teacher learning. Third, the teaching profession is being exhorted to be autonomous while at the same time it is under increasing surveillance by politicians and the community to be more accountable through standards regimes and rituals of verification (Power 1997). Resolving these paradoxes underpinning changes in education policy and practice brings into focus the importance of the role that CPD has in the development and renewal of the teaching profession.

The version of professionalism currently informing various policy documents and now mandated by the state is what we describe as 'managerial professionalism'; its attributes, intentions and purposes are elaborated below. While much of the content of the discourse informing managerial professionalism is obvious, other aspects of its form are left unsaid or silent but nevertheless inform practice.

Managerial professionalism

In some respects the discourse of managerial professionalism (Sachs 2003) has been the more dominant of the two discourses given its impact on the work of teachers. This is particularly the case with the consequences of reform initiatives such as organizational change, imperatives for teachers in schools to be more accountable and for systems to be more efficient and economic in their activities.

Sugrue's review of CPD provision in Europe (see Chapter 3) and Avalos' examination of South America (see Chapter 5) suggest that within the education sector recent policies promoting devolution and decentralization have provided sympathetic conditions for a discourse of managerialism to emerge and flourish. One of the consequences of this is the development of an alternative form of teacher professionalism – namely, managerial professionalism – which gains its legitimacy though the promulgation of policies and the allocation of funds associated with those policies. The new discourse attempts to redefine what is meant by teacher professionalism and how teachers practise it individually and collectively.

Where devolution and decentralization have been at the core of reform agendas the conditions are ripe for the development of what Brennan (1996: 22) describes as a corporate management model. This model emphasizes:

> A professional who clearly meets corporate goals, set elsewhere, manages a range of students well and documents their achievements and problems for public accountability purposes. The criteria of the successful professional in this corporate model is of one who works efficiently and effectively in meeting the standardised criteria set for the accomplishment of both students and teachers, as well as contributing to the school's formal accountability processes.

Clarke and Newman (1997: 92–3) argue that 'managerial discourses create the possibilities within which individuals construct new roles and identities and from which they derive ideas about the logic of institutional change'. In terms of teachers' professional development and the profession's moves to establish new and more active notions of teacher professionalism, the managerialist approach directly contrasts with democratic professionalism. Furthermore, advocates of each of these kinds of professionalism are often at loggerheads with each other because unions and other professional bodies champion democratic professionalism, while systems and employers advocate managerial professionalism.

Democratic professionalism

The second of the discourses circulating about teacher professionalism is that of democratic professionalism. Apple (1996) suggests that an alternative to state control is not traditional professionalism but a democratic professionalism which seeks to demystify professional work and build alliances between teachers and excluded constituencies of students and members of the community on whose behalf decisions have traditionally been made either by professions or by the state.

The core of democratic professionalism is an emphasis on collaborative, cooperative action between teachers and other educational stakeholders. It suggests that the teacher has a wider responsibility than the single classroom and includes contributing to the school, the system, other students, the wider community and collective responsibilities of teachers themselves as a group and the broader profession (Brennan 1996).

While it is not the intention to develop fully the dimensions of these two discourses here, for current purposes they can be summarized as shown in Table 1.1. These two discourses of teacher professionalism should not be seen as polarized or exclusive; rather, it is more likely the case that teachers make choices regarding which form they subscribe to. Indeed in practice in the case studies below it is apparent that variations of both forms are evident. It is likely that teachers move between the two, negotiating the contradictions and multiple demands that are placed on them in their busy and complex workplaces.

Common to both these forms of teacher professionalism is the desire to improve the performance and skills of teachers in schools and thereby improve student learning outcomes. How they go about doing this and who has control of the process is what distinguishes one from the other. As Warren Little reports in the USA (see Chapter 4), the focus has been on stimulating and supporting teacher learning and instructional decision making, bolstering teacher community, advancing whole-school reform and satisfying the

Table 1.1 Managerial and democratic professionalism compared

Managerial professionalism	Democratic professionalism
System driven/ends	Profession driven/ends
External regulation	Professional regulation
Drives reform agenda	Complements and moves beyond reform agenda
Political ends	Professional development
Competitive and market driven	Collegial and profession driven
Control/compliancy	Activism

demands of accountability. Here both discourses are informing practice. Grundy and Robison (see Chapter 6) report that a version of this is also occurring in Australia where teacher professional development was previously linked to restructuring in teaching and an industrial accord. However, more recently it has been concerned with satisfying the demands of the development of standards regimes and increased accountability from governments.

Interestingly, many of the cases (Australia, the USA, Europe) in this handbook provide evidence of the shift from locally designed and locally controlled reform initiatives to centrally defined imperatives linked to standards-based accountability. The shift has been not only to change the type of CPD that is made available to teachers but also the type of teacher professionalism that is seen as legitimate and supported by the state (see Sachs 2003). David Hargreaves (1994: 436) captures the requirements of a new professionalism, arguing: 'To improve schools, one must be prepared to invest in professional development; to improve teachers, their professional development must be set within the context of institutional development'.

Models of CPD

Over the last 20 years, in many countries, there has been a shift in the rhetoric of teacher training and development from one in which individual teachers have been able to choose at will from a 'smorgasbord' of (mainly) short one-shot workshops and lectures, to one in which lifelong learning is regarded as essential for all as a mandatory part of every teacher's needs. Hence in many countries, although the narrow 'INSET' model (in-service education and training) continues to be the principal means of accessing development (if for no other reason than it appears to be the most efficient and cost-effective way to reach the huge population of teachers), teachers must now engage in one way or another in learning oriented towards either maintenance, improvement or change.

Cochrane-Smith and Lytle (1999) identified three conceptions of knowledge associated with teachers' learning and development:

- *knowledge-for-practice:* formal knowledge generated by researchers outside the school (for example, research-based programmes, new theories of teaching, learning and assessment);
- *knowledge-of-practice:* generated by teachers critically examining their own classrooms and schools, alone or with others, in terms of broader issues of social justice, equity and student achievement;
- *knowledge-in-practice:* teachers' practical knowledge generated through their own systematic inquiry, stimulated by questions raised concerning their own classroom effectiveness.

Teaching is a passionate vocation (Fried 1995; Day in press). The person plays a large part in the work of the professional. So any conception of CPD needs to include in it the education of self, including the emotions. For this reason we would add to Cochrane-Smith and Lytle's conception:

- *knowledge of self:* generated by teachers engaging regularly in reflection in, on and about their values, purposes, emotions and relationships.

While these conceptions are important, they represent only a partial framework for conceptualizing, planning and analysing CPD, for they are entirely concerned with cognitive knowledge. Research continues to show that the best teaching involves a combination of cognition and emotion. Phillip Jackson's study of life in American classrooms (Jackson 1968) is only one of a plethora of research and writing which demonstrates this. As Andy Hargreaves (1998: 835) eloquently affirmed many years later:

> Good teaching is charged with positive emotion. It is not just a matter of knowing one's subject, being efficient, having the correct competencies, or learning all the right techniques. Good teachers are . . . passionate beings who connect with their students and fill their work and their classes with pleasure, creativity and joy . . .

The kinds of CPD which predominate at any given time often reflect views of teachers' needs by those outside the classroom. For example, long ago, Philip Jackson (1968) identified in CPD (then, mistakenly, understood as in-service training and development) a *deficit model* in which it was assumed that teachers needed to be provided with something (knowledge, skills) which they did not already have. This model remains firmly in place. (Witness the growth of the teacher competencies movements in all countries in which attempts are made to prescribe prescriptive national standards as if all teachers' circumstances are the same or as if there is a simple and direct cause and effect relationship between teacher learning and pupil progress.) However, alongside this is an *aspirational model* which acknowledges that teachers who are already effective at what they do can build on this, can 'improve' in a quest, for example, for schools to become learning communities. Such a model builds upon, on the one hand, research findings about effective and improving schools and teachers, and on the other about teachers' identity, commitment, work and lives. These models are not in conflict but rather complement one another, for they combine the instrumental, change-driven needs of employers with the broader educational purposes of those for whom teaching is more than delivering a product.

David Hargreaves (1994) identified a 'post-technocratic' model of professional development in which:

- teachers are understood to have lifelong professional learning needs;
- for continuity and progress to be realized, these must be assessed on a regular basis;
- school development plans must contain professional development opportunities;
- personal development needs must be reconciled with school needs.

This emphasizes a symbiotic relationship between individual and organizational needs, but on closer examination proves to be problematic. In practice, teachers in different phases of their career (Huberman 1995) and working in differing circumstances will have needs which may be distinctively different from those identified at any given time by their schools. For example, from a managerial perspective, raising the standard of students' work may be a legitimate priority; whereas from an individual teacher's perspective, sustaining enthusiasm or commitment in classrooms in which a significant minority of students do not wish to learn may be more important. Furthermore, since teaching is, we would suggest, a moral enterprise in the sense that it is always directed for the betterment of students, CPD needs, as a matter of course, to focus upon individual needs. There seem to be many in policy-making and managerial roles who have lost sight of the skill, knowledge and sheer emotional energy which teachers need in order to engage in intelligent planning and action in the classroom as agents of change (Fullan 1993).

The influence of individual and collective culture

Just as conditions in classrooms affect the ability of teachers to provide the best learning opportunities for students, so the school culture provides positive or negative support for its teachers' learning. A school's culture is 'moulded by the unique and shared experiences of participants, which are influenced by their class, race and neighbourhood as well as their school's history and its leadership . . .' (Finnan and Levin 2000: 89–90). Although various researchers have attempted to provide classifications or 'ideal types' (Nias *et al.* 1989; Rosenholtz 1989; Hargreaves 1994, 1995; Stoll and Fink 1996), each school's culture is unique and never static.

Most teachers still work in isolation from their colleagues for most of the time; opportunities for the development of practice based upon observation and critique of that practice remain limited; and, despite the best efforts of many school leaders to promote collegial cultures, these are almost always at the level of planning or talking about teaching rather than at the level of examining practice itself.

Moreover, although many teachers begin their careers 'with a sense that their work is socially meaningful and will yield great satisfactions', this is lost as 'the inevitable difficulties of teaching . . . interact with personal issues and vulnerabilities, as well as social pressure and values, to engender a sense of frustration and force a reassessment of the possibilities of the job and the investment one wants to make in it' (Farber 1991: 36).

Many teachers in mid to late career become disenchanted or marginalize themselves from learning, no longer holding the good of their pupils as a high priority. Low self-esteem and shame (at not achieving desired results) are directly correlated with less variety of teaching approaches and thus less connection with students' learning needs.

Teacher development through CPD, then, must take account of these and the psychological and social settings which can encourage or discourage learning – for example, the teachers' own personal life histories, their professional learning experiences, their expertise and school professional learning cultures, which provide the day-to-day contexts for their work.

Teachers' career phases

The most authoritative studies of teachers' career experiences and the most influential determinants within and outside the institution on them are those of Swiss secondary school teachers by Michael Huberman (1989, 1995), of English teachers by Sikes *et al.* (1985) and of American teachers by Fessler and Christensen (1992). Their work suggests that teachers pass through five broad phases:

1   Launching a career: initial commitment (easy or painful beginnings).
2   Stabilization: find commitment (consolidation, emancipation, integration into peer group).
3   New challenges, new concerns (experimentation, responsibility, consternation).
4   Reaching a professional plateau (sense of mortality, stop striving for promotion, enjoy or stagnate).
5   The final phase (increased concern with pupil learning and increasing pursuit of outside interests, disenchantment, contraction of professional activity and interest).

The final 10–15 years of a career is, theoretically, the phase of greatest expertise in teaching, albeit accompanied by the potential for increased personal health and family concerns. Yet it may also be the time of greatest 'conservatism'. Teachers in this phase complain more about the behaviour, commitment and values of students 'these days' (Peterson 1964; Prick 1986; Day and Bakioglu 1996), and are sceptical about the virtues of change. This is not surprising, given the huge investment of time, effort and expertise which these teachers are likely to have already made in their work. They are unlikely to be looking towards further promotion and may either be serenely moving towards a 'satisfactory' career end, or having to survive, dissatisfied, in an alien climate. These teachers may feel marginalized within the institution and embittered towards those whom they see as responsible for the condition of education, schooling and the declining standards of the students they must teach. They may work hard in their core acts of teaching, but this may not be accompanied by the levels of enthusiasm, emotional and intellectual commitment necessary for achieving excellence.

It is becoming increasingly clear from the literature on teachers' work, professional lives and development that expertise, capability, personal and professional biography, situational, emotional and psychological factors as well as the complexity of the pupils whom they teach, and changes over time and circumstance, affect their effectiveness. As Andy Hargreaves (1998: vii) argues:

> We are beginning to recognise that, for teachers, what goes on inside the classroom is closely related to what goes on outside it. The quality, range and flexibility of teachers' classroom work are closely tied up with their professional growth – with the way in which they develop as people and as professionals. Teachers teach in the way they do not just because of the skills they have or have not learned. The ways they teach are also rooted in their backgrounds, their biographies, and so in the kinds of teachers they have become. Their careers – their hopes and dreams, their opportunities and aspirations, or the frustrations of these things – are also important for teachers' commitment, enthusiasm and morale. So too are relationships with their colleagues – either as supportive communities who work together in pursuit of common goals and continuous improvement, or as individuals working in isolation, with the insecurities that sometimes brings.

Understanding how the interrelationships among these influences work and how they exert their effects is not easy.

Because we acknowledge the complexity of teachers' work and lives we have defined CPD in those terms. Thus in our view CPD is essentially not about particular forms of activity but rather about a range of activities – formal and informal – which meet the thinking, feeling, acting, life, context and change purposes of teachers over the span of their careers. It is about the short- and long-term development of the person, the professional, the classroom practitioner and the occupational role he or she occupies:

> Professional development consists of all natural learning experiences and those conscious and planned activities which are intended to be

of direct or indirect benefit to the individual, group or school and which contribute, through these, to the quality of education in the classroom. It is the process by which, alone and with others, teachers review, renew and extend their commitment as change agents to the moral purposes of teaching; and by which they acquire and develop critically the knowledge, skills and emotional intelligence essential to good professional thinking, planning and practice with children, young people and colleagues through each phase of their teaching lives.

(Day 1999: 4)

Ann Lieberman (1996) proposes an 'expanded view of professional learning', locating CPD in three settings:

1   *Direct learning* (through e.g. conferences, workshops, consultations).
2   *Learning in school* (through e.g. peer coaching, mentoring, critical friendships, active research, team planning and assessment, appraisal).
3   *Learning out of school* (through e.g. school-led renewal or reform networks, school-university partnerships, subject or phone-specific networks, professional development centres).

In today's world and in the foreseeable future, teachers will need to engage with all of these if they are to keep pace with and respond to changes in society, the demands of the results-driven standards agendas of governments and at the same time retain their energy, enthusiasm and commitment to high-quality teaching.

Strategies for delivery of CPD

A variety of strategies have been utilized across the cases to deliver CPD. School-based CPD, and the use of partnerships and networks have all contributed in various ways to the broad project of improving teacher performance and student learning.

School-based CPD

School-based teacher development programmes have featured consistently as a strategy for CPD but there have been varying degrees of its success. In Kenya, as Christie *et al.* point out (see Chapter 7), it was successful in its impact on the professional development of teachers, but unsuccessful in ensuring the institutionalization and operation of teacher advisory centres. Sugrue (see Chapter 3) claims that across Europe there are identifiable shifts in the structure of provision and the identities of the providers. Teacher centres tended to cater for individual preferences and needs, and local education authorities (LEAs) in England and Wales were the major providers through inspectors and advisory systems. Other European countries (such as Germany, Austria, Switzerland) continue to have dedicated regional institutes or centres dedicated to a range of CPD provision.

Sugrue argues that despite differences across Europe in terms of educational structures, all states appear to have bought into devolved decision making. He mentions the case of Ireland where all schools have six compulsory CPD days and England where the majority of these days are taken in school.

Grundy and Robison (see Chapter 6) report that in Australia the 1980s saw a move to the school as the appropriate site for professional development and a greater interest in educational reform by national government. This shift in focus to the school also had a strong democratic connection grounded in a critique of managerialism, yet acknowledging that schools needed to be sites of investigation and development. Nevertheless, it is worth remembering that improvement needed to take account of the context of practice as well as teaching practices themselves.

School-based study circles for teachers are now an important feature of the reforms of Ecuador, Guatemala and Paraguay. Cuba has also placed importance on school-based teacher professional development. As Avalos (see Chapter 5) notes, through these initiatives schools have a group of teachers that meets periodically to discuss teaching methods, produce learning materials, develop curriculum and exchange experience.

In various forms school-based CPD has been a consistent strategy for teacher renewal and professional learning. With varying degrees of success it has contributed to the broader education reform agenda across all of the cases presented.

Partnerships

Partnerships between schools, universities and other groups are represented across all of the cases. Furlong *et al.* (2000: 77–8) identify what they describe as ideal typical models of partnership. The continuum they present ranges from collaborative partnership at one end to complementary partnership at the other. These two types of partnership represent two very different strategies for linking work in schools with that of teacher education and other interested parties. According to Furlong *et al.* (2000: 80), in a complementary partnership the school and the university are seen as having separate and complementary responsibilities, but there is no attempt to bring these two dimensions into dialogue. Alternatively, a collaborative partnership:

requires the commitment by teacher-educators and school-based practitioners to develop a program where students are exposed to different forms of educational knowledge, some of which come from the school, some of which come from higher education or elsewhere. Teachers are seen as having an equally legitimate but perhaps different body of professional knowledge from those in higher education. Students are expected and encouraged to build up their own body of professional knowledge.

Not surprisingly, many of the outcomes of partnerships emerge, not from the planned or intended expectations, but rather by happenstance and serendipity. The list below is indicative of some possible outcomes facilitated by partnerships and collaborative relationships between teacher-educators and other educational stakeholders.

- negotiated expectations;
- collaborative planning;
- sharing of expertise;
- diversity of perspectives and viewpoints;
- knowledge generation;
- development of trust.

Effective partnerships are based on reciprocity, where both parties meet on equal grounds, with the desire to improve student learning outcomes and teacher practice at its core. At the same time it must be acknowledged that the development of a partnership needs to be based on the identification of a mutual need. Grundy and Robison's explication of the Innovative Links project and the Quality Schools project in Australia (see Chapter 6) are examples of where partnerships have been an effective means for both teacher and academic professional learning and where the above outcomes are evident.

Avalos (see Chapter 5) describes partnerships in Latin America which she claims generally involve courses dealing with subject-matter knowledge and teaching methods, delivered by institutions with which the government enters into a partnership. In Chile, for example, courses led by university academics are taught in the summer for the purpose of learning the new curriculum.

The important role to be played by universities working in partnership with schools and systems is made by Sugrue (see Chapter 3). He argues that universities, frequently marginalized from policy formulation and CPD, have a leading role to play in shaping the role of teachers as public sector intellectuals while simultaneously securing appropriate funding for professional learning and research efforts that collaboratively build understanding of, and contributions to, the knowledge base of lifelong learning for teachers.

Networks

Networks of teachers and schools have been an effective strategy to reduce the isolation and conservatism of teachers. These networks can be within school sites or they can be most expansive to include schools working across education districts, regions or even states, as the Innovative Links project in Australia indicated. Networks serve to link individual teachers with learning opportunities in the formation of a teacher community and collective strategy to work on instructional improvement at a school or individual classroom level. For Warren Little, the power of concentrating on colleagues working in school sites together is that they 'structure conversations around processes and participation goals rather than content area frameworks'.

Avalos (see Chapter 5) describes the teacher professional groups in Chile, which were established as meeting and learning contexts for teachers in secondary public schools. As part of this initiative schools were encouraged to set aside time once a fortnight for teachers to meet. The purpose of establishing the groups was to stimulate teachers to install their own professional development activities in schools, focusing on their own growth as people, professionals and members of a professional community.

In Singapore, the Teachers' Network is a system-initiated strategy for teacher CPD. The professional development activities seek to increase teachers' capacity to learn, cultivate collaborative inquiry, manage knowledge and value diversity. This is done through the establishment of learning circles comprising four to ten practitioners. Here teachers come together to identify and solve common problems and to address shared classroom concerns.

All research points to the complexity of teacher development which mirrors the complexity of the purposes and practices of teaching. Yet by and large, as the chapters in this book so aptly demonstrate, the dominant form of CPD remains the much-maligned short INSET course or workshop. In Chapter 2, Ray Bolam and Agnes McMahon provide a helicopter view of the territory occupied by CPD. In discussing system-level factors within emerging performativity contexts they focus upon changing policies, perspectives, work conditions and expectations which affect the provision, location, forms and processes of CPD; the role played by organizational contexts and external agencies in teacher learning; and the difficulties in establishing *continuing* professional development for all teachers. Their conclusion is that the plethora of research and writing which is often eclectic or draws upon different theoretical disciplines has resulted in different, and sometimes competing, understandings. There is little evidence of cumulative knowledge-building. There is a need, therefore, for more and better evaluations which focus upon outcomes and impact measures. More fundamentally, they recognize as axiomatic that CPD can only have an indirect impact on student learning. They conclude that national and international information bases on CPD would need to be improved, that comparative research needs to be undertaken so that there can be more productive sharing and learning, and that there is an urgent need for more clarity on the roles of the teaching profession in a social democracy and, thus, the nature of CPD appropriate to these.

In Chapter 3, Ciaran Sugrue discusses the growing emphasis placed by policy makers on CPD as a means of ensuring that their imposed change agendas for schools and classrooms are implemented efficiently and effectively. Sugrue suggests, however, that far from being a coherent thrust suited to purposes, the policies for CPD have been conceptually confused. This has resulted in both positive and negative consequences for teacher learning. Sugrue situates the discussion of policies and practice within Bourdieu's notion of power, positing that there is a 'subterranean set of power forces at work with important consequences for the manner in which teachers' learning and well-being are positioned and shaped'. He is thus able to contrast the globalized rhetoric of lifelong learning within which teachers are expected to be the principal role models of the engine for economic growth and competitiveness with the reality of teachers' work and lives, as the increasing politicization of education has challenged their sense of professionalism and identities and their roles have been expected to shift from expert knowledge-holders to facilitators of learning. Yet this professional change in rhetoric is set within schools which have decentralized sets of responsibilities within centralized policy prescriptions and increased public accountabilities based upon compliance with these. In a comprehensive and critical condemnation of the demands of new market-driven performativity agendas, Sugrue draws a complex mosaic of uneven use of ICT, school effectiveness and improvement agendas which ignores the importance of personhood in teaching, unresolved tensions between individual and organizational needs, the expansion of the responsibilities of most principals and the huge bureaucratic and social burden upon teachers. In exchange for these, there are in many countries across Europe five mandatory CPD days and a few embryonic nationally prescribed management training programmes.

In Chapter 4, Judith Warren Little uses the same lens of policy and power as Sugrue but from the micro-perspective of teachers' analysis of student work as emblematic of the possibilities and tensions in contemporary professional development in the USA. Like Sugrue, she points to the fragmentation and a lack of coherence in CPD and a nationwide centralist involvement towards linking CPD with narrowly conceived standards-based accountability agendas. Here, CPD, as in many other parts of the world, is dominated by conventional forms of 'training' which are not inquiry oriented. Within this, however, Warren Little identifies a movement led by the research community and teacher-educators to link CPD more closely to the demands of teaching practice through investigations of artefacts, accounts and examples of classroom activity by using, for example, case study, collaborative student assessment and teacher communication networks. The chapter introduces discussion of three broad purposes for CPD: to deepen teacher knowledge and strengthen individual practice; to build collective capacity for improvement of teaching and learning at school level in order to build cultures of inquiry; and to review student work as an instrument of standards implementation and external accountability. Such purposes appear to represent orientations which are complementary. However, like Sugrue, Warren Little identifies issues of power and control as privileging some purposes and forms of CPD over others. Thus each approach contributes something of importance (to teacher development) but each suffers from conceptual and design limitations.

In focusing attention upon and providing detailed illustrations of 'value added' contributions to knowledge and practice, Warren Little advocates CPD as a means of practising direct association between teachers as learners, teachers in practice and student learning. Because such work is self-selected, it creates a sense of ownership, relevance and collegiality and the development of communities of mutual inquiry focused upon practice. It may also enable, she concludes, a strategic convergence between research, practice and the continuing dominant agenda of public accountability.

In Chapter 5, Beatrice Avalos begins by locating CPD in the huge variety of contradictory cultural linguistic, social and political systems and educational opportunities which make up the 20 'developing' nations of Latin America. What is taken for granted educationally in Europe and the USA cannot be assumed to be the case in Latin America where, for example, 110 million people have not gone beyond an education of five years and where Peru's expenditure of $480 per pupil contrasts sharply with the $6,043 spent by the USA. The extent and quality of the pre-service training of teachers is also variable and CPD is not a term in common use. Rather, teacher development is variously referred to as 'skill training', 'improvement', 'upgrading' or 'refreshing'. It is not surprising, perhaps, that in this scenario, CPD is largely a centrally orchestrated deficit model of in-service training intended to provide knowledge and skills which teachers do not presently have.

Within this dominant model in which, as in Europe and the USA, most CPD is geared to the implementation of reform initiatives, Avalos identifies the growth of, for example, school-based professional development associated with non-governmental institutions and based upon action research. The dominant teacher development purposes which Avalos identifies show close correspondence with those centrally funded programmes described in the case studies of Europe and America. Within these there are initiatives which are particular to the social and economic needs of the countries in the Latin American region (that is, 'Education for All' equity concerns). Interestingly, one raft of CPD is overtly political, concerned with the 'improvement' of teachers by widening teacher understanding and perspectives about education issues and practices through programmes of local, national and international visits to other schools and school systems. In the majority of cases CPD is funded by national governments and the World Bank; and, more than in Europe and America, universities remain central to the design and delivery of INSET. There is limited but growing evidence of school-initiated, school-based CPD, in which teacher groups collaborate to form and develop their own learning agendas – though Avalos cautions against over-optimism for the development of such initiatives in environments where teachers have heavy workloads and little time to focus on their own improvement. She concludes by suggesting a need to develop a systemic approach to CPD in which initial and continuing teacher development go hand in hand.

In Chapter 6, Shirly Grundy and Judith Robison begin from the premise that 'development' is central to the profession of teaching and the retention of a highly committed teaching force; and that it serves three principal functions – that is, extension, renewal and growth – which are both systemic and per-sonal. They track the changes in provision, purposes and location of CPD in Australia from the 1960s to the present and chart its increasingly close rela-tionship to employers' notions of productivity. Unlike the Europe described by Sugrue in his chapter, however, although the 'threat' of a more narrowly defined accountability regime lingers, it is the principle of a broader notion of professional communities, in charge of their own development, which has gained the centre ground of CPD in Australia, with an emphasis upon personal motivation and an understanding that 'It is around the concept of change that systemic provision and personal motivation come together . . . that profes-sional life is not independent of the whole life experience'. The authors note seven themes for successful professional development: relevance (to teacher-identified need); control (by participants); access (to expertise of facilitation by others); collegiality; active learning; longer time frames for cycles of action and reflection; and acknowledgement of the need for school reform and restructur-ing as a basis of improvement alongside professional development and change. They provide examples of these in action in an optimistic account of CPD trends in Australia.

In stark contrast, in Chapter 7 Pam Christie, Ken Harley and Alan Penny discuss the nature, provision, purposes and outcomes of CPD across 41 coun-tries in sub-Saharan Africa in which two-thirds of the population of 630 million people live in rural areas with high levels of poverty and in which economic survival is heavily dependent upon international aid and foreign loans. They provide a picture of unevenness and considerable differences in CPD which, in some of the countries, does not exist. In many there is also a lack of demarcation between initial teacher education and CPD. In some coun-tries, there is no basic education for all children and a chronic shortage of new teachers. In Africa, CPD is not afforded the same priority as in the other regions represented in the accounts in this book. The contrast is stark as in some of the countries life expectancy is now less than 40 years and in others

AIDS-related illnesses outstrip the supply of new teachers. In these contexts, perhaps unsurprisingly, the authors identify rampant instrumentalism in CPD, with teachers cast in the role of technicians in contrast to those of reflective practitioners implied in varying degrees in accounts of Europe, South America, America, Asia and Australia. Furthermore, the traditional value systems which privilege teachers as authority figures provide obstacles to learner-centred reform; and much of existing CPD – whether a part of (PRESET) or not – is prescriptive. What the authors describe is schooling and CPD which are highly politicized in order to maintain existing forms of social organization rather than improve them – CPD here is for survival, not change. They provide examples, however, of two distinctively different countries' approaches to CPD – Kenya and South Africa. Kenya has established a school-based teacher development programme which combines school-based, tutor-supported distance strategies which aim to break the pattern of teachers as technical and the institutionalization of bureaucratic practices. However, the culture suggests that this will not be sustainable. In South Africa, too, the rhetoric of CPD which reflects democratic principles has been affirmed with a commitment for teachers to undertake 80 hours of INSET annually, though this has not yet been translated into practice. The authors point not only to the immense difficulties in establishing CPD which promises reflective practice of the kind espoused, for example, in Australia, but to problems of institutionalizing such initiatives in traditional bureaucratic, hierarchical educational cultures which subscribe to the rhetoric but are resistant to the realities of change through CPD in the face of overwhelming social, economic, health and cultural issues. Of all the accounts in this book, this is the most challenging for those who wish to promote CPD in order to raise and sustain the quality of teachers and thus teaching and learning.

In Chapter 8, David Tripp, drawing upon the work of Nicholas Tang Ning, describes and assesses a major initiative launched by the Singapore Ministry of Education in response to a recognition of the need to produce learning outcomes for pupils which go beyond the mastery of content in order to prepare them as thinkers and problem solvers. Its vision of the thinking teacher in learning organizations led to the founding of a 'Teachers' Network' which seeks to increase teachers' capacity to learn, cultivate collaborative inquiry, manage knowledge and value diversity. The Network provides a range of sustained opportunities for teachers to reflect critically on their practice. Tripp evaluates these and in doing so finds that changing teachers' individual and collective learning cultures and those of the schools in which they work is not always straightforward. The lack of network leadership roles, the complexity of skills needed by teachers to engage in reflection and action research and the intellectual and affective qualities essential to the kinds of sustained critical friendship required for supporting teachers in the range of learning activities combine to hinder the complete fulfilment of the aspirations of this innovative venture. There is a message here about the need to recognize the complexities of teacher learning and change, and in particular to take account of key knowledge-mediating roles and the importance of identity.

There are several recurrent themes across all of the cases presented. First and foremost is the challenge of how to sustain change at the system and individual level while at the same time ensuring that education bureaucracies have the capacity (resources and intellectual) to support the rhetoric and intent expressed in education reform agendas and ensuing policies. Changing teachers' practice through systemic curriculum reform requires significant investment by education bureaucracies. It is clear that one-off workshops, staff training days or what Mockler (2001) has referred to as 'spray-on CPD' do not change teachers' practice or beliefs about teaching, nor their competence as teachers.

All of the cases presented demonstrated what Sugrue has described as an intensification of reform initiatives, which he argues are frequently top-down driven. He suggests that there is a two-tier approach to CPD: national priorities that receive preferential funding and support which teachers and schools are expected to embrace; and individual needs which, he maintains, are consigned to what may be possible given an individual's time, resources and availability. These cases present ample evidence of the needs of state policy having ascendancy over teachers' individual needs.

Two recurrent themes are driving the reform agenda: systemic requirements and the personal requirements and needs of teachers. As Grundy and Robison observe, the systemic drivers are in response to the increasing age profile of teachers, the renewal of teachers' knowledge base and in some cases linking curriculum reform more closely with the needs of the state and government priorities. At the individual or personal level is the need for teachers to maintain their commitment to and enthusiasm for teaching and to be able to sustain and enhance their personal lives through intellectual and professional engagement.

For Avalos, reporting from South America, the search for efficiency has meant that the common features of education reform have targeted changes in management and funding of the education system (decentralization and privatization), and improvement of the quality of teaching and learning through textbooks, curriculum materials, computers and a lengthening of the school day and year. Likewise, recent reform agendas in Australia, the UK, the USA and elsewhere have served to challenge traditional conceptions of teacher professionalism, in particular issues of teacher autonomy and what responsibility the state has in providing CPD through the implementation of similar types of initiative.

Function and purpose of CPD

Broadly speaking the function of CPD may be seen to be one of three imperatives: to align teachers' practice with educational policies (see South America,
Europe, Africa, Singapore and Australia as exemplars of this); to improve the
learning outcomes of students by improving the performance of teachers; or
(less evident but more aspirational) to enhance the status and profile of the
teaching profession (see Sachs 2003).

Grundy and Robison identify three interconnected purposes of CPD:
extension, growth and renewal. Extension is through introducing new knowledge or skills into a teacher's repertoire, growth is by the development of
greater levels of expertise and renewal is achieved through transformation and
change of knowledge and practice. Elements of these three functions are evident in CPD provisions elsewhere, but what distinguishes the African and
South American cases from those of the USA, Europe and Australia is the move
of CPD from deficit theory (Avalos) to being a strategy to enhance teacher
professionalism through the use of evidence-based practice (Groundwater-
Smith 2000; Groundwater Smith and Hunter 2000) and research with teachers
by academics or by teachers themselves.

Avalos documents in some detail the various initiatives by governments
across South America to have teachers participate in skill training, upgrading
of qualifications or refresher courses. She suggests that in many instances, as
far as teachers were concerned initially, the focus was to 'teach the reform' but
over time courses developed which were oriented more towards general
teacher 'improvement' in content and pedagogic matters. In stark contrast,
referring specifically to Kenya, Christie and her colleagues observe that
developing a coherent strategic plan for CPD has never been a priority, in spite
of a relatively impressive record of short in-service training of teachers at various times.

Warren Little argues that two central impulses dominate the contemporary landscape of professional development in the USA. One impulse – to
organize teacher learning in and from practice – arises from the premise that
improvements will most likely come from teachers' deep understanding of
how children learn. The second impulse arises from the premise that
improvements in teaching can be wrought by clarifying expectations (standards), specifying practice and exercising sanctions.

Looking at student work has been an effective response to using CPD as a
strategy to improve student learning in the USA. Drawing on a developing
tradition of activities that focus on learning in and from practice, where
teachers rely on artefacts and accounts of classroom practice as central
resources in professional development, Warren Little claims that there is a
growing appeal of professional development linked closely to practice.

Evidence of the third purpose of CPD, that of reforming or enhancing teacher professionalism, can be found in the examples presented from Australia. The work of the National Schools Network and the Innovative Links project are examples that have attempted to bring together the broad education reform agenda with a revitalization of the teaching profession through CPD. While there are elements of these projects still in place, the jury is out as to how much they have influenced the professionalism of the large and fragmented teaching force in Australia.

In Chapter 9, Geert Kelchtermans identifies the historical absence of shared understandings of the concept itself. Because CPD can have many different meanings, its purposes, processes and impact are often undifferentiated and diffuse. Kelchtermans uses findings from a range of research to locate CPD as a learning experience bounded in time and context (working conditions) to address the related issue of how it may be organized most effectively. The first part of the chapter focuses on describing ways in which CPD may be understood in terms of teachers' professional selves (self-image, self-esteem, motivation, task perceptions, future perspective), identities and subjective theories. Kelchtermans relates these to the importance of shared power, authority and a decision-making culture, the necessity to provide opportunities for individual, autonomous development alongside collaborative work, and a recognition that the construction and reconstruction of meanings by teachers is not only a technical matter. It is also a moral one, because it takes place within both micro- and macro-political contexts which are, it seems, obsessed with efficiency and effectiveness defined in terms of raising standards in narrowly conceived areas. Contextualization is not only about person, place and politics but is also time-situated. Teacher learning at any given time, therefore, can only be properly understood in terms of earlier learning, present practice and expectations for the future – in other words, teachers' biographical contexts.

Kelchtermans locates these conditions and contexts for teacher learning in research on the tensions between individual and organizational development, noting that both the financial and social-organizational facets of work act as filters which privilege some learning activities while limiting others – one reason, perhaps, for the exercise of power by system managers which results in the domination of organizationally perceived over individually perceived needs when research clearly points to the need for encouraging both if teachers' personal and emotional commitment is to be nurtured. The different dimensions in teaching and teacher (and school) development should be seen as closely intertwined. Width is needed if one-sidedness is to be avoided. Yet the dominant discourse of CPD continues to reflect strong managerialist agendas and uses only those parts of the research findings which appear to support these. From this perspective, Kelchtermans subscribes to Sachs' view that the professional identity of teachers is 'individualistic, competitive, controlling and reflective, and externally defined' (2001: 157).

In the final part of the chapter, Kelchtermans discusses the relationship between research and CPD, citing Cochran-Smith and Lytle (1999), Desimone *et al.* (2002) and Wilson and Berne's (1999) writings on increases in teacher knowledge for, in and of practice which may result from CPD. He concludes that while effective CPD is social, interactive and context-related, if it is to challenge participants to critically review their beliefs and ideas it must be relevant to their agendas. Research demonstrates that the form and location of CPD itself are insufficient to achieve effectiveness. Rather, this will depend upon understanding by CPD designers of the significant influences on teacher learning and change of historical, social, cultural and institutional contexts as well as the quality of leadership. Definitions of effectiveness will also depend upon the kind of professionalism which is being encouraged – whether CPD is about nurturing on the one hand inquiry as a stance alongside activist identity, or on the other compliance and conformity to others' agendas.

In Chapter 10, Susan Groundwater-Smith and Marion Dadds argue that to have an impact beyond the classroom, practitioner inquiry (also known as action research and teacher research) needs to be embedded in school culture. In making this argument they provide a focus on five of the most important factors in CPD effectiveness identified by Kelchtermans and cited in the case studies in this book – that is learning through inquiry; the power of the school culture to affect teacher development positively or negatively; how the kinds of CPD available to teachers indirectly represent the kinds of professionals that teachers are expected to be or become; the importance of acknowledging values; and evidence-based practice as CPD. Groundwater-Smith and Dadds are clear in their advocacy of inquiry which 'places the research in the hands of those engaged in the educational enterprise as equal partners' and they distinguish this from action research which may be designed to pursue others' reform agendas. They also view schools as moral institutions, 'with a concern for ethicality, equity, social justice and transparency', and research and teaching as value-laden, moral work. Thus practitioner inquiry must, in their view, be strongly committed to the voices and perspectives of young people.

In writing about practitioner inquiry from the Australian and English contexts, Groundwater-Smith first describes two ground-breaking projects linking schools with universities, in the case of one in order to formulate and answer questions identified by schools and of the second to address a common question, 'What is it about the ways in which teachers' work is organized that gets in the way of learning?'. More recently, she identifies a trend towards 'evidence-based practice', a new form of practitioner inquiry. Dadds' description of the growth of a compliancy culture in the UK, in which 'knowledge production being pursued for the good of the profession is being replaced by knowledge production for policy solutions', is in sharp contrast.

The second part of the chapter provides exemplars of school-initiated, sustained school-university partnerships to enhance the role of schools as knowledge-creating organizations in order to expand teachers' professional learning through collegial engagement in evidenced-based practices; and a justification of evidence-based practice itself, the primary purpose of which is to increase understanding of practice rather than to seek 'best practice', a goal which the authors see in the context of the complexities of teaching and learning as both undesirable and impossible to achieve.

Perhaps understandably, the final part of the chapter focuses upon the tensions in forming and sustaining working relationships between individual teachers, schools and university personnel, whose worlds are often perceived as being akin to those of classroom teachers. There are questions of credibility, trust and commitment to be resolved in work which brings the two cultures together, and these have been discussed extensively elsewhere (Giddens 1990). Importantly, as the authors point out, such practitioner inquiry may be stimulated or discouraged by the broader policy cultures which affect schools. In so-called 'audit societies', for example, which use resources to achieve predetermined outcomes which themselves are measurable, it may also be appropriated by policy makers for the purpose of policy implementation. Yet this in itself provides an argument for the promotion of practitioner inquiry as a powerful means of professional development which enhances teachers as active professionals who are needed to engage young people in learning and achievement relevant to their own and society's needs.

In Chapter 11, John Elliott carefully dissects the efficacy and implications of teaching as an evidence-based profession. Groundwater-Smith and Dadds choose to interpret its purposes as ensuring that educational research, which is driven by practitioner inquirers with support from higher education, produces findings that are both relevant and useful to teachers in understanding and improving practice. Elliott agrees, but provides a second, more sinister interpretation: that evidence-based practice can also represent an attempt 'to co-opt teachers into a strictly instrumental view of practically relevant educational knowledge, and thereby disconnect it from fundamental questions about the ends of education in the wider society'. He sees these two interpretations as 'trajectories of meaning', in tension with each other across a range of policy initiatives which promote evidence-based practice and which seem either to empower teachers (and by implication limit the knowledge generation and production control exercised by much research from universities) or disempower teachers by only counting as important knowledge which can be instrumentally used to drive externally defined standards. Elliott provides a detailed analysis of a higher education schools consortium in England. In this illustration, research which is meaningful is that which engages teachers both *in* and *with* research, which addresses their concerns, which employs a range of different qualitative and quantitative research genres, which focuses upon enhancing their understanding of the triangular relationship between teaching, learning and subject matter in their particular contexts, and which challenges simplistic linear, cause and effect relationships between them. The chapter is located in the English experience of centralist policy thrusts which promote teacher-led research which serves policy agendas through small-scale experimental and normative process-product studies. Elliott's message, that what counts as 'useful' evidence cannot be defined independently of teachers, echoes Lawrence Stenhouse's notion that it is teachers who will change the world by understanding it (see Rudduck and Hopkins 1995: 124). It also provides a cautionary note for those in any country who would seek to impose learning and change agendas which are prescriptive or which demand simple cause and effect relationships in education.

One of the most neglected areas of CPD is that of evaluating its effects upon teachers, schools and student learning and achievement. While there is little doubt that establishing direct cause and effect relationships between CPD and, for example, improved student test outcomes, is problematic, it is reasonable to assume there will be a correlation between high-quality CPD (which is relevant to need, clear in its purposes and appropriate in its processes) and improved teaching. As yet, however, few rigorous 'fit for purpose' evaluation models which may be applied to different forms of CPD in order to determine worth and impact of all kinds have been developed. In Chapter 12, Daniel Muijs, Christopher Day, Alma Harris and Geoff Lindsay highlight the existing poor quality of CPD evaluation practices, suggesting that they do not yet take account of its different purposes and orientations or the complex inter-relationship between teacher learning, pupil learning, school improvement, conditions and factors, and the settings in which CPD occurs. While this dearth of good practice is not limited to the education sector, it does nevertheless prevent any systematic review of the short-, medium- and long-term impact of CPD, a valid consideration of 'cost effectiveness' and the development of 'best practice' CPD models. The authors cite Guskey's (2000) five-level evaluation model as being potentially the most useful means for developing a comprehensive framework for evaluating CPD, though even this lacks proper consideration of antecedents and the emotional challenges of change. The authors conclude by presenting a tentative framework for evaluation.

The message for CPD of all kinds which this chapter suggests, confirms those of others in this handbook: that identifying teachers' agendas is crucial to learning and change; that teacher learning needs to be inquiry oriented, personal and sustained, individual and collaborative, on and off site; that CPD means a range of learning opportunities appropriate to needs and purposes; that these need to be supported by school cultures of inquiry and be evidence-based where evidence is collected and interrogated which acknowledges the complex worlds of teaching and learning, teachers and learners; and, that if it is to be effective its direct and indirect results need to be systematically evaluated.

Conclusion

What then do these perspectives tell us about the state of CPD across developed and developing states? First and foremost, it is clear that governments and systems are using CPD as a means of achieving broader education reform agendas. CPD is political, and in this sense serves the interests of some groups better than others. Furthermore, depending on the political development of the state, CPD has been a strategy used by governments to align curriculum with broader political agendas. Given the significant investment of resources, time and energy this is not surprising.

All of the cases in this handbook provide evidence in various forms of the three functions of CPD: extension, growth and renewal. How these functions are operationalized and achieved is dependent on the resources available and the priorities of governments at the time. Certainly extension and growth of teachers' professional competencies, especially as these relate to curriculum content, is evident across all of the regions.

Importantly, despite the significant investment in CPD by governments, there is an uneven picture of how effective or economic many of these initiatives have been. The extent to which there have been systematic and careful evaluations of programmes is unclear. This is not to suggest the need for cost-benefit analysis but rather the need to gauge the benefit or the costs (personal and financial) of these expensive initiatives to the various constituencies. This is somewhat paradoxical given the increased regimes of accountability that have been imposed on various public sector instrumentalities or initiatives. Given this unevenness it is difficult for bureaucracies to identify what has been learned from generations of teacher professional development activities. Indeed, a focus on learning from previous systemic initiatives may reveal future possibilities in terms of the purpose, function, design and delivery of CPD initiatives.

Three major issues emerge. First is how to develop a teaching force in which CPD is the core value for all teachers whereby the systemic needs of government are achieved but the individual learning of teachers is not neglected. Surely an intelligent, educated and competent teaching force is in the best interests of everyone. Second is the sustainability of some CPD initiatives, in particular the work of networks and partnerships which require significant levels of trust and the development of new types of relationship. Here thought has to be given to long-term prospects and possibilities rather than short-term expedience. Finally, what role should the profession itself play in the provision of CPD? Cargo cult (or mendicant) mentalities often encouraged by governments and teachers who are seen as the grateful recipients of CPD do not provide the conditions for an intelligent and responsive teaching profession.

Each of the chapters examine CPD through a slightly different lens. For Avalos in South America the massive problem of ensuring that there are enough well-prepared teachers to contribute to extending the education of children and young people predominates. Yet within this, she points to the importance of development of teachers as critical thinkers. Groundwater-Smith and Dadds' advocacy of practitioner inquiry sits well with this as they provide an important illustration of the 'unsilencing' of teachers' voices through collaborative, self-selected and issue-focused CPD. Judith Warren Little provides a further illustration of how teachers can be encouraged and supported in their learning by kinds of CPD which focus directly upon inquiry into practice and which minimize the problems of transfer of practice so often associated with off-site programmes. Yet there are also dangers associated with work of the kind espoused by Little, Groundwater-Smith and Dadds in particular. The kinds of CPD evidence-based inquiry which they discuss may, for John Elliott, be used to promote the efficient, effective (and non-critical) implementation of policy. Sugrue warns of policy prescriptions which simplify the complexities of teaching and learning in a 'post-democratic' new world order, such that teachers' energies to pursue learning which is of direct relevance to their growth and their students' needs are sapped by the imperatives of externally imposed short-term goals and lack of time and funding. Kelchtermans rightly identifies the challenge by highlighting the need to answer the question concerning to what kind of *professionalism* CPD should contribute if teaching is to be an attractive occupation which is able to retain highly committed teachers. That the question needs to be asked by researchers, policy makers and teachers themselves implies that the definition of what being and behaving as a professional means is disputed.

And this is at the root of all CPD. The range of possible CPD experiences will all have different orientations according to purposes. Some will (inevitably and rightly) be concerned with policy implementation and some with authentic teacher inquiries into aspects of practice. Some (hopefully more) will be designed primarily to address the need for an understanding and management of emotions in the classroom as part of the ethic of care as well as effectiveness. Some may consist of short, inspirational lectures, some of sharing practice and thinking with others from other schools, and some will be sustained partnerships between schools, universities and others. Yet it is not only the variety and range of CPD or the promotion of schools as learning communities, or even the acknowledgement that teachers need time to learn over the whole course of their careers which will move CPD forward as a real and accepted part of every school and every teacher's learning and change agendas. If it is to move on, then governments, with policy makers, strategists, researchers, professional associates, teachers and parents, will need to engage in an ongoing dialogue about what kind of teachers are needed for the twenty-first century – and this will relate also to the kinds of citizenry that will be needed. Will it be the compliant teacher who promotes compliancy among students, who become passively unquestioning members of society? Or will it be the activist teacher who models critical thinking and intelligent emotion, who promotes the questioning student who then becomes an active, participative member of their local, regional, national and global communities?

The contributions to this handbook suggest that there are indications of a reduction in the disjuncture between what research internationally reveals about effective schools and effective teacher learning, development and change and the previously narrow understanding of CPD by policy makers, as expressed in its limited purposes and forms. For the optimists, there are signs of a new understanding among all educators that CPD will not, should not, and cannot always produce direct 'pay-off' in classroom learning and student achievements. There are simply too many other variables which prevent immediate transfer of learning. The increased investment in practitioner inquiry as a way of learning, in professional development schools, or networked learning communities, the renewed emphasis on creating and sustaining schools as learning communities under leaders who recognize the value of collaboration and place CPD at the heart of their school development efforts and who themselves are lead learners, are all signs that CPD is becoming understood to have a range of forms, locations and practices appropriate to its many purposes. Yet both time to learn and the right timing are essential to success. The pessimists will point to continuing resourcing difficulties and deterioration in teacher morale; to despair at what they see as the impossibly high expectations vested in CPD. This handbook, the first of its kind for more than 20 years, offers a message not of optimism or pessimism, but of hope: 'It is hope, above all, that gives us strength to live and to continually try new things, even in conditions which seem hopeless' (Havel 1993: 68).

What is clear is that there still remains a considerable gap in our knowledge of the effects of CPD, in all its forms, upon the thinking, planning and practice of individual teachers and schools as learning organizations; and a chasm between the economic 'haves' and 'have nots' across the world's regions. Nor do we know enough about the impact on students, their motivations, attitudes, work and achievements. There is a need for national and international conceived and funded longitudinal research which investigates the effectiveness of CPD of all kinds and in all locations over time and according to purpose. It is, after all, surprising that the form and effects of so large an enterprise, involving so many people, with such great aspirations, should continue to be so neglected.

Finally, if asked to give a statement on the health of CPD across the cases presented, one could say that it is alive, but not thriving. Whether or not teachers will prosper through the 'professional life support' they are given is up for debate.

References

Apple, M. (1996) *Cultural Politics and Education*. New York: Teachers College Press.

Brennan, M. (1996) *Multiple Professionalisms for Australian Teachers in an Information Age*. New York: American Education Research Association.

Clarke, J. and Newman, J. (1997) *The Managerial State*. London: Sage.

Cochrane-Smith, M. and Lytle, S. (1999) Relationships of knowledge and practice: teacher learning in communities, in A. Iran-Nejad and C. Pearson (eds) *Review of Research in Education*, 24(2): 251–307.

Commission on Global Governance (1995) *Our Global Neighbourhood: The Report of the Commission on Global Governance*. Oxford: Oxford University Press.

Day, C. (1999) *Continuing Professional Development*. London: Falmer Press.

Day, C. (in press) *A Passion for Teaching*. London: Routledge- Falmer.

Day, C. and Bakioglu, A. (1996) Development and disenchantment in the professional lives of headteachers, in I.F. Goodson and A. Hargreaves (eds) *Teachers' Professional Lives*, pp. 205–7. London: Falmar Press.

Day, C. *et al.* (1996) *Class Size Research and the Quality of Education: A Critical Survey of the Literature Related to Class Size and the Quality of Teaching and Learning*. Haywards Heath: National Association of Headteachers.

Desimone, L., Porter, A., Garet, M., Yoon, K.S. and Birman, B. (2002) Effects of professional development on teachers' instruction: results from a three-year longitudinal study, *Educational Evaluation and Policy Analysis*, 24(2): 81–112.

Farber, B. (1991) *Crisis in Education*. San Francisco: Jossey-Bass.

Fessler, R. and Christensen, J. (1992) *The Teacher Career Cycle: Understanding and Guiding the Professional Development of Teachers*. Boston, MA: Allyn & Bacon.

Finnan, C. and Levin, H.M. (2000) Changing school cultures, in H. Altrichter and J. Elliott (eds) *Images of Educational Change*. Buckingham: Open University Press.

Fried, R.L. (1995) *The Passionate Teacher: A Practical Guide*. Boston, MA: Beacon Press.

Friedson, E. (2001) *Professionalism: The Third Logic*. Cambridge: Polity Press.

Fullan, M. (1993) Why teachers must become change agents, *Educational Leadership*, 50(6): 12–17.

Furlong, J., Barton, L., Miles, S., Whiting, C. and Whitty, G. (2000) *Teacher Education in Transition*. Buckingham: Open University Press.

Giddens, A. (1990) *The Consequences of Modernity*. Cambridge: Polity.

Groundwater-Smith, S. (2000) *Evidence-based practice – towards whole school improvement*. Paper presented to the Annual Conference of the Australian Association for Research in Education, Sydney, 4–7 December.

Groundwater-Smith, S. and Hunter, J. (2000) Whole school inquiry: evidence-based practice, *Journal of In-Service Education*, 26(3): 583–600.

Guskey, T. (2000) *Evaluating Professional Development*. Thousand Oaks, CA: Corwin Press.

Hargreaves, A. (1998) The emotional practice of teaching, *Teaching and Teacher Education*, 14(8): 835–54.

Hargreaves, D. (1994) The new professionalism: the synthesis of professional and institutional development, *Teaching and Teacher Education*, 10(4): 423–38.

Hargreaves, D. (1995) School culture, school effectiveness and school improvement, *School Effectiveness and School Improvement*, 6(1): 23–46.

Havel, V. (1993) Never hope against hope, *Esquire*, October: 65–9.

Hoyle, E. (1980) Professionalisation and de-professionalisation in education, in E. Hoyle and J. Megarry (eds) *World Yearbook of Education, 1980: The Professional Development of Teachers*, pp. 42–56. London: Kogan Page.

Huberman, M. (1989) The professional life cycle of teachers, *Teachers' College Record*, 91(1): 31–57.

Huberman, M. (1995) Professional careers and professional development, in T. Guskey and M. Huberman (eds) *Professional Development in Education: New Paradigms and Practices*, pp. 193–224. New York: Teachers College Press.

Jackson, P. (1968) *Life in Classrooms*. New York: Holt, Rinehart & Winston.

Lieberman, A. (1996) Practices that support teacher development: transforming conceptions of professional learning, in M.W. McLaughlin and I. Oberman (eds) *Teacher Learning: New Policies, New Practices*, pp. 185–201. New York: Columbia University, Teachers College Press.

Mockler, N. (2001) *Professional Learning Portfolios: A Tool for the Reflective Practitioner*, Fremantle: AARE Notre Dame University, Annual Conference, Perth.

Nias, J., Southworth, G. and Yeomans, R. (1989) *Staff Relationships in the Primary School: A Study of Organizational Cultures*. London: Cassell.

Peterson, W. (1964) Age, teacher's role and the institutional setting, in B. Biddle and W. Elena (eds) *Contemporary Research on Teacher Effectiveness*, pp. 264–315. New York: Holt, Rinehart & Winston.

Power M. (1997) *The Audit Society: Rituals of Verification*. Oxford: Oxford University Press.

Prick, L. (1986) *Career Development and Satisfaction Among Secondary School Teachers*. Amsterdam: Vrije Universiteit.

Rosenholtz, S.J. (1989) Workplace conditions that affect teacher quality and commitment: implications for teacher induction programs, *The Elementary School Journal*, 89(4): 420–39.

Rudduck, J. and Hopkins, D. (eds) *Research as a Basis for Teaching: Reading from the Work of Lawrence Stenhouse*, p. 124. London: Heinemann.

Sachs, J. (2001) Teacher professional identity: competing discourses, competing outcomes, *Journal of Educational Policy*, 16(2): 149–61.

Sachs, J. (2003) *The Activist Teaching Profession*. Buckingham: Open University Press.

Sikes, P., Measor, L. and Woods, P. (1985) *Teachers' Careers: Crisis and Continuities*. Lewes: Falmer Press.

Stoll, L. and Fink, D. (1996) *Changing Our Schools: Linking School Effectiveness and School Improvement*. Buckingham: Open University Press.

Strathern, M. (ed.) (2000) *Audit Cultures*, London: Routledge.

Wilson, S.M. and Berne, J. (1999) Teacher learning and the acquisition of professional knowledge: an examination of research on contemporary professional development, in A. Iran-Nejad and P.D. Pearson (eds) *Review of Research in Education*, pp. 173–209. Washington: The American Educational Research Association.

2 Literature, definitions and models: towards a conceptual map

Ray Bolam and Agnes McMahon

This chapter's aim is to provide a brief critical overview of recent developments in the conceptualization, purposes, forms and processes of continuing professional development (CPD). It does so by reviewing selected literature, concentrating on experience in the developed world, reported in English and published since the mid-1980s. Experience from England is used as a running illustration partly because it is the system with which we are most familiar but also, more importantly, because it exemplifies some significant recent trends. Largely because of limitations of space, there are some aspects of CPD that we either do not deal with or only do so summarily. For example, we do not deal with in-service training directed at upgrading unqualified teachers, an essential feature of teacher education policy in some developing countries (Brock 1996) or with studies on induction, even though they raise many important issues (Tickle 2001). Nor do we deal with issues related to the design and implementation of CPD (for example, Hall and Oldroyd 1991; Craft 1996); rather we adopt a more systemic perspective.

Introduction

Several terms related to CPD are found in the literature including, for example, teacher development, in-service education and training (INSET), staff development, career development, human resource development, professional development, continuing education and lifelong learning. Unfortunately, these terms often have overlapping meanings and are defined very differently by different writers. There are also many different models in the literature. Sparks and Loucks-Horsley (1990) proposed five models of what they called staff development: the individually guided staff development model; the observation/assessment model; the development/improvement process model; the training model; and the inquiry model. Tillema and Imants (1995) distinguished between four models of training: training for conceptual change; cognitively guided training; study groups; and promoting change in teaching practice. Sparks and Hirsh (1997) asserted that sustained implementation of new practices requires a new form of professional development affecting not only the knowledge, attitudes and practices of individual teachers, administrators and so on, but also the cultures and structures of the organizations in which they work. They argued that teachers must have opportunities to discuss, think about, try out and hone new practices by taking new roles, creating new structures, working on new tasks and creating a culture of inquiry; hence, staff development linked to a reform agenda must support a learner-centred view of teaching and a career-long conception of teachers' learning. Fullan (1995) portrayed teachers as not only crucial to successful improvement efforts but also as key initiators, arguing that the rapid pace of change today imposes upon teachers moral and cultural imperatives that compel them to be active change agents. Hargreaves (1995: 126) took this a step further, arguing that, as well as addressing technical competence, professional development should include 'the place of moral purpose in teaching, political awareness, acuity, and adeptness among teachers, and teachers' emotional attachment to and engagement with their work'.

In seeking to take account of these perspectives and models, and the dilemmas implicit in them, this chapter adopts a working definition proposed by Day (1997: 4):

> Professional development consists of all natural learning experiences and those conscious and planned activities which are intended to be of direct or indirect benefit to the individual, group or school and which contribute, through these, to the quality of education in the classroom. It is the process by which, alone and with others, teachers review, renew and extend their commitment as change agents to the moral purposes of teaching and by which they acquire and develop critically the knowledge, skills and emotional intelligence essential to good professional thinking, planning and practice with children, young people and colleagues through each phase of their teaching lives.

Helpful as it is, this definition is far from being unproblematic, as we shall see in discussing how CPD is researched and theorized, since the various perspectives and theories often overlap and are difficult to disentangle. These features are necessarily reflected in what follows.

Furthermore, this complexity is compounded by the fact that teacher learning and CPD are influenced by the changing contexts – policy, practice and professional culture – in different countries. Meanwhile, developing theory and research are extending, and sometimes complicating, our understanding of the processes of teacher learning and CPD. The next two sections consider the nature and impact of two aspects of these wider contextual factors on teacher learning and CPD and are followed by a review of changes in CPD itself. Further sections focus on organizational and individual processes as they relate to teacher learning and CPD. The final section identifies some key issues and makes some suggestions for future work in theorizing and researching CPD and in clarifying the nature of teacher professionalism.

System-level factors affecting teachers' work, learning and CPD

CPD policies and practices are necessarily rooted in the particular context of a single educational system and, indeed, are often the product of unique and dynamically changing sets of circumstances – political, economic, social, cultural, historical, professional and technical – in that system. Macro changes in society and the economy over which governments have limited control – like the growth of information technology, the knowledge economy and globalization, increases in immigration and refugees (Williams 2001), as well as natural disasters like the HIV/AIDs epidemic, in addition to those introduced by governments themselves – like the nature and extent of centralization and regulation (Karstanje 1999), giving greater priority to secondary and vocational education, social inclusion and increased access to higher education – all influence the aims and processes of education, schools and schooling and have their impact on CPD.

Nevertheless, the continuing centrality of CPD to the improvement of educational performance is evident from the importance attached to it over several decades in the developed world (for example, CERI 1982, 2001; OECD 1998) and in the developing world (for example, Delors 1996; World Education Forum 2000; UNESCO 2001). In the former, the developments that have most powerfully influenced CPD have been those associated with the extensive national and state-level reforms in the 1990s. As a result, teachers and school leaders increasingly work in a political context in which external, 'restructuring' changes, initiated by national, state or local authorities to raise standards of achievement, exert priority over their own vision of desirable improvements. Unsurprisingly, governments are primarily concerned to ensure that CPD enhances education quality. Thus, many countries adopted the same broad 'steering' strategies, often based on dedicated or categorical funding, to couple professional development tightly to the implementation of their reform policies. Indeed, this approach has probably become the dominant paradigm for systemic change in Organization for Economic Cooperation and Development (OECD) member countries (Halasz 2000).

A good example of this was the introduction of the national literacy and numeracy strategies in England. The curricula and pedagogical content of these innovations were specified very tightly by central government agencies as, too, was the associated training, and the outcomes were reported to be very successful (see www.standards.dfee.gov.uk). However, the danger of generalizing from this experience is apparent from Little's (2001: 23) analysis of school reform in the USA. She stated that the kinds of pedagogical, curricular and organizational changes envisioned by reformers in the 1980s and 1990s (for example, teaching for understanding) could not easily be expressed in terms of specific transferable skills and practices:

> to make headway on ambitious but broadly defined aims and principles would require adequate opportunities to learn (experiment, consult, evaluate) that were embedded in the routine organisation of teachers' work day and work year. That is, such reforms would require less of a conventional training model and more of a consultation, problem solving, and programme development model.

Thus, it appears that the nature and specificity of the reforms and the associated CPD may be critical determinants of success.

School effectiveness and improvement research does, however, have some relevant messages for CPD. Most of the factors that correlate with effective school outcomes have direct implications for teachers (Sammons *et al.* 1995) and indirect ones for teacher learning and CPD. Teachers in effective schools are reported to work collegially and to collaborate to achieve shared goals; they have high expectations of their students, teach purposively, monitor student work and give positive feedback (Teddlie and Reynolds 2000). The literature on improving schools indicates that they have learned to manage multiple change and are moving towards the concept of a learning organization. Fullan (1993: 138) argued that planned change strategies are not the solution because: 'reality under conditions of dynamic complexity is fundamentally non-linear'. He suggested that learning teachers are the key to a learning organization and that this will require inner learning (intrapersonal sense-making) as well as outer learning (relating to and collaborating with others); one means of promoting this is to invest in teacher professional development. Similarly, Gray *et al.* (1999: 144) concluded that a common theme of schools that were improving more rapidly was that 'they had found ways of facilitating more discussion among colleagues about classroom issues than hitherto'.

In an historical overview, Hopkins and Reynolds (2001) argued that the current phase of school improvement research emphasized the need for schools to create an infrastructure, especially collaborative patterns of staff development, to enable knowledge of best practice and research findings to be shared and utilized.

Changes in teachers' work and professionalism affecting teachers' learning and CPD

A distinctive feature of CPD in teacher education is its focus on an occupational group whose professional status and conditions of service vary between countries and, indeed, over time in any one country. Hence, any discussion of continuing professional development must consider what it means to be a professional and the extent to which professionals should be able to exercise autonomy in their work. For example, Eraut (1995) argued that the professional development of teachers cannot be separated from the development of schools as professional institutions that create, monitor and review educational programmes and policies. He also argued that, while the professionalization of schools is necessary, such a development is dependent upon appropriate modes of accountability. Specifically, schools must give special attention to the impact of their programmes and policies on the progress of individual students, a proposal that raises feasibility questions in centralized systems. Nevertheless, it is surely axiomatic that, no matter the degree of centralization or decentralization, issues such as whether the individual teacher or the employer has the main responsibility for ensuring staff receive CPD, what should be its focus and content, and how it should be provided are all influenced by teachers' conditions of service and by perceptions of teachers as professionals.

National reforms in the 1990s certainly impacted on teachers' and headteachers' roles and conditions of work, with considerable implications for their professionalism and CPD. In England and Wales, for example, the 1990s saw the introduction of government-imposed national salary scales, conditions of service, career ladders and performance-related pay for all teachers and headteachers in 25,000 schools. Currently, a controversial new contract designed, in part, to give a teaching role to teaching assistants is being negotiated. This reform agenda resulted in extensive and radical changes in the roles and responsibilities of teachers, headteachers and other senior staff in general in what was, in effect, a cultural shift in schools and the teaching profession. Weindling (1999) reported that 90 per cent of a cohort of British secondary headteachers said their role had changed significantly over the previous five years, while a European study found that Welsh heads were much more likely than their counterparts in the Netherlands, Norway and Spain to see government reforms as causing them substantial problems (Bolam *et al.* 2000). There were also substantial changes in teachers' workloads and motivation. Campbell and Neill (1994: 68) reported that their sample of teachers 'actually work significantly longer hours than most other non-manual and manual workers in Great Britain and Europe'.

The number of vacancies, especially for headteachers, increased, mainly due to early retirements caused by stress, ill health and workload pressure, all of which had a negative impact on teachers' motivation and morale (School Teachers' Review Body 1996: 15; Travers and Cooper 1996). A small-scale study (McMahon 2000) reported that teachers' lesson preparation, classroom management and assessment of pupil work all suffered when they were working under undue pressure. Unsurprisingly, teacher retention is problematic – up to 40 per cent of teachers with three years' experience leave the profession (Smithers 2001) which itself is ageing – more than 40 per cent of teachers are aged 40 or more (Department for Education and Employment 1999).

This situation is not unique to Britain. According to Darling-Hammond (1990), CPD in the USA is being influenced by changes in the nature of the teaching force – for example, it contains more women, has an increasing age profile and there are severe recruitment problems. In New Zealand, teachers also reported high levels of stress and a decline in morale (Whitty 1997: 305). A comparative study of teachers' experience in Australia, New Zealand, the UK and the USA referred to the 'erosion of the profession', key features of which included decreased status, external interference, excessive change and increased workload (Scott *et al.* 2000). In the USA, according to one commentator, 'individual merit pay, career ladders and similar schemes have failed miserably' (Fullan 2001: 258). Policy makers are well aware of the importance of these developments. At the time of writing 24 OECD countries are engaged in a collaborative project entitled 'Attracting, Developing and Retaining Effective Teachers', one main objective of which is to investigate the policies and conditions, including the role of CPD, that promote the retention of effective teachers in schools (see www.oecd.org/els/education/teacherpolicy).

The links between continuing professional development and notions of professionalism and accountability are also apparent, although the factors involved are often complex. In most of the 16 European countries studied by Le Metais (1997), teachers are civil servants, with rigorous competition for entry but also security of tenure and high status throughout their professional careers, limiting the demand for CPD. However, demographic changes meant that almost two-thirds of teachers were over 40 years of age, increasing the pressure for CPD from governments, given that so many changes are occurring in education. As a result, in most countries CPD was regarded as a professional right and duty, although the extent of these obligations was rarely defined precisely. There were, reportedly, four main reasons for teachers to undertake CPD: to improve individual performance, identified either by performance appraisal or through personal initiative; to enhance their ability to meet changing needs; to train for new roles or promotion; as a preparation for management. In eight of the countries, attendance for certain purposes was compulsory, mainly during school hours.

Specific issues arise in particular countries. In the unusual circumstances of Greece, where a gap of up to ten years often occurs between qualification and first appointment, CPD is compulsory for all new appointees (Le Metais

1997). In China and several African countries, 'particularism' and 'universalism' impact on staff selection and CPD:

> In particularist approaches selection is shaped by the personal affiliation of the players, for example kinship, religion, ethnic or political similarities. The particularist approach of appointing people to posts as a reward for support or in recognition of affiliation can be adopted both by government agencies or departments, and by individual managers in schools and colleges.
>
> (Foskett and Lumby 2003: 70)

In the Netherlands, CPD is apparently problematic for quite other reasons, because of 'the tradition of teachers' professional freedom in determining whether or not they take part in such activities . . . Teachers' traditional autonomy has posed problems for Dutch headteachers wishing to introduce a policy on professional development' (Karstanje 2000: 30).

These issues can be located in the broader analytical framework of managerialism or new public management (NPM), concepts adapted from the private sector (Clarke and Newman 1997) and applied across the public sector in health, social services and housing. In education, the main features of NPM include increased centralization of strategic decision making to the national level, reduced collegial involvement in national policy-making, decentralization of operational decision making to the site level, an increased emphasis on line management and managerial control of teachers' work in the interests of efficiency, the weakening of teacher autonomy, the creation of new managerial roles, skills and responsibilities and the emergence of more distinct managerial layers in schools. In addition, it is often associated with various forms of market-oriented mechanisms together with an increased emphasis on target setting, 'rational' management and accountability. Variants on NPM have been adopted in the UK and in other developed countries (Smyth 1995; Moos and Dempster 1998). Moreover, because NPM is supported by governments and international agencies like the OECD, it will probably continue to exercise a considerable influence on education and CPD.

Questions about the nature of a profession are complex but also culture-bound (Le Metais 1997; Whitty 1997). In the UK, Hoyle and John (1995: 16) distinguished between professionalism, professionality and professionalization in stressing the importance of considering 'questions about the *nature* of teachers' autonomy, knowledge and responsibility, as these relate to effective practice'. They also cast light on another theoretical perspective on CPD – the sociological distinction between professional and organizational socialization. The former is seen as an individual's cumulative, career-long experience of the wider practices and values of the broader profession, while the latter is that individual's socialization into the practices and values of a single organization. Both may be used as conceptual tools to analyse CPD. Thus, Weindling (1999: 98) described the organizational socialization of new headteachers as 'a critical period when the new head's notions of headship meet the reality of a particular school'.

Changes in CPD policy and practice affecting teachers' learning

Against this background, approaches to CPD have varied considerably between countries over the past 20 years (CERI 1982; OECD 1998). From a US perspective, Sparks and Hirsh (1997: 12) identified several major shifts in staff development, including:

- from individual development to individual and organization development;
- from fragmented, piecemeal improvement efforts to staff development driven by a clear, coherent strategic plan for school district, each school and its departments;
- from district-focused to school-focused approaches to staff development;
- from a focus on adult needs and satisfaction to a focus on student needs and learning outcomes and changes in on-the-job behaviours;
- from training conducted away from the job as the primary delivery system for staff development to multiple forms of job-embedded learning;
- from an orientation toward the transmission of knowledge and skills to teachers by experts to the study by teachers of the teaching and learning processes;
- from staff development directed toward teachers as the primary recipients to continuous improvement in performance for everyone who affects student learning;
- from staff development for individual teachers to the creation of learning communities in which all – students, teachers, principals and support staff – are both learners and teachers.

Similar changes are evident in England and Wales, where the funding arrangements from the 1960s to the early 1980s gave primacy to enabling individual professionals to attend external courses. In the late 1980s, new national policies for the financing of CPD changed this situation dramatically. The most important changes were the introduction of five compulsory training days for all teachers; the creation of a regulated market in which schools received annual funding to provide and buy training and consultancy services (Harland *et al.* 1993); a framework of national priority topic areas linked to the national reforms; a substantial reduction in the capacity of local authorities to deliver training; the demise of local teachers' centres; a substantial increase in the number of professional associations and unions, private trainers, consultants and other commercial agencies offering training; more flexible, market-driven, university-based, masters-level provision (for example, modularization, credit transfer and accumulation, accreditation of prior learning and experience, professional development profiles, distance and open learning programmes); and a substantial increase in the number of taught doctorates, especially the Ed.D. In recognition of the importance of CPD in school improvement the recent trend in national policy is to set a strong regulatory framework. The national contract of service required all teachers to participate in CPD activities using an annual grant and with an emphasis on reform-related activities. Within this framework, responsibility for implementing CPD was largely delegated to the school level. Emerging policies have acknowledged the importance of balancing system and individual needs by increasing investment in CPD for individual teachers (Department for Education and Employment 2000). Thus, professional bursaries are being paid directly to teachers to help them achieve their individual career goals – for example, by studying for a masters degree – and £3 million was allocated for individual research scholarships, again paid directly to teachers, to carry out research in partnership with a university and/or other schools.

The intended model of CPD consequential on these changes can be characterized roughly as follows: self-developing, reflective teachers, in self-managing schools with devolved funding and five training days, design, implement and evaluate professional development programmes aimed at meeting an appropriate balance of individual teacher, school and national needs and priorities. From a practical perspective, tools for implementing these and related ideas are widely available. They include professional development profiles (Day 1999), action research (Elliott 1991), action learning (Wallace 1991), coaching (Joyce and Showers 1988), mentoring and peer-assisted learning (Bolam *et al.* 1995), and the overall management of CPD (Craft 1996). The most recent addition to this repertoire is performance management (Middlewood 2002).

However, there is evidence to indicate that the impact on CPD of successive education reforms made it difficult to implement this model successfully. For example, McMahon (1999) reported on a study of CPD based on a sample of teachers in 66 secondary schools in four English local education authorities (LEAs). She found that the operation of the CPD market was substantially influenced by the schools' geographical location, rural schools having poorer access to provision than their urban counterparts, and by the considerable variation that existed in the size of individual CPD budgets, certain schools sometimes having three times more money than others. The five training days were most often used for administrative purposes (for example, departmental planning) and based on needs derived from the schools' development plan; only 28 per cent of schools allocated them for individual professional development needs. The aims and content of all training activities were primarily driven by the national reform agenda with most activities taking the form of short training courses which, as research has demonstrated over the years, are weak at promoting sustained change. McMahon concluded that this tendency for the training agenda to be centrally determined was increased by the government's emphasis on training teachers to meet the national numeracy and literacy targets and by the policy of linking the funding for university-provided in-service training programmes to national priorities, as a result of which several programmes had their funding removed. These findings, which are broadly consistent with earlier research (for example, Harland *et al*. 1993), indicate that the notion of site-based management of CPD within a regulated market did not, and probably still does not, operate widely in practice. Rather, the CPD agenda was determined largely by the needs of centrally imposed reforms and by the needs of the schools and departments to implement them. This left little scope, given their limited resources and access to provision, for schools to meet the professional development needs of individual teachers. Thus, Bottery and Wright (2000) concluded that greater market influence led to less choice and more central state direction to improve school performance.

Consistent with this pattern of centralization and regulation, several countries have introduced national standards of professional practice for teachers and headteachers. One of the first examples was in the USA, where the National Board of Professional Teacher Standards (NBPTS) developed standards and assessment procedures for 30 subject areas based on five principles whereby teachers: are committed to students and their learning; know the subjects they teach and how to teach those subjects to students; are responsible for managing and monitoring students' learning; think systematically about their practice and learn from experience; and are members of learning communities (NBPTS 1993). In England and Wales, the Teacher Training Agency (TTA) introduced a comprehensive 'national curriculum' framework for initial and in-service teacher education based on four sets of national standards: for newly qualified teachers, special needs teachers, subject leaders and headteachers. The Standards for Qualified Teacher Status were in four sections: knowledge and understanding of subject matter; planning, teaching and class management; monitoring, assessment, recording, reporting and accountability; other professional requirements, including CPD (TTA 1998). At present there is little research evidence about the usage or impact of these standards but they undoubtedly attract much criticism because of their close links with competencies-based learning (Day 1999).

Significant changes are also evident in leadership development. The National College for School Leadership (NCSL) has formulated a leadership development framework targeted at over 120,000 professionals and encompassing five stages: emergent leadership, which includes subject and specialist leadership roles; established leadership, comprising experienced deputy and assistant heads who do not wish to be headteachers; entry into headship, which embraces the preparatory National Professional Qualification for Headship and a revised induction programme (Headlamp); advanced leadership, for heads with four or more years' experience (the Leadership Programme for Serving Headteachers); and consultant leadership (Newton 2003). Activities and programmes related to all five stages are coordinated by the NCSL, a government-funded organization, not university-based, with an annual budget of £60 million (NCSL 2002).

The NCSL is unquestionably a major institutional innovation, not simply in terms of its implications for school leadership development, which are clearly considerable, but also because its innovative use of a range of technologies and methods has much broader implications for CPD in general. Perhaps the most influential, widespread and recent technical innovation in CPD has arisen with the advent of the worldwide web and e-learning (see the National College website for a good example: www.ncsl.org.uk). According to Johnson and Everett (2001) 'e-learning and online instruction [are] delivered through the Internet or Intranet or personal computer, providing a visual environment, interactive experience and customised learning process (enhanced by audio, video, and animation)'. The European Training Foundation (1997) located e-learning in the wider context of information technology, which it defined as also including one-way television, interactive television, computer-aided instruction, simulations and games, virtual reality, the internet, intranets, computer and video conferencing, broadband multimedia and just-in-time learning. It offered a rationale for the expansion of technology, including e-learning, arguing that it can enhance the teaching and learning process by helping students to move from a receiving to a creative role in the learning process; by taking learners from the isolation of their classroom into interaction with the wider world; by providing access to simulations, case studies and learning laboratories; and by improving communication between students, between faculty and between the two (p. 83).

A second major NCSL innovation is its extensive support for networked learning communities. At the time of writing there are approximately 80 networks and 1000+ schools in operation (see www.ncsl.org.uk). The rationale for the network approach, according to Lieberman (2000), is that schools are being asked to educate a growing and diverse population, yet school systems that are organized bureaucratically and function traditionally have difficulty adapting to change. Lieberman argued that educational reform networks are particularly well suited to making use of new technology and institutional arrangements. They are flexible, borderless and innovative, able to create collaborative environments, focus and develop agendas that grow and change with participants. Moreover, networks are said to give teachers the opportunity to create as well as receive knowledge (Jackson 2002). Variants on networking practice include those which are university based (Fullan 1995; Day 1999) and attempts to extend the role of professional development schools mainly concerned with initial training to embrace CPD (Stallings and Kowalski 1990).

The roles of external agencies in CPD are evidently changing as these new processes and methods emerge. In several countries the numbers of private trainers and consultants have increased. In England and Wales this increased marketization of CPD provision was accompanied by a reduction in the roles of LEAs and universities and the demise of teachers' centres. The decrease in LEA involvement is due to government policy and is probably peculiar to England and Wales, where LEAs are in the process of seeking a new identity and role (Hemsley-Brown *et al.* 2003; *Times Educational Supplement* 2003). The issues with respect to universities are more complex and diverse. An ongoing OECD study found that in many countries there is greater involvement of universities in teacher education, with England and Wales being the major exceptions (Coolahan 2002). An earlier OECD study (CERI 2001) found a wide diversity of approaches to leadership and management development in terms of content, delivery mode, timing and institutional framework and, once again, universities were playing a key role, except in England and Wales where there are, in effect, two parallel systems operating – in universities and in the NCSL programmes (Bolam 2003). Changed central financial regulations and new modes of assessment and accountability, reinforced by the increased financial rewards for research and publications and the recruitment of international students, have been particularly influential in reducing universities' role in CPD for local teachers. Moreover, few universities and schools of education have had the vision to rethink their approach to teacher education and establish professional schools. According to one commentator:

> Universities and colleges therefore urgently need to review the position of professional education in their institution; in particular they need to review the position of staff with professional rather than academic qualifications and devise ways of recruiting, rewarding and developing such staff; work collaboratively, both regionally and nationally, to promote the position of professional education within higher education.
>
> (Furlong 2000: 33)

Changes in school-level processes affecting teacher learning and CPD

This section opens with several perspectives on CPD at the school level, which sometimes overlap with, and sometimes run counter to, one another. Perhaps the most familiar is the instrumental stance associated with the management or staff development perspective. For instance, in a sample of OECD countries, professional development was accepted as being 'central to the way principals manage schools, in at least two respects: first, as instructional leaders, principals may be expected to coordinate professional progression of their staff; second, they need to manage the learning community as a whole, using development as part of school change' (CERI 2001: 27). This finds support in international research and experience. For example, of approximately 700 new primary and secondary headteachers in five European countries, 25 per cent rated 'promoting professional development' and 20 per cent rated 'regular formal appraisal of teachers' as a 'serious or very serious problem' (Bolam *et al.* 2000: 28).

A typical definition of staff development associated with this perspective is one from Hong Kong:

> Different types of programmes and activity which aim to empower teachers and administrators to develop positive attitudes and beliefs about education and management, become more effective individuals and teams, be competent in teaching students and managing the school process, as well as helping the school adapt to its changing environment.
>
> (Tam and Cheng 1996: 17)

Similarly, Hall and Oldroyd (1991) described a typical UK approach using a CPD coordinator to manage a cyclic model with the following stages: policy and strategic planning; identification of needs and priorities at individual teacher, group and whole-school levels; planning, implementing and evaluating the annual programme. In the UK this approach has found its most sophisticated and elaborate expression in the Investors in People programme, for which about 20 per cent of schools have been recognized (see www.iipuk.co.uk). The staff development perspective is firmly rooted in the human resource management (HRM) tradition, characterized recently as follows: 'An overriding assumption in the literature is that the purpose of HRM is to help organizations achieve their objectives, which are essentially in terms of performance' (Kamoche 2001: 1). However, writers on HRM are well aware of the dangers of an approach that is too instrumental (for example, Beardwell and Holden 1994).

The actual operation of CPD varies according to a wider range of organizational factors. One very basic variable is school size. Thus, Southworth and Weindling (2002) concluded from a study of 26 large (401–600) primary schools in England that, compared to smaller schools, they were characterized by more staff expertise, more opportunity for peer support, more internal communication difficulties, more delegation, more reliance on middle managers and more use of teams. Less tangibly, the nature of the school as a workplace also has a powerful influence on their attitudes to learning and professional development.

The culture and ethos of the school, the quality of leadership and administration, the availability of resources, whether or not there is a calm and orderly atmosphere, and the level of workload will all influence whether teachers have any space or energy to devote to their professional development (Sparks and Loucks-Horsley 1990). Joyce *et al.* (1999) proposed a model of school improvement in which the school is a learning community for teachers as well as students. The micro-, school-level cultures that these writers argue are associated with teacher growth and learning are ones in which teachers feel able to experiment and take risks, where collaboration is valued and time is allocated to facilitate shared work, where information is used as a basis for joint inquiry and investigation and where sharing and partnership rather than competition between teachers is encouraged. How are such cultures established? Case studies of schools that appear to be moving in this direction show that changing the culture takes prolonged effort by many people over several years and that it is possible to regress as well as move forward (McMahon 2001).

The concept of school culture is a very slippery one. Questions abound about whether the culture of an organization can be viewed holistically; about how it can be identified and the extent to which it can be managed and changed. Schein (1985: 9) argued that culture is:

> a pattern of basic assumptions – invented, discovered or developed by a given group as it learns to cope with its problems of external adaptation and integration – that has worked well enough to be considered valid and, therefore has to be taught to new members as the correct way to perceive, think and feel in relation to those problems.

However, others have argued that such definitions give too much emphasis to values and the holistic nature of organizational culture, which is better seen as 'a tool kit that provides strategies for action that members of the culture can use in many different ways' (Firestone and Louis 1999: 299). This interpretation gives room for individual creativity and recognizes that the culture may not be uniform and that individuals and groups will draw differentially on what Firestone and Louis term the 'cultural codes'. There are likely to be a number of subcultures that reflect cultural differences between the various groups of people (for example, teachers, pupils, parents) and the subgroups (for example, the science teachers) who form the school community.

This links directly with the concept of community of practice (COP), for which Wenger (1999) proposed the following indicators: sustained mutual relationships, whether harmonious or conflictual; shared ways of doing things together; rapid flow of information; the absence of introductory preambles in conversations because they are assumed to be continuations; and knowing what others know and what they can do. He also argued that a whole organization may be too large a social configuration both for individuals to relate to as a COP and also for analytic purposes. Treating them as a single COP would gloss over discontinuities, which are integral to their structure; they are better viewed as constellations of interconnected practices. Constellations share historical roots, have related enterprises, belong to the same institution, face similar conditions and have members in common. The potential applications to departments and other teams and groups in schools are apparent.

Building on this and on the more familiar idea of a learning organization (Senge *et al.* 2000), a related perspective is that of the professional learning community, which is also informed by literature on what it is to be a professional, adult learning and the meaning of community. According to several writers (for example, Hargreaves 1994; Stoll *et al.* 2002) a new form of professionalism is emerging in which teachers work more closely and collaboratively with colleagues, students and parents, linking teacher and school development. Thus, King and Newmann (2001) argued that teacher learning is most likely to occur when teachers: can concentrate on instruction and student outcomes in the specific contexts in which they teach; have sustained opportunities to study, to experiment with and to receive helpful feedback on specific innovations; and have opportunities to collaborate with professional peers, both within and outside their schools, along with access to the expertise of researchers.

Similarly, Smylie (1995) drew upon a range of adult learning theories to identify conditions of effective workplace learning, including opportunities for teachers to learn from peer colleagues in collaborative group work settings, with open communication, experimentation and feedback. The focus on community emphasized mutually supportive relationships and the development of shared norms and values, whereas the focus in the literature about professionals and professionalism emphasized the acquisition of knowledge and skills, orientation to clients and professional autonomy (Louis *et al.* 1995). These developments have strong echoes of earlier ideas on school-focused in-service training as a mechanism for promoting school improvement (CERI 1982: 20; Fullan 2001: 255), which continue to resonate with practitioners, for example in Israel (Sabar and HaShar-Francis 1999). Moreover, they are entirely congruent with related perspectives like learning organizations and capacity building.

Enquiry-based, or evidence-informed, practice is increasingly seen as an important feature of effective professional learning communities. Cochran-Smith and Lytle (2001) proposed that a legitimate and essential purpose of CPD is the development of an enquiry stance on teaching that is critical and transformative, a stance linked not only to high standards for the learning of all students but also to social change and social justice, and to the individual and collective professional growth of teachers (p. 46). According to Stoll *et al.* (2002), three broad, interconnected approaches are open to schools wishing to promote evidence-informed practice. They can promote systematic research and evaluation in the school, in departments and by individual classroom teachers; adopt a more systematic approach to the collection, analysis and use of 'routine' data (for example, in relation to students' examination results, value-added data and external school inspection reports); and search for and use externally generated research. None of these modes is unproblematic, but there is evidence (for example, Joyce *et al.* 1999; Jackson 2002) to suggest that the strategy can promote both professional development and school improvement. The concept of an effective professional learning community is currently under investigation in the UK (Stoll *et al.* 2003).

Changing perspectives on the processes of teacher learning and CPD

In contrast to the systemic and organizational perspectives on CPD adopted so far in this discussion, several perspectives focus on the needs and aspirations of individual teachers and headteachers. Here, too, some overlaps are evident. One perspective focuses on job and career stages – initial, induction, in-service and school leadership – and their implications for CPD needs. Thus, Burden's (1990: 314) view was that knowledge of teacher characteristics and stages of development is important for teacher-educators, since it can help them understand the needs and abilities of teachers at different points in their careers:

> Teacher career development deals with changes that teachers experience throughout their careers in a) job skills, knowledge and behaviours in such areas as teaching methods, disciplines and techniques, curriculum, lesson plans, rules and procedures etc. b) attitudes, expectations and concerns in such areas as attitudes toward self and others, images of teaching, professional confidence and maturity, commitment to teaching and satisfaction, beliefs and concerns c) job events in such areas as changes in grade level, school or district.

This is sometimes linked with a lifelong learning perspective. For example, Coolahan (2002: 7) highlighted the emergence of widespread international support for the idea of lifelong learning, citing a wide range of reports and policy statements and the implications for teacher education, concluding that 'the move towards lifelong learning is essentially a people-centred movement. It reflects a deeply humanistic concern that learning be seen to be integrated as a continuing feature of human experience from the cradle to the grave'.

However, an alternative interpretation is to see it as the logical adaption of the instrumental, market-driven approach that sometimes characterizes HRM at the organizational level (for example, European Training Foundation 1997) to the system level: 'A key to the twenty-first century, learning throughout life will be essential for adapting to the evolving requirements of the labour market and for better mastery of the changing time frames and rhythms of individual existence' (UNESCO 1996: 100).

Parallel changes in our understanding of professional learning and development are also emerging, a perspective that is well established in HRM more generally (see Collin 1994). Clearly, teachers need specialized knowledge and a repertoire of pedagogical skills. Eraut (1995: 230) distinguished between four types of process knowledge: processes for acquiring information; routinized action and skilled behaviour; deliberative processes such as planning, decision making and problem solving; and meta-processes such as assessing, evaluating and controlling. The underlying concept of the teacher as reflective practitioner has been widely adopted and central to it is the need for teachers to develop the ability to reflect critically on their behaviour, alone or with the help of colleagues, so as to develop a deeper understanding of the learning process and how it can be improved. From a developmental perspective, it is clear that individual learning needs will also be shaped by factors such as length of experience, level of responsibility and, perhaps, by gender and ethnicity. Huberman (1995) explored the relationship between teachers' professional lives and their professional development, arguing that their motivation for development will be influenced by the stage and position they have reached in their careers, and this in turn will influence their willingness to seek out professional development opportunities. Thus, self-evidently, the professional development needs of a beginning teacher are likely to be very different from those of an expert teacher in mid-career who is taking on a senior leadership role.

Borko and Putnam's (1995) perspective on teachers' professional growth is grounded in cognitive psychology and based on the premise that one important component of teachers' ongoing learning is the expansion and elaboration of their professional knowledge base. Following an analytic account of three CPD courses based on their own model, they concluded that:

> persons who wish to reform educational practice cannot simply tell teachers how to teach differently. Teachers themselves must make the design changes. To do so, they must acquire rich knowledge of subject matter, pedagogy, and subject specific pedagogy; and they must come to hold new beliefs in these domains. Successful professional development efforts are those that helped teachers to acquire or develop new ways of thinking about learning, learners, and subject matter, thus constructing a professional knowledge base that will enable them to teach students in more powerful and meaningful ways.
>
> (1995: 60)

Clearly, however, other factors are also important. Maurer and Tarulli (1994) identified the following factors affecting the voluntary involvement in development activities of workers in general: perceptions of the working environment; perceptions and beliefs about the benefits of development; judgement of senior management support; personality factors like identification with work; personal concept of career; and sense of self-efficacy, particularly how confident the individual is about learning new skills. Building on this work, Ruohotie's (1996) study concluded that boring, repetitive and dependent work discourages professional development and growth whereas challenging, variable and independent work encourages it; personal factors and life changes can cause individuals to reconsider career priorities and goals – for instance, when the career routine is broken or personal circumstances change significantly, this can result in the initiation of a personal learning cycle which, in turn, can be reinforced by external feedback and support. Thus, Ruohotie links the individual, personal dimension to the idea of a learning organization (p. 439).

Day (1999: 48 ff.) reviewed a wide range of models of teacher development. These included one with three components – career cycle, personal environment and organizational environment – which postulated that teacher development is a function of a 'dynamic ebb and flow . . . with teachers moving in and out of stages in response to environmental influences from both the personal environment and the organisational environment' (Fessler 1995: 187). Day (1999: 68) concluded by rejecting linear models of development as too simplistic and explored the utility of a framework for career-long development planning, using a 'personal development profile' (p. 102 ff.) as a means of engaging in purposive and proactive development. His approach highlights a key issue in CPD. Logically it seems essential for *continuing* professional development to be cumulative: a personal development profile offers one important means of achieving this.

Such an approach must, however, take account of Hargreaves' (1993) perspective which embraces wider societal trends. He criticized the idea of teacher development as self-development especially when it ignores the moral framework and wider context of teaching. He argued that it can be self-indulgent, for instance when researchers and professional developers prefer to work with teachers who share their own values; or politically naïve, for example when they encourage reflection on personal biographies without relating them to the broader social/historical context; or misleadingly grandiose, for example when researchers promote an excessive belief in the transformative power of personal knowledge and personal change. Developing this argument, Hargreaves (1995) stressed the importance of social and moral purposes in CPD and in teachers' work generally: despite the lip-service currently being granted to teacher professionalism, such CPD overlooks and undermines the place of purpose and goals in teachers' work and as a result ends are separated from means.

Discussion and conclusions

This chapter has reviewed developments in CPD over the last 20 years or so. It is striking just how much has changed. Technically the emergence of the worldwide web and of e-learning have made possible CPD methods and approaches – for example, network learning groups made up of schools several miles apart – that were previously unthinkable. The increased emphasis on school-focused CPD which was evident in the 1980s has developed into a much more sophisticated approach which takes account of school culture, work-based learning and professional learning communities. The increased importance attached to teacher learning as the core process of CPD and of self-directed learning as the main goal, perhaps using personal development profiles as the main tool, has transformed our understanding of the whole process. Increased emphasis on the moral purposes of teaching, and hence of CPD, have had a similar impact.

At the same time, certain well-documented issues and dilemmas remain, although recent theoretical perspectives offer new insights. For example, NPM theory throws new light on the potential tension between CPD directed towards meeting the needs of individuals and the organization (CERI 1982: 11). Certainly, the issue of how to strike an appropriate balance between meeting the needs of individual professionals on the one hand and of the school and national policy on the other has been, and still is, alive. The evidence from research and experience in several countries demonstrates that national needs have been dominant since the mid-1980s. Furthermore, the boundaries of CPD remain somewhat problematic. Clearly, staff development and work-related training are part of CPD. But what place, if any, should there be in CPD for professional education, like university masters degrees, and liberal education, as advocated in initial teacher education (Liston and Zeichner 1991)? What, exactly, is meant by lifelong learning in this context? Is it exclusively intended for vocational and instrumental purposes or does it have a liberal education component? What of the idea of personal development, of the person in the professional (Day 2000)? How reasonable is it to argue that teachers need professional education at all stages of their careers and liberal education throughout their lives? And who should pay what proportion of the costs for such education, and when and how should it be provided and accessed? What part, if any, can CPD play in reducing stress and achieving an appropriate work/life balance? At present, the answers to these questions are implied in the various definitions of CPD and teacher learning reviewed in this chapter, but the underlying value positions are usually left implicit and unexamined. Resolving such dilemmas and answering such questions are complex tasks. We conclude with some reflections and proposals regarding theory, research and the teaching profession that we see as important steps towards doing so.

Theorizing CPD: the need for a conceptual map

One obvious conclusion from this selective review is that literature on CPD is itself problematic. Even a cursory reading reveals a mundane but considerable practical problem: that it is so very extensive. Reports, articles in academic journals, books and chapters in books are being published at an overwhelming rate. More worryingly, these numerous and burgeoning publications are rarely mutually informing and, indeed, are often contradictory. In part, this is because they are written from diverse perspectives, for instance focusing on individual teacher self-development, classroom or subject teaching, school organization and leadership, national policy-making or theoretical development. It is also because they draw upon a range of theoretical subfields, some of which have a strong discipline base (for example, sociology, cognitive psychology, social psychology and occupational psychology) and some of which are more eclectic (such as teacher education and training, andragogy, evaluative research, change theory, management studies and policy studies). One consequence is that there are too many rather than too few approaches and theories, a problem characterized as 'conceptual pluralism' in the related field of educational administration (Bolman and Deal 1997). Whereas this latter field has undergone a lengthy process of self-criticism and development – from the early atheoretical approaches, via the so-called 'theory movement' through to the current state of pluralistic approaches (see Griffiths 1988; Bush *et al.* 1999) – there has been nothing comparable in CPD studies. The underlying problem, according to Guskey and Huberman (1995: 2–3) is that:

> Those familiar with the professional development literature generally are aware that these differences in perspectives exist. Nevertheless, few understand the precise nature of the differences. In large part this is because no attempt has been made in the professional development field to lay bare these differences. There has been no systematic effort to clearly illustrate the conceptual grounds from which each perspective is derived or to show the connections between the prescriptions each offers for practice.

As discussed in the opening section, various writers offer typologies of CPD, but each start from their own assumptions and adopt their own focus. For example, Sparks and Loucks-Horsley (1990) excluded state or district level models; Huberman and Guskey (1995) identified two tensions in the literature – between deficit and growth models and between individual and institutional models; and Cochran-Smith and Lytle (2001: 49) concentrated on three different conceptions of teacher learning that coexist and are used to justify quite different ideas and approaches to improving teaching and learning – knowledge-for-practice, knowledge-in-practice and knowledge-of-practice. Partly in recognition of these dilemmas, Day (1997: 41) emphasized the importance of conceptualizing CPD as 'multidimensional, a dynamic interplay between teachers' stages of biographical and situated experience, environmental factors, career, life and lifelong learning phases'.

We conclude that a broad framework or conceptual map is needed to make sense of these complex and diverse issues. Experience in the related field of educational administration may offer possible ways forward. Thus, adapting Bolam's (1999) provisional framework, it may be helpful to distinguish between four categories of CPD literature: the 'knowledge for understanding' literature, which includes theoretical and critical policy analysis; the 'knowledge for action' literature, which includes evaluations; the 'policy makers' literature, which includes national- and state-level policy statements; and the 'practitioner' literature, which includes two subsets – instrumentalist and reflexive – and consists mainly of accounts of practice and methods (for an alternative approach see Gunter and Ribbins 2002).

Researching CPD: strengthening and managing the knowledge base

Another striking feature of the literature is that, after several decades of research, there is little evidence of CPD's impact on policy and practice yet, despite this, numerous CPD schemes and programmes are constantly being introduced throughout the world. Moreover, they are often claimed to be new and innovative when it is clear from the literature that they are not. We conclude that the knowledge and evidence base for CPD needs to be strengthened in several respects.

First, there continues to be an urgent need for better evaluations focused on outcomes and impact measures and directed as closely as possible at student learning. Very few published evaluation studies make any reference to impact on teacher behaviour or student learning outcomes. Most rely on teacher perceptions. The underlying reason is that such evaluations have been acknowledged as problematic for some time for, as Guskey (1995: 117–18) pointed out: 'Because of the powerful and dynamic influence of context, it is impossible to make precise statements about the elements of an effective professional development program'. Yet such evaluations are certainly possible, provided the aims are specific and the research tools are appropriate, as Joyce *et al.* (1999), for example, have demonstrated. Guskey (2000) offered a comprehensive review and compelling rationale for CPD evaluation. He proposed five critical levels at which professional development evaluation information needs to be gathered: participants' reaction; participants' learning; institution support and change; participants' use of new knowledge and skills; and student learning outcomes. He concluded that 'tracking . . . effectiveness at one level tells you nothing about the impact of the next' (2000: 86). Incidentally, it should be recognized as axiomatic that CPD, like school leadership (see

Hallinger and Heck 1999; Silins and Mulford 2002) can only have an indirect impact on student learning.

A second, more fundamental issue is that, unlike research in the natural sciences, the CPD field shows only limited evidence of cumulative knowledge-building (Hargreaves 1996) and, hence, has produced few uncontested findings, well exemplified in numerous studies of induction in the past 30 years (Bolam 1994). There are, however, some encouraging developments. At the time of writing, the first systematic, international review of studies designed to evaluate the impact of CPD is underway, under the auspices of the Evidence for Policy and Practice Information Centre (see www.eppi.ioe.ac.uk). More such systematic reviews are needed to assess the utility of various methodologies – outcome evaluation, process evaluation, economic evaluation, intervention description, methods, needs assessment, review and descriptive study – in CPD research and evaluation, using the underlying criterion of 'fitness for purpose'.

Third, clarification is needed of the role of theory in the study of CPD, on the one hand, and in its practice, on the other. The implicit assumption in much research and writing on CPD as a field of study is that the underpinning theoretical framework is drawn from the social sciences. This is most evident in evaluation studies (for example, Guskey 2000) and in policy analyses (for example, Hargreaves 1995). The position is less clear with respect to writing about the practice of CPD. Here too, lessons may be learned from the related field of educational administration in which, for example, Hodgkinson (1991) distinguished between three modes of action: *theoria*, theory which abstracts and generalizes by induction, deduction and hypothesis; *techne*, technique or technology which applies and interacts with theory; and *praxis*, purposeful, ethical action in a political context. He went on: 'Praxis . . . suggests . . . conscious, reflective intentional action . . . as opposed to mere reflex or mechanical responses to stimuli' (p. 43). Similarly, Argyris *et al.* (1985) proposed action science as an underpinning theoretical perspective to inform a range of action modes, which presumably could include CPD (see Eraut 1995; Day 1999).

Fourth, there is a related, strategic need to improve national and international information bases on CPD. Policy statements and comparisons are woefully short on facts and figures about the scale of provision, who does what, costs, numbers on courses, how CPD is funded, how the funds are allocated, how they are actually spent and how value for money is measured. In most countries, no single organization collects and publishes adequate monitoring data about the nature and scope of this diverse, extensive and costly national enterprise. Unsurprisingly, therefore, adequate comparative international data are not available. If policy decisions are to be properly informed, good data about actual, as opposed to projected, provision, expenditure, take-up and impact should be collected, published and analysed on a routine basis.

Fifth, comparative research and data also need to be strengthened so that productive sharing and learning can take place. For example, the CPD literature in education tends to be inward-looking. There is only limited reference to experience and research in related fields and disciplines like human resource management, occupational psychology and CPD for other professions (see Tomlinson 1997). There is more evidence of attempts to learn from international experience but this is far from being unproblematic. Caution is essential when we seek to understand, learn from and adapt international experience and research. At the same time, writers and researchers in developed countries also need to recognize the potential lessons to be learned from developing countries (Dimmock and Walter 2002; Harber and Davies 2003). Some approaches may be unique to a particular country, culture or setting; on the other hand, certain developments appear to be similar in various countries and some techniques are certainly adaptable across systems. Guskey (1995) argued that the powerful and often ignored influence of context consistently thwarts efforts to find universal truths in professional development. He suggested that, instead of looking for abstract elements that can be applied across contexts, we should find an optimal mix of processes and technologies that can be adapted to unique context characteristics. Drawing from research on CPD and individual change he outlines a series of guidelines for doing so. Certainly, it is probably safest to assume that technical developments, like mentoring or the use of information technology, are more easily adaptable across cultures than institutional innovations, like a national college, or professionally controversial ones, like performance management, but such assumptions must be tested.

CPD policy and teacher professionalism

The nature of the school as an organization is likely to change in the years ahead. Teachers have come to expect regular curriculum renewal but other factors such as the widespread use of information technology and moves to employ more staff as aides or auxiliary helpers suggest that in future they will act more as facilitators of learning and managers of a team of support staff than as direct instructors. There is no evidence of a reduction in the pace of change and teachers will need to update their knowledge and skills through CPD if they are to be effective. Furthermore, in several countries, the image of the teacher as an autonomous professional is being replaced by the concept of the school as a learning community in which the teacher works collectively as a member of a wider group of staff in a joint effort to improve the quality of learning.

Against this background, several writers have argued the need for a new concept of teacher professionalism (for example, Day 1999: 5; Whitty 2000). Some definitions require teachers to take responsibility for their own learning and to receive appropriate support to do this within an accountability framework. It is encouraging that these issues are being addressed at the level of policy and practice. One example is the professional code for teachers developed by the English General Teaching Council in 2001, based on a model of teachers as reflective practitioners, enhancing their knowledge and skills so as to adapt their teaching to new knowledge and technologies. It is also notable that the Scottish qualification for headship takes professional values as its starting point. The first standard is called 'Professional Values' and requires headteachers 'to hold, articulate and argue for professionally defensible educational values . . . based on the professional obligations of headteachers to serve the interests of children and young people in schools' (Scottish Qualification for Headship Development Unit 1998: 4).

More fundamentally, these issues and criticisms generate a series of questions about the role of the teaching profession in a social democracy and what this implies for CPD. For example, is it not reasonable to assume that the longer-term health of schools and students depends on well-educated teachers, not just well-trained and well-informed ones? Indeed, in an open, democratic society, should it not be seen as essential for professional educators themselves to be educated to exercise evidence-informed judgements and not simply trained to implement centrally determined policies? What part should democratic values play in CPD?

References

Argyris, C., Putnam, R. and McLain Smith, D. (1985) *Action Science*. London: Jossey-Bass.

Beardwell, I. and Holden, L. (eds) (1994) *Human Resource Management: A Contemporary Perspective*. London: Pitman Publishing.

Bolam, R. (1994) The impact of research on policy and practice in continuing professional development, *British Journal of In-service Education*, 20(1): 35–46.

Bolam, R. (1999) Educational administration, leadership and management: towards a research agenda, in T. Bush, L. Bell, R. Bolam, R. Glatter and P. Ribbins (eds) *Educational Management: Re-defining Theory, Policy and Practice*. London: Paul Chapman Publishing.

Bolam, R. (2003) Models of leadership development: learning from international experience and research, in M. Brundrett, N. Burton and R. Smith (eds) *Leadership in Education*. London: Sage.

Bolam, R., McMahon, A. Pocklington, K. and Weindling, R. (1995) Mentoring for new headteachers: the British experience, *Journal of Educational Administration*, 33(5): 29–44.

Bolam, R., Dunning, G. and Karstanje, P. (eds) (2000) *New Headteachers in the New Europe*. Munster/New York: Waxman Verlag.

Bolman, L.G. and Deal, T.E. (1997) *Reframing Organizations: Artistry, Choice, and Leadership*, 2nd edn. San Francisco: Jossey-Bass.

Borko, H. and Putnam, R.T. (1995) Expanding a teacher's knowledge base: a cognitive psychological perspective on professional development, in T.R. Guskey and M. Huberman (eds) *Professional Development in Education: New Paradigms and Practices*. New York: Teachers College Press.

Bottery, M. and Wright, N. (2000) *Teachers and the State: Towards a Directed Profession*. London: Routledge.

Brock, C. (ed.) (1996) *Global Perspectives on Teacher Education*. Wallingford: Triangle Books.

Burden, P.R. (1990) Teacher development, in W.R. Houston (ed.) (1990) *Handbook of Research on Teacher Education*. London: Macmillan.

Bush T., Bell, L., Bolam, R., Glatter, R. and Ribbins, P. (eds) (1999) *Educational Management: Re-defining Theory, Policy and Practice*. London: Paul Chapman Publishing.

Campbell, R.J. and Neill, S.R. (1994) *Secondary Teachers at Work*. London: Routledge.

CERI (Centre for Educational Research and Innovation) (1982) *In-service Education of Teachers: A Condition for Educational Change*. Paris: OECD.

CERI (Centre for Educational Research and Innovation) (2001) *New School Management Approaches*. Paris: OECD.

Clarke, J. and Newman, J. (1997) *The Managerial State*. London: Sage.

Cochran-Smith, M. and Lytle, S.L. (2001) Beyond certainty: taking an enquiry stance on practice in A. Lieberman and L. Miller (eds) *Teachers Caught in the Action: Professional Development that Matters*. New York: Teachers College Press.

Collin, A. (1994) Learning and development, in I. Beardwell and L. Holden (eds) *Human Resource Management: A Contemporary Perspective*. London: Pitman Publishing.

Coolahan, J. (2002) *Teacher Education and the Teaching Career in an Era of Lifelong Learning: OECD Working Paper No 2*. Maynooth: Education Faculty, National University of Ireland.

Craft, A. (1996) *Continuing Professional Development: A Practical Guide for Teachers and Schools*. London: Routledge and the Open University.

Darling-Hammond, L. (1990) Teachers and teaching: signs of a changing profession, in W.R. Houston (ed.) *Handbook of Research on Teacher Education*. London: Macmillan.

Day, C. (1997) In-service teacher education in Europe: conditions and themes for development in the 21st century, *Journal of In-service Education*, 23(1): 39–54.

Day, C. (1999) *Developing Teachers: The Challenge of Lifelong Learning*. London: Falmer Press.

Day, C. (2000) Stories of change and professional development: the costs of commitment, in C. Day, A. Fernandez, T.E. Hauge and J. Moller (eds) *The Life and Work of Teachers: International Perspectives in Changing Times*. London: Falmer Press.

Delors, J. (1996) *Learning: the Treasure Within. Report of the International Commission on Education for the Twenty-first Century*. Paris: UNESCO.

Department for Education and Employment (DfEE) (1999) *Eighth Report of the School Teachers Review Body*. London: HMSO.

Department for Education and Employment (DfEE) (2000) *Professional Development: Support for Teaching and Learning*. London: DfEE.

Dimmock, C. and Walter, A. (2002) School leadership in context – societal and organizational cultures, in T. Bush and L. Bell (eds) *The Principles and Practice of Educational Management*. London: Paul Chapman Publishing.

Elliott, J. (1991) *Action Research for Educational Change*. Buckingham: Open University Press.

Eraut, M. (1995) Developing professional knowledge within a client-centred orientation, in T.R. Guskey and M. Huberman (eds) *Professional Development in Education: New Paradigms and Practices*. New York: Teachers College Press.

European Training Foundation (1997) *Re-designing Management Development in the New Europe – Report of the Torino Group*. Luxembourg: Office for Official Publications of the European Communities.

Fessler, R. (1995) Dynamics of career stages, in T.R. Guskey and M. Huberman (eds) *Professional Development in Education: New Paradigms and Practices*. New York: Teachers College Press.

Firestone, W.A. and Louis, K.S. (1999) Schools as cultures, in J. Murphy and K.S. Louis (eds) *Second Handbook of Research on Educational Administration*. San Francisco: Jossey-Bass.

Foskett, N. and Lumby, J. (2003) *Leading and Managing Education: International Dimensions*. London: Paul Chapman Publishing.

Fullan, M. (1993) *Change Forces*. London: Cassell.

Fullan, M. (1995) The limits and the potential of professional development, in T.R. Guskey and M. Huberman (eds) *Professional Development in Education: New Paradigms and Practices*. New York: Teachers College Press.

Fullan, M. (2001) *The New Meaning of Educational Change*, 3rd edn. London: Routledge-Falmer.

Furlong, J. (2000) *Higher Education and the New Professionalism for Teachers: Realising the Potential of Partnership*. London: CVCP.

Gray, J., Hopkins, D., Reynolds, D., Wilcox, B., Farrell, S. and Jesson, D. (1999) *Improving Schools: Performance and Potential*. Buckingham: Open University Press.

Griffiths, D. (1988) Administrative theory, in N. Boyan (ed.) *Handbook of Research on Educational Administration*. London: Longman.

Gunter, H. and Ribbins, P. (2002) Leadership studies in education: towards a map of the field, *Educational Management and Administration*, 30(4): 387–416.

Guskey, T.R. (1995) Professional development in education: in search of the optimal mix, in T.R. Guskey and M. Huberman (eds) *Professional Development in Education: New Paradigms and Practices*. New York: Teachers College Press.

Guskey, T.R. (2000) *Evaluating Professional Development*. New York: Corwin Press.

Guskey, T.R. and Huberman, M. (eds) (1995) *Professional Development in Education: New Paradigms and Practices*. New York: Teachers College Press.

Halasz, G. (2000) System regulation changes in education and their implications for management development. Keynote paper presented at the Annual Conference of the European Network for the Improvement of Research and Development in Educational Management (ENIRDEM), 23 September, Tilburg University, the Netherlands.

Hall, V. and Oldroyd, D. (1991) *Managing Staff Development*. London: Paul Chapman Publishing.

Hallinger, P. and Heck, R. (1999) Can leadership enhance school effectiveness? in T. Bush, L. Beu, R. Bolam, R. Glatter and P. Ribbins (eds) *Educational Management: Re-defining Theory, Policy and Practice*. London: Paul Chapman Publishing.

Harber, C. and Davies, L. (2003) Effective leadership for war and peace, in M. Brundrett, N. Burton and R. Smith (eds) *Leadership in Education*. London: Sage.

Hargreaves, A. (1993) Teacher development in the postmodern age: dead certainties, safe simulation and the boundless self, in P. Gilroy and M. Smith (eds) *International Analyses of Teacher Education: JET Papers One*. Carfax: Carfax Publishers.

Hargreaves, A. (1994) *Changing Teachers, Changing Times: Teachers' Work and Culture in the Postmodern Age*. London: Cassell.

Hargreaves, A. (1995) Development and desire: a post-modern perspective, in T.R. Guskey and M. Huberman (eds) *Professional Development in Education: New Paradigms and Practices*. New York: Teachers College Press.

Hargreaves, D.H. (1996) *Teaching as Research-Based Profession: Possibilities and Prospects – The Teacher Training Agency Annual Lecture 1996*. London: TTA.

Harland, J., Kinder, K. and Keys, W. (1993) *Restructuring INSET: Privatisation and its Alternatives*. Slough: NFER.

Hemsley-Brown, J., Wilson, R., Easton, C. and Sharp, C. (2003) *Research into Practice: The Role of the LEA in Facilitating the Use of Research for School Improvement*. Slough: NFER.

Hodgkinson, C. (1991) *Educational Leadership: The Moral Art*. Albany, NY: SUNY Press.

Hopkins, D. and Reynolds, D. (2001) The past, present and future of school improvement: towards the third age, *British Educational Research Journal*, 27(4): 459–76.

Houston, W.R. (ed.) (1990) *Handbook of Research on Teacher Education*. London: Macmillan.

Hoyle, E. and John, P.D. (1995) *Professional Knowledge and Professional Practice*. London: Cassell.

Huberman, M. (1995) Professional careers and professional development: some intersections, in T.R. Guskey and M. Huberman (eds) *Professional Development in Education: New Paradigms and Practices*. New York: Teachers College Press.

Huberman, M. and Guskey, T.R. (1995) The diversities of professional development, in T.R. Guskey and M. Huberman (eds) *Professional Development in Education: New Paradigms and Practices*. New York: Teachers College Press.

Jackson, D. (2002) *The Creation of Knowledge Networks: Collaborative Enquiry for School and System Improvement*. Nottingham: NCSL.

Johnson, D.R. and Everett, R.E. (2001) *Alternative delivery sources for e-learning*. Paper presented at the Annual Conference of the British Educational Leadership, Management and Administration Society.

Joyce, B. and Showers, B. (1988) *Student Achievement through Staff Development*. London: Longman.

Joyce, B., Calhoun, E. and Hopkins, D. (1999) *The New Structure of School Improvement: Inquiring Schools and Achieving Students*. Buckingham: Open University Press.

Kamoche, K.N. (2001) *Understanding Human Resource Management*. Buckingham: Open University Press.

Karstanje, P. (1999) Decentralisation and deregulation in Europe: towards a conceptual framework, in T. Bush, L. Bell, R. Bolam, R. Glatter and P. Ribbins (eds) *Educational Management: Re-defining Theory, Policy and Practice*. London: Paul Chapman Publishing.

King, M.B. and Newmann, F.M. (2001) Building school capacity through professional development: conceptual and empirical considerations, *International Journal of Educational Management*, 15(2): 86–93.

Le Metais, J. (1997) Continuing professional development: the European experience, in H. Tomlinson (ed.) *Managing Professional Development in Schools*. London: Paul Chapman Publishing.

Leithwood, K. and Hallinger, P. (eds) (2002) *The Second International Handbook of Research on Educational Leadership and Administration*. Dordrecht: Kluwer.

Lieberman, A. (2000) Networks as learning communities: shaping the future of teacher development, *Journal of Teacher Education*, 51(3): 221–7.

Liston, D.P. and Zeichner, K.M. (1991) *Teacher Education and the Social Conditions of Schooling*. London: Routledge.

Little, J.W. (1993) Teachers' professional development in a climate of educational reform, *Educational Evaluation and Policy Analysis*, 15(2): 129–51.

Little, J.W. (2001) Professional development in pursuit of school reform in A. Lieberman and L. Miller (eds) *Teachers Caught in the Action: Professional Development that Matters*. New York: Teachers College Press.

Louis, K.S., Kruse, S.D. *et al.* (1995) *Professionalism and Community: Perspectives on Reforming Urban Schools*. Thousand Oaks, CA: Corwin Press.

McMahon, A. (1999) Promoting continuing professional development for teachers: an achievable target for school leaders? in T. Bush, L. Bell, R. Bolam, R. Glatter and P. Ribbins (eds) *Educational Management: Re-defining Theory, Policy and Practice*. London: Paul Chapman Publishing.

McMahon, A. (2000) Managing teacher stress to enhance student learning. Paper presented at the AERA Annual Conference, New Orleans, April.

McMahon, A. (2001) Fair Furlong Primary School, in M. Maden (ed.) *Success Against the Odds – Five Years On: Revisiting Effective Schools in Disadvantaged Areas*. London: Routledge-Falmer.

Maurer, T.J. and Tarulli, B.A. (1994) Investigation of perceived environment, perceived outcomes and personal variables in relationship to voluntary development activity by employees, *Journal of Applied Psychology*, 79(1): 3–14.

Middlewood, D. (2002) Appraisal and performance management, in T. Bush and L. Bell (eds) *The Principles and Practice of Educational Management*. London: Paul Chapman Publishing.

Moos, L. and Dempster, N. (1998) Some comparative learnings from the study, in J. MacBeath (ed.) *Effective School Leadership: Responding to Change*. London: Paul Chapman Publishing.

NBPTS (National Board for Professional Teaching Standards) (1993) *What Should Teachers Know and Be Able to Do?* Detroit, MI: NBPTS.

NCSL (National College for School Leadership) (2002) *Corporate Plan 2002/2006*. Nottingham: NCSL.

Newton, P. (2003) The National College for School Leadership: its role in developing leaders, in M. Brundrett, N. Burton and R. Smith (eds) *Leadership in Education*. London: Sage.

OECD (Organization for Economic Cooperation and Development) (1998) *Staying Ahead: In-service Training and Teacher Professional Development*. Paris: OECD.

Ruohotie, P. (1996) Professional growth and development, in K. Leithwood, J. Chapman, D. Corson, P. Hallinger and A. Hart (eds) *International Handbook of Educational Leadership and Administration*. Dordrecht: Kluwer Academic Publishers.

Sabar, N. and HaShar-Francis, A. (1999) School-focused in-service training: the key to restructuring schools, *Journal of In-service Education*, 25(2): 203–24.

Sammons, P., Hillman, J. and Mortimore, P. (1995) *Key Characteristics of Effective Schools: A Review of School Effectiveness Research. A report by the Institute of Education for the Office for Standards in Education*. London: Institute of Education.

Schein, E. (1985) *Organisational Culture and Leadership*. San Francisco: Jossey-Bass.

School Teachers' Review Body (1996) *Fifth Report*. London: HMSO.

Scott, C., Stone, B. and Dinham, S. (2000) International patterns of teacher discontent: Paper presented at the AERA annual conference, April.

Scottish Qualification for Headship Development Unit (1998) *The Standard for Headship in Scotland*. Stirling: University of Stirling, Institute of Education.

Senge, P., Cambron-McCabe, N., Lucas, T., Smith, B., Dutton, J. and Kleiner, A. (2000) *Schools That Learn*. London: Nicholas Brealey.

Silins, H.C. and Mulford, W. (2002) Leadership and school results, in K. Leithwood and P. Hallinger (eds) *Second International Handbook of Educational Leadership and Administration*. London: Kluwer Academic Publishers.

Smithers, R. (2001) Teacher shortage: staff praise Ofsted chief, *Guardian*, 29 August: 4.

Smylie, M.A. (1995) Teacher learning in the workplace: implications for school reform, in T.R. Guskey and M. Huberman (eds) *Professional Development in Education: New Paradigms and Practices*. New York: Teachers College Press.

Smyth, J. (1995) Teachers' work and the labour process of teaching: central problematics in professional development, in T.R. Guskey and M. Huberman (eds) *Professional Development in Education: New Paradigms and Practices*. New York: Teachers College Press.

Southworth, G. and Weindling, D. (2002) *Leadership in Large Primary Schools: A Report for the Esmee Fairbairn Foundation*. Reading: University of Reading School of Education.

Sparks, D. and Hirsh, S. (1997) *A New Vision for Staff Development*. Alexandria, VA: Association for Supervision and Curriculum Development and National Staff Development Council.

Sparks, D. and Loucks-Horsley, S. (1990) Models of staff development, in W.R. Houston (ed.) *Handbook of Research on Teacher Education*. London: Macmillan.

Stallings, J. and Kowalski, T. (1990) Research on professional development schools, in W.R. Houston (ed.) *Handbook of Research on Teacher Education*. London: Macmillan.

Stoll, L., Bolam, R. and Collarbone, P. (2002) Leadership for and of change: building capacity for learning, in K. Leithwood and P. Hallinger (eds) *The Second International Handbook of Research on Educational Leadership and Administration*. Dordrecht: Kluwer.

Stoll L. *et al.* (2003) *Creating and Sustaining Effective Professional Learning Communities*. www.eplc.info

Tam, W.M. and Cheng, Y.C. (1996) Staff development for school education quality, *Training for Quality*, 4(4): 16–24.

Teddlie, C. and Reynolds, D. (2000) *International Handbook of School Effectiveness Research*. London: Falmer Press.

Tickle, L. (2001) Teacher probation resurrected: England 1999–2000, *Journal of Education Policy*, 15(6): 701–13.

Tillema, H.H. and Imants, J.G.M. (1995) Training for the professional development of teachers, in T.R. Guskey and M. Huberman (eds) *Professional Development in Education: New Paradigms and Practices*. New York: Teachers College Press.

Times Educational Supplement (2003) *100 years of LEAs*, special supplement.

Tomlinson, H. (1997) Continuing professional development in the professions, in H. Tomlinson (ed.) *Managing Professional Development in Schools*. London: Paul Chapman Publishing.

Travers, C.J. and Cooper, C.L. (1996) *Teachers Under Pressure: Stress in the Teaching Profession*. London: Routledge.

TTA (Teacher Training Agency) (1998) *National Standards for Qualified Teacher Status*. London: TTA.

UNESCO (1996) *Learning: The Treasure Within*. Paris: UNESCO.

UNESCO (2001) *International Expert Meeting on General Education in the Twenty-first Century: Trends, Challenges and Priorities*. Paris: UNESCO.

Wallace, M. (1991) *School-centred Management Training*. London: Paul Chapman Publishing.

Weindling, D. (1999) Stages of headship, in T. Bush, L. Bell, R. Bolam, R. Glatter and P. Ribbins (eds) *Educational Management: Re-defining Theory, Policy and Practice*. London: Paul Chapman Publishing.

Wenger, E. (1999) *Communities of Practice: Learning, Meaning and Identity*. Cambridge: Cambridge University Press.

Whitty, G. (1997) Marketisation and the teaching profession, in A.H. Halsey, H. Lauder, P. Brown and A. Stuart Wells (eds) *Education: Culture, Economy and Society*. Oxford: Oxford University Press.

Whitty, G. (2000) Teacher professionalism in new times, *Journal of In-service Education*, 26(2): 281–96.

Williams, J.H. (2001) On school quality and attainment, in J. Crisp, C. Talbot and D.B. Cipollone (eds) *Learning for a Future: Refugee Education in Developing Countries*. Geneva: UNHCR.

World Education Forum (2000) *The Dakar Framework for Action – Education for All: Meeting our Collective Commitments*. Paris: UNESCO.

PART 2
Regional Case Studies

3 Rhetorics and realities of CPD across Europe: from cacophony towards coherence?

Ciaran Sugrue

As the pace of change – economic, social and cultural – quickened perceptibly throughout the decade of the 1990s, national education policy makers responded to a cacophony of calls for educational reforms – curricular, pedagogical and organizational – by increasing the emphasis on teacher professional development. As globalization, market forces and information and communication technologies (ICTs) increasingly made their presence felt within a consequent cauldron of educational reform, restructuring and reconceptualization, calls for renewed and redoubled educational reform efforts became more shrill, persistent and pervasive. Provision of professional support for teachers became a major growth 'industry', an end in itself. If school reform was the perceived problem, teacher professional development was increasingly becoming the proprietary prescribed educational prophylactic, the panacea of choice, the prozac of the education system.

Introduction

In a headlong hurtle designed to facilitate each country 'staying ahead', the Organization for Economic Cooperation and Development (OECD) reports that 'the impact of teacher development is that it is very clearly a necessary condition for educational change, it is not, by itself, sufficient' (1997: 59). Behind this 'spin', however, lurks a more murky, muddied, muddled and contested set of policies and practices with positive and negative consequences for teacher learning, their well-being and career trajectories, but also with an emerging consensus around the following:

> Professional development for teachers has a poor track record because it lacks a theoretical base and coherent focus. On the one hand, professional development is treated as a vague panacea – the teacher as

continuous, lifelong learner. Stated as such, it has little practical meaning. On the other hand, professional development is defined too narrowly and becomes artificially detached from 'real-time' learning. It becomes the workshop, or possibly the ongoing series of professional development sessions. In either case, it fails to have a sustained cumulative impact.

(Fullan 1995)

Brussels too, as the 'eye in the sky' of the European Union's (EU) 15 member states, began to formulate and disseminate a rhetoric of lifelong learning as a means of providing leadership to national governments. Towards this end, 1996 was designated the year of lifelong learning in all member states. Governments, in their turn, have sought to play out these rhetorics within national borders. What emerges is a series of overlapping, intersecting, conflicting and contradictory rhetorics, policies and practices, where new thinking collides with more traditional and often outmoded structures and practices.

Shaping the task: considerations and constraints

The process of determining the scope and direction of this chapter led to a number of considerations beyond the contents of other contributions to the handbook, as well as limitations on length. While induction and mentoring of beginning teachers into the profession has received significant attention in recent years, particularly since there is growing awareness of 'attrition' from teaching in the early years and through seeking early retirement or respite from increasing frustrations and role diffusion (Darling-Hammond 1997; Sharp and Draper 2000; Wilhelm et al. 2000), this vital early career stage (Schein 1978, 1990; Huberman et al. 1993) is not a concern here. Rather, the focus is on more mainstream concerns regarding continuing professional development (CPD) of the vast majority of teachers beyond initiation, while readily conceding that in a more comprehensively reconceptualized notion of CPD, cognizance of this vital phase is a necessity.

The focus is on European countries, but this is not confined to EU or western European countries only, particularly since the cartography of the EU itself as well as many eastern region emerging nations is about to change radically or has recently undergone profound alterations. Additionally, in recognition of a growing international 'interdependence' (Barber 1996; Homer-Dixon 2001), literature from outside this axis is not excluded, but is drawn on selectively as a means of lending further ballast to policy and practice within the main orbit of my focus. Studies of particular merit, landmark studies that have been seminal in the field are referenced, while much of the literature reviewed in this chapter has its origins and axis of influence in the European theatre of engagement, with particular emphasis on studies conducted and reported during the past five years. The intention is to provide a comprehensive review of this rather fragmented literature, to bring some 'situated certainty' (Hargreaves 1994) to the terrain, while seeking also to lend coherence to the field of CPD, as well as set significant agendas for further investigation, with the express purpose of strengthening the knowledge base in a fractured and fledgling dimension of teachers' lives and work.

While there is a significant and growing literature on several aspects of CPD, other literatures also have a shaping influence. These include educational change (Fullan 1991, 1992; Fullan and Hargreaves 1992; Hargreaves and Fullan 1998; Hargreaves *et al.* 1998; Altrichter and Elliott 2000), school leadership (Grace 1995; Leithwood *et al.* 1996, 1999; Southworth 1996; Hopkins and Harris 1997; MacBeath 1998; Day *et al.* 2000; Sergiovanni 2001), school effectiveness (Mortimore 1988, 1998; MacBeath and Mortimore 2001; Reynolds *et al.* 2002) and school improvement (Hopkins *et al.* 1994; Mortimore 1998; Gray *et al.* 1999). These competing and sometimes conflicting literatures intersect at various points, and to a greater or lesser degree, with concerns about the conceptualizations, policies, practices and purposes of CPD. Connections will be made with these offerings at various points to illuminate emergent concerns, while the focus on CPD is maintained throughout a nested review.

Power, policies and practice

Within this general landscape, the particular focus in this chapter is on power relations locally, nationally and transnationally, and their impact on CPD policy and practice, while seeking also to identify innovations to ground potential initiatives on these emerging issues, to recognize the 'glocalizing' tendency in reform initiatives (Beck 2000).[1] However, it is important to recognize that power relations between the local and global are frequently asymmetrical. Consequently, teachers are often relatively powerless to shape their own and their students' futures in the face of prescriptive, government-led or -driven reform agendas. Bourdieu makes this point when he states: 'we cannot grasp the dynamics of a field if not by a synchronic analysis of its structure', while adequate understanding of such a structure needs 'a historical . . . genetic analysis of its constitution and of the tensions that exist between positions in it, as well as between this field and other fields, and especially the field of power' (Bourdieu and Wacquant 1992: 90). For Bourdieu, this entails a 'structural history' which documents 'each successive state of the structure under examination, both the product of previous struggles to maintain or to transform this structure, and [its] subsequent transformations' (p. 91). The forces at play in shaping CPD provision in a European context constitute a 'field', 'a space of play and competition', where the social agents and institutions . . . all possess the determinate quantity of special capital (economic and cultural capital in particular) sufficient to occupy the dominant positions within their respective fields. At any one time within a field, what is happening is a division of the work of domination.

(Bourdieu and Wacquant 1992: 76, n.16)

Following Bourdieu, therefore, between the rhetorics, policies and practices of CPD, within this field, 'the structure of social space', there is 'its dominant and its dominated, its struggles for usurpation and exclusion, its mechanisms of reproduction . . .' (p. 106). Within local, national and global rhetorics there is a subterranean set of power forces at work with important consequences for the manner in which teachers' learning and well-being are positioned and shaped.

Power forces: policy rhetorics

The dominant international force is globalization, a world without borders where 'a postmodern capitalist economy' produces an endless supply of goods (and services) that are 'marketable through promotion, spin, packaging, and advertising' (Barber 1996: 59). In this 'brave new world', image is everything, and education too is falling prey to 'shadow rather than substance'. When this globalizing tendency is capitalized on (no pun intended) by what Barber (1996: 100–36) calls the 'infotainment telesector', this combination of forces can, he suggests, 'guarantee a market without bounds' wherein it is possible to 'deconstruct and then reassemble the soul' (p. 83). The commodification of everything through a process of 'imagineering' has an infantalizing impact on consumers, while a small number of media moguls compete for monopolistic control over powerful images with potential 'to sell a certain lifestyle, a certain culture, certain products and certain ideas' (p. 82). For these and other reasons, Homer-Dixon (2001: 49) concludes that we are already on the threshold of 'a fundamentally new world' that dramatically raises 'the complexity, unpredictability, and pace of events around us'. Barber's consequent concern is for citizenship and the health of democracy, while Homer-Dixon's primary concerns are environmental. Educational concerns in the present context need to take cognizance of these shaping influences and mores.

The major change forces identified above, have had, and continue to have, a profound impact on, and implications for, education policy-making. First, education is increasingly perceived as an engine for economic growth and international competitiveness. Second, as the pace of change has gathered momentum, market and private sector thinking have taken hold of policy mindsets, and complexity has become a byword to describe systems. Devolution of decision making and local autonomy have become new policy orthodoxies with profound consequences at the level of the school. Third, in this increasing state of flux and uncertainty, demands for new thinking and practices have increased, where there is a growing realization that 'business as usual' is no longer adequate, with consequent demands for continuous learning on the part of teachers (Little 1993, 2001). Fourth, these forces have coalesced into a new and emergent policy rhetoric of lifelong learning for all, and teachers in particular are expected to be role models of lifelong learning for their students (OECD 1998). In such circumstances, apart from growing complexities in the role of teachers, opportunities for learning – formal and informal – both inside and outside the school, have increased exponentially in most jurisdictions and in many instances are increasingly being perceived by teachers as a further demand and burden on their time and energies, rather than being facilitative, empowering and supportive (Sugrue *et al.* 2001). Recently, the European Commission declared that 'Europe has indisputably moved into the Knowledge Age'. Consequently, it declares, 'patterns of learning, living and working are changing apace' (European Commission 2001: 3). The working definition it adopts states that: 'all purposeful learning activity, undertaken on an ongoing basis with the aim of improving knowledge, skills and competence' qualifies as lifelong learning (2001: 3).

This state of affairs is in sharp contrast to the realities of teachers' lives and work, even relatively recently. Less than a decade ago, in-service courses, rather than CPD, were a somewhat anarchic, serendipitous form of episodic engagement, primarily 'a matter for individuals to involve themselves in if they chose to undertake some form of education that might influence their teaching or enhance their prospects of promotion' (Lee 1997: 9). Teachers' participation in such courses was voluntary, idiosyncratic and frequently hinged on personal interest, availability, accessibility and timing rather than direct concern for the quality of teaching and learning (see Gough 1997; Sugrue and Uí Thuama 1997; Sugrue *et al.* 2001). Nevertheless, despite a state of benign serendipity that pertained into the 1990s, Bolam (2000: 278) argues that:

> the ultimate aim of CPD is to improve student learning. This is not, and to my mind never has been, in dispute. The issue has been and still is how to strike an appropriate balance between meeting the needs of individual professionals, on the one hand, and of the school and national policy on the other.

As the press of the postmodern has intensified, thus accelerating the pace of change, global competitiveness, market forces and a general trend of political conservatism often characterized as a move to the 'right' evident in many European countries and beyond, teachers' identities and sense of professionalism have been challenged (Huberman 1995; Castle 1997; Graham 1998; Retallick 1999; Hargreaves 2000a; Sachs 2000; Sharp and Draper 2000; Whitty

2000). This new frontier for teachers has resulted, according to Day (2000: 101), in teachers having 'to bear an increased workload' to the extent that 'energy levels and motivation remain at best "frayed around the edges", as the threat of increased class sizes, teacher redundancies and teacher shortages grows'. In Ireland, by contrast, where class sizes have decreased during this period, exponential increases in professional learning opportunities and teacher shortages pose serious challenges, and the feelings of being over-burdened are no less apparent (Sugrue *et al.* 2001).[2]

Teacher professionalism

In response to these changing and challenging times, Hargreaves has suggested that there is evidence of, as well as necessity for, an emerging 'post-modern professionalism' (Hargreaves and Goodson 1996; Hargreaves 2000a). He is in agreement with Whitty (2000) that centralized prescriptions have tended in England and Wales in particular, as well as in Ontario, Canada, towards a 'deprofessionalization' of teachers. Whitty indicates that while some professionals have a 'licensed autonomy', others, teachers among them, are increasingly circumscribed by a 'regulated autonomy' (p. 283).[3] For this reason, he advocates 'new' or 'democratic professionalism' so that teachers reclaim, reconstruct and re-establish what he sees as their professional right, something that will 'require continuing efforts to maintain a more broadly defined sense of common professional identity' (p. 291), to be 'in control of their own future' (Sachs 2000: 87). However, in order to become 'profession-ally stronger', Hargreaves (2000: 176) argues that teachers need to become more proactive rather than reactive, more outward-looking than being defen-sively introspective, to embrace the 'paradoxical challenge' of becoming 'pro-fessionally stronger' by becoming 'more publicly vulnerable and accessible', while Graham (1998: 25) enthusiastically advocates that 'teaching urgently needs to become a profession of international standing' (see also Bascia 1998). The extent to which teachers are cast as 'restricted' or 'extended' professionals (Stenhouse 1975) is determined by the manner in which international rhetor-ics imbue and inform national political dynamics as they interact at school, local, regional and national levels within existing and changing structures and processes.

National policies

While national governments generally have embraced the rhetoric of lifelong learning, its major impact is most apparent in terms of changing institutional and programme structures where 'pathways' to personal learning and advancement are being created. Apart from signalling the potential of ICT for facilitating learning, Brussels advocates 'a major shift towards user-oriented learning systems with permeable boundaries across sectors and levels' (European Commission 2000: 13). Towards this end, teacher identities are expected to shift significantly from more traditional modes of 'teaching as telling' (Britzman 1986; Holt-Reynolds 1992; Johnson 1992; Kagan 1992; Pajares 1992) to one where they will 'support learners [to] take charge of their own learning' to the extent that they are already being expected to 'develop and practice . . . participatory teaching and learning methods' as 'an essential professional skill for educators . . . in both formal and non-formal settings' (European Commission 2000: 14). However, this European rhetoric is frequently supplanted at national level by increasing regulation of curriculum content, pedagogy, prescription of targets and benchmarks and the regular measurement of 'outcomes'. Aspirant members of the EU such as Slovenia, as well as some of its neighbours, have been engaged in 'policy borrowing' (Halpin and Tronya 1995), particularly in relation to accountability measures to 'prove' their ingratiation with western power-brokers, as well as to indicate membership of an 'audit culture', and to engage in 'comparability' studies (Trnavcevic 2002). Despite these homogenizing tendencies, it is important to recognize and to document significantly different policy traditions and trajectories of CPD within national borders.

Due to the rapidity of change, acquiring systematic and up-to-date information about changing patterns of policy and practice in a rapidly changing field such as CPD is problematic. By the time of publication, snapshots in time are already dated if not redundant. Consequently, and consistent with Bourdieu's notion of documenting deep structures, this section seeks to identify trends within various traditions as reflected in reported policy-oriented publications, for, as the OECD (1997: 32) asserts: 'the sheer weight of tradition still dictates much of what happens in in-service training and development'. But existing orthodoxies are being challenged under new and emerging demands, expectations and aspirations. When breaking old moulds, continuities as well as changes must be identified.

Policies: traditions, trends, continuities and change

Policy-borrowing and homogenizing tendencies notwithstanding, there is benefit from comparative analysis while readily recognizing that 'no country has found a perfect way of giving teachers sufficient control and ownership over their development . . . while . . . maintaining a coherent system-wide policy strategy' (OECD 1997: 13). However, it is reasonable to aspire to finding a 'golden mean' from a meta-analysis of national trends and traditions. It is necessary to recognize that internationally, CPD is 'no longer a privately pursued optional extra but a publicly implicit, accountable part of every teacher's regular working life' (Day 1993: 87–8). With intensification due to continuous reform initiatives, and an espoused policy of decentralization and devolved decision making, the school is increasingly being perceived as the locus and focus of reform.

Despite considerable differences in terms of educational structures – local education authorities (LEAs) in England and Wales, federalist cantons in Austria and Germany, highly centralized policy-making in Sweden (until very recently), a strong tradition of municipal democratic decision making in Norway and Denmark, France and Ireland with a strong tradition of policy-making at the centre but the latter without any regional structures – all appear to have bought into devolved decision making. Consequently, depending on the political and economic climate, schools are positioned increasingly in a contradictory and decentralized set of responsibilities within a highly centralized or recentralized set of policy prescriptions. When 'school-based' and 'school-focused' curriculum development was advocated in the 1980s (see Skilbeck 1985, 1990, 1998), additional requirements of budgetary management (local management of schools as in England and Wales), of accountability, benchmark testing, specification of learning outcomes, as well as transformation of schools from nineteenth-century institutions into twenty-first-century learning organizations, were not part of the package of responsibilities. However, all of these requirements, and the imposition of private sector thinking and management practices on schools, have become commonplace during the intervening years.

England has become synonymous with extreme versions of recentralization with attendant infamy attaching to privatized school inspection via the Office for Standards in Education (Ofsted), league tables, and a new vocabulary that includes such terms as 'naming and blaming', 'failing' and 'sink' schools, as well as a return to versions of 'payment by results' and a general preoccupation with test scores that measure a narrow range of competencies, typically in literacy and numeracy. As the package of reforms becomes increasingly intensified and overloaded, as the pace of change and demand for reforms become more frenetic, there is a general tendency on the part of policy makers to grow more impatient and become increasingly prescriptive, despite a rhetoric of decentralization and devolved decision making. Colleagues 'on the ground' in many of the countries mentioned above report increasing tensions and power struggles between individual schools, municipal, local or regional authorities and central governments, with these power plays being shaped significantly by such factors as the status and remuneration of teachers as well as the 'muscle' of their unions, and the general economic and political climate. However, there is a growing feeling that as the forces of global economic competition intensify, teachers will become the front-line troops in 'the mother of all battles' for the soul of education and the heart of civil society. It may be the case that, while teachers are increasingly expected to be flexible, adaptable, enquiring collaborative critical thinkers, characteristics and skills that they should model for their students (OECD 1997), schools may have a much more crucial role as 'free spaces in which it is possible to live not only as consumers but as citizens' (Barber 1996: 300). The primary or primal force that drives the dilemma of decentralization/recentralization is economic competitiveness in a global economy, where citizens, including teachers and their students, are pawns in an international 'premier' league where the prize is measured in 'market share', and increased and increasing efficiency. Effectiveness and 'bottom lines' are the only outcomes that merit attention, and are the only criteria that determine location on this particular 'league table'.

ICTs

Another dominant element of national education policies, as part of equipping teachers and students with the necessary skills to survive and thrive in the new economic environment, is ICT (OECD 1997). While some governments have been slower than others to seize on this necessity, schools have been equipped with a range of hardware and software, and teachers have been provided with a range of professional support. For example, in a White Paper on Education (Ireland Government Office 1995), there is no mention of ICT, but since then there has been a series of national initiatives that embrace education and training with many initiatives, national and transnational, securing EU funding (see European Commission 2000: 25–30). However, while these major national initiatives have increased awareness of the potential of ICTs, the extent to which use of personal computers (PCs) and the internet have become embedded in curricular and pedagogical routines is, so far, disappointing, even in contexts where high levels of provision are the norm (Cuban *et al.* 2001). During the past few months, I have visited more than 70 student teachers in as many classrooms and several schools, and while PCs were present in virtually all of these classrooms, in the vast majority of instances they were not turned on and never in use. Marx *et al.* (1998: 50) conclude that:

> Teachers will not profit from the technology nor will it be self-sustaining unless infrastructure capacity is developed, including attention to resources and maintenance . . . [to] how teachers will be given the time to use it, and what support will be provided to help teachers continue to up-grade their skills and understanding.

These authors also conclude that a considerable barrier to adaptive implementation may be significant discrepancies between, for example, the espousal of constructivist approaches to staff development, teaching and learning, and a pervasive behaviouristic drill and practice approach to software development, where there is considerable 'value dissonance' between teachers' beliefs and market-determined technological tools (Day *et al.* 2000; Sergiovanni 2001).

Perhaps, more importantly, technological changes are one aspect only of the changing context, orientation of, and expectations for, schooling.

Collaboration

As pressures for reform of schooling have intensified, school effectiveness and improvement literatures have tended to focus more on the nexus between 'teacher competence' and 'student outcomes' (OECD 1997).[4] Consequent on the international trend of devolved responsibility, there is a growing tension between the individual needs of teachers, their collective responsibility from a 'whole-school' perspective and system needs as identified in (prescriptive) policy statements (McLaughlin and Talbert 1993; Kelchtermans and Vandenberghe 1994, 1996; Joyce and Showers 1996; Hopkins and Harris 1997; Hopkins et al. 1998; Kwakman 1998; Clement and Vandenberghe 2000; McLaughlin 2002). Consistent with market-place values attaching to team-work, teachers are expected to collaborate with colleagues to the extent that creating a 'collaborative culture' has become the *sine qua non* of school reform (Hargreaves 1992, 1994). The teacher as 'artisan' (Eraut 1994) is frequently portrayed as a dinosaur, while others advocate the necessity for 'principled disagreement' in place of 'contrived collegiality' (Little 1990, 1993, 1999, 2001; Hargreaves 1994).

These policy-determined tensions play out very differently in different contexts. In Germany, Switzerland, Austria and Luxembourg, for example, where traditional academic education has remained separate from technical and vocational schooling, teachers in the former continue to place a premium on professional 'upgrading' that is primarily focused on content knowledge, while efforts are being made to promote cross-curricular pedagogical approaches (OECD 1997). However, under a rhetoric of diversity of provision and inclusion, market forces as well as downward demographic trends are enabling some parents to be more selective in school choice (Ball 1990, 1994; Lawton 1992). Consequently, there is growing concern, and increasing evidence, that a competitive market approach to education policy-framing is contributing to and exacerbating social inequalities.

Adding to these tensions considerably, policy requirements that alter the roles of schools and teachers significantly are also evident. While the combination of school effectiveness, improvement, market forces and parental choice collectively contrive, along with government policies, to focus narrowly on academic results, teachers' brief has been expanded to include 'care' for learners (Noddings 1992), to attend to their 'moral formation' and education for 'citizenship' (Lawn 1996; Helsby 1999; Arnot and Dillabough 2000). As a consequence of these competing, conflicting and sometimes contradictory demands on teachers, the intensity of the 'emotional labour' of teaching has increased exponentially (Hoschild 1983; Beatty 2000, 2001; Hargreaves 2000b;

Hargreaves *et al.* 2001). When this occurs, there is greater necessity to attend to the personal as well as the professional needs of teachers (Day *et al.* 2000). However, in practice the person in the professional is frequently marginalized, and this is partly a consequence of a lack of consensus on where 'this [expanded] mission starts and stops'. While there is growing recognition among teachers that lack of 'regard for students' well-being is a poor basis for learning' (OECD 1997: 26), testing and a relentless pursuit of pre-specified learning outcomes frequently militate against teachers' commitment to care as well as the development of the aesthetic, affective and holistic elements in learners.

As market forces combined with sustained criticisms of the public sector have become more pronounced during the past two decades, and schools have been construed as the 'units of production' of the educational enterprise, two other policy trends have emerged, namely greater emphasis on school leadership and public-private partnerships. These are discussed separately, though all these elements are part of an emerging pattern in national and transnational educational policy landscapes.

Leadership

An OECD visiting team to Ireland in 1991 was highly critical of the absence of adequate management training for school principals and middle-managers (OECD 1991). In their view, such professional development would be essential if devolution of decision making to schools were to be realized. Currently, a programme called Leadership Development for Schools (LDS) is being planned and this follows on similar developments such as the Scottish National Qualification for Headship (SNQH), as well as the more recently established National Leadership College at the University of Nottingham. These developments are mirrored by similar concerns in Denmark and Norway, thus giving rise to significant tensions between central and municipal authorities as to whom should fund such programmes and control their content and delivery. Slovenia too has its 'National Leadership School' (Er ulj 2002), and universities across Europe are increasingly making provision for postgraduate diplomas and degrees with administration, management and leadership in their titles (Sugrue *et al.* 2001). However, the primary concern here is to understand the function and impact of these policy emphases.

While the term 'leadership' is much contested (Smyth 1993; Dimmock 1996) teachers and principals are increasingly subject to role expansion. Principals are becoming instructional and transformational leaders (Leithwood *et al.* 1996, 1999), while sharing the burdens of leadership with colleagues is also part of this extended brief. Whole-school development planning is frequently the conduit for such collective endeavours. The necessity to schedule regular meetings as well as produce a plethora of policy documents has led to impossible demands on time as a very finite resource as well as on the energy levels of teachers, often with negative consequences for their motivation and commitment. It is worth noting that in Asian countries, where social continuity and cohesion as well as more broadly shared value systems are still evident, the role of school principals does not appear to be as significant as in western countries, where much greater efforts are necessary to create shared visions, values and goals (Reynolds *et al.* 2002). There is a sense, therefore, in which the diversified roles of school leaders and their teaching colleagues are a compensatory requirement, where schools as moral communities, as places of calm, of ordered discipline, are dissonant with, and different from, the values of the market-place and the 'infotainment' world in which they are situated. Countries such as Germany, Luxembourg, Austria and Switzerland, with traditions of strong regional and national government, are inured to some extent against such requirements, but the general tendency towards the school as the unit of production is altering this pattern (OECD 1997). This creeping homogenization may be attributed to globalizing tendencies, thus resulting in the mixed message of care, concern and citizenship while continuing to place a premium on examination results.

Partnerships

The Irish government refers in policy documents to those directly involved in education as 'the partners', and identifies 'parents, patrons/trustees/owners/ governors, management bodies, teachers, the local community and the State' among them, while 'the social partners, businesses and the professions should also be recognized as having legitimate interests in the system' (Ireland Government Office 1995: 7). While this partnership approach is often heralded as distinct and different from more adversarial and top-down approaches to reform, the rhetoric tends to cloak the influence of those with most power, thus maintaining the status quo rather than creating more democratic and participatory decision making (Sugrue forthcoming). This specific example reflects a more general 'profusion of contacts between schools and local businesses/employers' (OECD 1992) and between 'schools and the families of their pupils' (OECD 1997: 28).

There are various levels to these partnerships and responsibilities that are worth identifying:

1   Teachers, *in loco parentis*, have a responsibility to communicate and engage with parents regularly in the best interests of children's education.

2   As inclusion and multiculturalism become more of a reality in schools and communities, the role of the class teacher becomes more complex and necessitates dealing with a range of support staff – heritage/ mother-tongue teachers, teachers of English as a second language

(ESL), home, school-community liaison personnel and other support agencies.

3 Local partnerships serve a number of functions. They provide work experience to teenagers, share expertise between teachers and private sector personnel, provide funding for particular initiatives or innovations such as computer use, and provide placements in industry for teachers as a means of extending their management and linguistic skills.

4 There are more ambitious partnerships also that seek to transform the nature of schools and schooling such as the Sizer Coalition of Essential Schools. Gerstner *et al.* (1994), chairman and chief executive of IBM, harbours the more ambitious mission of reinventing education. His perception is that public schooling has failed to reform because it enjoys a monopoly. Private sector practices and thinking he sees as a solution: 'a business perspective not only sheds light on the nature of the problem, it suggests strategies for a solution' (p. 15), though this appears to be strongly motivated by ideology rather than the virtues of the 'private'!

There are many examples of these partnerships at local, regional, national and international levels that readers can readily identify. However, the more important issue in the present context is the impact of these coalitions of interest on the lives and work of teachers and school leaders, and the consequent demands to expand their repertoires of skills and expertise, as well as deal with expanding roles and responsibilities, while continuing to manage their time. It is not surprising that the number of applicants for school principalship is in dramatic decline internationally (Sugrue 2003), and that the 'myth of the superprincipal' is increasingly suspect (Copland 2001).

Provision and providers

As policy rhetorics of decentralized and devolved decision making take hold, there is a corresponding need for professional support for teachers and principals as the school becomes the fulcrum of reform. There is general consensus internationally that, until recently, pre-service teacher education has been the major focus of national governments to the relative neglect of CPD, with negative consequences in terms of fragmentation, funding and lack of coherence (OECD 1997). Another immediately identifiable trend is towards greater homogenization of provision, even in Germany with a strong tradition of autonomy in each *Länder*: 'the in-service agenda is remarkably similar even in Lander under different political control and is moving towards the whole school perspective . . .' (OECD 1997: 65).

Another commonplace of CPD provision is the emergence of five days as the magic number whereby teachers can absent themselves from schools (this applies in England and Wales, Austria, Switzerland, Germany and Sweden) (see OECD 1997; Schratz and Resinger 2002). However, in some jurisdictions some of these days are merely taken as additional holidays (for example in Austria – Schratz and Resinger 2002), while in Ireland, due to a centrally planned revised curriculum implementation strategy, all schools have six CPD days that are effectively compulsory. However, school closure for these days is highly disruptive to the extent that teachers are increasingly embarrassed to inform parents of yet another closure and further erosion of teaching time (Sugrue *et al.* 2001).

In England the majority of these days are now taken in school, and there is additional international variation also in the extent to which supply cover is provided for these release days, as such financial provision adds significantly to the cost of CPD. In general, therefore, the emergence of CPD days across systems may be regarded as indicative of recognition by policy makers that teachers need time to learn, and as the consequence of pressure from teacher unions. However, there is considerable debate about the benefits of one-day provision interspersed throughout the school year, and a general lack of evidence about the impact of such 'respite' days (Bates *et al.* 1999). Nevertheless, there is increasing recognition that 'improving teachers' knowledge, skills and practice, are legitimate and essential dimensions of teacher work, not simply add-ons or organizational frills' (Bredeson 2000: 63). Acknowledging learning as a legitimate element of teachers' work, however, leaves open questions of its timing and location for maximum benefit to teachers and their students. Another consequence of intensification of reform initiatives that are frequently top-down driven is a two-tier approach to CPD. National priorities receive preferential funding and support, and teachers and schools are expected to 'buy into' them. Individual needs (and even school agendas) on the other hand are consigned to what may be possible at the individual's discretion – time, resources and availability being major constraints. Such scenarios, intended or not, create the impression that system goals take priority over personal professional needs. Consequently, while there may be increased learning opportunities for teachers, their impact, apart from possible overload, may be to communicate a sense of being less valued and cared for by the system.

There are also identifiable shifts in the structure of provision and the identities of providers. As already indicated, in less pressured times, teachers' centres tended to cater for individual preferences and needs (Gough 1997; Lee 1997), and LEAs in England and Wales were the major providers through their inspectors and advisory systems. Other European countries, partly as a consequence of federation (Germany, Austria, Switzerland are good examples) continue to have dedicated regional institutes or centres dedicated to a range of CPD provision. Luxembourg has the services of a national centre, while in Sweden, universities enjoy a strong presence in this field (OECD 1997). By contrast, in the UK and Ireland, the role of the universities and colleges has become more marginal to government policies, while there is a growing distinction also between accredited courses provided by these institutions and an increasing number of shorter non-credit courses being availed of by teachers (Bates *et al.* 1999; Sugrue *et al.* 2001). However, in other jurisdictions, Slovenia, Austria and Luxembourg among them (OECD 1997; Schratz and Resinger 2002; Trnavcevic 2002), courses for credit are a recognized and required means of salary enhancement and career advancement. Such courses are identified as lacking in Yugoslavia (Zindovic-Vukadinovic 2002). The amount of credit available for courses tends to distort their attractiveness for teachers, thus creating another version of privileged and marginalized courses, regardless of personal preference or need, as well as policy-driven priorities. On the other hand, there is growing discontent among teachers that despite making significant sacrifices in terms of time, personal energy and resources to invest in their professional development, there are few if any tangible rewards.

There are identifiable distinctions also between traditions in primary and secondary teaching. In the latter, despite efforts to promote interdisciplinary and whole-school approaches to teaching and learning, professional identities formed around subject specialisms remain steadfast, and subject associations, an important source of professional support in many jurisdictions, tend to focus on knowledge content, while a focus on pedagogical concerns occupies a more prominent position in provision for primary teachers. In Ireland, in particular, teacher unions have become significant providers, and, in a sector that lacked infrastructure and personnel until very recently, secondment of teachers on an ad hoc basis has become a major conduit for delivery of professional support (Sugrue *et al.* 2001). As CPD gains in significance internationally, there is growing awareness of the needs of providers as a distinct group with its own particular professional development needs that are generally unrecognized and even more poorly supported (OECD 1997). There are newly identifiable career patterns beginning to emerge, while these public sector 'educational entrepreneurs' are increasingly in competition with a growing number of private consultants (Sugrue 2003). New networks of learners are also emerging, where there is greater emphasis on inquiry and learning through sharing of expertise, a combination of support and challenge (Wenger 1998). There are increases, therefore, in both formal and informal means of supporting ongoing professional learning. The former is largely state funded, voluntary and quasi-compulsory, while the latter is voluntary and predominantly self-financing. The spectrum of provision is categorized by the OECD (1997) as formal (accredited), non-formal (non-accredited and occasional), and informal (non-taught learning activities in all settings).

Funding

While there is little doubt that activity generally in the CPD domain has increased significantly in recent years, an increase that is common in all jurisdictions, it is not necessarily the case that this increase has been matched by correspondingly larger budgets. It is extremely difficult to establish with accuracy the impact of funding in the sector, and calculations are complicated by a number of factors. While in the early 1990s, Norway appears to have been top of this particular league table, spending 2 per cent of its education budget on in-service training, with Sweden next at 1.5 per cent, the vast majority of other European countries were spending significantly less than 0.5 per cent of their respective education budgets on CPD (UNESCO 1992). In countries such as Germany and Ireland, for example, where there is virtually no provision made for substitute cover, relatively modest budgets can have significant impact. However, with increased activity in the sector, there are opportunity costs that generally do not enter into calculations, such as loss of teaching time and learning opportunities for students. Additionally, in the Irish context, where provision is dependent to a significant extent on seconded classroom teachers, their salaries become a major burden on CPD and at the same time they are disruptive of staffing schedules with consequences for learners.

In England, in the period post the 1988 Education Act, there has been significant recentralization, with funding for the sector being controlled by quangos such as the Teacher Training Agency (TTA) and traditional providers such as LEAs being marginalized (Bates *et al.* 1999). While this is offset, to a limited extent, by providing some funding as part of school budgets, this leaves CPD in a very vulnerable position due to local management of schools (LMS) constraints. In general, there is considerable difference between having dedicated centres (the European norm), typically located regionally, with considerable resources and expertise, and 'going to the market' for the best value for money. The former approach is more likely to build and sustain capacity in the system, while the latter, with an emphasis on immediate priorities, may actually deplete capacity, thus undermining sustainability at a time when there is every indication that more regular and ongoing professional support will be a vital necessity if teachers are to become model lifelong learners.

Competitive bidding for funding CPD, coupled with clearly identified government priorities, can have further negative consequences. First, it is less likely that career-stage-sensitive courses are provided, and more likely that 'one fit for all' programmes are perpetuated, when there is increasing recognition of their inappropriateness. Second, it becomes difficult for providers to make medium- or long-term plans to develop the sector when funding is allocated on an annual, biennial or triennial basis. Thus, emphasis shifts from sustainable capacity building within systems to an emphasis on service. While service may be immediately more cost effective, in the longer term a system's capacity to support and sustain lifelong learning is actually reduced. Third, CPD is rather like a public transport system; not every route is self-financing. Consequently, competition may actually reduce access to professional support depending on the geographical location of teachers, thus creating inequities in the system, while putting some students at a considerable disadvantage in comparison with their peers. Fourth, a strongly prescribed top-down approach to CPD also has considerable potential to foster and perpetuate a 'dependency culture' (Coolahan 1994) among teachers that is the very antithesis of becoming a lifelong learner. Fifth, if national priorities are allocated the lion's share of CPD funding for 'recognized' or 'taught' courses, then personal needs and interests may be marginalized or entirely ignored, with important consequences for teacher morale, motivation and commitment. Sixth, since the school has become *de facto* the locus and target of reform endeavours, teachers are obliged to plan their professional development – an additional responsibility that consumes time. However, the litmus test of any provision is 'where the rubber meets the road'. Consequently, it is necessary to turn to practice as a means of completing the picture.

CPD practice: examples and evaluation

There are a plethora of reasons why CPD provision is so fragmented, and why it is poorly researched and evaluated, none of which need detain us here. However, it is difficult in such circumstances to paint some worthwhile pictures of practice in an effort to bring some 'situated certainty' or coherence to the field (Hargreaves 1994). In an effort to provide an initial map of the field, a categorization of provision is constructed using the framework identified above: formal, non-formal and informal, and this is reproduced in Table 3.1.[5] Provision in each category should not be understood as entirely discrete. Rather, the three categories are more profitably thought of as a continuum, with activities being understood as belonging primarily in one rather than another, but with varying degrees of overlap and commonality across boundaries. Very recently, the European Commission has made the addition of 'random learning' as a fourth category, but this has not been included here (European Commission 2001). The term 'lifewide' learning is also being promoted as a more inclusive notion than its antecedent, lifelong, learning.

As already indicated above, until relatively recently, teachers' professional learning was largely serendipitous and individual. Table 3.1 suggests that, as pressures for reforms have intensified, idiosyncrasy is being supplanted by

Table 3.1 The nature of CPD practice

Formal	Non-formal	Informal
Taught courses, credit and non-credit by university personnel and CPD experts/ facilitators including short 'in-service' as well as extended postgraduate course modules for awards (diplomas/degrees).	Emphasis is on inquiry/ learning. School-based/ focused. Partnerships: school/university. Networks: interests, subjects, innovations. Communities of practice: professional support, sharing expertise, knowledge generation, action-oriented.	Individual, private. Includes: staffroom conversations; occasional lectures; family/close friends; reading professionally related journals/ magazines; TV/video. Unplanned/opportunistic conversations. Hobbies/interests.

more prescribed, collective professional endeavours with a general social constructivist orientation, where participation is increasingly a requirement or perceived as a necessity without attracting the label 'compulsory'. There is very little evidence of a systematic nature relating to teachers' informal learning, but this is worthy of systematic inquiry. It may be the case that as activities in the other two categories increase, the informal and more personal dimensions of personal and professional renewal are squeezed to the margins, thus diminishing personal satisfaction and well-being despite greater participation in collective learning. It is necessary to know much more about an appropriate trade-off between these different spheres of professional support and challenge and how they complement and conflict with one another. Analysis of recently published research in addition to my own and work in the CPD field (Sugrue *et al.* 2001; Sugrue 2002) suggests a convergence around learning and how this is inhibited or supported.

Teacher learning in practice

Comments here are intended to be succinct, perspicacious and provocative as a means of pushing the field to grapple with some of its major dilemmas and contradictions. There are ongoing tensions within systems between mandated, centrally prescribed changes and the accompanying 'compulsory' professional learning that is provided as part of such reform 'packages'. Consequently, even when and where professional support is provided it begins to feel like further coercion, having one's space and time colonized by the puppet masters of the system to the point of alienation. Even within formal accredited learning scenarios, teachers as learners realize that it is the informal networks in and around the 'set piece' formal contact hours of such courses that the 'real' learning is made to happen, often through sustained engagement with peers. In such scenarios they are taking control of their own learning, beginning to feel empowered in the process, and acquiring a new and emerging confidence to meet new challenges head on and in ways that previously they did not imagine were possible. Such learning is career-stage sensitive, and requires time and space as well as conducive conditions that also need to alter with time, while the external climate creates a context that impinges in marked ways on such cocoons or oases of learning.

Teacher learning thrives on an unpredictable combination of formal stimulation or input in the form of texts, lectures and presentations followed by time for debate, reflection and experimentation. The conception of experimentation is often regarded as the hands-on element of such learning scenarios, but it may also include playing with ideas and inventing a language of practice in which to include new thinking into one's repertoire of teaching intentions and actions. As part of this learning it may be important to endorse Barth's (1990) notion of schools as places of learning for teachers as well as pupils. Yet, it is important to acknowledge also that professional learning needs additional support from networks outside school communities and that the combination of this complementary networking changes the pattern, intensity and level of involvement at various stages. Much more research is needed so that we can begin to map these patterns of teacher learning more adequately as well as seek to optimize their learning potential. Such networks are the products of coercive, centralized prescriptions for school reform, as much as they are creative coping strategies by teachers for the times we live in. The emergence of CPD as a phenomenon of increasing significance must also be understood and researched as a manifestation of contemporary educational forces, nationally and internationally, as well as of the ongoing insatiable desire for learning that is also part of the human condition and can be enhanced or suppressed by an external climate of rewards, risks and routines.

Conclusions

Comments in this section are brief. Remarks are at three levels: policy, practice, research and evaluation, with an emphasis on seeking some coherence.

Governments' recent interest in CPD and their articulated policies are driven by concern for, and preoccupation with, economic competitiveness in the global economy. Despite a rhetoric of devolved responsibility and decision making, recentralization, increasing homogenization and prescription of what counts as 'successful' educational outcomes are eroding teacher autonomy and undermining career commitments and trajectories as well as changing significantly more traditional employment patterns in the sector. These policies place a premium on service, on immediate short-term goals that may be inimical to building capacity in the sector that is more likely to construct appropriate infrastructure that challenges and supports life-wide learning for teachers. In the 'post-democratic' new world order of global competition and the info-tainment telesector, it is necessary for teachers and researchers, along with other partners in education, to build coalitions of interest that recognize their knowledge-producing potential. While the pace of change and the continuous avalanche of policy directives militate against 'real time' learning for teachers, unless they wish to be consigned to the 'service sector', what Barber (1996: 79) describes as 'the third world of the services domain, with its dependency at the lower end of relatively unskilled labor and uncomplicated work', they need to grasp the challenge of becoming knowledge producers, shapers of images, signs and symbols, that reshape and reposition their identities and influence within the 'new information' sector of the global economy. There is a basic policy contradiction, therefore, at the heart of many recent reform efforts. While the rhetoric is of increasing complexity in school and classroom ecology, policies tend to rationalize such complexities and reduce them to a series of relatively uncomplicated prescriptive solutions, and provide courses for teachers to instruct them in implementation strategies. Universities in particular, frequently marginalized from policy formulation and CPD, have a leading role to play in shaping the role of teachers as public sector intellectuals while simultaneously securing appropriate funding for professional learning and research efforts that collaboratively build understanding of, and contributions to, the knowledge base of lifelong learning for teachers, emerging patterns of leadership and professionalism.

Time emerges as the single most intractable difficulty in the practice of real-time learning for teachers. However, an exclusive focus on issues of time is unlikely to deal with more fundamental concerns. Evidence tentatively suggests that current pressures and possible overload on teachers' willingness and capacity for continuous learning and improvement have shifted their learning away from more individual and idiosyncratic pursuits and towards more formulaic, frequently prescribed learning routines. Their lives as well as their learning become distorted, and the growth in, and popularity of, emergent learning networks and communities of practice indicates that they are seeking safe spaces where they can begin to exercise more control over their learning, lives and work. While the growth of such support groups may (potentially) constitute significantly more than an anarchic 'Jihad' (see Barber 1996) response to globalizing tendencies and policy prescriptions, the voices of teachers need to be heard beyond the confines of these creative coping cells. There is much to be learned about the nature of life-wide learning for teachers. Documenting in much greater detail, and in career-sensitive ways, the optimum balance between formal, non-formal and informal learning emerges as a potentially fruitful place to begin to construct this vitally important knowledge base.

It is abundantly evident that lifelong learning for teachers is relatively uncharted territory. Published evaluations tend to document specific interventions such as the teaching of ICTs, science or mathematics. Personal interests and lack of strategic and more adequate funding for CPD and its ongoing evaluation, conspire to ensure that support for particular innovations is short and often transitory, as well as preaching to the converted, so that outcomes typically advocate more of the same for other teachers which in many instances falls on deaf ears. Such outcomes frequently leave practitioners and policy makers alike with little or no evidence about the longer-term impact on the quality of teaching and learning. Apart from the necessity to document the nature of teacher learning in a more holistic, life-wide manner, there are potential benefits also from revisiting notions of career stages and career patterns, as these too are already altering in response to rapidly changing contexts of schooling. There is an obvious need also to provide more in-depth accounts of the manner in which CPD is funded as well as how such funds are disbursed and spent.

Finally, how power is exercised within national systems, how global forces are refracted within national and local politics and policies, have enormous consequences for the lives and work of teachers. It is crucially important for all concerned to acknowledge the core contradiction at the heart of current rhetorics on school reform: at a time when knowledge generation is being promoted as crucial for maintaining international competitiveness, teachers, in an increasing number of jurisdictions, are being regarded as technicians of teaching, mere clerks of the global empire, rather than as professionals who generate insights and understandings that contribute to the knowledge base of teaching and learning. Teachers themselves have a crucial role to play, and researchers need to be more adept at enabling their voices to be heard as key players in the creation of new knowledge, in a new generation of learners and in community with teaching colleagues, locally, nationally and internationally.

Notes

1   I concur with Beck's (2000) preference for the notion of glocalization, where the local meets the global, in opposition to Giddens' (1991) more linear notion of the McDonalization of the world.

2   By way of illustration, at the annual conference (February 2002) of the Irish Primary Principals' Network, itself a manifestation of the increasing burden on principals, the president of the network called for a complete moratorium on in-service courses for the revised primary curriculum (introduced in 1999), to enable teachers and principals to consolidate learning gains rather than being rushed headlong into further requirements by predetermined implementation schedules devised by the government.

3   The VITAE research project currently being undertaken by the University of

Nottingham and the London Institute of Education is a very prominent example of this confluence of forces, where, over a period of three years, efforts are being made to connect teacher professional development with student learning.

4   This classification corresponds favourably with the German classification of 'taught learning', 'deliberate learning' and 'random learning' (Federal Statistics Office of Germany, January 2001).

5   For definitions and criteria being applied to these categories, see European Commission (2001: 9–14).

References

Altrichter, H. and Elliott, J. (eds) (2000) *Images of Educational Change*. Buckingham: Open University Press.

Arnot, M. and Dillabough, J. (2000) *Challenging Democracy: International Perspectives on Gender, Education and Citizenship*. London: Routledge.

Ball, S. (1990) *Politics and Policy-Making in Education*. London: Routledge.

Ball, S. (1994) *Educational Reform: A Critical and Post-Structural Approach*. Buckingham: Open University Press.

Barber, B.R. (1996) *Jihad vs. McWorld*. New York: Balantine Books.

Barth, R. (1990) *Improving Schools from Within: Teachers, Parents and Principals Can Make a Difference*. San Francisco: Jossey-Bass.

Bascia, N. (1998) Teacher unions and educational reform, in A. Hargeaves, A. Lieberman, M. Fullan and D. Hopkins (eds) *International Handbook of Educational Change*, pp. 895–915. Dordrecht: Kluwer.

Bates, T., Gough, B. and Stammers, P. (1999) The role of central government and its agencies in the continuing professional development of teachers: an evaluation of recent changes in its financing in England, *Journal of In-service Education*, 25(2): 321–36.

Beatty, B. (2000) Teachers leading their own professional growth: self-directed reflection and collaboration, and changes in perception of self and work in secondary school teachers, *Journal of In-service Education*, 26(1): 73–98.

Beatty, B. (2002) Emotion matters in educational leadership. Unpublished doctoral thesis, University of Toronto.

Beck, U. (2000) *What is Globalization?* Cambridge: Polity Press.

Bolam, R. (2000) Emerging policy trends: some implications for continuing professional development, *Journal of In-service Education*, 26(2): 267–80.

Bourdieu, P. and Wacquant, L.J.D. (1992) *An Invitation to Reflexive Sociology*. Chicago: University of Chicago Press.

Bredeson, P.V. (2000) Teacher learning as work and at work: exploring the content and context of teacher professional development, *Journal of In-service Education*, 26(1): 63–72.

Britzman, D. (1986) Cultural myths in the making of a teacher: biography and social structure in teacher education, *Harvard Educational Review*, 56(4): 442–56.

Castle, J. (1997) Towards understanding professional development: exploring views across a professional development school, *Teachers and Teaching: Theory and Practice*, 3(2): 221–42.

Clement, M. and Vandenberghe, R. (2000) Teachers' professional development: a solitary or collegial (ad)venture? *Teaching and Teacher Education*, 16: 81–101.

Coolahan, J. (ed.) (1994) *Report on The National Education Convention*. Dublin: The National Education Convention Secretariat.

Copland, M.A. (2001) The myth of the superprincipal, *Phi Delta KAPPAN*, 82(7): 528–33.

Cuban, L., Kirkpatrick, H. and Peck, C. (2001) High access and low use of technologies in high school classrooms: explaining an apparent paradox, *American Educational Research Journal*, 38(4): 813–34.

Darling-Hammond, L. (1997) *The Right To Learn*. San Francisco: Jossey-Bass.

Day, C. (1993) Reflection: a necessary but not sufficient condition for professional development, *British Educational Research Journal*, 19: 83–93.

Day, C. (2000) Teachers in the twenty-first century: time to renew the vision, *Teachers and Teaching: Theory and Practice*, 6(1): 101–36.

Day, C., Harris, A., Hadfield, M., Tolley, H. and Beresford, J. (2000) *Leading Schools in Times of Change*. Buckingham: Open University Press.

Dimmock, C. (1996) Dilemmas for school leaders and administrators in restructuring, in K. Leithwood, J. Chapman, D. Corson, P. Hallinger, and A. Hart (eds) *International Handbook of Educational Leadership and Administration*, vol. 2, pp. 135–70. Dordrecht: Kluwer.

Er ulj, J. (2002) Collective learning in 'Networks of Learning Schools'. Unpublished manuscript, Kranji.

Eraut, M. (1994) *Developing Professional Knowledge and Competence*. London: Falmer Press.

European Commission (2001) *Report of the Eurostat Task Force on Measuring Lifelong Learning*. Brussels: European Commission, Statistical Office of the European Communities.

Fullan, M. (1991) *The New Meaning of Educational Change*. London: Cassell.

Fullan, M. (1992) *What's Worth Fighting for in Headship?* Buckingham: Open University Press.

Fullan, M. (1995) *Successful School Improvement*, 2nd edn. Buckingham: Open University Press.

Fullan, M. and Hargreaves, A. (1992) *What's Worth Fighting for in Your School?* Buckingham: Open University Press.

Gerstner, L.V. with Semerad, R.D., Doyle, D.P. and Johnston, W.B. (1994) *Reinventing Education: Entrepreneurship in America's Public Schools*. New York: Dutton.

Giddens, A. (1991) *Modernity and Self-identity: Self and Society in the Late Modern Age*. Stanford, CA: Stanford University Press.

Gough, B. (1997) Teachers' centres as seen through the pages of the *British Journal of In-service Education, Journal of In-service Education*, 23(1): 23–30.

Grace, G. (1995) *School Leadership: Beyond Educational Management*. London: Falmer Press.

Graham, J. (1998) From New Right to New Deal: nationalism, globalisation and the regulation of teacher professionalism, *Journal of In-service Education*, 24(1): 9–30.

Gray, J., Hopkins, D., Reynolds, D., Wilcox, B., Farrell, S. and Jesson, D. (1999) *Improving Schools: Performance and Potential*. Buckingham: Open University Press.

Guskey, T.R. and Huberman, M. (eds) (1995) *Professional Development in Education: New Paradigms and Practices*. New York: Teachers College Press.

Halpin, D. and Tronya, B. (1995) The politics of education policy borrowing, *Comparative Education*, 31(3): 303–10.

Hargreaves, A. (1992) Cultures of teaching: a focus for change, in A. Hargreaves and M. Fullan (eds) *Understanding Teacher Development*. London: Cassell.

Hargreaves, A. (1994) *Changing Teachers, Changing Times*. London: Cassell.

Hargreaves, A. (2000a) Four ages of professionalism and professional learning, *Teachers and Teaching: Theory and Practice*, 6(2): 151–82.

Hargreaves, A. (2000b) Mixed emotions: teachers' perceptions of their interactions with students, *Teaching and Teacher Education*, 16: 811–26.

Hargreaves, A. and Fullan, M. (1998) *What's Worth Fighting for Out There?* New York: Teachers College Press.

Hargreaves, A. and Goodson, I.F. (1996) Teachers' professional lives: aspirations, and actualities, in I.F. Goodson and A. Hargreaves (eds) *Teachers' Professional Lives*, pp. 1–27. London: Falmer Press.

Hargreaves, A., Lieberman, A., Fullan, M. and Hopkins, D. (1998) *International Handbook of Educational Change*. Dordrecht: Kluwer.

Hargreaves, A., Earl, L., Moore, S. and Manning, S. (2001) *Learning to Change: Teaching Beyond Subjects and Standards*. San Francisco: Jossey-Bass.

Helsby, G. (1999) *Changing Teachers' Work: The 'Reform' of Secondary Schooling*. Buckingham: Open University Press.

Holt-Reynolds, D. (1992) Personal history-based beliefs as relevant prior knowledge in course work, *American Educational Research Journal*, 29(2): 325–49.

Homer-Dixon, T. (2001) *The Ingenuity Gap*. Toronto: Vintage Canada.

Hopkins, D. and Harris, A. (1997) Understanding the school's capacity for development: growth states and strategies, *School Leadership and Management*, 17(3): 401–11.

Hopkins, D., Ainscow, M. and West, M. (1994) *School Improvement in an Era of Change*. London: Cassell.

Hopkins, D., Beresford, J. and West, M. (1998) Creating the conditions for classroom and teacher development, *Teachers and Teaching: Theory and Practice*, 4(1): 115–42.

Hoshschild, A.R. (1983) *The Managed Heart: The Commercialization of Human Feeling.* Berkeley, CA: University of California Press.

Huberman, M. (1995) Networks that alter teaching: conceptualisations, exchanges and experiments, *Teachers and Teaching: Theory and Practice*, 1(2): 193–212.

Huberman, M., Grounauer, M., Mati, J. and Huberman, A. (1993) *The Lives of Teachers.* New York: Teachers College Press.

Ireland, Government Office (1995) *Charting Our Education Future: White Paper on Education.* Dublin: Government Publications.

Johnson, S. (1992) Images: a way of understanding the practical knowledge of student teachers, *Teaching and Teacher Education*, 8(2): 123–36.

Joyce, B. and Showers, B. (1996) Staff development as a comprehensive service organisation, *Journal of Staff Development*, 17(1): 2–5.

Kagan, D. (1992) Professional growth among pre-service and beginning teachers, *Review of Educational Research*, 62(2): 129–69.

Kelchtermans, G. and Vandenberghe, R. (1994) Teachers' professional development: a biographical perspective, *Journal of Curriculum Studies*, 26(1): 45–62.

Kelchtermans, G. and Vandenberghe, R. (1996) *Becoming Political: A Dimension in Teachers' Professional Development. A Micro-political Analysis of Teachers' Professional Biographies.* ERIC no. ED395921.

Kwakman, K.H. (1998) Professional learning on the job of Dutch secondary teachers: in search of relevant factors, *Journal of In-service Education*, 24(1): 57–72.

Lawn, M. (1996) *Work, Professionalism and Citizenship in Teaching.* London: Falmer Press.

Lawton, D. (1992) *Education And Politics In The 1990s: Conflict or Consensus?* London: Falmer Press.

Lee, M. (1997) The development of in-service education and training as seen through the pages of the *British Journal of In-service Education, Journal of In-service Education*, 23(1): 9–22.

Leithwood, K., Chapman, J., Corson, D., Hallinger, P. and Hart, A. (eds) (1996) *International Handbook of Educational Leadership and Administration.* Dordrecht: Kluwer.

Leithwood, K., Jantzi, D. and Steinbach, R. (1999) *Changing Leadership for Changing Times.* Buckingham: Open University Press.

Little, J.W. (1990) The persistence of privacy: autonomy and initiative in teachers' professional relations, *Teachers College Record*, 91(4): 509–36.

Little, J.W. (1993) Teachers' professional development in a climate of educational reform, *Educational Evaluation and Policy Analysis*, 15(2): 129–51.

Little, J.W. (1999) Teachers' professional development in the context of high school reform. Unpublished manuscript, San Francisco.

Little, J.W. (2001) Locating learning in teachers' communities of practice: opening up problems of analysis in records of everyday work. Unpublished manuscript, San Francisco.

MacBeath, J. (ed.) (1998) *Effective School Leadership: Responding to Change*. London: Paul Chapman Publishing.

MacBeath, J. and Mortimore, P. (eds) (2001) *Improving School Effectiveness*. Buckingham: Open University Press.

Marx, R., Blumfeld, P. and Krajcik, J. (1998) New technologies for teacher professional development, *Teaching and Teacher Education*, 14(1): 33–52.

McLaughlin, M. and Talbert, J. (1993) Contexts that matter for teaching and learning. Unpublished manuscript, Stanford University Center for Research on the Context of Secondary School Teaching.

McLaughlin, M.W. (2002) Sites and sources of teachers' learning, in Sugrue, C. (ed.) *Developing Teachers and Teaching Practice*, pp. 95–115. London: Routledge-Falmer.

Mortimore, P. (1988) *The Road to Improvement: Reflections on School Improvement*. Lisse: Swets & Zeitlinger.

Mortimore, P. (1998) The vital hours: reflecting on research on schools and their effects, in A. Hargeaves, A. Lieberman, M. Fullan and D. Hopkins (eds) *International Handbook of Educational Change*, pp. 85–99. Dordrecht: Kluwer.

Mortimore, P., Sammons, P., Stoll, L., Lewis, D. and Ecob, R. (1988) *School Matters: The Junior Years*. London: Paul Chapman Publishing.

Noddings, N. (1992) *The Challenge to Care in Schools: An Alternative Approach to Education*. New York: Teachers College Press.

OECD (1991) *Reviews of National Education Policies for Education: Ireland*. Paris: OECD.

OECD (1992) *Schools and Business: A New Partnership*. Paris: Centre for Educational Research and Innovation, OECD.

OECD (1997) *Staying Ahead: In-service Training and Teacher Professional Development*. Paris: Centre for Educational Research and Innovation, OECD.

OECD (1998) *Lifelong Learning to Maintain Employability*. Paris: OECD.

Pajares, M. (1992) Teachers' beliefs and educational research: cleaning up a messy construct, *Review of Educational Research*, 62(3): 307–22.

Retallick, J. (1999) Teachers' workplace learning: towards legitimation and accreditation, *Teachers and Teaching: Theory and Practice*, 5(1): 33–50.

Reynolds, D., Creemers, B., Stringfield, S., Teddlie, C. and Schaffer, G. (eds) (2002) *World Class Schools: International Perspectives on School Effectiveness*. London: Routledge-Falmer.

Sachs, J. (2000) Rethinking the practice of teacher professionalism, in C. Day, A. Fernandez, T.E. Hauge and J. Moller (eds) *The Life and Work of Teachers: International Perspectives in Changing Times*, pp. 76–90. London: Falmer Press.

Schein, E.H. (1978) *Career Dynamics: Matching Individual and Organizational Needs*. Reading, MA: Addison-Wesley.

Schein, E.H. (1990) *Career Anchors: Matching Individual and Organizational Needs*. San Diego, CA: Pfeiffer.

Schratz, M. and Resinger, R. (2002) Austria: a national case study, in B. Moon (ed.)

Institutional Approaches to Teacher Education in the European Region: Current Models and New Developments. Bucharest: UNESCO-CEPES.

Sergiovanni, T. (2001) *Leadership: What's in it for Schools?* London: Routledge-Falmer.

Sharp, S. and Draper, J. (2000) Leaving the register: Scottish teachers lost to the profession, 1997–98, *Journal of In-service Education*, 26(2): 247–66.

Skilbeck, M. (1985) *School Based Curriculum Development*. London: Paul Chapman Publishing.

Skilbeck, M. (1990) *Curriculum Reform: An Overview of Trends*. Paris: OECD.

Skilbeck, M. (1998) School-based curriculum development, in A. Hargreaves, A. Lieberman, M. Fullan and D. Hopkins (eds) *International Handbook of Educational Change*, 121–44. Dordrecht: Kluwer.

Smyth, J. (ed.) (1993) *A Socially Critical View of the Self-managing School*. London: Falmer Press.

Southworth, G. (1996) *Looking into Primary Headship*. London: Falmer Press.

Stenhouse, L. (1975) *An Introduction to Curriculum Research and Development*. London: Heinemann.

Sugrue, C. (2002) Irish primary principals' professional development experiences: lessons from a support group, in F. Rauch and C. Biott (eds) *Challenges and Support for School Leadership*. Austria: Studienverlag.

Sugrue, C. (2003) Principals' professional development: realities, perspectives & possibilities, *Oideas*, 50.

Sugrue, C. (forthcoming) Whose curriculum is it anyway? Power, policies and politics in primary curriculum reform, in C. Sugrue (ed.) *Ideology and Curriculum: Irish Experiences, International Perspectives*. Cork: Collins Press.

Sugrue, C. and Uí Thuama, C. (1997) Lifelong learning for teachers in Ireland: policy, provision and vision, *British Journal of In-service Education*, 20: 213–26.

Sugrue, C., Morgan, M., Devine, D. and Rafferty, D. (2001) *The Quality of Professional Learning for Irish Primary and Secondary Teachers: A Critical Analysis*. Dublin: Department of Education & Science.

Trnavcevic, A. (2002) Personal correspondence.

UNESCO (1992) *UNESCO Statistical Year Book 1992*. Paris: UNESCO.

Wenger, E. (1998) *Communities of Practice*. Cambridge: Cambridge University Press.

Whitty, G. (2000) Teacher professionalism in new times, *Journal of In-service Education*, 26(2): 281–96.

Wilhelm, K., Dewhurst-Savellis, J., and Parker, G. (2000) Teacher stress? An analysis of why teachers leave and why they stay, *Teachers and Teaching: Theory and Practice*, 6(3): 291–304.

Zindovic-Vukadinovic, G. (2002) Teacher education, institutional approaches within higher education: a case study on Yugoslavia, in B. Moon (ed.) *Institutional Approaches to Teacher Education in the European Region: Current Models and New Developments*. Bucharest: UNESCO-CEPES.

4 'Looking at student work' in the United States: a case of competing impulses in professional development

Judith Warren Little

'Looking at student work' enjoys growing popularity as a vehicle of professional development in the USA. Yet the phrase 'looking at student work' masks multiple practices, shaped by diverse and potentially contradictory purposes: stimulating and supporting teachers' learning and instructional decision making; bolstering teacher community; advancing whole-school reform; and satisfying demands for public accountability. This chapter portrays 'looking at student work', with its varied practices and purposes, as emblematic of two current impulses and tensions in contemporary professional development in the USA. One impulse – to root teacher learning in and from practice – arises from the premise that improvements in teaching will result from teachers' deep understanding of how children learn. The second impulse – toward greater external control of teaching and teacher education – arises from the premise that improvements in teaching can be wrought through policy by specifying expectations (standards), controlling practice and exercising sanctions. Available research suggests that close examination of student work yields benefits for teacher learning in specific subject domains, but few studies illuminate the actual practices of teachers engaged in looking at student work and most rapidly expanding activities – those associated with school reform and public accountability – deserve more attention from researchers.

Introduction

Envision a group of teachers gathered together to examine samples of students' school work – essays in literature or history, laboratory reports in science, displays of problem solving in mathematics, a videotape of musical performance – and consider how the ensuing conversation might constitute an occasion for teachers' professional development. Such activity enjoys a growing popularity in the USA. Through publications, websites and conferences, various organizations and groups urge educators to come together to look closely at student work.[1] Yet the phrase 'looking at student work' masks a multi-faceted set of practices, bent toward and shaped by diverse and sometimes contradictory purposes: stimulating and supporting teacher learning and instructional decision making, bolstering teacher community, advancing whole-school reform and satisfying demands for public accountability.

It is precisely this constellation of purposes that makes looking at student work of particular interest in the landscape of teachers' continuing professional development (CPD). Embedded in the arguments for looking closely and collectively at student work, and embodied in the conception and design of specific approaches, these purposes reflect certain prevailing interests and emerging tensions in teachers' work and teacher development more generally. In this regard, looking at student work is a case emblematic of contemporary professional development in the USA.

This analysis draws on two sets of resources to analyse looking at student work as a case illustrative of recent developments and tensions in teachers' professional development. First, it makes use of documents published in print and online, in which designers, users and advocates of various approaches identify the purposes and justifications they embrace. These documents serve rhetorically to position selected practices both educationally and politically, and to illuminate the assumptions connecting purpose to practice. They also typically supply examples of specific practices and guidelines for their use.

Second, the chapter takes stock of a small but growing body of empirical research that focuses on looking at student work as an element of professional development activity. Some of the available research attests to the potential benefits for teachers and students that may reside in such activity; however, the professional development approaches targeted by those studies represent only part of the broader landscape of practice.

The chapter begins by situating the case of looking at student work in relation to two central impulses in teaching and teacher development in the USA: an impulse to locate and support teacher learning more fully in and through practice; and a countervailing impulse to direct and control teacher practice more firmly through instruments of external accountability. It then elaborates on looking at student work as a set of practices joined to three particular purposes: as a resource for teacher learning in specific subject matter domains; as a resource for teacher community and reform-oriented collaboration at the school level; and as a vehicle for public accountability. These same configurations of purpose and practice then serve as the organizing frame for a review of the available research.

The climate of contemporary professional development in the USA

Teachers' CPD in the USA remains in many respects no less fragmented and disconnected from practice than Conant (1963) charged four decades ago and than other critics have echoed thereafter (Little 1989; Wilson and Berne 1999). Amid this diffuse array, some teachers succeed in developing a professional development trajectory of remarkable coherence and vigour, while others derive little or nothing from professional development experiences, either by avoiding participation or by failing to find much of value in the available activities. (Little *et al.* 1987; Henke *et al.* 1997).

Responses to this long-standing fragmentation and superficiality have pushed professional development in two quite different directions. One response, mounted largely by the research community and by teacher-educators themselves, has been to seek professional development that is joined more closely to the genuine demands and resources of teaching practice (Ball and Cohen 1999). A second response, emerging primarily from the policy community, has been to seek greater coherence in professional development activity and a closer link to curriculum policy (Porter 1989; Cohen and Hill 2000). In recent years, developments in professional development policy have also mirrored a broader policy shift from locally-designed and locally-controlled reform initiatives to centrally-defined imperatives linked to standards-based accountability. The growing appeal of looking at student work – and the particular ways in which it has taken shape in practice – owes a debt to both of these responses.

Learning in and from practice

As a site for teacher development, looking at student work exemplifies efforts to root teacher learning more consistently and deeply in dilemmas of practice. The central argument for concentrating professional development more fully in practice derives from the intellectual shortcomings and strategic flaws characteristic of most in-service activity – especially when seen against the recurrent demands for reforms in teaching and learning:

> Rarely do these in-services seem based on a curricular view of teachers' learning. Teachers are thought to need updating rather than opportunities for serious and sustained learning of curriculum, students, and teaching . . . *Hence we propose new ways to understand and use practice as a site for professional learning, as well as ways to cultivate the sorts of inquiry into practice from which many teachers could learn.*
>
> (Ball and Cohen 1999: 3–4, 6, emphasis added)

Central to what Ball and Cohen term 'learning in and from practice' (p. 10) are teachers' investigations of student learning and teaching practice:

> Crucial questions about teaching and learning would be one part of the frame of such work, and evidence of professional work – teaching and learning – would be another part. Investigating such questions and bringing salient evidence to bear would be central activities in the acquisition and improvement of professional knowledge. Thus the pedagogy of professional education would in considerable part be a pedagogy of investigation.
>
> (p. 13)

By comparison with the sheer volume of traditional professional development activities, organized opportunities for learning in and from practice seem sparse (Little 1993; Wilson and Berne 1999). Yet some activities, such as the Bay Area Writing Project and other practice-centred teacher networks, boast a long history (Lieberman and Wood 2001), and the range of examples has widened steadily in recent years: video clubs (Frederiksen *et al.* 1998); case-based investigations of student learning (Barnett 1998; Greenleaf and Schoenbach 2001); lesson study (Lewis 2000; Fernandez 2002); collaborative student assessment (Falk and Ort 1998; Roberts and Wilson 1998); teacher research networks (Buchanan 1993; Ershler 2001); and the orchestrated use of multimedia archives of teaching (Lampert and Ball 1998; Kerr 2000; see also DeMonner 1998). In each of these activities, teachers rely on artefacts and accounts of classroom practice – stories told, samples of student work, classroom tasks and assignments, videotapes of classroom activity – as central resources in professional development. Together, these examples offer a substantial body of useful precedents and offer testimony to the growing appeal of professional development linked closely to practice.

Escalating accountability pressures

Professional development programmes that emphasize learning from and in practice – and the teachers who engage in them – reside in a policy and reform environment marked by shifting definitions of what constitutes 'good teaching' and by external pressures for 'improvement'. For the last decade, those definitions and pressures have coalesced in centrally defined accountability demands, with corresponding expectations for professional development specifically aligned to state academic standards and testing regimes. The growth of the standards movement has compelled attention to student achievement while also fuelling debates over what constitutes adequate and appropriate evidence of student learning.

In the realm of professional development, the standards movement appears to have resulted in a general push toward conventional training and away from inquiry-oriented activity. Professional development policy and practice thus manifest growing tensions between professional and bureaucratic control of teaching. These tensions play out in competing conceptions of what constitutes good professional development, and in turn, in funding and design. Activities that entail the close, collective examination of student work are particularly vulnerable to these tensions.

In summary, two central impulses dominate the contemporary landscape of professional development in the USA. One impulse – to organize teacher learning in and from practice – arises from the premise that improvements in teaching will most likely result from teachers' deep understanding of how children learn. The second impulse – toward greater external control of teaching and teacher education – arises from the premise that improvements in teaching can be wrought by specifying expectations (standards), controlling practice and exercising sanctions. Together, they help account for the wide range of meanings attached to the practice of looking at student work.

Looking at student work: profiles of purpose and practice

Approaches to looking at student work are distinguished from one another by their guiding purposes and values, their underlying assumptions and premises and their defining features of practice. The following discussion introduces three broad purposes that have served as the *principal rationales* for looking at student work and that in turn have structured *programmatic choices*. The first purpose is to deepen teacher knowledge and strengthen teachers' instructional practice in specific subject domains. A second set of purposes focuses on collective capacity for improvement in teaching and learning at the school level; it joins school reform goals with an emphasis on professional community. Finally, a third set of purposes aligns directly with the growing accountability movement, employing reviews of student work in the service of standards implementation and external accountability. Each of these purposes positions student work differently, and orients teachers differently in relationship to that work. Yet regardless of its declared purpose and emphasis, any particular approach plays out in a contemporary climate of professional development shaped by both of the competing impulses and tensions outlined above.

Student work as a resource for deepening teacher knowledge

In some respects, of course, all of the activities that come under the broad banner of looking at student work reflect an interest in the benefits that accrue to individual teachers and to classroom practice. Those who design or facilitate such activities express hopes that teachers' participation will strengthen the knowledge, skill and confidence they bring to classroom practice, and bolster their commitments to instructional improvement.

In a subset of those activities, however, teachers' knowledge and under-standing – what Shulman (1986, 1987) encompasses in a typology including subject knowledge, pedagogical content knowledge and knowledge of students – forms the central focus of programme goals and strategies. By design, programme activities employ examples of student work deliberately and spe-cifically as a means of deepening teacher knowledge and strengthening teachers' practice in specific subject domains – most often mathematics, but also in science, history, social studies and literacy. Such programmes typically rest on a foundation of research focused on subject learning and teaching, with researchers taking an active role in their design and leadership. The resulting activities serve dual purposes, as sites for teachers' professional development and as sites for ongoing research.

A description of one programme – the Strategic Literacy Initiative (SLI) – illustrates programmes of this type.[2] The SLI links an inquiry-oriented programme of professional development to a research-grounded model of 'reading apprenticeship' in middle and high school classrooms (Greenleaf and Schoenbach 2001; Greenleaf et al. 2001; Greenleaf and Katz in press). Pro-gramme designers posit that teachers will be better able to develop students' skill and confidence as adult readers – and especially their ability to grapple successfully with difficult texts across subject disciplines – if they deepen their understanding of the metacognitive strategies on which they themselves rely as readers, and if they become adept in uncovering and strengthening their students' awareness and use of such strategies. Each element of the pro-gramme's design thus creates conditions for teachers to render their tacit knowledge, and that of their students, explicit and accessible as a resource for instruction and assessment. Teachers meet regularly in network groups, where they engage in case inquiry activities focused successively on: their own read-ing processes; analysis of various texts for the demands they place on a reader's comprehension; analysis of student reading processes, using both prepared cases and samples from teachers' own classrooms; and classroom applications.

When examining samples of student work from their own classrooms, teachers make use of a 'protocol' – a set of steps and guidelines designed to focus attention first on the teacher's intentions ('What did you want students to learn from this?'), then on the reading task ('What reading knowledge/ strategies does the student need to accomplish this task?'), and finally on a few samples of student work ('What, if anything, is surprising or unexpected in this student work? What can we learn about the student's reading from this work sample?'). Having examined the student work for what it reveals about the student's understanding or difficulties, the participants turn their atten-tion to implications for instruction and assessment.

More formally structured cases of 'reading apprenticeship' developed by programme staff include text materials, videotaped student reading perform-ances and print and video excerpts from interviews with students about their literacy histories. Case designers specify: 'The video excerpts are selected to present teachers with contrasting performances from individual students, thereby complicating the domain of reading literacy and making it less likely that teachers can form easy generalizations about a particular student's read-ing ability' (Greenleaf and Schoenbach 2001: 2).

The programmatic elements of the SLI respond directly to Ball and Cohen's (1999) appeal to organize professional development activity in and from practice. Programme leaders propose that 'these case materials and the supportive protocols we have designed for inquiry comprise a type of "record of practice" around which participating teachers can begin to build a profes-sional discourse' (Greenleaf and Schoenbach 2001: 3). Yet in a climate of growing accountability demands and in the face of competing ideas about adolescent literacy, programme leaders also employ standardized measures of students' reading comprehension and reading fluency to assess and document gains in students' achievement.

Programmes like SLI that emphasize growth in teacher knowledge and practice differ in their design elements: in the specific place that student work occupies and the way that teachers engage with it; the degree to which they rely on student work from participants' own classrooms, or on cases built from work collected elsewhere; the degree to which they introduce frameworks for structuring discussion of student learning, or invite a more inductive process for arriving at shared frameworks or understandings; and even their under-lying theories of teacher change.[3] However, they share a premise that deepen-ing teachers' knowledge of subjects, subject pedagogy and student learning plays a central part in instructional improvement.

Student work as a catalyst for professional community and school reform

For advocates of whole-school reform and for educators seeking to remedy teacher isolation, engaging teachers in looking together at student work pro-vides a means to anchor a school's professional community in meaningful talk about teaching and learning. Approaches emphasizing teacher community differ from the subject-oriented programmes described above both in purpose and in characteristic design elements: they canvass a multidisciplinary terrain rather than delving into single subjects; they concentrate on colleagues within school sites rather than building networks or cohorts of interested individuals from many schools; and they structure conversation around process and par-ticipation goals rather than content area frameworks. Specific programmes and sites vary in numerous ways – their affiliation with particular reform ini-tiatives, their grounding in traditions of child study or teacher research, their orientation toward individual teacher interests or collectively defined goals. Across the board, however, programme designers tend to espouse a principled commitment to a school-based community conducive to inquiry into learning and teaching.

Consistent with this broad commitment to school-based professional community and a culture of inquiry, teacher study groups of various sorts form the prototypical context for looking at student work. Among the well-known examples in the USA are critical friends groups (CFGs), school-based teacher groups first developed and promoted in the mid-1990s by two national school reform organizations – the Coalition of Essential Schools (CES) and the Annenberg Institute for School Reform (AISR). Such groups typically involve teachers from multiple disciplines and grade levels, who are thus positioned by expertise, experience and interest to respond to student work in quite different ways and with quite different resources. Looking closely together at student work as well as artefacts of teacher work – lesson plans, written assignments, unit designs and so on – constitutes part of what CES and AISR term a 'cycle of inquiry' targeted toward instructional improvement and whole-school reform.[4]

The activities of school-based teacher groups differ in certain respects, especially with regard to the part played by scoring or otherwise assessing the student work.[5] Some schools and reform organizations have organized student performance assessment as a pivotal component of whole-school reform and a primary focus of teacher study groups. Collaborative student assessment activities at the school level arise from pragmatic concerns with the quality of assessment practice in reforming schools, and reformers' interests in building local capacity for multiple measures of student learning and school improvement. Examples range from the collective use of the primary language record to chart and support children's language development in elementary schools to the public presentation and review of student portfolios or senior projects at the high school level. In each case, teachers' collaborative work involves deliberations over standards and expectations, shared use of common assessment methods, and joint review of students' work (Darling-Hammond *et al.* 1995; Falk and Ort 1998).

Other groups and organizations eschew an assessment stance, inviting teachers instead to suspend or delay judgement as they consider what might be learned in open-ended consideration of student work. The 'evidence process' developed by Harvard Project Zero is premised on the notion that student work offers a window into children's thinking. At the core of the evidence process is the belief that structured conversation and close attention to student work will provide teachers with new insight into how students learn and will inspire new possibilities for instruction (Allen 1998; Seidel *et al.* 2001).

Despite internal variations, however, these activities all reflect an assumption that instructional improvement will result from bringing teachers together to focus on questions and problems of teaching and learning and to pool resources of teacher expertise, experience and mutual support. Each of these activities links teachers' individual learning opportunities to the formation of teacher community and the collective capacity to work on instructional improvement at the school level.

Student work as an instrument of external accountability

The emphasis on student learning makes the activity of looking at student work ripe for embrace by district or school officials in the interests of external accountability.[6] The most prominent and visible example, developed by the Education Trust as a component of its 'Standards in Practice' (SIP) programme, differs in crucial ways from activities in the preceding categories by its primary focus on the evaluation and improvement of academic tasks, assignments and instructional strategy, and by its orientation to accountability demands. As described by the Education Trust: 'Standards in Practice (SIP) is a professional development strategy to ensure that all activities in classrooms are aligned with standards . . . SIP is a quality control that can be used to evaluate classroom assignments, projects, courses, curricula, even teachers' and administrators' performances' (www.edtrust.org).

In differentiating SIP from other approaches, the Education Trust emphasizes that reviews of student work and teaching assignments are explicitly aligned with standards. A training videotape prepared by the Trust explains: 'Standards in Practice is the connection between instruction and standards . . . There are two elements to SIP that make it different from other professional development activities looking at student work. One, it focuses on assignments. And two, it is tied to standards' (Education Trust 2002).

On the premise that 'students can do no better than the assignments they are given', the SIP process joins a review of student work with close scrutiny of the corresponding classroom assignment. Participants in school-based teacher groups bring an academic task and samples of the student work that resulted from it. They begin by completing the assignment themselves, analysing the learning demands embedded in it and the degree to which it is linked to relevant standards. Using the assignment and standards, they develop a scoring guide for assessing the student work and pose the question of whether a given sample of student work would 'meet the standards'. The eventual aim of reviewing student work is to turn attention back to instructional strategy, and specifically to the design of appropriate academic tasks.

Multiple purposes – complementary or competing?

In principle, these three purposes are complementary. Yet selected profiles of activity show how purposes compatible in principle prove difficult to reconcile in practice, with markedly different rhetorical stances and programmatic emphases. Specific professional development activities tend to privilege one of the rationales over others.

Of course, the correspondence between purpose and activity is neither complete nor neatly specified. Nor are the purposes entirely independent from one another. Multiple purposes operate simultaneously and often in tension (for example, the tension between teacher-defined inquiry and compliance with external standards, or the tension between introducing a research-based model and honouring teachers' own interests and expertise). This portrait of purposes becomes further complicated when one takes the perspective of the individual teacher, for whom these purposes operate not as discrete frames of reference but as simultaneous and overlapping sensitivities. Yet the actual practices in which teachers engage tend to foreground particular purposes in ways that mask or subordinate others.

I argue that each of these purposes and related practices constitutes a partial resource for improvements in teaching and learning. Each approach supplies certain conditions that might render looking at student work a generative resource for improvements in teaching: depth of understanding in particular subject domains; professional norms of mutual support and critique; expectations for both internal and external accountability regarding students' opportunity to learn. Yet none of the specific approaches supplies all of these resources. Rather, each contributes something of importance and each suffers from limitations of conception and design.

Thus, activities focused on teacher knowledge and understanding may go a long way towards equipping teachers to strengthen their classroom teaching, but the effects of these activities may be weakened by tenuous school-level supports and by local norms or state imperatives that embody competing expectations for 'good teaching'. Activities in the 'professional community' category place their faith in the generative power of teacher exchange and interaction as a resource for instructional improvement within school-based cohorts. Project designers tend to be neutral regarding the content or substance of teachers' work together, despite evidence that professional development that takes serious account of subject resources proves more effective than professional development that relies only on innovations in form (Ball and Mosenthal 1991; Kennedy 1998). One consequence of this programmatic stance is to make participating teachers and programme facilitators relatively inattentive to subject area resources that might help teachers to capitalize on the strengths of growing teacher community at the school site.

Finally, activities directly driven by standards and accountability may orient teachers to common expectations regarding curriculum priorities and student performance on particular tasks. However, the focus on classroom tasks may leave little time (or permission) to grapple with how and why students came to produce a particular kind of work. (Just designing tasks well does not ensure student learning, but a well-designed task may help to reveal the source of students' struggles.) Further, the emphasis on external accountability may lead teachers to suppress expressions of their own uncertainty, especially in the absence of supportive teacher community and other resources for instructional improvement. In the current climate of bureaucratic and corporate accountability – what some have termed the 'audit society' (Groundwater-Smith and Sachs 2002) – professional development linked tightly to accountability demands necessarily introduces and highlights issues of power and control.

I acknowledge that any design choices inevitably constitute a set of constraints, and that inherent in the choice to foreground or pursue particular purposes is a corresponding choice to constrain or forgo other possibilities. However, I press the point here as a way of suggesting that those choices matter and that they may not be apparent to the educators who elect to participate in one or another project in which looking at student work is an organizing activity.

Contributions and limitations of research

The broad array of practices subsumed under the banner 'looking at student work', together with the different purposes underlying those practices, stimulate interest in the contributions of the available research. How has research on these practices been framed – what are its central questions and problems? To what extent has it illuminated how looking collectively and systematically at student work might contribute to intended outcomes for teachers and their students?

In the summary that follows, each of the studies focuses in some way on programmes, practices or contexts in which teachers' joint review of student work formed a central part of their collaborative practice.[7] Taking stock of this body of work, I put forward the following summary observations: (1) some evidence exists to show benefits to teaching and learning when looking closely at student work forms a key element of professional development activity; (2) yet few studies do much to illuminate the actual practices of teachers engaged in that activity; and (3) the scope of empirical research is poorly matched to the range of practice, with the best-developed body of research heavily centred on professional development in specific subject domains.

'Value added': contribution to teacher knowledge and practice

The available evidence does provide support for professional development activity in which looking at student work occupies a prominent place. Although the body of relevant research is small, findings from the available studies indicate that the collective examination of student work, where it is designed to focus teachers' attention closely on children's learning, may have a positive effect on outcomes of interest: teacher knowledge, teaching practice and (in some cases) student learning. This evidence of 'value added' derives particularly from a small subset of quasi-experimental studies that investigate the relationships among teachers' participation in subject-specific professional development, changes in their teaching practice and the learning demonstrated by their students. My colleagues and I came to call these 'triangle studies' by virtue of their attempt to investigate the relationships between teacher development, classroom practice and student learning; these relationships might be considered to form a professional development triangle that parallels the more commonly described instructional triangle (teacher, student, curriculum).

These studies, discussed in greater detail below, provide evidence that groups whose members systematically examine student work and student thinking were associated with higher student learning gains, more self-reported and observed change in teaching practice and more growth in teacher knowledge than comparison groups where looking at student work was not a central activity. Such studies remain concentrated almost exclusively on programmes of subject-focused professional development and related programmes of collaborative student assessment, where the governing professional development purpose is deepening individual teacher knowledge. Of the studies we reviewed, four were designed to supply evidence of a link between teachers' professional development activity and student learning.

A quasi-experimental three-group design provided the basis for project researchers in the Integrating Mathematics Assessment (IMA) project to examine changes in teaching practice and student learning for teachers in each of the project's three professional development configurations (Gearhart *et al.* 1999; Saxe *et al.* 2001). The 'experimental' configuration employed student work to illuminate students' mathematical thinking and development, embedded in a sequence of activities focused on teachers' mathematics, children's mathematics, children's motivation and student assessment. A comparison 'collegial support' configuration provided teachers with curriculum materials and organized a less intensive, but regularly scheduled, collegial support group. A third group of teachers employed the existing curriculum with no supplemental professional development. Evidence of student learning included both conventional measures of change in computational ability or familiarity with arithmetic facts, and measures of change in problem-solving and conceptual understanding. The most significant effects on student learning and the most uniform shifts in teaching practice were associated with the experimental group.

Project researchers associated with the Science Education for Public Understanding Program (SEPUP) also employed a quasi-experimental three-group design to evaluate contributions to teacher knowledge, teaching practice and student learning in science (Roberts and Wilson 1998; Wilson and Sloane 2000). Teachers in the experimental group received support in designing and refining curriculum-embedded assessments in science, forming a 'community of judgment' (Wilson 1994) through participation in a process termed 'moderation':

> Moderation is the process in which teachers discuss student work and the scores they have given that work, making sure that the scores are being interpreted in the same way by all teachers in the moderation group. In moderation sessions, teachers discuss the scoring, interpretation, and use of student work and make decisions regarding standards of performance and methods for reliably judging student work related to those standards. Moderation sessions also provide the opportunity for teachers to discuss implications of the assessment for their instruction, for example, by discussing ways to address common student mistakes or difficult concepts in their instruction.
>
> (Wilson and Sloane 2000: 201)

A second group of teachers received curriculum and assessment materials, but did not participate in the moderation process. A third group, selected for similar experience and qualifications in science, taught the existing science curriculum. Results of the three-group study showed student learning gains to be highest in classrooms of teachers from the experimental group – that is, where teachers participated in collaborative assessment activity involving scoring of student work samples and related discussion of integrated approaches to curriculum, instruction and assessment.

Similarly, researchers affiliated with Cognitively Guided Instruction (CGI) have compared changes in subject matter knowledge and student performance for teachers participating in CGI activity, with its use of a research-based framework for children's mathematical development, and teachers in a comparison (non-participating) group.[8] Studies conducted by CGI focus primarily on changes in teacher knowledge and practice, and on associated gains in student learning. Students in classrooms of CGI participants showed more knowledge of basic arithmetic facts and more problem-solving strategies than students in non-CGI comparison classrooms (Franke *et al.* 2001). Programme researchers attribute sustained teacher learning in part to the contribution of sustained 'communities of learning that focus on children's thinking': 'The learning communities these teachers create include their classrooms. These communities provide a basis for teachers to engage in inquiry focused on children's mathematical thinking with their students, their colleagues, and themselves' (Franke *et al.* 1998: 23).

Although research on the SLI has not made use of comparison groups, it has employed a pre-post design in following several cohorts of participating teachers and their students. Pre- and post-test data on the nationally-normed Degrees of Reading Power (DRP) instrument provide evidence of changes in students' reading comprehension in classrooms of participating teachers (Greenleaf *et al.* 2001). To gauge changes in teachers' understanding and teaching practice, project researchers videotaped teacher network meetings, collected teacher journals, and conducted pre and post interviews they describe as 'practice-grounded'.[9] Among the results reported by the project: participating teachers became more aware of their tacit knowledge as skilled readers and more able to make tacit knowledge available as a resource for instruction; teachers shifted from focusing on students as deficient or unmotivated readers to focusing on students' unfamiliarity with particular kinds of reading texts and tasks; and teachers shifted their classroom roles and practices in ways consistent with the notion of 'reading apprenticeship' and away from conventional remedial roles and practices (Greenleaf and Schoenbach 2001).

Inside the practice of looking at student work

In the light of long-standing norms of privacy in teaching and long-standing complaints about professional development disconnected from practice, teachers' approaches to looking at student work would seem of substantial interest. Yet few studies investigate the actual practices employed by teachers as they examine student work and investigate students' thinking or understanding. Rather, claims regarding teachers' interactions rest nearly exclusively on interview or survey testimony from teachers regarding the value of the collaborative activity, or on observers' summary process descriptions of teachers' participation in selected activities.[10] On the whole, the 'triangle studies' employ experimental and comparison group designations as proxies for the direct observation of teacher experience.

Of more than 20 studies reviewed for this analysis, five delve inside practice by constructing detailed observational records to tap teacher experience. Two of the available studies focus on teacher interaction within structured programmes of subject-specific professional development and represent an exception in the larger body of research on those programmes. The remaining studies concentrate on programmes where strengthening teacher community or advancing school-level reform is a central goal.[11]

Videotape records of teacher network events, supplemented by the teachers' written journal entries and by practice-grounded interviews, enabled researchers affiliated with the SLI to examine teachers' participation in case inquiry (Greenleaf and Schoenbach 2001; Greenleaf and Katz in press). Researchers used discourse analysis of videotape segments and content analysis of case discussions, interviews and journals to construct trajectories of participation and learning for 29 teachers, and to create more intensive case profiles of eight focus teachers over a two-year period. In a paper devoted to the dynamics of teacher interaction and processes of sense-making within the case inquiry groups, Greenleaf and Katz (in press) show how teachers selectively appropriate the ideas, materials and practices of a reading apprenticeship model. Teachers draw on their own and others' resources of knowledge, experience and disposition, rethinking to different degrees and moving in different ways to imagine 'new pedagogical selves' (p. 1). Speculating aloud to one another about a student case, the teachers 'are offered, and take up, positions as theorists, exploring possible accounts for a phenomenon of interest' (p. 13). The SLI studies highlight the role of active sense-making in teachers' professional development, and illuminate how that sense-making unfolds as teachers co-construct the meaning of student work. The central contribution of the SLI analysis is to show how specific elements of professional development design – in this instance, a case inquiry process – become 'generative' by interrupting or unsettling teachers' assumptions about student work and teaching practice, and by supplying resources for rethinking those assumptions and practices.

In another investigation 'inside practice', Kazemi and Franke (2003) trace the development of discourse among elementary teachers over a one-year period as they examine their students' responses to mathematical tasks and activities. The researchers draw on the well-established precedent of cognitively guided instruction (Franke *et al.* 2001) for a substantive focus – a framework for children's mathematical development in primary grades – but have modified the professional development approach to focus more consistently and centrally on samples of student work and on teachers' accounts of children's thinking as it was evident in the work and in teachers' reports of classroom activity:

> We hoped that looking at student work would allow teachers across the grade levels to build a framework for interpreting different mathematical ideas inherent in operating on numbers, particularly ways children come to understand and use their knowledge of the base ten system. Looking at student work, then, would enable us to build ideas about children's thinking in mathematics from the ground up.
>
> (Kazemi and Franke 2003: 5)

Kazemi and Franke's research was premised on the idea that the teachers' learning trajectories should be evident in the way that they talked with one another as they took up particular artefacts and moments of classroom teaching and learning: 'Teachers' talk, we claim, should be a key source of evidence about the new ideas they are noticing in their students' work and the questions their discussions with colleagues inspire about teaching and learning mathematics' (Kazemi and Franke 2003: 8).

In a paper built from analysis of audiotape transcripts for one teacher group (8 meetings with 11 teachers in a single school, spanning one school year), the researchers examine how investigations of student work strengthened teachers' grasp of children's understanding and its relationship to common teaching practice in their classrooms. First, student work alone proved insufficient as a resource for generating new insights into children's thinking; rather, these insights emerged when teachers began paying close attention to specific details of student thinking and problem-solving practice as those were revealed in the *combination* of classroom talk and samples of student work. Teachers' inferences from physical artefacts of student work about what students 'must have been thinking' were challenged when the teachers started to pay close attention to what the students were actually doing and thinking as they solved problems. Second, close attention to students' problem-solving strategies fuelled the gradual emergence and evolution of a mathematical agenda in the group. Thus, in the second meeting, 'we initiated what would become a bigger focus for the group, the idea that place value was not just about identifying columns. Rather, it meant being able to understand and operate with "ten as a unit"' (p. 23). With the mathematical agenda in mind, and recourse to detailed representations and artefacts of children's reasoning, teachers were able to reconsider some of their habitual instructional practices.

In both of these studies, student work was employed consistently by the organizers of professional development activity as a means of opening up new insights into subject matter learning and teaching. Taken together, these studies demonstrate that simply convening teachers to look at student work may have modest effect on teachers' understanding and practice. The studies begin to illuminate precisely how and under what conditions looking at student work might be expected to influence teacher thinking and practice in subject domains.

The three remaining studies yield a different but complementary set of discoveries. Each points to the likelihood that the recent enthusiasm for looking at student work will translate into established practices in schools, and further, that those practices will result in teacher learning and school improvement. On the whole, these studies confirm that looking at student work may open important opportunities for locating teacher development in and from practice, but they also offer testimony to the rather tenuous place occupied by 'looking at student work' practices, even in groups organized to promote them.

Two studies focus on activities of CFGs. Both show that CFGs vary in the amount and type of attention they actually devote to student work, even when looking at student work is one of the expressed aims of teachers' activity. Matsumura and Steinberg (2001) charted specific activities and the amount of time devoted to them in a sample of 11 CFGs, finding that teachers devoted less time to looking at student work (less than 20 per cent of meeting time) than estimated by group leaders (up to 44 per cent). Although it is not entirely clear what the researchers mean by this term, they also report having observed 'high quality feedback' in only 3 of 11 groups observed, suggesting that teachers refrain from pushing one another on matters related to student performance and teaching practice. In a second study of CFGs (Nave 2000), groups that most consistently engaged in looking at student work had introduced practices for doing so early in their history and sustained them over time. Groups that delayed in introducing routines for looking at student work found it difficult to do so later, suggesting that building the 'trust' for tackling questions of teaching and learning may be a product of attempting and persisting with these practices rather than a precondition for them.

In a third study, researchers conducted a video-based investigation of four teacher groups looking at student work, each in collaboration with one of three national reform organizations (Gearhart *et al.* 2002; Little *et al.* in press). In an overview of findings from that investigation, the researchers characterize three conditions that, where present, helped to focus attention on the student work and to deepen the discussion of teaching and learning (Little *et al.* in press). First, teachers were more likely to focus deeply on student work where they adopted a flexible, creative stance towards structured processes ('protocols') and crafted them to their local purposes. Second, explicit attention to the subject content of any given piece of student work, and to related questions of student learning and teaching practice, was an important contributor to what a group was able to accomplish by looking at student work. This observation was significant because none of the observed teacher groups formed with the explicit aim of pursuing professional development in a particular subject area. Their purposes were broader (a general concern for enhancing professional community and supporting instructional improvement), and they typically considered student work from several subject areas during any one meeting.

Finally, sustaining close attention to student work called for a balance between comfort and challenge. Protocols and process guidelines proved to have some power to help groups get past cultural norms of privacy and non-interference – getting a conversation started and focusing it on student or teacher work – but by themselves such structures could not bear the burden of cultural change in schools and in teachers' professional relationships. Where observers saw evidence of group norms built on open discussion, constructive questioning and critique, it was where individuals took the initiative to establish a different kind of conversation – for example, when a facilitator made moves to open up a question or persist with a difficult point, or a presenter invited feedback by being self-critical or disclosing problems openly, or a participant took the risk to broach a controversial topic. Groups varied with regard to these conditions, and thus in their resources for opening up and sustaining generative discussion of student learning and related questions of teacher knowledge and practice.

Thus, where research has delved inside the practice of looking at student work, it reveals what might be summed up as meaningful variations in 'opportunity to learn' at the level of practice. Together, these studies reveal how groups and events vary in their ability to bring student work onto the table for consideration in the first place. They also depict how groups vary in their resources for opening up and sustaining generative discussion of student learning and related questions of teacher knowledge and practice. In doing so, they illuminate some of the characteristic problems that arise in translating the notion of 'learning in and from practice' into formal programmes of CPD. One recurrent issue lies in the representation of classroom practices of learning and teaching in out-of-classroom contexts in which teachers come together for purposes of professional development. How much of students' thinking or learning is made evident by the student work available for consideration, and what additional resources enable teachers to make the most from looking at student work?

A second recurrent issue centres on traditions of professional practice, especially as they bear on collective scrutiny of classroom practice. Systematic attention to student learning and related questions of teaching practice requires discourse among teachers that runs against the grain of prevailing professional norms and habits. Research on the formation of teacher community suggests that teachers deepen their understanding of teaching and learning as groups develop practices and norms conducive to disclosure of problems, expressions of uncertainty and tolerance for public disagreement (Pfeiffer and Featherstone 1996; Lampert 2000; Grossman *et al.* 2001). In effect, such groups create an environment in which serious scrutiny of one another's practice is rendered legitimate and fruitful, essentially displacing or modifying traditional norms of privacy.

Limited scope of research, expanding the scope of practice

Finally, the landscape of research maps incompletely on the landscape of practice. That developments in practice have outpaced developments in research (or that practice and research have developed largely independently from each other) is hardly news in education. In this instance, the most rapidly expanding activities – those associated with school reform and public accountability – are less well represented in the published research than activities focused on specific dimensions of teaching knowledge and practice. While the 'triangle studies' represent a series of related investigations of selected programmes, spanning years and generating many publications, the 'inside practice' studies tend to be recent, smaller in scale, and more likely to be single studies.

Whatever the explanation for these patterns, the result is an asymmetrical distribution of research interest and investment across the landscape of practice. The result: a growing arena of practice that remains weakly positioned to capitalize on research, and research weakly attentive to expanding contexts of practice.

Conclusion

The growing enthusiasm for looking at student work reflects certain converging interests in teacher development rooted firmly in practice and sensitive to its complexities, and in school reform that capitalizes on the collective insights and expertise of teachers. It also reflects certain converging pressures to take serious account of student learning and to demonstrate student achievement. In this regard, looking at student work is emblematic of the possibilities and the tensions in contemporary professional development in the USA.

Arguably, the multiple purposes associated with looking at student work might be served by a more deliberate and strategic convergence between research and practice, coupled to a stance on professionalism that Bacon *et al.* (2000) have termed both 'activist' and 'accountable'. They describe a solution to the prevailing crisis of legitimization in teaching and other professions: 'It is our argument that the most efficacious response will come from addressing directly the heart of the matter, the core of the field – the methodologies of practice . . . which puts a special premium on practitioner or action research as an incisive form of reflexivity in practice' (p. 6).

Such a stance stands to bridge the now countervailing impulses to inquire deeply into practice and to satisfy public interests in accountability. A central aim of this chapter has been to stimulate reform advocates, professional developers and researchers to make headway towards such a convergence.

Notes

1 For example, Allen (1998), McDonald (2001), Seidel *et al.* (2001); see also www.lasw.org; www.essentialschools.org; www.annenberginstitute.org; http://www.pz.harvard.edu/Research/Evidence.htm; http://www.edtrust.org.

2 A comprehensive inventory of such programmes is beyond the scope of this chapter, but I draw on studies of five related programmes in characterizing this set of activities and in a review of the available research: cognitively guided instruction (Franke *et al.* 1998, 2001); Mathematics Case Methods project (Barnett and Friedman 1997; Barnett 1998); Integrating Mathematics Assessment project (Saxe *et al.* 2001); Science Education for Public Understanding

Program (Roberts and Wilson 1998); and Writing What You Read (Gearhart and Wolf 1994; Wolf and Gearhart 1997).

3 For example, Nelson (1997), introducing *Mathematics Teachers in Transition*, describes the chapters as representing four different (though related) positions on the process of changing teacher practice. (See also Kennedy 1998.)

4 In addition to these well-known examples, Japanese Lesson Study has attracted growing interest in the USA. However, it remains in its fledgling stages both with regard to established practice and to a corresponding body of research and thus is not treated in depth in this chapter. See Stigler and Hiebert (1999); Yoshida (1999); Lewis (2000); Lewis *et al.* (2001); Fernandez (2002).

5 McDonald (2001) differentiates approaches to looking at student work on the basis of their orientation towards judgement. The 'wondering' stance embraced by Seidel (1998) requires teachers to suspend judgement and thereby presumably affords them the opportunity to generate unexpected insights. Subject-oriented programmes emphasize investigation of student work as a means for exploring student thinking (Kazemi and Franke 2003). Judgement is most centrally at issue in projects focused on collaborative assessment (making informed and defendable judgements), and those organized to chart students' progress towards defined academic standards (as in the Education Trust model).

6 Excluded from consideration here are those activities in which teachers are convened for the sole purpose of scoring student work to determine the students' performance level on a local or state assessment. Teachers may derive some professional development benefit from the scoring activity, but professional development is not the espoused purpose.

7 Some programmes, such as cognitively guided instruction, have been the object of a sizeable research programme and numerous papers. Rather than supply a count of discrete publications, I have attempted to characterize both the range of research that is available and the substantive findings.

8 For summaries of research findings, see: Fennema *et al.* (1996); Franke *et al.* (1998); and Franke *et al.* (2001).

9 Practice-grounded interviews are conducted at the beginning and end of the school year. Teachers bring a sample of a text that they will use or have used in the classroom, together with any related materials or lesson plans and samples of student work if available. The interview begins with a detailed 'walk-through' of how the teacher employs the text and other materials in the classroom, and what thinking informs the teacher's choices. It also encompasses the teacher's approach to assessment and observations about students' responses. In the end-of-year interview, teachers are also asked about their perception of any changes in their own thinking or practice during the year. Researchers view these interviews as an advance over conventional self-report accounts: 'Rather than providing merely teachers' self reports, these interviews, anchored in classroom teaching through the lesson materials and student work samples, provided us with a type of performance assessment of

the range of reading activities, learning activities, and roles individual teachers afforded the students in their classrooms' (Greenleaf and Schoenbach 2001: 5).

10 To pursue this kind of analysis introduces new conceptual and methodological challenges that we have explored more fully elsewhere (Gearhart *et al.* 2002; Little 2002). Conceptual challenges centre on definitions of learning and opportunity to learn within an ongoing stream of discourse and interaction; methodological challenges range from problems in the sampling of practice to problems of inference in discourse analysis.

11 We found only one study – a programme evaluation – focused on the role of looking at student work for purposes of standards implementation and accountability (Laguarda 1998). The study relies on teacher interviews and surveys to summarize teachers' responses to the SIP process, but does not meet the standard of the triangle studies for evidence of a relationship between participation and outcomes, nor does it examine teachers' actual participation in professional development practices.

References

Allen, D. (ed.) (1998) *Assessing Student Learning: From Grading to Understanding*. New York: Teachers College Press.

Bacon, W., Groundwater-Smith, S., Nash, C. and Sachs, J. (2000) *Legitimating profes-sionalism?* Paper presented to the British Educational Research Association Annual Conference, Cardiff.

Ball, D.L. and Cohen, D.K. (1999) Developing practice, developing practitioners: toward a practice-based theory of professional education, in L. Darling-Hammond and G. Sykes (eds) *Teaching as the Learning Profession: Handbook of Policy and Practice*. San Francisco: Jossey-Bass.

Ball, D.L. and Mosenthal, J.H. (1991) *The construction of new forms of teaching: subject matter knowledge in inservice teacher education*. Paper presented at the annual meeting of the American Educational Research Association, Chicago.

Barnett, C. (1998) Mathematics teaching cases as a catalyst for informed strategic inquiry, *Teaching and Teacher Education*, 14(1): 81–93.

Barnett, C. and Friedman, S. (1997) Mathematics case discussions: nothing is sacred, in E. Fennema and B.S. Nelson (eds) *Mathematics Teachers in Transition*. Mahwah, NJ: Lawrence Erlbaum Associates.

Buchanan, J. (1993) Listening to the voices, in M. Cochran-Smith and S.L. Lytle (eds) *Inside/outside: Teacher Research and Knowledge*, pp. 212–20. New York: Teachers College Press.

Cohen, D.K. and Hill, H.C. (2000) Instructional policy and classroom performance: the mathematics reform in California, *Teachers College Record*, 102(2): 294–343.

Conant, J.B. (1963) *The Education of American Teachers*. New York: McGraw-Hill.

Darling-Hammond, L., Ancess, J. and Falk, B. (1995) *Authentic Assessment in Action: Studies of Schools and Students at Work*. New York: Teachers College Press.

DeMonner, S. (1998) *SLATE: Space for Learning and Teaching Exploration*. http://soe.umich.edu/resources/techserv/slate/slat.htm.

Education Trust (2002) *Looking at Teacher Work: Standards in Practice* (videotape). Washington, DC: Collaborative Communications Group.

Ershler, A.R. (2001) The narrative as an experience text: writing themselves back in, in A. Lieberman and L. Miller (eds) *Teachers Caught in the Action: Professional Development that Matters*. New York: Teachers College Press.

Falk, B. and Ort, S. (1998) Sitting down to score: teacher learning through assessment, *Phi Delta Kappan*, 80(1): 59–64.

Fennema, E., Carpenter, T.P., Franke, M.L., Levi, L., Jacobs, V.R. and Empson, S.B. (1996) A longitudinal study of learning to use children's thinking in mathematics instruction, *Journal for Research in Mathematics Education*, 27: 403–34.

Fernandez, C. (2002) Learning from Japanese approaches to professional development: the case of lesson study, *Journal of Teacher Education*, 53(5): 393–405.

Franke, M.L., Carpenter, T., Fennema, E., Ansell, E. and Behrend, J. (1998) Understanding teachers' self-sustaining, generative change in the context of professional development, *Teaching and Teacher Education*, 14(1): 67–80.

Franke, M.L., Carpenter, T., Levi, L. and Fennema, E. (2001) Capturing teachers' generative change: a follow-up study of professional development in mathematics, *American Educational Research Journal*, 38: 653–90.

Frederiksen, J.R., Sipusic, M., Sherin, M. and Wolfe, E.W. (1998) Video portfolio assessment: creating a framework for viewing the functions of teaching, *Educational Assessment*, 5(4): 225–97.

Gearhart, M., Saxe, G.B., Fall, R., Schlackman, J., Nasir, N., Ching, C.C., Bennett, T.R., Rhine, S. and Sloan, T. (1999) Opportunities to learn fractions in elementary mathematics classrooms, *Journal for Research in Mathematics Education*, 30: 286–315.

Gearhart, M., Little, J.W., Curry, M. and Kafka, J. (2002) *'Looking at student work': locating opportunities for teacher learning in the context of practice*. Paper presented at the annual meeting of the American Educational Research Association, New Orleans.

Greenleaf, C.L. and Katz, M. (in press) Ever newer ways to mean: authoring pedagogical change in secondary subject-area classrooms, in S.W. Freedman and A.F. Ball (eds) *New Literacies for New Times: Bakhtinian Perspectives on Language, Literacy, and Learning for the 21st Century*. Cambridge: Cambridge University Press.

Greenleaf, C.L. and Schoenbach, R. (2001) *Close Readings: A Study of Key Issues in the Use of Literacy Learning Cases for the Professional Development of Secondary Teachers*. San Francisco: Strategic Literacy Initiative, WestEd.

Greenleaf, C.L., Schoenbach, R., Cziko, C. and Mueller, F.L. (2001) Apprenticing adolescent readers to academic literacy, *Harvard Educational Review*, Spring: 79–129.

Grossman, P., Wineburg, S. and Woolworth, S. (2001) Toward a theory of teacher community, *Teachers College Record*, 103(6): 942–1012.

Groundwater-Smith, S. and Sachs, J. (2002) The activist professional and the reinstatement of trust, *Cambridge Journal of Education*, 32(3): 341–58.

Henke, R., Choy, S., Chen, X., Geis, S. and Alt, M.N. (1997) *America's Teachers: Profile of a Profession: 1993–94*. Berkeley, CA: MPR Associates.

Kazemi, E. and Franke, M.L. (2003) *Using Student Work to Support Professional Development in Elementary Mathematics*. Seattle, WA: Center for the Study of Teaching and Policy, University of Washington.

Kennedy, M.M. (1998) *Form and Substance in Inservice Teacher Education*. East Lansing, MI: College of Education, Michigan State University.

Kerr, S.T. (2000) *Technology and the quality of teachers' professional work: redefining what it means to be an effective educator*. Paper prepared for the CCSSO Educational Technology Conference, January 2000.

Laguarda, K.G. (1998) *Partnerships for Standards-based Professional Development*. Washington, DC: Policy Studies Associates.

Lampert, M. (2000) *Issues in the representation of teaching practice: difficulties and opportunities in multimedia archives*. Paper presented at the annual meeting of the American Educational Research Association, New Orleans, for the Symposium on Issues in the Representation of Teaching Practice.

Lampert, M. and Ball, D.L. (1998) *Teaching, Multimedia, and Mathematics: Investigations of Real Practice*. New York: Teachers College Press.

Lewis, C. (2000) *Lesson study: the core of Japanese professional development*. Invited address, Special Interest Group in Mathematics Education, American Educational Research Association annual meeting, New Orleans.

Lewis, C., Fernandez, C. and Stigler, J. (2001) *Three Perspectives on Lesson Study* (videotape). Oakland, CA: Regents of the University of California.

Lieberman, A. and Wood, D. (2001) When teachers write: of networks and learning, in A. Lieberman and L. Miller (eds) *Teachers Caught in the Action: Professional Development that Matters*. New York: Teachers College Press.

Little, J.W. (1989) District policy choices and teachers' professional development opportunities, *Educational Evaluation and Policy Analysis*, 11(2): 165–79.

Little, J.W. (1993) Professional development in a climate of educational reform, *Educational Evaluation and Policy Analysis*, 15(2): 129–51.

Little, J.W. (2002) Locating learning in teachers' communities of practice: opening up problems of analysis in records of everyday work, *Teaching and Teacher Education*, 18(2): 917–46.

Little, J.W., Gerritz, W.H., Stern, D.S., Guthrie, J.W., Kirst, M.W. and Marsh, D.D. (1987) *Staff Development in California: Public and Personal Investment, Program Patterns, and Policy Choices*. San Francisco: Far West Laboratory for Educational Research and Development.

Little, J.W., Gearhart, M., Curry, M. and Kafka, J. (in press) 'Looking at student work' for teacher learning, teacher community, and school reform, *Phi Delta Kappan*.

Matsumura, L.C. and Steinberg, J.R. (2001) *Collaborative, School-based Professional Development Settings for Teachers: Implementation and Links to Improving the Quality of Classroom Practice and Student Learning.* Los Angeles: National Center for Research on Evaluation, Standards, and Student Testing (CRESST), University of California at Los Angeles.

McDonald, J.P. (2001) Students' work and teachers' learning, in A. Lieberman and L. Miller (eds) *Teachers Caught in the Action: Professional Development that Matters.* New York: Teachers College Press.

Nave, B. (2000) *Critical Friends Groups: Their Impact on Students, Teachers, and Schools: Results of a Two Year Qualitative Study of the National School Reform Faculty Program.* Providence, RI: Annenberg Institute for School Reform.

Nelson, B.S. (1997) Learning about teacher change in the context of mathematics reform: where have we come from?, in E. Fennema and B.S. Nelson (eds) *Mathematics Teachers in Transition*: Mahwah, NJ: Lawrence Erlbaum Associates.

Pfeiffer, L.C. and Featherstone, H.J. (1996) *'Toto, I don't think we're in Kansas Anymore': Entering the Land of Public Disagreement in Learning to Teach.* East Lansing, MI: National Center for Research on Teacher Learning, Michigan State University.

Porter, A.C. (1989). External standards and good teaching: the pros and cons of telling teachers what to do, *Educational Evaluation and Policy Analysis*, 11(4): 343–56.

Roberts, L. and Wilson, M. (1998) *Evaluating the Effects of an Integrated Assessment System: Changing Teachers' Practices and Improving Student Achievement in Science.* San Diego, CA: AERA.

Saxe, G.B., Gearhart, M. and Nasir, N. (2001) Enhancing students' understanding of mathematics: a study of three contrasting approaches to professional support, *Journal of Mathematics Teacher Education*, 4: 55–79.

Seidel, S. (1998) Wondering to be done: the Collaborative Assessment Conference, in D. Allen (ed.) *Assessing Student Learning: From Grading to Understanding.* New York: Teachers College Press.

Seidel, S., Blythe, T., Allen, D., Simon, D.D., Veenema, S., Turner, T. and Clark, C. (2001) *The Evidence Process: A Collaborative Approach to Understanding and Improving Teaching and Learning.* Cambridge, MA: Project Zero, Harvard University Graduate School of Education.

Shulman, L. (1986) Paradigms and research programs in the study of teaching: a contemporary perspective, in M.C. Wittrock (ed.) *Handbook of Research on Teaching.* New York: Macmillan.

Shulman, L.S. (1987) Knowledge and teaching: foundations of the new reform, *Harvard Education Review*, 57(1): 1–22.

Stigler, J.W. and Hiebert, J. (1999) *The teaching gap: Best Ideas from the World's Teachers for Improving Education in the Classroom.* New York: Summit Books.

Wilson, M. (1994) Community of judgment: a teacher-centered approach to educational accountability, in Office of Technology Assessment (ed.) *Issues in*

Educational Accountability. Washington, DC: Office of Technology Assessment, United States Congress.

Wilson, M. and Sloane, K. (2000) From principles to practice: an embedded assessment system, *Applied Measurement in Education*, 13(2): 181–208.

Wilson, S.M. and Berne, J. (1999) Teacher learning and the acquisition of professional knowledge: an examination of research on contemporary professional development, *Review of Research in Education*, 24.

Yoshida, M. (1999) *'Lesson Study'* (*Jugyokenkyu*) *in elementary school mathematics in Japan: a case study*. Paper presented at the annual meeting of the American Educational Research Association.

5 CPD policies and practices in the Latin American region

Beatrice Avalos

As the train takes us from the historical city of Cuzco through the squalor of its surrounding dwellings, into the magnificent scenery leading down to the 'heights of Machu Picchu', the image of Latin America's contradictions hits us powerfully. The inheritors of the great civilizations of the Incas and the Mayas today are the poor, while the inheritors of the invaders still hold power and riches despite well-known exceptions. These contradictions form the context in which assessments about education and teaching need to be located.

Introduction

The 20 nations of Latin America (excluding the anglophone Caribbean) differ in size, climate, languages and cultures, income, natural resources and political systems. The fact that Spanish is usually understood to be the unifying factor is of course not true of the over 160 million inhabitants of Brazil, nor of Haiti, though it clearly is the dominant language that makes regional communications and economic alliances possible.

All Latin American nations are considered to be 'developing' countries, though some are richer than others. The greatest contrast is between Haiti's $US490 gross national product (GNP) per capita, Chile's $US4600 or Argentina's $US7550 (United Nations Population Division Statistics 1999). Many people in Latin America do not speak Spanish as their first language. Aymara is spoken by around 2 million people in the Bolivian, Peruvian and Chilean *Altiplano* and these people have more to share among themselves than with the country to which they belong. The eight dialects of Quechua are spoken by more than 8 million people in the Andean highlands of six countries. Mexico has 6.5 million people from many ethnic groups speaking different languages and sharing different cultures. Paraguay is practically a bilingual country (Spanish and Guarani). There are 21 Maya languages spoken in Guatemala and more than a hundred dialects, besides Spanish.

Education opportunities and educational achievement are not the same for all Latin Americans.[1] Around 39 million people (15 per cent) of the population are totally illiterate. They are found among the poor, the indigenous populations, women and rural people. But there are differences between countries. The highest literacy rates (more than 90 per cent) are found in Cuba, Uruguay, Chile, Argentina and Costa Rica, and the lowest (68.1 per cent) in Haiti, Nicaragua and Guatemala. Functional illiteracy is also high, with 50 per cent of the adult population performing very low in the main skills of prose, reading of documents and maths (UNESCO 2001). In Latin America 110 million people have not gone beyond an education of five years, and even in countries with good opportunities 40 per cent of the population over 25 years old are in this situation (Chile, Argentina and Costa Rica). Children in many countries repeat the school year more than once, taking between 8 and 50 per cent additional time to complete their basic school education.

Countries do not spend similar amounts on education at the primary level. Higher spending is found in Chile, Argentina, Uruguay, Brazil, Cuba and Peru. But Peru's $US480 per pupil is far removed from the $US6,043 that the USA spends on its children.

Teachers in Latin America also have unequal opportunities of being prepared for their task and in general are rewarded inadequately in terms of salaries and working conditions. While primary and secondary teachers in Chile are prepared in four- to five-year higher education programmes (also in Peru), primary teachers in Argentina for the most part are trained in three-year programmes at teachers' colleges (non-university) and in Guatemala primary teacher education is of secondary level. Untrained teachers are found in many countries (in Haiti over 70 per cent). In the poor rural northeast of Brazil 57.1 per cent of teachers have less that eight years of schooling (Delannoy 2000). However, on the whole, teachers' education programmes have over the last 20 years raised their requirements and level from secondary to tertiary status (UNESCO 2001).

The stronger awareness achieved in the early 1990s that economic, social and cultural development in the Latin American region would require a very strong push in the direction of improving education (ECLAC 1992) coloured the educational policies of that decade, centred on equity and quality – in tune with 'Education for All' policies (UNICEF 1990).

It is in this context then that policies concerning teachers and teachers' development need to be examined.

Continuing teacher professional development in Latin America: an eclectic concept and fragmented practices

At national or regional education policy meetings, it is common to hear actions regarding teacher development variously referred to as *capacitaciõ* (skill training), *perfeccionamiento* (improvement), *actualizaciõ* (upgrading or refreshing) or as in-service preparation. Less referred to but also used is the concept of 'permanent' or 'continuing' teacher education. To a certain extent the use of these concepts reflects the underlying assumptions that have marked teacher education over the past 20 or so years. Initial teacher education has a long history of development in Latin America starting with the first 'Normal School' for primary teachers founded by the Argentinean educator Domingo Faustino Sarmiento in Chile in 1842, and the Instituto Pedagógico to prepare secondary teachers at the University of Chile in 1889. These institutions, especially the Normal School, served as models for teacher education throughout the region and were established on the assumption that they would provide teachers with all they would need throughout a lifetime of teaching. Other actions related to teacher education were not considered important except in relation to specific needs as they arose in the course of educational changes.

A major shift in this concept of haphazard teacher in-service education was the establishment in 1965 of the National In-Service, Research and Educational Experimentation Centre (Centro de Perfeccionamiento, Experimentación e Investigaciones Pedagógicas) at the Chilean Ministry of Education, with the purpose of delivering a major education reform. The Centre contracted a first-class staff in the all the main curriculum areas and with the universities organized courses to inform and prepare teachers to teach the new curriculum. With international assistance, especially from the United Nations Educational, Scientific and Cultural Organization (UNESCO), the Centre also organized courses for different educational specialities such as educational technology or educational management and planning, attended by educators from throughout the Latin American region.

Though initially the main rationale of the Centre, as far as practising teachers were concerned, was to 'teach the reform', over time it developed other courses oriented to more general teacher 'improvement' in content and pedagogic matters. Both these concepts to a large extent have stood behind most of teacher education initiatives in other Latin American countries.[2] And in a way they reflect what is known as 'deficit theory' (see Huberman and Guskey 1995): teacher education activities for in-service teachers are organized on the basis of providing something teachers are considered not to have, be this knowledge or skills.

Outside of the governmental sphere, there were always teacher educational experiences that different groups or institutions organized – for example, for indigenous or rural teachers. However, in the 1980s the effect of dictatorships in countries such as Chile, Argentina and Uruguay on teacher morale and professionalism brought about a new concept and new developments in the form of teacher workshops. Associated to non-governmental research institutions in these countries and led by committed and imaginative educators, teachers gathered in workshops to review their practice and carry out small action research projects on the effect of the innovations or changes they introduced. Funding for some of these experiences was provided by the Canadian International Development and Research Centre (IDRC), which also supported regional meetings of those involved in these experiences. The following description by Vera (1990: 116) shows how much these experiences were approximating what we now conceptualize as school-based professional development based on action research:

> Educators' workshops are based on a number of guiding ideas of professionalisation, group formation, and autonomous learning. First, they attempt to provide an opportunity for research by participants themselves, leading to critical reflection on their own teaching practice and the real situation in their schools. Second, they attempt to serve as an opportunity for research and learning about how to learn in small groups, which differs from the methods which predominate in the school system. Third, they attempt to provide an opportunity for professional development, for teachers to learn how to learn spontaneously, analysing problems in the teaching practice of participants and connected with the group experience they are undergoing.

The experience of the teacher workshops helped to produce a revision among educators of the concept of in-service education as overcoming 'lacks' and promote a move towards the concept of teacher professionalism and professional development. Research in Mexico at the education research centre of the Instituto Politécnico Nacional (IPN) in the 1980s also assisted this new understanding. Researchers carried out the first classroom research studies with an ethnographic approach focusing on teachers' pedagogical knowledge (see Ducoing and Landesmann's 1996 review of educational research in the 1980s in Mexico). Through the master's programme conducted at the IPN other Latin American researchers were introduced to these concepts of teacher professionalism and teacher pedagogical knowledge, taking them in turn to their own countries. The programme also helped to prepare the researchers who did one of the first ethnographic studies of classrooms and teachers in four Latin American countries (Avalos 1986).

In their review of the 20 years of the Major Project of Education, UNESCO considered that most teacher education activities in the period were geared to the implementation of reform initiatives (UNESCO 2001). These were generally short courses that did not consider what teachers knew about their practice nor their needs. Looking more specifically at continuing education for science and mathematics teachers, a study by the Organization of Iberoamerican States (OEI 1994) concluded also that activities were not embedded in national policies and were fragmented and often out of touch with teachers' real needs.

Despite this assessment, in the 1990s and into the new century there are initiatives that merit attention, including some efforts to produce comprehensive policy frameworks for continuing teacher education. To a certain extent, these initiatives mix conceptualizations derived from deficit theory with concepts that are closer to professional development and teacher empowerment.

CPD in the decade of national reforms

In the 1990s, practically no Latin American country failed to engage in changes of some scale in their educational system. These reforms shared common elements influenced by national concerns to provide effective and efficient education to all citizens and by the policies of lending agencies such as the World Bank and the Interamerican Development Bank (Coraggio and Torres 1997). Reforms in the 1990s wanted primarily to improve and distribute education equitably to all beneficiaries of public school systems. The rationale behind this purpose was a newer version of human capital theory and of modernity theory. An important joint document by the Latin American Economic Commission and UNESCO pointed to the need for deep-rooted reforms in education to provide the kind of learning opportunities needed for productive involvement in modern society. All children and young people should at least acquire what were termed the 'cultural codes of modernity' (ECLAC 1992).

In the search for efficiency the common features of educational reforms targeted changes in the management and funding of the education system (decentralization and privatization), and improvement of the quality of teaching and learning through textbooks, curriculum materials, computers and lengthening of the school day and year. To stimulate teachers' and school principals' willingness to change, various incentive policies were put in place such as monetary rewards for the best improvement projects developed by school communities (Chile and Colombia) and systems of national assessments (of language and mathematics attainment at least) in almost all countries of the region, aimed at comparing effectiveness among schools and even countries (PREAL 2001a).[3] These common reform features are reflected in the titles given to several of the reforms funded by the World Bank, expressed as variations of the concept of improvement of the quality and equity of education.

Despite the commonality of these features, a number of the Latin American countries developed national responses to their particular needs. Thus Bolivian educational reform is focusing on intercultural-bilingual education and has developed curriculum and teaching materials in the four main languages of the country. Chile, on the basis of non-government institution involvement with poor children during the military dictatorship, maintains a programme aimed at the poorest schools and children, known as the 900-Schools' Programme (see Filp 1993; Carlson 2000). Some countries, such as Argentina, carried out deep-seated structural and curricular reforms.

What is the situation of in-service teacher education in the context of these reforms?

While the traditional forms of in-service education such as centralized or decentralized courses continue to be offered in all countries in distance or face-to-face modes (by government and university institutions), other forms have emerged as a result of reform needs or in the context of ongoing reform programmes. These are described in the following sections in terms of their purposes, forms of delivery, management and organization, funding and evidence of their results.

Purposes

Although the teacher programmes referred to below all share purposes related to reform targets in their countries, they can be organized into three groups according to their emphases. In the first group we find those actions directed towards learning and putting into operation major reform changes such as a new curriculum. The second group includes teacher development activities that focus on equity and quality, or that respond to what is known internationally as Education for All (UNICEF 1990). The third group comprises actions specifically geared to teacher personal, social and professional development. Table 5.1 lists these programmes, of which some will be described later.

Responding to reform needs

A most complex requirement of reforms is to assist teachers in taking on a new curriculum, using its materials and working with suggested methodologies. The challenge is all the more serious when teachers have not participated in the framing of the curriculum. Most countries undertaking curriculum change usually allow little time to prepare teachers before the new curriculum is actually implemented. So the easiest form of dealing with the issue is to organize massive courses aimed at 'informing' teachers about what is new and what

Table 5.1 Types of teacher development programmes in teacher in-service activities

Implementation of reforms	Education for All concerns	Teacher development (personal, social, professional)
Being informed about a new curriculum (PPF, Chile; subject courses in Argentina). Understanding the contents of a new curriculum (PRONAP, Mexico; PLANCAD, Peru). Learning, understanding, trying out reform materials and curriculum (*Asesoría Pedagógica*, Bolivia).	Learning and implementing bilingua/intercultural curriculum (*Asesores Pedagógicos*, Bolivia). *Escuela Bilingüe Activa* with a focus on rural bilingual areas and the preparation of teachers working in Teacher Circles (Guatemala).	Updating knowledge and professional skills, innovating and doing classroom research (PFPD, Colombia; Centre for In-Service Education and the CERPs, Uruguay). Empowering teachers in isolated rural one- or two-room schools (*Microcentro Rurales*, Chile and Colombia).
Using ICT in schools (ENLACES, Chile) and the Educational Technology Programme in Costa Rica.	Understanding and developing materials and strategies for work with poor populations (P900 School Teacher Workshops, Chile; PAREB, Mexico). *Programa de Educaçao Continuada* for work with 'accelerated classes programme' (Brazil).	Empowering secondary public school teachers (Teacher Professional Groups, Chile). School-based study circles (Ecuador and Guatemala). *Colectivo Pedagógico* (Cuba), *Círculos de Aprendizaje* (Paraguay).
Response to urgencies (changes that are not working); modelling through visits to good classrooms, Chile).		Widening teacher understanding and perspectives about education issues and practices: country expeditions (Colombia); visits abroad (Chile); *Centros de Maestros* (Mexico). Support networks for teacher development (Colombia, Latin America).

they must do. The Perfeccionamiento Fundamental Programme (PPF) in Chile is a good example of this. The original purpose of this programme was to offer courses led by university professors dealing with key and complex topics in the various subject areas. However, before this approach had a chance to be tried out, the PPF had to change focus in order to prepare teachers to apply the new primary and secondary curriculum. Following the pace with which the syllabuses for each year were written, courses were organized and delivered just before the beginning of the corresponding school year. Every summer, from 1999, about 40,000 teachers have attended 60-hour courses, on a voluntary basis. These courses are conducted by university teams contracted by the Ministry of Education and include two short follow-up meetings during the year.[4]

Mexico used a more comprehensive system to deal with the same need. In the early 1990s the government established the Programme for Teacher Upgrading (PEAM), with the purpose of strengthening in the short-term teachers' knowledge level and of enabling them to participate in reform initiatives (Tatto and Vélez 1997). In time, and with the experience gained, the government widened the scope of its activities and established in 1995 the Programa Nacional para la Actualización Permanente de los Maestros de Educación Básica en Servicio (PRONAP) to support the new curriculum. Addressed to primary or basic education teachers PRONAP uses different forms of delivery (courses, workshops, classroom support) as well as teacher resource centres.

In Peru, PLANCAD (Teacher Up-grading Programme) is similar in its purpose and approach to the Mexican programme. It is aimed at preparing teachers, principals and administrators of the educational system in a nine-month programme of workshops (centralized and at school level) to understand and apply changes established by the Ministry of Education, including the new curriculum.

The Asesores Pedagógicos (Pedagogic Assistants) is the main system used by the Bolivian educational establishment to communicate reform. With a special focus on the needs of the intercultural-bilingual curriculum and therefore on the large rural and poor population, the programme covers both the purposes of reform communication and Education for All concerns. The *Asesores Pedagógicos* are teachers selected on the basis of their training, skills and linguistic background, who are prepared in a six-month course to work with teachers at classroom level in the implementation of reform. The concept is new in Bolivia, even though it might be likened to the pedagogical role of supervisors in other countries.

The introduction of an information and communication technology (ICT) network in schools in Chile was a novelty throughout the region. In the early part of the 1990s, and with support of a World Bank loan, Chile began gradually to provide primary schools (and later, secondary schools) with computers. Today only those primary schools in remote areas without telephone connections are not part of the programme known as ENLACES. To provide technical assistance for the operation of ENLACES and to prepare teachers, the Ministry of Education entered into agreements with universities throughout the country. For two years, the university specialists prepared teachers in each of the schools to work with the computers and to assist their colleagues. The

Educational Technology Programme in Costa Rica, which predates ENLACES, used a different method to prepare teachers for computer usage. There was no face-to-face contact, only facilitation and monitoring in the use of modular materials delivered to teachers electronically (Navarro and Verdisco 1999).

Reform implementation is always fraught with problems. Often these are not necessarily the result of the reform but the effect of contextual factors that were not adequately accounted for. However, they are food for attacks by political opponents and, in the logic of governments, they require prompt responses. In Chile, where results in assessment tests did not live up to expectations after ten years of reform, rapid decisions have been taken to provide correction. On the assumption that the problem lies with the teachers, a recent initiative based on the concept of learning by models will involve teachers' visits to 'exemplary classrooms' in the country. Another programme due to start shortly adapts the literacy and numeracy campaign in Great Britain for use in schools that fail to improve despite all reform efforts.

Not only are teacher education programmes and policies developed to support reforms, but also to support entirely new institutions. Such is the case of Uruguay, where there was only one secondary teacher training institution in Montevideo that also provided in-service training. To widen the offer throughout the country, the government established an innovative Centre of Education for Teachers and Teacher Training (Centro de Capacitación y Perfeccionamiento Docente) in Montevideo and four regional teacher education centres (CERPs) throughout the country, for the initial and in-service preparation of secondary teachers (Vaillant and Wettstein 1999).

Education for All concerns

The assertion that by focusing on general education needs everyone will be served equally is clearly not true, as school retention indicators or assessment of school results among poor populations show. Thus, a number of Latin American governments have over time developed special education programmes for poor populations. However, only in the educational reforms of the 1990s do we find what we might call overt 'affirmative action' or compensatory programmes directed to such groups of children and young people. The Bolivian Asesores Pedagógicos programme referred to above has as one of its purposes the assistance of teachers in bilingual regions to teach in the languages of their students: Aymara, Quechua, Guarani or Spanish. Teachers will not only have to know the language but must develop cultural understanding and sensitivity as well as skills to facilitate the transition into Spanish.

Chile's 900 Schools Project was one of the first reform initiatives undertaken when the country returned to democracy in 1990. The poorest and most vulnerable schools (900 initially) were selected for targeted action to support success rather than criticize failure. Besides investment in classrooms, books and materials, time was allocated for teachers to meet on a weekly basis in order to familiarize themselves the curricular emphasis and teaching materials developed for these schools and to improve their teaching practices.

Accelerated classes were originally introduced in the State of Maranhão, Brazil in 1994 with the purpose of stopping over-age students (Grades 1 to 3) from dropping out of school (Oliveira 1999). Teachers were assigned to work with these students in classrooms of 20 to 25 pupils for the same four hours a day as ordinary classes. But they were provided with special materials and given a 40-hour specific training for their use. They got on-site support from the school principal and supervisors in carrying out their tasks. The success of the programme has caused it to be extended to many other states of the country and to receive the UNESCO prize for Child and Peace (Garrido 2001).

The Mexican PAREB (Programme to Redress School Repetition or Delay) is implemented by the State Co-ordination Group of the National Council for Education Development (CONAFE). It serves primary school populations that traditionally have been difficult to reach through the educational services. The programme improves infrastructure (builds classrooms) and provides educational materials and teacher preparation. Teachers learn within the framework of a constructivist pedagogy to work with children in both their own and the Spanish languages (Tatto and Vélez 1997).

Teacher personal, social and professional development

These programmes are also oriented towards implementing reforms or changes brought about by the educational system. However, they focus primarily on the teachers as people who often work in isolation and stand in need of interaction with colleagues, or who feel diminished as professionals, justifiably or not, because of public perceptions and difficult working conditions. They also consider that teachers develop better as professionals in situations where their experience and prior knowledge counts, something that does not always happen in the traditional format of in-service courses. There are a good number of such programmes in Latin America, either in the context of government or non-government action.

Borrowing on the experience of Colombia's one-classroom rural schools and the concept of school cluster teacher meetings, the Rural Microcentres developed in the isolated rural areas of Chile as a way of bringing teachers together from neighbouring multi-grade schools for monthly professional development meetings.

The Teacher Professional Groups in Chile were gradually established as meeting and learning contexts for teachers in the secondary public schools involved in the Secondary Improvement Project of the Ministry of Education (Avalos 1999). School-based study circles for teachers are now an important feature in the reforms of Ecuador, Guatemala and Paraguay. Cuba puts strong emphasis on school-based teacher development. Every school has a *colectivo pedagógico* (group of teachers) that meets periodically to discuss teaching methods, produce learning materials, develop curriculum and exchange experiences (Gasperini 2000).

Most teachers have little opportunity to learn about what happens beyond their own schools or towns. A few programmes are in place that are geared to what we might call the 'opening of vistas' and learning about 'how others do it', both inside and outside teachers' own countries. In 2001 a group of over 440 Colombian teachers were involved in the *Expedición Pedagógica Nacional* (National Pedagogic Expedition). This involved trips throughout the country, visiting schools, talking to other teachers and asking themselves questions such as 'How do our schools fare? What sort of teachers are we? How are we being trained? Are we doing research?' (Unda *et al.* 2001).

In 1996 the Chilean president, Eduardo Frei, announced a major programme to strengthen the teaching profession. It included among other initiatives a fund to allow teachers on a competitive basis to visit school systems and classrooms abroad. The programme, which initially was criticized by the Teachers' Union as being elitist, has now reached more than 4000 teachers, offering them not only the two-month visits originally planned for, but longer study periods in their various specialization areas.

In Mexico the *Centros de Maestros* (close to 500) are resource centres for teachers with a library of 5000 volumes, tapes, computers, multimedia and internet connection. At the centres, teachers from the surrounding schools find trainers and facilitators who can deal with their questions and requests for assistance. A similar experience is starting in Bolivia.

Teacher networks are also growing in Latin America. They are stimulated by universities, as is the case with RED-CEE, supported by the National Pedagogic University in Colombia (Unda *et al.* 2001), or by regional organizations such as the Major Education Project of UNESCO,[5] or have developed from school-based teacher groups, as in Chile.

Forms of delivery, management and organization of CPD activities

There are three main levels of responsibility, organization and control over teacher professional development activities: the national state level (generally, departments within ministries of education), regional states or provinces in federal systems (this may include local government such as municipalities) and non-governmental activities conducted by universities, independent centres or other institutions such as teacher unions.

National and state or provincial government activities

Most of the programmes developed by governments in the 1990s (or continuing from earlier periods) serve to illustrate the following three types of organization and management:

1   Partnerships with institutions for direct delivery of the programmes to teachers. These institutions are accredited to do so (for example, the Argentine Federal Network, the Chilean formal in-service courses), are successful in bidding for the purpose (for example, the Chilean PPF courses and the Peruvian PLANCAD), or have worthwhile programmes to offer local government for funding.
2   Cascade procedures to prepare teacher trainers at different levels to reach teachers in their specific locations or schools. This form has been used in programmes in Paraguay, Guatemala, Mexico and to a certain extent in the *Asesores Pedagógicos* programme of Bolivia.
3   Centrally coordinated or decentralized actions for schools by means of the system of school supervisors. This form was mainly developed in the teacher development activities linked to reform programmes in Chile.

Partnerships

These activities generally involve courses dealing with subject matter knowledge and teaching methods, delivered by institutions with which the government enters into partnership. The Chilean PPF courses taught in the summer vacations for the purpose of learning the new curriculum are an example. These courses are delivered by university teams that bid for the task. The Ministry of Education sets the terms of reference and the institutions must organize the course in line with the new syllabuses. There has been no direct evaluation of this programme, which is scheduled to last until the last set of new syllabuses is published (2002). PLANCAD in Peru uses a host of institutional agents to execute the teacher continuing education programme (a nine-month strategy) which involves centrally organized workshops, school-based support and follow-up activities. There are also good examples of state-level initiatives, generally in partnership with universities or other non-government institutions. Cardoso and Scarpa (2001) report on Escola Que Vale (School that Counts), an ongoing programme since 1999 with six municipalities and collaboration of academics from CEDAC (an education centre at the University of Sao Paulo). The programme engages teachers in the development of classroom projects in reading and writing and monitors them using former schoolteachers, who are part of the university centre involved. To stimulate critical analysis of their teaching, participants use narrative accounts and videos to report on their classroom events. During the workshops, teachers get classroom examples similar to their own experience that also serve the purpose of analysis. There is a distance component consisting of electronic reviews by the regional coordinator of work done by the teachers (video clips, narratives and classroom observations). Teachers have access to these communications at a local 'teachers' house' installed by the municipality, which is also a meeting place and a resource centre.

Cascade programmes

The cascade system experiences are used in multi-layered training programmes that aim to reach teachers in schools. An experience extensively studied and evaluated (Tatto and Vélez 1997; Tatto 1999; PREAL 2001b) is PAREB in Mexico. It was conceived as a five-year action in four of the poorest states in Mexico (Chiapas, Guerrero, Hidalgo and Oaxaca). It has since been widened to cover preschool and basic education (primary level) in most of the other states, where poor or indigenous populations require extra educational support. Trainers are prepared nationally using a cascade system and they in turn prepare supervisors and school principals. On the basis of a constructivist approach to teaching and learning, PAREB uses a combination of face-to-face contact by means of intensive summer courses and semi-schooled courses throughout the year, and work at school level. Participants are encouraged also to meet twice a month in their schools. As described by Tatto (2000), 'the course is carried out through contact sessions, team and group work, and self-instructional time including readings and written exercises. The experience of the teacher is seen as the beginning point for instruction'.

The Círculos de Calidad Docente (Teaching Quality Circles) in Guatemala also use a cascade system to prepare trainers to reach teachers. The Círculos are voluntary meetings of teachers who work on adapting the curriculum to local needs. The groups work on the basis of a set of nine modules prepared nationally:

> In general, the modules are designed to enable teachers to offer solutions to daily problems encountered in the classroom and schools, stimulated by narratives or vignettes. They are asked to examine proposed methods for work with the children and encouraged to try them out. Towards the end of each module, teachers are asked to specify actions they are willing to try out the next day in their classroom.
>
> (Ortega 1998)

The training of trainers occurs at three levels. The first is directed to departmental heads (ministry authorities), in-service coordinators and other local authorities (to secure their understanding of the programme). Their task is to organize the process in their own locations. They meet once every three months to assess progress and correct problems. The second level is directed to school supervisors, in-service trainers as well-school counsellors and other specialists. Specialists from the national reform programme conduct this training. The third level takes place at the teachers' circle meetings facilitated by supervisors initially and then by school principals.

Supervisor-facilitated teacher workshops

These activities are in reality forms of the cascade system, but with fewer intermediary stages. In Chile, three of the reform programmes have established teacher groups or workshops at school level. The Rural Microcentres are monthly meetings of teachers for a whole day. As documented by supervisors, who facilitate the meetings, the participant teachers usually organize cultural and recreational activities for teachers and pupils, learn cooperatively through means of language and maths texts, and try out extracurricular activities with their children such as micro-journalism or local history gathering. A specific methodology has developed that includes committee work, collection of information and of materials to be used in their projects. The teacher workshops, part of the 900 Schools Project, are weekly meetings of teachers in each school, assisted by supervisors prepared by national staff from the Project. In the first years of operation only teachers in the first four grades were involved. They worked to improve their conceptual and practical knowledge of language and mathematics teaching, using sets of materials especially prepared for the purpose. Since 1997, however, all teachers in the school participate and the contents of the meetings have been widened accordingly. The teacher professional groups function in the secondary schools and initially were also facilitated by supervisors prepared nationally for the task. This programme will be described in more detail below.

Non-governmental activities

Non-government institutions have always organized teacher education activities in Latin America. Fe y Alegría is a well-known programme linked to a Catholic Church system of schools for the poor. This programme began in Venezuela but extended to other Latin American countries such as Bolivia. The philosophy of its teacher development activities rests on the assumption that real teacher growth occurs when teachers are able to improve *in situ* their practice. Fe y Alegría teachers work on the basis of a problem-solving and team-oriented approach, often in collaboration with school administrators and members of the community at large. They focus on the realities of classroom and community, inquiring into the causes of problems and proposing solutions (Navarro and Verdisco 1999). There is continuous monitoring by supervisors who are former teachers of the Fe y Alegría schools.

In Brazil there are many non-governmental initiatives. The Centre for Studies and Research into Education, Culture and Action (CENPEC), based in Sao Paulo, has over ten years of experience working with schools and teachers in the country. One of their documented activities was the Reading and Writing Project developed in five schools of the city of Sao Paulo (CENPEC 1998). The workshops involved an initial analysis of teachers' needs, and then a 16-hour face-to-face set of meetings. These were followed by monthly meetings of 4 hours throughout the school year. Teachers were stimulated to write and reflect by means of literature texts. The programme also involved the preparation of coordinators who visited teachers' classrooms and discussed with them their progress and problems. On request by the state of Sao Paulo, CENPEC has held in-service activities for school principals and subject teachers (language, maths, science, history and geography) (CENPEC 1998).

Also in Brazil initiatives are undertaken by academics in universities (Garrido 2001). Fiorentini and Miorim's work with teachers in Campinas (2001) is an interesting example. Their starting point was a one-year university-based course offered for in-service teachers in the arts, physics and maths, that involved reading and discussing written texts and curriculum innovation experiences. Teachers continued to work for another two years after the course was ended, undertaking classroom innovation projects and eventually producing a collaborative book: *Por Trás da Porta: Que Matemática Acontece? (Behind the Door: What Mathematics Takes Place?)*. In the second year they planned and developed their projects while keeping narrative accounts and journals of the process and meeting for report and discussion. In the third year, they put the book together, working through the information they had gathered and discussing critically the products as they developed.

Funding of CPD activities

A large part of the activities organized and delivered by national or state/local governments are funded from the national education budgets. However, many of the countries involved in major reforms have additional funds from bank loans (World Bank and International Development Bank) as well as from other bilateral donor agencies. During the 1990s around 18 countries entered into such loans (UNESCO 2001). Rivero (1999) states that between 1990 and 1994 the joint loans of both banks amounted to $US2000 million.

Specifically, the World Bank supported the early stages of the compensatory programmes in Mexico (including PAREB) and the ICT programmes in Costa Rica and Chile. Bilateral donor agencies from European countries (Sweden, Germany and Spain among others) contributed especially to teacher-related and other actions directed to the purpose of Education for All. Such was the case of the 900 School's Project in Chile in its first years (Cox and Avalos 1999) and is still the case for the projects that support decentralization in Bolivia and school-based teacher improvement. USAID assisted the pilot projects that led to the current teacher continuing education programme in Guatemala. Loans to countries like Chile and Argentina are granted at higher interest rates than those to poor countries such as Nicaragua and Bolivia. Once the loans run their course, the programmes need to be inserted in the recurrent budgets of the countries involved, which means a lowering of funding levels and some operational problems.

Brazil established in January 1998 a fund for basic education and teacher support known as FUNDEF (Fondo de Mantención y Desarrollo de la Educación Fundamental y Valorización del Magisterio). The system is aimed at redistributing national resources more equitably among states and municipalities. Among its requirements is that 60 per cent of the funds in each state and municipality go to teacher salaries (in many other countries this amounts to about 90 per cent) and the other 40 per cent to teacher in-service development and other expenditures related to schooling requirements such as materials for teaching, school infrastructure, scholarships and so on. The funds for teacher education are intended mainly to certify untrained teachers and upgrade those with less than eight years of education. The effects of FUNDEF on the situation of teachers in poor regions have been very important. Teacher salaries in the northeast, for example, have gone up almost 50 per cent (Delannoy 1999).

Private foundations also contribute generally to projects jointly carried out by non-governmental organizations or university centres and municipal or state governments.

Evaluations

Most of the national and state level continuing development programmes have not been evaluated in terms of their effects on teachers and students. The analysis of the 20 years of UNESCO's Major Education Project is rather grim in its assessment that there is little evidence of the effect of most traditional teacher in-service courses (UNESCO 2001).

However, some of the innovations in the 1990s have been evaluated, bearing in mind that most of them are still young. The impact of the Mexican PAREB on children's learning was evaluated in 1998 using performance tests designed by the Ministry of Education. It showed effects on learning indicators such as increased learning for average, rural and indigenous students as well as lowering of repetition and drop-out rates (Tatto 1999; PREAL 2001b). PAREB's teacher components were studied in its early phase by Tatto (1999), who used an ethnographic design for the purpose. Her findings show that the programme raised teachers' awareness about starting from pupils' existing knowledge in order to build meaningful and contextually relevant learning experiences and that it supported teachers working together with each other and with supervisors on their improvement. However, she noted the following shortfalls:

> The PARE fell short of its constructivist aims by failing to teach teachers in the manner they were expected to teach pupils, by allowing concerns with efficiency and accountability to stand in the way of implementing a more in depth training program for teachers and supervisors (e.g. short-term courses prevented more in depth understanding of subject matters; use of cascade technique diluted the PARE's constructivist message; lack of classroom follow-up resulted in reversion to traditional ways of teaching; constrained curriculum offerings prevented the development of other contextually relevant courses), and by reinforcing the top-down structure of authority in the Mexican educational system (e.g. using supervisors and principals as the main vehicles for teacher education) rather than enabling teachers – and indeed whole shools – to become vehicles of their own life-long transformation.
>
> (Tatto 1999)

Tatto's conclusions could easily be extrapolated to other similar programmes carried out in the region, but it is also true that the subjects of many of these programmes are teachers with a low cultural basis and inadequate initial training. It is also true that given the budgets and resources available to the governments concerned, resorting to supervisors as facilitators is the only means at hand.

The Chilean school-based programmes relying on supervisors for their implementation have all been externally evaluated. Particularly, the Rural Microcentres show important effects of teacher-related action on student results – for example, an improvement in performance of 12 per cent in reading, writing, maths, social and natural studies (Avalos 2001). Teacher development in the case of the secondary improvement project, according to external evaluation (reported in MINEDUC 2001), has produced important effects on teacher capacity to develop curricular materials. Student learning has also improved, as shown by their use of different sources of information available for their school work (library, internet), behaviours that show understanding, problem solving capacities and more peer collaboration. The teacher workshops of the 900 Schools' Project also show teacher learning, although problems such as those related by Tatto for the Mexican programme are also found here (Avalos 2001).

Internal reports on programmes such as the Teacher Circles in Guatemala lay emphasis on the importance of such activities actually taking place (given they are voluntary). This said, it appears that such programmes are changing teachers' work habits with children (using available materials, organizing classroom learning corners and so on), and that teachers now work better with members of the local community (Ortega 1998).

The Peruvian PLANCAD programme, though not officially evaluated, has shown improvements according to those responsible at the Ministry of Education (Escobar 1998; DINFOCAD 2001). Teachers want to be part of the programme, the teacher development strategy is a great improvement over former ones and teachers have been able to start adapting curricular materials to local needs.

A closer look at two experiences

The Federal Network for Continuing Teacher Education in Argentina (1994–99)[6]

Faced with the need to develop a massive system of continuing education in the context of a federal and decentralized system (as exists in Argentina) and to 'reconvert' teachers to the new education structure, the Ministry of Education established by law the Federal Network of accredited institutions. The unregulated and unequal status of the programmes at provincial and local level as well as the lack of articulation between initial and continuous teacher education were also reasons behind this initiative.

At the start of the 1990s most initial teacher education was delivered in over 1200 Institutos de Formación Docente (Teacher Education Institutions), while in-service teachers selected from a market of courses offered by a variety of institutions that might give them credit for promotion and salary raises. In-service education being a provincial responsibility, there was little guidance and monitoring of these courses at national level. The quality and provision of courses was also unequal as not all provinces undertook the task of seeing that there was sufficient provision for all teachers. Most courses also required teachers to pay for them.

The new federal law enacted in 1993 stated the need to establish a structure of continuing education for all teachers in the country (over 600,000 at the time). Besides declaring the right and obligation of teachers to continue their education, it affirmed the need for national involvement in the provision of teacher continuing education opportunities. In practice, this meant a national commitment of 80 per cent of total costs for such a scheme during a period of five years. The general purposes of the teacher education proposals emphasized the following:

> Teacher continuing education should lead to a critical review of practice, the strengthening of their work and renewed teacher motivation and professional attitudes.

It should provide teachers with an opportunity to learn about educational policy and its relation to social and institutional demands.

It should support innovation in policy, education, subject-matter areas. Opportunities for teacher development should be institutionalised and teachers should have professional recognition for their work. It should take place at the work place during school hours or out of school but paid. It should also cover all teachers without their having to pay for the courses.

(Serra 2001)

The Network was organized under a national headship and provincial headships. The national headship's task was to coordinate the implementation of the programme, evaluate its achievements and provide the funding. The provincial headships in turn had to formulate the criteria for in-service activities in the province, set priorities, accredit and register institutions in the province as deliverers, provide information on these institutions and evaluate them. The process was started in 1996 with public calls for institutional providers of in-service activities, evaluation and selection of those considered appropriate and the establishment of a Federal Register of Evaluation, Projects and Teacher Certification (REFEPEC).

Until 1999 the provinces organized and implemented the system. This was done by sending information each year to schools about the available offer, asking schools to prioritize their needs and select activities. Schools were required to ensure that at least 40 per cent of their teachers took the courses together with someone from the school administration.

The courses offered were organized in different groups depending on whom they were directed at: preschool level, general basic education (primary and lower secondary), the *'polimodal'* level (diversified upper secondary) or school administrators. Most courses in practice were offered for the initial and general basic education level. Ninety-four per cent of courses were face-to-face, with a duration of 45 hours delivered in a maximum of five weeks, divided into two periods. Only 2 per cent were entirely distance courses. Most of the institutions with approved courses to be put on offer were teacher training institutes (53 per cent), followed by non-government institutions (14 per cent), universities (7 per cent), teacher unions (4 per cent) and others. The courses were monitored by national staff and also by the provinces. This involved looking at management issues as well as delivery, by means of observation. However, between 1995 and 1999 only 2.5 per cent of courses were monitored.

The funding of the scheme was through transferral of national funds to the provinces and it amounted to 0.76 per cent of the total allocation for education in the period 1994–99. According to Serra (2001) it is difficult to judge exactly how many of the total number of teachers in the system were covered, because of problems of double counting. However, Serra estimates that around 100 per cent of preschool teachers and 89 per cent of basic education teachers were covered, while the other levels covered about 35 per cent.

In his assessment of the system as a whole, Serra (2001) considers that it was a good effort to provide national coverage of in-service opportunities to teachers and that the institutional networks established at provincial level were a real innovation. The experience also greatly stimulated the development of interesting offers of professional development opportunities on the part of the institutions. In particular, the work done by the teacher training institutes should remain and in time should produce the necessary links between initial and continuing teacher education.

It does seem, however, that the whole focus and structure of the scheme was geared to 'reconversion' – that is, based on a 'deficit' theory of teacher professional development. According to Serra there are 'strong indications' that the adopted strategies did not move in the direction of promoting teacher development, as they did not consider sufficiently in the framing of courses the views, needs and conditions of teachers.

The Secondary Level Teacher Professional Groups in Chile

In 1995, with the beginning of the secondary education improvement programme (MECE-Media), schools were encouraged to form teacher workshops. This meant setting aside time once a fortnight for teachers to meet for two hours approximately to engage with materials and activities suggested by the national coordinators of the improvement programme. To get this started, secondary school supervisors were prepared as facilitators. Their role was to assist the groups only for the time needed to get them off the ground (generally, the first year), after which the school pedagogic leader would take on this task. For the first year and a half, more or less, teachers in the group worked on the basis of a group handbook that included readings, activities and suggestions for reflection and experimentation that followed a similar project carried out in New Zealand (Bell and Gilbert 1994; Avalos 1998). This handbook was followed by a second one that focused more closely on curriculum development and assessment in the classroom. A third handbook was written by different specialists and required teachers to break up what originally was an interdisciplinary group into subject groups. These materials addressed key concepts and curriculum issues related to subject teaching (areas of science, history, literature, maths and so on), though they were not linked specifically to the school syllabuses.

The purpose of establishing the groups was to stimulate teachers to install their own professional development activities in their schools, focusing on their growth as persons, professionals and as a teacher community. Being part of the MECE-Media programme that was implemented gradually, the groups also developed gradually and in the course of time moved on to initiatives that were not even thought of at the start. The Seminarios Didácticos were one of these. From 1997 onwards teachers from different groups who shared the same specialization and curriculum interests began to participate in national, regional or local meetings to discuss issues related to subject matter teaching. The number of teachers participating in these meetings grew from 1131 in 1997 to over 7000 in the year 2000.

Another important outcome of the Secondary Teacher Groups has been their effort to communicate their classroom experiences. Teachers send accounts of these experiences to the national coordinators at the Ministry of Education to be included in a periodic publication called *Páginas Didácticas* (*Pages on Teaching*). Since the first issue in 1996 there have been seven more with examples of classroom work. The latest development arising from these groups is the organization of teacher networks. The first one, in 1997, gathered physics teachers in a region in the north of Chile. By the year 2000 there were 87 other networks in operation, mostly in the north and the metropolitan region (Santiago), with a few operating also in the south of Chile. The main topics discussed in the networks meetings refer to curriculum implementation, classroom innovations, teaching and assessment strategies, computer usage and classroom management (Ministerio de Educación 2001).

The MECE-Media programme as a whole was evaluated externally, and the contribution of these teacher group activities was found to be important, especially as far as implementing the educational reforms were concerned. There are problems, however, that have not been sufficiently addressed even though there is awareness about them. One of these is teachers' time. Only recently have teachers had this time recognized in their contractual conditions. However, teachers who work in more than one school are not always able to participate in these activities or are not given time to do so.

Keeping this programme going even after the World Bank funding was finished (in 2000) has been an important achievement, but the programme still operates in isolation from other in-service opportunities. The teacher activities are largely handled by the teachers themselves, with limited support regarding improvement of their content knowledge. The national coordinators are really facilitators and mediators of what teachers do; but their position is fragile until the programme is well inserted in a national policy for continuing education. That policy still has not been formulated.

Discussion issues and conclusions

This brief overview of teacher continuing education activities in Latin America in the 1990s points to developments in the direction of what international experience considers as good practice. There is a growing understanding that if teachers are to become better (both as far as knowledge and teaching capacities are concerned), they must decide themselves on the need for change and collaborate in producing such change. This explains the number of initiatives focusing on teacher groups at school level. To a certain extent, this emphasis is due to changes in the way ministries are dealing with the matter. Capable and experienced as well as innovative staff are contracted to lead these programmes (some of these leaders were part of the workshops in the 1980s described earlier). In several cases, they do not belong to the permanent government bureaucracies. In Chile, for example, all the improvement programmes of the 1990s operated on the basis of contract staff (on a temporary basis).

But, having said this, many of these programmes are inserted in old-fashioned systems, where norms and regulations often curtail the possibility of innovation. They are also inserted in contexts where teachers' working conditions are not adequate. Many teachers in Latin America get poor salaries and as a result have other jobs to make ends meet. In some countries they have heavy teaching loads and little time is allocated for preparation, meeting with parents and participating in teacher development activities. In the countries with ongoing reforms, these place constant and different demands on the same teachers. All this points to the fact that, as has been noted in other reform contexts, teachers in Latin America have little time for their own improvement.

The policies and reforms of the 1990s focused on improving pupil learning, especially that of children and young people in usually excluded populations. Thus there is a certain pressure for results and a growing demand for teacher accountability in this respect. While there are teachers who do not work well, who are absent from classrooms or do not care to improve, many teachers still find it difficult to achieve what is required from them. Their own schooling has been insufficient and they do not have access to appropriate continuing education programmes that could support, for example, their subject matter understanding. The quick information courses on curricular reforms are not enough. What is needed are more comprehensive programmes that give time and opportunity for teachers to learn and improve. There are good initiatives in this direction such as PLANCAD in Peru and the Teacher Regional Centres in Uruguay. The Argentinean Federal Network may not have national funding to continue in this decade, but it nevertheless created a useful structure for teacher continuing education. The Mexican system has established a structure and varied programmes of continuing teacher education. But most countries still have many activities that are not part of a national, comprehensive policy and that therefore may or may not be useful to the population they reach.

It would seem then that in a new phase of teacher education policies, countries need to develop a systemic approach. Teacher initial and teacher in-service provisions need to go hand in hand. As in Argentina, teacher-educators should not only prepare teachers at the initial phase, but also work with in-service teachers. The right to continuing education needs to be recognized more forcefully so that all teachers have an opportunity for further learning that is free (this is especially valid in a context where teachers hardly earn more than $US100 per month). Incentives for voluntary improvement on the part of teachers should not be a mechanical addition of points for courses done in order to get salary improvement, but linked to proper teacher evaluation and career stages.

The above comments are part of discussions all over Latin America: at the UNESCO level; among ministry of education staff who work with teachers; among teacher-educators; and among teachers. Yet, the tendency is still to start a new programme in order to solve a problem, rather than review the opportunities as a whole and decide on a comprehensive and sufficiently flexible teacher education policy with middle-term and longer-term ends in view.

Table 5.2 Teacher education activities and policies in Latin American countries

Country	Teacher CPD actions	Comprehensive policy for teacher education (initial and continuing)
Argentina	Red Federal de Formación Docente Continua	Red Federal
Bolivia	Asesores Pedagógicos	Being developed
Brazil	Programa de Educacao Continuada: accelerated classes	Referenciales para la formación de profesores
Chile	Rural Microcentres (rural schools) Teacher professional development groups (secondary) Teacher workshops (primary)	Being considered
Colombia	Expedición Pedagógica Nacional	Sistema Nacional de Formación de Educadores
Costa Rica	Educational Technology Programme Programa Especial de Formación Docente	No information
Cuba	Colectivo Pedagógico	Sistema Nacional de Formación Inicial y Continua de Docentes
Ecuador	Circulos de Estudio	Red Nacional de Formación Docente
El Salvador	Initiatives linked to EDUCO programme	Formación en Servicio (only in-service)

Continued

Table 5.2 *Continued*

Country	Teacher CPD actions	Comprehensive policy for teacher education (initial and continuing)
Guatemala	Círculos de Calidad Docente	Sistema Nacional para la Formación Educativa
Haiti	No information	Plan Nacional de Educación y Formación
Honduras	Centros para la Capacitación Docente	No information
México	Programa Nacional para la Actualización	Acuerdo Nacional para la Modernización de la Educación Básica
	Permnente de Maestros (PRONAP)	
	Programa para rebatir el rezago educativo (PAREB)	
Nicaragua	Small initiatives linked to reform programmes	No information
Panamá	No information	Sistema Nacional de Formación Docente
Paraguay	Círculos de Aprendizaje	No information
Perú	Programa de Capacitación Docente (PLANCAD)	Being developed
Dominican Republic	No information	Sistema Nacional de Formación y Desarrollo del Personal Directivo, Docente, Técnico y Administrativo
Uruguay	Centro de Capacitación y Perfeccionamiento Docente	Política Nacional de Formación Inicial y Continua
	Centros Regionales de Profesores (CERP)	
Venezuela	Centro Regional de Apoyo al Maestro	No information

Notes

1   The latest figures are found in UNESCO's account of the 20 years of the Major Project of Education in Latin America and the Caribbean (2001). See also PREAL (2001a).

2   For example, in the early 1980s in response to demands for better teacher preparation Brazil established the Centros de Formacao e Aperfeiçoamento do

Magistério (CEFAMs) with the collaboration of the Ministry of Education and other institutions, aimed at the education of primary teachers in terms of upgrading, the development of innovative practices and the improvement of teaching. Having been established with greater or lesser success in several states, it was expected that they might become centres for all forms of teacher education (Secretaria de Educaçao Fundamental 1998).

3   Although two or three countries participated in the TIMMS (Third International Mathematics and Science Study), only Chile has published its results. But 13 countries participated in UNESCO's First International Comparative Study of School Results in Language and Maths (2000).

4   Secondary teachers engaged in technical-vocational schools have experienced a very radical change of the curriculum, and they are being prepared with a slightly more complex programme: 60 hours of face-to-face instruction and 20 hours spent in a work setting (industry, business).

5   Towards the end of the 1990s, one of these networks (PICPEMCE) oriented to the improvement of teacher education and exchange of experiences had the participation of 20 countries in the region and 33 teacher education institutions. Each country had its own network that included the teachers' unions (UNESCO 2001).

6   This description follows closely the paper prepared by Juan Carlos Serra for the CRESUR Project (2001) that addresses reforms in Argentina, Chile and Uruguay in the 1990s.

References

Avalos, B. (ed.) (1986) *Teaching Children of the Poor: An Ethnographic Study in Latin America*. Ottawa: International Development Research Centre.

Avalos, B. (1998) School-based teacher development: the experience of teacher professional groups in secondary schools in Chile, *Teaching and Teacher Education*, 14(3): 257–71.

Avalos, B. (2001) *La Formación de Profesores y su Desarrollo Profesional: Prácticas Innovadoras en Busca de Polícas. El Caso de Chile*. Report prepared for the project on Educational Reforms in Argentina, Chile and Uruguay. Santiago: CRESUR Project.

Cardoso, B. and Scarpa, L. (2001) Posibles caminos para el desarrollo profesional del maestro. Paper presented at the 46th ICET World Assembly, Santiago, July.

Carlson, B. (2000) *Achieving Educational Quality: What Schools Teach Us. Learning from Chile's P900 Primary Schools*. Serie Desarrollo Producitvo. Santiago: ECLAC.

CENPEC (1998) *10 Años. Una Década Promoviendo a la Escuela Pública*. Sao Paulo: Centro de Estudos e Pesquisas em Educaçao, Cultura e Açao Comunitária (CENPEC).

Coraggio, J.L. and Torres, R.M. (1997) *La Educación Según el Banco Mundial. Un Análisis de sus Propuestas y Métodos.* Buenos Aires: Miño y Dávila.

Cox, C. and Avalos, B. (1999) Educational policies, change programmes and international co-operation: the case of Chile, in K. King and L. Buchert (eds) *Changing International Aid to Education: Global Patterns and National Concerns.* Paris: UNESCO.

Delannoy, F. (2000) *Brazil: Teachers Development and Incentives: A Strategic Framework.* Report no. 20408-Br., Latin America and the Caribbean Regional Office. Washington: The World Bank.

Ducoing, P. and Landesmann, M. (eds) (1996) *La Investigación Educativa en los Ochenta. Perspectivas para los Noventa. Sujetos de la Educación y Formación Docente.* México: Consejo Mexicano de Investigación Educativa.

ECLAC (1992) *Education and Knowledge: Basic Pillars of Changing Production Patterns with Social Equity.* Santiago: ECLAC-UNESCO.

Escobar, N. (1998) Modernización de la formación docente, *Revista Latinoamericana de Innovaciones Educativas* (Argentina), X(30): 91–119.

Filp, J. (1993) *The 900 Schools Programme: Improving the Quality of Primary Schools in Impoverished Areas of Chile.* Paris: IIEP Research and Studies Programme.

Fiorentini, D. and Miorim, M.A. (2001) Investigando y escribiendo en la educación continuada de profesores de matemáticas. Paper presented at the 46th ICET World Assembly, Santiago, July.

Garrido, E. (2001) Innovative experiences and public policies related to pre-service and in-service teacher education programmes in Brazil. Paper presented at the 46th ICET World Assembly, Santiago, July.

Gasperini, L. (2000) *The Cuban Education System: Lessons and Dilemmas.* Washington: The World Bank, LCSHD Paper Series.

Huberman, M. and Guskey, T.R. (1995) The diversities of professional development, in M. Huberman and T.R. Guskey (eds) *Professional Development in Education: New Paradigms and Practices.* New York: Teachers College Press.

MINEDUC (2001) *Desarrollo Profesional Docente en el Liceo: Programa MECE-Media 1995–2000.* Santiago: Ministerio de Educación Chile.

Navarro, J.C. and Verdisco, A. (1999) Teacher training in Latin America: innovations and trends. Paper presented at the Conference on Teachers in Latin America: 'New Perspectives on their Development and Performance', San José de Costa Rica, June 28–30.

OEI (1994) *Diagnóstico sobre la Formación Inicial y Permanente del Profesorado de Ciencias y Matemática en los Países Iberoamericanos.* Madrid: Ministerio de Educación y Ciencia and OEI.

Oliveira, J.B. (1999) Learn as you teach: the accelerated learning program in Brazil and its approach to teacher education. Paper presented at the Conference on Teachers in Latin America: 'New Perspectives on their Development and Performance', San José de Costa Rica, June 28–30.

Ortega, M.E. (1998) El programa nacional de capacitación en Guatemala, *Revista Latinoamericana de Innovaciones Educativas (Argentina)*, X(29): 133–64.

PREAL (2001a) *Quedándonos Atrás. Un Informe del Progreso Educativo en América Latina*. Informe de la Comisión Internacional sobre Educación, Equidad y Competitividad Económica en América Latina y el Caribe, Santiago, December.

PREAL (2001b) Mexico: 10 años de programas compensatorios, *Formas y Reformas de la Educación: Serie Mejores Prácticas*, 3(7).

Rivero, J. (1999) *Educación y Exclusión en América Latina. Reformas en Tiempos de Globalización*. Buenos Aires: Miño y Dávila.

Secretaria de Educaçao Fundamental (1998) *Referenciais para Formaçao de Professores*. Brasilia: Ministério de Educaçao e do Desporto.

Tatto, M.T. (1999) Conceptualizing and studying teacher education across world regions, an overview. Paper presented at the Conference on Teachers in Latin America: 'New Perspectives on their Development and Performance'. San José de Costa Rica, June 28–30.

Tatto, M.T. and Vélez, E. (1997) Teacher education reform initiatives: the case of Mexico, in C.A. Torres and A. Puigross (eds) *Latin American Education: Comparative Perspectives*. Boulder, CO: Westview.

Unda, M.P., Martínez, A. and Medina, M.J. (2001) La experiencia de expedición pedagógica y las redes de maestros: ¿Otros modos de formación? Paper presented at the 46th ICET World Assembly, Santiago, July.

UNESCO (2001) *Overview of the 20 Years of the Major Project in Education in Latin America and the Caribbean*. Santiago: UNESCO.

UNICEF (1990) *World Conference on Education for All: Meeting Basic Learning Needs*, final report. Thailand: Jomtien.

Vaillant, D. and Wettstein, G. (1999) *Centros Regionales de Profesores. Una Apuesta al Uruguay del Siglo XXI*. Montevideo: Editorial Fin de Siglo.

Vera, R. (1990) Case study: educators workshops in Chile: participative professional development, in V.D. Rust and P. Dalin (eds) *Teachers and Teaching in the Developing World*. New York: Garland Publishing.

6 Teacher professional development: themes and trends in the recent Australian experience

Shirley Grundy and Judith Robison

This chapter presents an exploration of themes and trends in recent teacher professional development around two interrelated concepts – function and drivers. The authors argue that there are three principal functions served by professional development – extension, renewal and growth – and that there are two drivers – systemic and personal. Within the systemic driver there is a strong emphasis upon the 'renewal' function of professional development. The authors explore the recent trends in systemic provision of professional development through a review of changes in the emphasis of professional development programmes over the last few decades and through a consideration of some recent Australian Commonwealth professional development programmes. The personal driver refers to the personal desire and motivation by teachers to sustain and enhance their professional lives. The relationship between professional development driven by personal preference and the three functions of extension, growth and renewal is more problematic. The personal dimensions of professional development are explored through a theoretical mapping of various theories of personal career development (stage theory and life event responses).

Introduction

Teaching is forever an unfinished profession. Thus, professional development is intrinsic to the vocation of teaching. By its very nature, teaching is never complete, never conquered, always being developed, always changing. Far from signalling some flaw, the centrality of development to the profession of teaching should be viewed as a badge of honour.

Perhaps nothing signals the centrality of professional development to teaching more than the fact that many teachers begin their career, not by teaching, but by participating in professional development. In many schools in Australia the school year begins with one or more 'pupil free' days devoted to planning and professional development. Hence, before they even begin to teach, beginning teachers may well participate in professional development. Of course, not only does this example signal to novice teachers that professional development is central to their work, but its positioning first in the school calendar for many teachers signals its ongoing importance throughout a teacher's career.

This recognition of the centrality of 'development' to the profession of teaching is the position from which we propose to begin this discussion of themes and trends in recent professional development experiences in Australia. That is, we do not intend to argue whether or not professional development *ought* to be important for the teaching profession, but rather to accept that it is and to describe and disentangle some of the threads of the experience. By accepting professional development as a 'given', however, we are not wanting to argue that the place and value of professional development within schools, systems and the profession more generally is unambiguous. On the contrary, most of the practices that constitute the trends we identify are located within contradictory and contested spaces in the educational discourse.

The chapter presents the exploration of themes and trends around two interrelated concepts – function and drivers. We argue that there are three principal functions served by professional development – extension, renewal and growth – and that there are two drivers – systemic and personal. We identify the ageing of the teaching profession as a factor that is strongly influencing systemic professional development provision (often expressed as 'PD programmes'). Within this driver (systemic provision in response to an increasing age profile), there is a strong emphasis upon the 'renewal' function of professional development. This might express itself as a concern for the renewal of teachers' knowledge base (particularly in areas of information and communication technologies or ICTs, science and mathematics) or renewal of enthusiasm and commitment. We will explore the recent trends arising in relation to systemic provision of professional development through a review of changes in the emphasis of PD programmes over the last few decades and through a consideration of some recent Australian Commonwealth professional development programmes.

The other driver in relation to professional development themes and trends is personal engagement and/or commitment. This driver refers to the personal desire and motivation by teachers to sustain and enhance their professional lives. The relationship between professional development driven by personal preference and the three functions of extension, growth and renewal is more problematic. We explore the personal dimensions of professional development through a theoretical mapping of various theories of personal career development (stage theory and life event responses). Again, the theme of ageing is pertinent, but we query whether the deficit implications of the systemic drivers are as pertinent when considering personal drivers.

The functions of professional development

As noted above, there are three basic functions of professional development: extension, growth and renewal.

By 'extension' we mean introducing new knowledge or skills into a teacher's repertoire. A prime example of such extension is the introduction of ICTs into schools and classrooms. When computers were first introduced into schools, most teachers had no experience with them at all, let alone having an understanding of their application to classroom learning and teaching. Professional development to extend teachers' knowledge and skills has been a major focus for schools and education systems in Australia, as elsewhere, for the last decade and a half. Between 1984 and 1986 the Commonwealth Schools Commission oversaw the $A18 million National Computer Education Program. The professional development of teachers was a central concern for that programme. The evaluators of the National Computer Education Program commented upon the 'extension' function of its professional development aspect:

> Whatever model for the professional development of teachers is used, the use of computers in schools for educational purposes is clearly an innovation . . . computing is like other innovations in that it provides teachers with an opportunity to either support and extend their traditional teaching methods, or, alternatively, to question and change some of their existing practices and hence explore the opportunity for different pedagogies provided by the new technology.
>
> (Grundy *et al.* 1987: 43)

If 'extension', to adopt a housing metaphor, is a process of 'building on', then 'renewal' is akin to 'renovation'. That is, the old and worn out is replaced with an updated version. The need for teacher 'renewal' has recently been linked to the ageing of the teaching profession. The median age of teachers in Australian schools rose from 33 to 40 in the decade 1986–96 (Australian Council of Deans of Education 2002: 115). Presumably, by 2006 this median age will have risen to 50. While this age profile clearly gives the teaching profession depth of experience, there are concerns that it is also leading to a lag in teachers' professional knowledge base. Thus, the Quality Teacher Program (QTP), introduced in 2000 and to which we will return later in the chapter, has identified teachers with older qualifications as a target group for professional development:

> The Quality Teacher Programme will support the updating and improvement of the knowledge and skills of teachers who completed initial teacher education ten or more years ago, teachers re-entering the workforce and casual teachers in the priority areas of literacy, numeracy, mathematics, science, information technology and vocational education in schools.
>
> (Department of Employment, Education, Training and Youth Affairs 2000)

We will note later that this assumption that teachers with older qualifications are in particular need of 'renewal' has created some fundamental implementation problems for the QTP.

For the majority of teachers, however, professional development is an intrinsic part of the growth and development cycle of a professional career. Sachs (2000: 79) argues:

> One of the hallmarks of being identified externally as a professional is to continue learning throughout a career, deepening knowledge, skill and judgement, staying abreast of important developments in the field and experimenting with innovations that promise improvements in practice.

Thus, extension through educational innovation, growth through the development of greater levels of expertise and renewal through transformation and change of knowledge and practice are key functions of teacher professional development that will form the focus of our discussion here.

The systemic driver: promoting growth and renewal through professional development

The question of how to promote teacher change or renewal has long been of central interest to educators and educational systems. This question has also become an increasingly vital one for governments as the teaching workforce ages and fewer young people are attracted into teaching as a career (Dinham 1996). During the last decade, the desire of governments, including the Australian federal and state authorities, to create an efficient and flexible workforce to support economic reform has focused attention on teacher renewal as a component in the wider restructuring of education (Ashenden 1992; Kenway *et al.* 1993; Marginson 1993, 1997; Down 1994; Beare 1995; Preston 1996; Alford 1998).

It has generally been accepted by educational authorities that the process of teacher renewal can be promoted by effective professional development.

Teacher professional development is usually claimed to improve the learning outcomes for students by providing teachers with greater knowledge or skills which can be applied directly to their own practice (Hargreaves and Fullan 1992: 1). Professional development is an integral part of the lifelong learning of teachers which begins with initial or pre-service education. The term 'professional development' is applied to numerous forms of education for teachers, varying from one-hour workshops through to extended courses. It may have a number of different purposes ranging from specific training in the implementation of a particular teaching strategy, such as 'whole language' approaches to learning, or the implementation of a curriculum package, to a focus on the long-term development of a broader range of skills, for instance the management of educational change. Professional development has various dimensions, including planning, implementation and evaluation. It may be organized by a variety of education stakeholders, such as government and non-government education systems, teacher unions, professional associations and tertiary institutions, each pursuing independent initiatives or cooperating in 'partnership' arrangements.

During the 1960s and 1970s 'in-service education', as 'professional development' was then known, was predominantly aimed at keeping individual teachers up to date with current changes and developments in discipline, content or pedagogy. Such in-service education was usually organized either by state-based education systems or by professional associations. The most common formats were one-day or half-day workshops, held at sites remote from the classroom, with little follow-up to support teachers or to evaluate the effectiveness of the programme in bringing about change. The model was that of 'delivery'. That is, new information, knowledge or skills were identified and delivered to teachers, who in turn would be expected to apply their newly acquired knowledge or competencies in the classroom.

The 1980s saw a move to the school as the appropriate site for professional development and a greater interest in educational reform by national governments. The political agenda which underlay this support for change was the conviction that education should be more economically efficient and effective and that the way to achieve this was by organizing education according to business and market principles. Schools were challenged to rethink what knowledge, attitudes and competencies the citizens of the future would need and produce educational 'products' that could meet those needs. This shift in focus to the school also had a strong democratic connection grounded in a critique of managerialism, yet acknowledging that schools needed to be sites of investigation and development (Grundy 1992).[1] It was acknowledged that improvement needed to take account of the context of practice as well as teaching practices themselves. Questions were raised about how the organization, the relationships and the practices that characterize the work of teaching and learning in schools contribute to or impair students' learning outcomes.

This move signalled a bringing together of school development and professional development.

In the early 1990s, professional development began to emerge as a component of industrial agreements, rather than a personal decision taken by an individual teacher aimed at improving qualifications or better responding to the needs of students in their classes. At the state level in Australia, the previous emphasis on teaching and learning was largely replaced by a more indirect reform strategy in which the practices of organizing educational work became the prime focus for change (Brown *et al.* 1996: 313). At the national level, it was argued that the development of a highly competent teaching workforce must be linked with restructuring in teaching (Porter *et al.* 1994). The implications of the linking of teacher development, school restructuring and industrial reform are described as follows by Angus (1992: 115):

> For employers the message of greater productivity that underpins award restructuring has a timely ring. It is entirely consistent with the rhetoric surrounding the devolution reforms in which all states are presently engaged: improvements to the quality of education will come from rethinking the way in which work is done in schools . . . the key to better schools is to allow those most directly involved in teaching to exercise more direct control over the management of their work environment; the rules and regulations negotiated by employers and unions which circumscribe how work is done must be rethought and made more responsive to school proposals for improvement.

Although the emphasis of this new industrial/educational environment was reform, restructuring and improvement, with a commensurate emphasis on reward (through salary increases linked to award restructuring and educational reform), there was also a strong implicit element of accountability:

> Every government school system in Australia is engaged in some form of decentralisation whereby the responsibilities for school management are being devolved from central office to the school site. In theory schools are being given greater latitude to determine how they can best improve student learning; in return they are being held more directly accountable for their results.
>
> (Angus 1992: 115)

In the early 1990s the new emphasis upon teacher accountability became rather simplistically linked to notions of teacher appraisal. This followed from the application of a technical approach to the development of competencies. Once a narrow industrialist view of skill development and accountability for 'productivity improvement' was introduced, appraisal of the acquisition and application of professional competencies against a set of teaching standards was a small step.

The relationship between teacher appraisal and the development of teachers' professional knowledge in improving teacher quality became an area of debate within the educational community in Australia in the 1990s, as it had been in Britain during the latter part of the 1980s. Writing in response to the British government's proposed models for improving teacher quality, Richard Winter (1989) and John Elliott (1989) developed critiques of the managerial model of teacher appraisal. Winter noted that most appraisal schemes are designed to serve two purposes: on the one hand to provide reliable knowledge about teachers' professional activities, and on the other as a means of achieving greater managerial control. Elliott's analysis showed how such managerial models undermine the teacher's ability to act educationally by producing knowledge that can be used to create hierarchical forms of teacher surveillance and control. Both writers provided alternative approaches to improving teacher quality, which included collaboration, reflexivity, practical knowledge and professional culture.

Interestingly, despite the strengthening of the discourse of accountability that became associated with teacher professional development in the early 1990s, the fears of a narrow technicist approach to the ongoing professional development of teachers did not eventuate. Indeed, the decade became more noted for the development of an emphasis upon collaborative, reflexive, site and practice-based teacher and school development.

In the Australian context, the federal Labour government became a central player in the debate on teacher quality in the late 1980s with the publication of John Dawkins' *Strengthening Australia's Schools* (1987) policy document. Associated publications by the Schools Council (1989) presented the view that high-quality teaching demanded systematic and relevant professional development, purposeful appraisal, an integrated career structure and improved workplaces. Such documents, and subsequent Commonwealth-funded programmes aimed at improving the quality of teaching and learning, recognized that the quality of teachers depended more on a lifelong commitment to learning than on the imposition of a narrow regulatory system. The National Professional Development Program (NPDP)[2] encouraged a considerable amount of cooperation between state and federal educational bureaucracies as well as the development of partnerships between teacher professional associations, employers from both government and non-government sectors, teacher unions and higher education institutions for teacher professional development.

The experiences of the NPDP projects and much recent research on the effectiveness of various approaches to professional development has led to some consensus on the principles which underlie 'best practice' in professional development. The 1995 evaluation of the NPDP published a summary of the work of a number of researchers which identified four areas of professional development: *planning*, which included the principles that it should be based on teachers' needs and relevant to their experience and interests; *facilitation*, which included the principles that it should involve leaders with expert knowledge, provide high-quality, user-friendly resources and be located in an appropriate setting; *implementation*, which included the principles that it should demonstrate a clear relationship between theory, research and practice, should provide opportunities for active engagement, use a variety of presentation styles, involve modelling exemplary practice, and build knowledge and ownership through action research; and *application*, which included the principles that it should involve planned follow-up, translate into practice the knowledge and skills gained, support teachers' accountability for student outcomes and reward participation in some manner, such as academic credit (National Education Forum and DEET 1995: 87). The evaluations of individual NPDP projects tended to confirm these principles – for example, participants in the Innovative Links[3] project referred to such factors as ownership and local relevance, the importance of location and the provision of time to engage in professional development; they valued opportunities to work collaboratively, the input of external educational advisers and the recognition of their work through opportunities for appraisal and accreditation (Southern Cross Evaluation Team 1996: 80–2).

These principles reflect those of earlier reviews of the literature on successful professional development such as that by the Department of Employment, Education and Training (DEET) titled *Teachers Learning – Improving Australian Schools through Inservice Training and Development* (1988) which identified ten principles of good learning including concern for adult learning principles, effective delivery modes, teacher control, worthwhile subject matter and conscientious evaluation. A review by Dunlop (1990, cited in National Board of Employment, Education and Training 1993: 21) also identified the importance of a sense of ownership by teachers, a recognition of adult learning principles, use of an appropriate site, content based on teacher needs and the 'practicality ethic' of teachers and some form of incentive or reward for participation. A Queensland Department of Education document, *Professional Development: A Review of Contemporary Literature* (1990), emphasized principles such as sound leadership, a sense of ownership, recognition of adult learning principles, worthwhile content and access to resources, incentives for commitment and adequate and appropriate time. All of these elements of exemplary professional development practices are consistent with the wider literature. Clandinin and Connelly (1994), for instance, have pointed to the importance of self-knowledge and self-understanding as a key to professional growth. Christopher Clark (1992: 77) argues that adult development is likely to be more successful if it is voluntary rather than coercive, and that many teachers already design their own professional development programmes.

Much recent research has confirmed the efficacy of the workplace model of professional development (for example, National Board of Employment, Education and Training 1993; Hager 1996; Retallick *et al.* 1999). Retallick *et al.* (1999) argued that workplace learning enables teachers to translate theory into practice by meeting the needs of teachers in particular school situations and encourages action research. Most of the principles for best practice in professional development are present in workplace learning situations. A National Board of Employment, Education and Training (NBEET) (1995: 91–2) study into workplace learning concluded that it is more likely to be sustained in a culture of collegial support and collaboration which fosters critical reflection among teachers; that it is ongoing and usually self-directed; that teachers recognize the importance of ideas from outside, though they tend to validate their worth in terms of the outcomes produced in the classroom; and that workplace learning takes place over a considerable period of time.

The decade of the 1990s was clearly one in which there was considerable tension and contestation around the improvement of educational outcomes for students and the improvement of the quality of teachers and teaching. This contestation had implications for the systemic drivers of professional development. The question that had to be addressed was 'What should be the focus of systemically driven professional development – the enhancement of skills and competencies, defined by the employer and related to productivity improvement (improvements in student learning) or a broader notion of a professional community, in charge of their own development?' It was the latter view that won out (although the threat of a more narrowly defined accountability regime that links monetary reward or even budgetary allocation to performance still lingers). We see in the major systemic professional development programme of the new century, the QTP (which will be discussed in more detail below) the acknowledgement that quality must be linked to a form of development that encapsulates the professional development principles discussed above. Furthermore, the move across all states of Australia to introduce some professional body that will have responsibility for teacher registration, professional standards and professional development further attests to the winning out of the professional discourse of teacher professional development over the industrial. However, the dual responsibility that teacher professional bodies have for professional development and for the maintenance of professional standards shows how the professional discourse has been tied to the new discourse of individual accountability.

It must be remembered, however, that despite the importance of the policy debates, systemic concerns are not the only drivers for teacher professional development. Of importance also, perhaps of prime importance, is the driver of individual motivation – the personal driver.

Personal drivers: career stages and life experiences

In *Understanding Teacher Development* Hargreaves and Fullan (1992) acknowledged that teacher development is also a process of personal development and that factors to do with personal development may hinder the achievement of professional development goals. Teachers who are at different points in their life cycle, so this argument goes, have characteristically different orientations to change and improvement as well as different needs with respect to their growth and development. Just as human development theorists have posited consistent patterns of human development across populations, so also a number of educational researchers have argued that stages of professional development are also identifiable in the professional lives of teachers.

Evidence from studies of teachers' professional life cycles indicates that there are important changes in teachers' concerns, relationships with pupils and relationships with colleagues that suggest differentiated learning interests and processes throughout their careers (Ball and Goodson 1985). According to Huberman's research (1989, 1993), most teachers see themselves as achieving mastery of different pedagogical competencies at various moments in their careers. Huberman also observed that teachers sought different sources of knowledge and learnt in different ways at different times in their careers, although with a general preference for informal discussions with colleagues.

Maclean and McKenzie (1991: 25) conceived of teachers' careers as being the passage of individuals through five main stages of work-related social roles over the length of their working lives as schoolteachers. These stages can be identified as: choice of teaching as an occupation; the pre-service training period; induction into teaching – the first four to five years; the teaching career proper – five years to end of career; and preparation for exit and exit from the occupation.

Huberman's research (1989, 1992, 1993) also pointed to teachers' careers as typically characterized by a number of definable phases or stages. These can be differentiated partly by the achievement of pedagogical competencies but they also parallel life cycle changes. Huberman differentiates a number of stages within what Maclean and McKenzie call 'the teaching career proper'. Huberman's first stage is *survival and discovery*, the phase of career entry. The survival theme has to do with the reality shock associated with confronting the complexity of instructional management, the gulf between professional ideals and the grind of daily classroom life, the fragmentation of tasks. The discovery theme refers to the initial enthusiasm of having one's own pupils and one's own classroom as well as feeling like a colleague among peers. The next phase is identified as *stabilization* and is characterized by personal and administrative affirmation – a personal commitment to teaching as a career and the administrative granting of tenure or permanency. This stage is also characterized by an affiliation to a professional community, freedom from direct supervision and greater instructional mastery and comfort. A stage of *experimentation/activism* follows stabilization. This is the time when teachers are typically ready for new challenges and stimulation, and experience a desire to increase their impact. The *experimentation* stage may be followed by a stage of *taking stock, self-doubt* when some form of mid-career crisis might become evident. Huberman proposed that this is usually between the twelfth and twentieth year of teaching and may be connected to a feeling of monotony or lack of challenge. Alternatively, self-doubt may be engendered from a sense of failure of attempts to influence or reform practice at the school or district level. Career changes are often considered at this time. If a teacher continues to teach, a period of *serenity* (characterized by more mechanical, but also more relaxed, self-accepting activity) may follow or perhaps a stage of *conservatism* (characterized by resistance to innovation). Huberman's final stage is *disengagement* during which there may be a trend towards increasing withdrawal and gradual disengagement from work towards more interest in outside pursuits.

Related to this notion of stages in the career cycle, Floden and Huberman (1989) also proposed 'seasons' in the professional life of a teacher. These are appropriate or favourable moments for carrying out specific tasks or reorienting one's career. Changes in schools and educational policy, the cohort of pupils taught, the projects in which teachers become involved are the sort of 'seasonal fluctuations that may trigger a move to the next phase of a teacher's career' (Floden and Huberman 1989: 463). The idea that change, growth and development are related more to life events than stages is supported by Goodson (1992: 117). He noted that research on teachers' careers points to the fact that there are critical incidents in teachers' lives, and specifically their work, which may crucially affect perception and practice. Other researchers suggest that there are a variety of intersecting factors which may influence the progress of teachers through their careers and their readiness to embrace change (Hargreaves and Fullan 1992).

The idea of stages of professional development is, therefore, a contested one. It is interesting to note that the interest in 'stage theory' for professional development was at its height around the beginning of the 1990s, when the median age of teachers in Australia was less than 40. It would be interesting to test whether the later stages of 'conservatism' and 'disengagement' are as clearly identifiable in today's teaching population in which the majority of teachers are in the later career stage. Certainly, participants in the National Conference on Quality Teaching (2001) did not think so. Reporting on a national study of professional development conducted under the auspices of the QTP (McRae *et al.* 2001), the conference noted:

> Experienced teachers are not jaded and in retreat from professional development. They do nearly twice as much professional development

as the group of least experienced teachers (and more than any other 'experience' group), pay much more (on average about six times as much) and self-reportedly get a great deal more out of it.

(Boucher and McRae 2002: 60)

Stage theory of professional development tends to constitute the teacher as passive in the developmental process. It is always something else that triggers growth and receptivity to change is induced by a set of life circumstances rather than through individual predilection.

Various researchers have studied the connections between teachers' lives and their willingness to embrace change in their professional lives. Knowles (1992: 102) argued that because biography, which he defined as 'those formative experiences of pre-service and beginning teachers which have influenced the way they think about teaching and, subsequently, their actions in the classroom' (1992: 99), influences teacher perspectives it is important to understand teachers' own experiences as schoolchildren. Raymond *et al.* (1992: 150) found that pre-training experiences such as the teacher's family background and their own schooling experiences often have a long-lasting influence on the way they teach and remain the core of their developmental process throughout their careers. They also argued, however, that teacher professional development is a process that is inseparable from the construction and expression of the teacher's personal identity. Various influences (parents, teachers, home, gender, ethnicity, religion and location) from the teacher's pre-professional life history are continually evoked and reconstructed to establish a firm moral and emotional ground that helps form teachers' professional commitment and identity. Informal and formal professional activities, challenging innovations or teaching experiences all seemed to be assessed against this personal ground.

It is around the concept of change that systemic provision and personal motivation come together. It is important to understand that professional life is not independent of the whole life experience. There are pressures and influences that at different times of the cycle of life affect people's work life. The review of professional development literature referred to above, however, suggests that the personal drive towards professional development is more likely to be influenced by life events than predictable career stages. The drive to change professional practice is often an interaction between personal and systemic drivers. That is, life events and personal challenges interact with systemic demands and professional advances to create the conditions in which change is embraced, whether freely or in response to systemic requirements. The challenge for those with the responsibility to promote professional development is to provide opportunities that take account of individual and unique needs and aspirations, the life and social contexts of the work of teachers, as well as the needs of the profession as a whole and the systems within which teachers work in order to provide extension, renewal and/or growth as appropriate.

In the next section we move away from a synoptic consideration of research and policy relating to the provision of professional development to consideration of some recent Australian Commonwealth examples of professional development provision at the systemic level. We argue that such programmes reflect the elements of effective professional development identified in the literature and, as such, signal the continued professionalization of teaching in Australia.

Recent themes and trends in teacher professional development

From the review of systemic provision through the latter decades of the twentieth century, we noted a number of themes for successful professional development. The most important of these were:

- relevance to the needs identified at the school level by teachers;
- control of the professional development programme by participants;
- access to expertise to facilitate learning rather than deliver programmes;
- adoption of collegial and collaborative programme organization;
- action learning principles (that is, development is a learning process, which is in turn grounded in investigations of practice and critical reflection upon change processes);
- longer time frames to allow development through cycles of action and reflection;
- acknowledgement of the need for school reform and restructuring as a basis of improvement as well as professional development and change.

Two recent and major Australian national professional development programmes – the Innovative Links project and the QTP – exemplify the application of these themes. The former was a systemically driven programme conducted under the auspices of the NPDP from 1994 to 1996. The latter is another systemic provision, which, like the NPDP, was designed to provide professional development to teachers in all systems (government, Catholic and independent) in all states and territories. The QTP was put into place in 2000 and is fully operational at the time of writing.

Innovative Links

The Innovative Links project (like its parent programme, the NPDP) reflected the trends in professional development identified above. It linked professional development to wider issues of educational reform and school restructuring. The inclusion of the education unions as joint partners in the programme and in all facets of the Innovative Links structures was also in keeping with the industrial relations link with respect to professional development that we noted earlier in the chapter.

The objectives of the Innovative Links project demonstrate how the themes and trends identified above were incorporated into the operational principles and practices of the project. The project had the following objectives:

- to develop schools as learning communities in which research, rethinking and renewal are regarded as normal and essential work practices;
- to examine and improve the work organization practices of schools and to enhance teacher competence;
- to provide participating schools with access to advice and expertise on current research findings and strategies relating to the area of concern for the school;
- to increase the skills of university-based teacher-educators to develop, in partnership with schools and members of 'Roundtables', research-based processes of professional development;
- to enhance university-based teacher-educators' understanding of school reform, national issues relating to schools, current classroom practice, and the needs of educators and leaders in schools;
- to explore new possibilities for ongoing teacher education and professional development.

Innovative Links was organized through a series of 'Roundtables' located around Australia in both metropolitan and regional sites. A Roundtable consisted of teachers from affiliated schools and teacher-educators from a participating university together with employer, union and National Schools Network representatives. The Roundtables enabled schools to be networked at the local level and linked nationally.

The principle of partnership between universities and schools was at the heart of Innovative Links. At the school level, university-based colleagues were teamed with school-based colleagues to engage in action research around issues identified by the school. The expertise that each partner brought to the issues under investigation contributed to mutual growth and development. Time was provided through the project for reflection, planning and evaluation. The partnership was not one that advantaged only schools and teacher professional development. University colleagues benefited from the partnership relationship with schools in a number of significant ways. One group of teacher-eductors who participated in the project reflected upon the mutual professional development that arose from it:

> While the focus of the Innovative Links project is the professional development of school teachers, it has become clear during its implementation that the developing role of the 'academic associate' demands a reassessment of the predominant positioning of universities and schools in the provision of professional development. The relationships developing in the project are ones which challenge traditional forms of interaction between university academics and school teachers . . . There now seems to be emerging a new form of partnership, which positions both academics and classroom practitioners as co-researchers and joint producers of professional knowledge.
>
> (Grundy *et al.* 1999: 37)

Thus Innovative Links not only provided an example of a systemically driven professional development project that incorporated the key themes identified above, but it also broke new ground in terms of the broad partnership principles that underpinned all elements of the project. The evaluators commented on this feature:

> What is peculiar and distinctive to Innovative Links is that its core feature is the idea of partnership between practising teachers on a whole school basis and university-based teacher-educators to foster teacher professional development. This is the first time that a formal and explicit partnership of this kind has been seen as central to the renewal and development of teacher professionalism.
>
> (Yeatman and Sachs 1995: 16)

The Quality Teacher Program

The QTP incorporated many of the principles and practices that were intrinsic to Innovative Links. As such it represents a continuation into the 2000s of many of the themes and trends of the 1990s. In particular, the QTP affirmed 'the value of professional development, where it is identified and implemented within the school context to meet the needs of their teachers and students, for the continuous improvement of professional practice' (Department of Employment, Education, Training and Youth Affairs 2000). Practitioner relevance, professional control, expert facilitation, collaborative and collegial organization, action learning and cyclical programme development were all themes that continued to inform the development and implementation of the QTP.

There are, however, also some fundamental differences that signal a shift back to the concepts of individual accountability for development, away from the more holistic orientation of the earlier programmes. As we noted above, the professional context of the 1990s located professional development within a wider social and industrial context. Thus, professional growth and enhancement was only one aspect of educational change and quality improvement. The other aspect was the school and systemic context. Thus improvements in individual practice needed to take place in a context of wider educational reform and school restructuring. Quality was dependent upon systemic as well as personal drivers.

The QTP had its genesis within a different political context, however. With the change from a federal Labor to a Liberal government came an ideological swing back to a focus on the individual. Thus, the co-dependence of professional development upon systemic reform and school restructuring gave way to a re-emphasis of the responsibility of the individual practitioner for improvement and quality practice. The language of 'standards' and accountability is obvious within the rationale of the new programme. In the following quotation from the rationale for the QTP, although the emphasis upon collaborative and collegial action is clear, it is also clear that individual accountability for identifiable outcomes and the achievement of standards is a strong theme:

> Central to [the] effectiveness [of a professional development program] is:
>
> - the support provided from education systems and schools to embed professional development effectively in conventional work practices;
> - the extent to which professional development is centred on the curriculum and agreed student learning outcomes; and the willingness of teachers to take responsibility for their own professional growth, to reflect upon their practices, trial new approaches and make collaborative decisions about future strategies and priorities.
>
> In addition, international research points to the value of helping individual schools understand and translate national standards into local contexts. The process of weaving internal and external expectations together can be greatly assisted when schools and teachers are provided with the capacity to refine and improve teaching practice in order to progress towards the achievement of improved school and student outcomes.
>
> (Department of Employment, Education,
> Training and Youth Affairs 2000)

It is not surprising, therefore, that alongside the professional development strand of the QTP there has been an emphasis upon the development of professional standards.

The other theme that is apparent in the discourse of professional development at this time is that of 'renewal'. As noted at the beginning of this chapter, there is now a concern about the ageing of the teaching force, and the need to revitalize and renew the knowledge and competencies base of the teaching profession has come to the fore. This emphasis upon renewal is also clear in the rationale for the QTP:

> The Quality Teacher Program will support the updating and improvement of the knowledge and skills of teachers who completed initial teacher education ten or more years ago, teachers re-entering the workforce and casual teachers in the priority areas of literacy, numeracy, mathematics, science, information technology and vocational education in schools.
>
> (DEETYA 2000)

Anecdotal reports from a number of managers of QTP projects and a search of QTP websites has revealed that renewal of long-serving teachers has slipped away as a prime focus of the programme. This has been partly because of the difficulty of singling out teachers who completed initial teacher education qualification more than ten years ago and identifying them as in need of professional development. Such an approach was in danger of stigmatizing a large proportion of the teaching force. Instead, extension and growth of the professional knowledge base of all teachers across a number of key focus areas has become central. These key areas are: literacy, numeracy, mathematics, science, information technology and vocational education and training. While there is still a strong rhetorical emphasis upon action research and action learning principles that place a premium on improvement through practitioner-initiated actions, a review of the many and varied programmes across states and schooling sectors reveals a strong swing back to programme delivery in the predetermined focus areas. In particular, information technology has become an overriding theme. Online delivery of professional development is becoming a preferred medium. The Teacher Learning Support Network (TLSN) in Western Australia is an example of the move to online professional development support: 'The TLSN is an interactive website which has been designed to provide support to teachers undertaking self-directed professional development' (http://qtp.eddept.wa.edu.au/ifs/files/deploy/tlsn/jsp/main.jsp).

The QTP continued to emphasize the importance of links with universities and teacher-educators. However, we see a move away from the partnership framework of Innovative Links, which emphasized joint learning and development, to a positioning of university colleagues as professional development providers. Indeed, the re-emphasis upon delivery and provision has signalled a reinvigoration of a professional development industry as private providers have offered courses in the key focus areas.

Conclusion

In this chapter we have argued that teacher professional development is influenced and informed by both systemic and personal drivers. The systemic drivers are concerned with the provision of appropriate professional development programmes for the teaching force as a whole or for subgroups within it. Personal drivers recognize life histories, personal circumstances and career trajectories as prime determinants of receptiveness to and enthusiasm for professional development. It is interesting to note that, while the provision of professional development in the new millennium provides evidence of a swing back to more individualistic development, we are not seeing a resurgence of personal interest-driven professional development. Rather, the drivers of systemic priorities strongly determine the focus areas for professional development programmes. Personal engagement and commitment is increasingly being fostered through stronger accountability demands – accountability for student outcomes and for professional standards. While such a trend might appear to meet systemic demands, a lack of attention to personal drivers may yet come at a cost. Retention of teachers within the profession is an increasing problem. Retaining a highly committed and competent teaching force might depend more upon taking account of personal drivers and influences upon teacher professional development than upon demanding that teachers develop in systemically predetermined ways.

Notes

1   An earlier version of this paper was delivered as a conference paper in 1990 and provides a critique of the market ideology that characterized the late 1980s educational discourses.
2   The National Professional Development Program was funded by the Australian federal government Department of Employment, Education and Training (DEET). Between 1993 and 1996, it provided about $A60 million for a variety of projects aimed at renewing teachers' discipline knowledge and teaching competencies.
3   Innovative Links Between Universities and Schools for Teacher Professional Development was part of the NPDP funded by the Australian federal government between 1994 and 1996.

References

Note: The authors have made every endeavour to acknowledge all sources cited or quoted in this chapter. If any text has been inadvertently cited without acknowledgement, we request that our oversight be made known to us.

Alford, K. (1998) Redefining education to serve the economy: competencies for teachers and students, *Unicorn*, 24(3): 15–26.

Angus, M. (1992) Award restructuring and school reform, in D. Riley (ed.) *Industrial Relations in Australian Education*, pp. 237–48. Wentworth Falls, NSW: Social Science Press.

Ashenden, D. (1992) Award restructuring and productivity in the future of schooling, in D. Riley (ed.) *Industrial Relations in Australian Education*. Wentworth Falls, NSW: Social Science Press.

Australian Council of Deans of Education (2002) *New Learning: A Charter for Education in Australia*. Canberra: Australian Council of Deans of Education.

Ball, S.J. and Goodson, I. (1985) *Teachers' Lives and Careers*. London: Falmer Press.

Beare, H. (1995) New patterns for managing schools and school systems, in C.W. Evers and J.D. Chapman (eds) *Educational Administration: An Australian Perspective*. St Leonards, NSW: Allen & Unwin.

Boucher, S. and D. McRae (2002) *Continuing professional development*. Paper presented at the national conference on quality teaching: Improvement or Transformation, Canberra, Australian College of Educators.

Brown, L., Seddon, T., Angus, L. and Rushbrook, P. (1996) Professional practice in education in an era of contractualism, *Australian Journal of Education*, 40(3): 311–27.

Clandinin, J.D. and Connelly, F.M. (1994) Personal experience methods, in N.K. Denzin and Y.S. Lincoln (eds) *Handbook of Qualitative Research*. Thousand Oaks, CA: Sage.

Clark, C.M. (1992) Teachers as designers in self-directed professional development, in A. Hargraves and M. Fullan (eds) *Understanding Teacher Development*. New York: Teachers College Press.

Dawkins, J.S. (1987) *Strengthening Australia's Schools: A Consideration of the Focus and Content of Schooling*. Canberra: Parliament House.

Department of Employment, Education and Training (DEET) (1988) *Teachers Learning – Improving Australian Schools Through Inservice Training and Development*. Canberra: Department of Employment, Education and Training.

Department of Employment, Education, Training and Youth Affairs (DEETYA) (2000) *Teachers for the 21st Century – Making the Difference: A Commonwealth Government Quality Teacher Initiative*. Canberra: Department of Employment, Education, Training and Youth Affairs. www.dest.gov.au/schools/Publications/2002/t21.htm.

Dinham, S. (1996) In loco grandparentis? The challenge of Australia's ageing teacher population, *International Studies in Educational Administration*, 24(1): 16–30.

Down, B. (1994) Human capital theory and secondary education, *Unicorn*, 20(3): 54–61.

Elliott, J. (1989) Knowledge, power and teacher appraisal, in W. Carr (ed.) *Quality in Teaching: Arguments for a Reflective Profession*. London: Falmer Press.

Floden, R. and Huberman, M. (1989) Teachers' professional lives: the state of the art, *International Journal of Education Research on Teachers' Professional Lives*, 13(4): 455–66.

Goodson, I. (1992) Sponsoring the teacher's voice: teachers' lives and teacher development, in A. Hargraves and M. Fullan (eds) *Understanding Teacher Development*. New York: Teachers College Press.

Grundy, S. (1992) Beyond guaranteed outcomes: changing the discourse for educational praxis, *Australian Journal of Education*, 36(2): 157–69.

Grundy, S., Bigum, C. *et al.* (1987) Teaching teachers: educational computing and the professional development of teachers, in C. Bigum, S. Bonser, P. Evans *et al. Coming to Terms with Computers in Schools*. Geelong, Victoria: Deakin Institute for Studies in Education.

Grundy, S., Jasman, A., Mountford, A., Newbound, P., Phillips, A., Robison, J., Strickland, L. and Tomazos, D. (1999) Exploring an emerging landscape: a metaphor for university academics working with, in and for schools, *The Australian Educational Researcher*, 26(3): 37–56.

Hager, P. (1996) Professional practice in education: research and issues, *Australian Journal of Education*, 40(3): 235–47.

Hargreaves, A. and Fullan, M. (eds) (1992) *Understanding Teacher Development*. New York: Teachers College Press.

Huberman, M. (1989) On teachers' careers: once over lightly, with a broad brush, *International Journal of Education Research on Teachers' Professional Lives*, 13(4): 347–62.

Huberman, M. (1992) Teacher development and instructional mastery, in A. Hargraves and M. Fullan (eds) *Understanding Teacher Development*. New York: Teachers College Press.

Huberman, M. (1993) *The Lives of Teachers*. London: Cassell.

Kenway, J. in association with Bigum, C. *et al.* (1993) New education in new times: Paper presented at the Australian Curriculum Studies Association Biennial Conference, Brisbane.

Knowles, J. (1992) Models for understanding pre-service and beginning teachers' biographies: illustrations from case studies, in I. Goodson (ed.) *Studying Teachers' Lives: Problems and Possibilities*. New York: Teachers College Press.

Maclean, R. and McKenzie P. (1991) *Australian Teachers' Careers*. Melbourne: ACER.

Marginson, S. (1993) *Education and Public Policy in Australia*. Cambridge: Cambridge University Press.

Marginson, S. (1997) *Markets in Education*. St Leonards, NSW: Allen & Unwin.

McRae, D., Ainsworth, G. *et al.* (2001) *Professional Development 2000 Australia: A National Mapping of School Teacher Professional Development*. Canberra: Commonwealth Department of Education, Training and Youth Affairs.

National Board of Employment, Education and Training (NBEET) (1993) *Workplace Learning in the Professional Development of Teachers*, commissioned report No. 24. Canberra: AGPS.

National Education Forum and Department of Employment, Education and Training (DEET) (1995) *National Professional Development Program: Mid-term review of NPDP Projects*. Canberra: DEET.

Porter, P., Lingard, B. and Knight, J. (1994) Changing administration and administering change: an analysis of the state of Australian education, in F. Crowther, B. Caldwell, J. Chapman, G. Lakomski and D. Ogilvie (eds) *The Workplace in Education: Australian Perspectives*. Sydney: Edward Arnold.

Preston, B. (1996) Professional practice in school teaching, *Australian Journal of Education*, 40(3): 248–64.

Queensland Department of Education (1990) *Professional Development: A Review of Contemporary Literature*. Brisbane: Research Services, Division of Curriculum Services, Department of Education.

Raymond, D., Butt, R. and Townsend, D. (1992) Contexts for teacher development: insights from teachers' stories, in A. Hargraves and M. Fullan (eds) *Understanding Teacher Development*. New York: Teachers College Press.

Retallick, J., Groundwater-Smith, S. and Clancy, S. (1999) Enhancing teacher engagement with workplace learning, *The Australian Educational Researcher*, 26(3): 15–36.

Sachs, J. (2000) Rethinking the practice of teacher professionalism, in C. Day, A. Fernandaz, T. Hauge and J. Møller (eds) *The Life and Work of Teachers*. London: Falmer Press.

Schools Council (1989) *Teacher Quality: An Issues Paper*. Canberra: Australian Government Publishing Service.

Southern Cross Evaluation Team (1996) *Partners in Research: Teachers and Teacher-Educators Learning Together*. Murdoch University, Innovative Links Project.

Winter, R. (1989) Teacher appraisal and the development of professional knowledge, in W. Carr (ed.) *Quality in Teaching: Arguments for a Reflective Profession*. London: Falmer Press.

Yeatman, A. and Sachs, J. (1995) *Making the Links: A Formative Evaluation of the First Year of the Innovative Links Project Between Universities and Schools for Teacher Professional Development*. Murdoch University, School of Education.

7 Case studies from sub-Saharan Africa

Pam Christie, Ken Harley and Alan Penny

This chapter argues that the provision of continuing professional development (CPD) in sub-Saharan Africa needs to be understood in relation to broader issues of education, the state and development. The state in Africa and its relationship to education have historically specific dynamics; and African models and expectations of CPD need to be understood in a context which often differs from CPD in states in the West/North. The first section of the chapter illustrates the ways in which the purposes and foci of CPD in sub-Saharan Africa, as well as issues such as management, funding and evaluation, are shaped by these contextual forces. In particular, we highlight the importance of donor funding and the devastating impact of HIV/AIDS (with teachers being a high-risk group). The second section of the chapter provides more fine-grained case studies of two very different countries, Kenya and South Africa, showing in greater depth and detail the links between context and CPD practices. In both cases, a key issue is how to institutionalize and sustain CPD initiatives within national systems and their local structures. In our account of CPD in Africa, we argue for the specificity of the African experience, as against either absorbing Africa into an existing corpus of theory, or viewing it as exceptional and exotic. We attempt to work against these binaries in providing an account of broad patterns of CPD and specific case study examples of practices in two countries. In conclusion, despite the difficulties facing CPD in Africa, we argue against a position of Afro-pessimism, suggesting rather the importance of active engagement with the specific dynamics of state formations and their education systems.

Introduction

In his study of contemporary Africa and the legacy of late colonialism, Mahmood Mamdani (1996) argues convincingly for the specificity of the African experience. Working against the binaries of an 'abstract universalism' which would absorb an analysis of Africa into an existing broad corpus of theory, and an 'intimate particularism' which would view it as exceptional or exotic, Mamdani proposes an historical approach to understanding the specific dynamics of state formations in Africa. This is important in identifying possibilities for change, as well as avoiding 'Afro-pessimism'. The same holds true for any account of education in Africa, including the continuing professional development (CPD) of teachers.

As a continent, Africa represents considerable geographic and economic diversity. As a region, sub-Saharan Africa comprises 41 countries which form a coherent operational zone for organizations such as the World Bank. In 1998, two-thirds of the sub-Sahara's 630 million people were living in rural areas, with high levels of poverty. Manuel Castells (2000) provides a coherent but depressing analysis of Africa at the turn of the millennium. At the same time as globalization and informational capitalism are in the ascendancy, he argues, most of Africa's economies have collapsed, a number of states have disintegrated and societies are wracked by famines, epidemics, civil wars and violence. In the last two decades of the twentieth century, the relative position of sub-Saharan Africa declined *vis-à-vis* all other areas of the world in terms of trade, investment, production and consumption. Under these conditions, economic survival has been heavily dependent on international aid and foreign borrowing. Private appropriation of state resources by elites is widespread, as is a patronage system of distribution. Castells notes that many African nation states have had a 'destructive role' on their economies and societies (2000: 95–6), and in a number of cases, including Zaire, Liberia, Sierra Leone and Somalia, there has been 'the disappearance of the nation-state for all practical purposes' (2000: 104).

Avoiding the determinism of 'Afro-pessimism', Mamdani's analysis grounds these conditions in the particular state formations that developed under colonialism. He argues that colonial rule in Africa bifurcated state power between racialized civic structures and tribalized structures of customary authority. After independence, African states generally managed to achieve deracialization, but most did not succeed in dismantling the tribal powers of customary authority which colonialism had bolstered, or in establishing fully-fledged democracies. African states have both 'modern' citizens and 'traditional' subjects. In this context, economic development has proved elusive, held back by interethnic and urban–rural tensions. Mamdani argues that resolving these tensions – particularly urban–rural tensions – is the historical challenge faced by African states. This challenge will be evident in our analysis of CPD in Kenya and South Africa later in this chapter.

The chapter argues that the provision of CPD in sub-Saharan Africa needs to be understood in relation to broader issues of education, the state and development. The first section of the chapter illustrates the ways in which the purposes and foci of CPD in sub-Saharan Africa, as well as issues such as management, funding and evaluation, are shaped by these contextual forces. The second section provides more fine-grained case studies of two very different countries, Kenya and South Africa, showing in greater depth and detail the links between context and CPD practices.

Provision of CPD in sub-Saharan Africa

Given the unevenness of state formations in sub-Saharan Africa, it is not surprising that education systems are also uneven, and there are considerable differences in the nature and provision of CPD. In countries such as the Democratic Republic of Congo, where the formal education system has broken down, CPD does not exist. In similarly underdeveloped but more politically stable countries where teacher development does take place, information may be elusive because of poor record-keeping, a lack of indigenous African research and the fact that much of what is written on CPD takes the form of evaluation reports on donor projects. With reference to Africa, Lewin (1999: 4) notes that 'studies of the comparative costs and benefits of different methods of training teachers are not readily available'. Sayed (2001: 6) argues that 'effective CPD requires sustained monitoring and evaluation. In this respect, much of the literature about effective CPD tends to rely on anecdotal evidence and focus on how teachers experience CPD'. Moreover, many African countries have policies in which initial teacher education is not clearly demarcated from CPD, and CPD initiatives frequently have their origins somewhere in the inscrutable terrain between the government education departments and foreign donors. What little research there is suggests that quality of classroom supplies is important (Ross and Postlethwaite 1992), and that a combination of teacher guides and textbooks has been 'a very effective form of in-service training for poorly trained teachers' (Farrell 1993: 33). Under these conditions, a discussion on CPD in Africa is as much about the context of CPD as it is about the nature of CPD itself.

Following Boyle (1999), we argue that educational development in sub-Saharan Africa occurred in three phases. In the first phase, prior to the 1960s, formal schooling was introduced by religious organizations and colonial administrations. Schools catered for expatriates and very limited numbers of Africans. In the second phase, that of independence and between the 1960s and the 1980s, newly independent countries responded to the demand for vastly expanded educational opportunity and provision. However, population growth and financial crises severely curtailed these ambitions in the third period, which was one of austerity following the 1980s. Patterns of primary school enrolments reflect these trends: 43.2 per cent in 1960; 79.5 per cent in 1980; and 76.8 per cent in 1997 (World Bank 2001: 8). Not only the consumers of education felt the effects of financial crises. Since the 1970s, teaching as a profession has declined in status and in the real value of wages. In some countries, teachers have approached the poverty line (ILO 1991: 138). Nevertheless, in the majority of sub-Saharan countries, teacher salaries account for over 90 per cent of the education budget (Makau and Coombe 1994).

In a context of financial austerity and underdevelopment, competing claims for funding within education systems are inevitable. Where there is lack of funding for basic education, CPD is readily displaced as a priority area, and is more likely to be narrowly targeted. This is illustrated in the following comment from a study in Malawi: 'Opportunities for in-service training for teachers and tutors arise only as a means of orienting them to new syllabuses or curricula . . . There is also lack of a professional development ethos at the school level' (Kunje and Chimombo 1999: 32). Because of backlogs in teacher supply, among other more pressing priorities, the World Bank estimates that teachers 'often underpaid and underqualified, rarely achieve the support and supervision they need to be effective' (World Bank 2001: 1).

The leverage of donor aid cannot be underestimated in the establishment of educational priorities in African states, particularly since Africa is more aid-dependent than other regions. In 1997, official development assistance represented 6.7 per cent of Africa's gross national product (GNP). In 1996, 42 per cent of the $668 million Africa received in aid went to basic education (World Bank 2001: 18). Donor funding enables provision of education beyond the budgets of nation states; however, it also means that outside agencies influence education agendas for good or ill. Moreover, aid is often accompanied by other agendas, and the World Bank in particular has been heavily criticized for the human capital assumptions that underpin its aid interventions. Since the Jomtien Declaration of the World Conference on Education for All (1990) and the Dakar Framework for Action adopted at the World Education Forum (2000), more than 40 governments have prepared action plans to achieve 'Education for All', supported by donor aid. Even though pupil enrolments are declining in many countries, there is a shortage of new teachers, which means that initial teacher preparation has more immediacy than in-service education, and CDP is often not a priority.

The impact of HIV/AIDS is nothing short of devastating in Africa, which has two-thirds of the world's 33.4 million AIDS sufferers (UNAIDS 1999). With HIV/AIDS ravaging Africa to a greater extent than other continents, and with professional classes being a high-risk group, the demand on teacher supply is exacerbated. According to World Health Organization reports, life expectancy is now less than 40 in Botswana, Malawi, Mozambique and Swaziland. In Zambia, teacher deaths from AIDS-related illnesses outstrip the output of the country's training colleges. HIV/AIDS compounds the teacher supply problem in another way: 'The shorter the professional lifetime of teachers in the system the higher are the real costs of providing an adequate number of trained teachers' (Lewin 1999: 19). Again, circumstances encourage an emphasis on pre-service education and training (PRESET) rather than CPD.

Typologies of CPD

According to Fullan (1991), professional development for teachers has a poor track record because it lacks a theoretical base and coherent focus. Discussion in this chapter relies on two ideal type conceptualizations of CPD drawn from the distinction in current discourse between teacher as 'technician' and teacher as 'reflective practitioner' (Stuart and Kunje 2000: 5).

While the teacher as technician has its origin firmly in the needs of systems or institutions, the reflective practitioner has its roots in beliefs about the teacher as a person and a professional. These roots are evident in Britzman's (1991) ground-breaking study which introduced the teacher's biography to teacher education. Others, such as Zeichner (1998), have built models on the principles of personal and professional identity. In a suitably personal comment, Day observes: 'I have learned that what I am as a person should not and cannot always be entirely separated from what I am as a professional. The one is nested in the other' (1995: 110). The capacities for reflection lie in a sense of agency, realized through inquiry and CPD.

The typologies of teacher as technician (rooted in institutional or system needs) and reflective practitioner (rooted in the personal-professional domain) can be augmented by two approaches to teacher development identified by Jackson (1971, cited by Eraut 1987). The 'defect' approach to teacher development sees the teacher as being inefficient and obsolete, having had limited training, or not being up to date. The 'growth' view of teacher development is embedded in an image of teaching as a complex activity, requiring teachers to develop creative responses to the challenge of circumstance.

Our typologies are thus:

The teacher as a . . .	CPD is directed at . . .	CPD rooted in images of . . .
Technician	Institutions and systems	Teacher 'defect'
Reflective practitioner	The personal domain	Teacher 'growth'

Although the term CPD is inappropriate for descriptions of 'one-off' short courses and workshops which teachers may attend, in this chapter it is used as a convenient shorthand term for all forms of teacher development activity.

Pressures for CPD

From the discussion thus far, it is clear that we infer that CPD in Africa may assume forms that differ from models in (Western) literature. Its instrumentality alone means that in terms of the typologies above, CPD in Africa casts the teacher into the role of technician as opposed to reflective practitioner, and, we argue, is rooted in an image of teacher 'defect'.

CPD in Africa has drawn its rationale from changing national priorities that were mediated, if not overwhelmed at times, by donor priorities in terms of the scale of CPD activity. This is evident from a closer examination of the history of education in Africa outlined earlier.

In the second phase of development identified by Boyle (1999) above, the rapid expansion of education provision was accompanied by curriculum changes aimed at aligning the curriculum with the vision of newly independent nations. For example, Guinea and Ghana placed strong emphasis on using schools to promote nationalism, and curriculum structure and content were to correspond to local knowledge and needs (Harber 1989). Education was to serve the cause of socialist transformation in Zimbabwe and Mozambique; socialism and self-reliance in Tanzania; humanism in Zambia; and 'unity in diversity' to deal with ethnicity in Nigeria. As Dorsey comments, 'Strategies for achieving mass education appear to be similar throughout sub-Saharan Africa despite differing ideologies. The problems that have ensued also bear a remarkable resemblance from country to country' (1989: 40).

Inadequately supported by human and financial resources, these visions did not materialize in the forms in which they had been intended. Again, while a clear agenda was set for teacher development, this took place only in limited ways within the routine but overextended role that school inspectors could play. In a climate of financial stringency, local visions gave way to dependence on donor aid and the imperatives of globalization.

The literature on CPD presents a consensus on the desirability of a PRE-SET/in-service education and training (INSET) continuum. However, in the period of austerity from the 1980s, INSET in many African countries became a way of completing PRESET, rather than being part of a continuum. Guinea and Malawi provide examples of the use of INSET to allow untrained teachers to become qualified. In 1998, Guinea estimated that it would need 25,000 new teachers over the next 12 years to achieve its goal of Education for All. To do this, two new approaches were introduced:

- short-term, intensive summer courses leading to provisional registration, with INSET then leading to permanent certification;
- an intensive year-long programme focusing on classroom practice (with student teachers spending 30–40 per cent of time in

primary school classrooms) followed by teacher mentoring and INSET.

By August 1999, 3000 new teachers had been trained – 20 times more than the output of the year before training started (World Bank 2001: 39). Similarly, despite its title, the Malawi Integrated In-Service Teacher Education Programme (MIITEP) is actually an INSET programme which is an integral part of PRESET. This is an intensive programme designed to certify 18,000 unqualified primary teachers over two years, through a combination of three months in a residential college and 20 months teaching under supervision of headteachers, the local primary education adviser (PEA), and their college tutors. Staff from the Malawi National Examinations Board and the Teacher Development Unit have a monitoring role. During this period, students study at a distance and attend seminars within their local zone. Finally, they return to college for revision and examination (Stuart and Kunje 2000).

The Malawian ministry is also putting in place a programme aimed at reducing the number of unqualified teachers from an estimated 50 per cent in 1997 to 30 per cent in 2002, to 10 per cent by 2012. The aim is for a quality, integrated INSET programme for primary teachers, with all having at least three days of INSET per year. The intention is to strengthen inspection, INSET and advisory services (Sayed 2001).

Donor-funded projects have arguably contributed more practical CPD than state bureaucracies. Donor activity has focused strongly on development within the primary school sector, effective management and the improved teaching of English, mathematics and science. In a number of cases, donor-funded projects have promoted learner-centred pedagogy, as with the MIITEP programme described above. It could be argued that in the African context where basic education needs relegate CPD to 'add on' status, donor-funded projects often 'add on' learner-centred pedagogy to the more instrumental priorities derived from human capital theory.

Teacher as technician vs. teacher as reflective practitioner

There is empirical evidence to suggest that there is a difficulty in moving teachers from the role of technician to that of reflective practitioner. In Botswana, Tabulawa (1997) attributes the failure of reform to its oversight of historically entrenched authoritarianism on the part of teachers. The new learner-centred pedagogies threatened teachers' taken-for-granted classroom worlds. In Tabulawa's study, teachers defined teaching as a process of imparting school knowledge and making sure there was sufficient classroom order to make this possible. Students' descriptions of their roles were consistent with their understanding of learning as a process of receiving the teachers' knowledge (1997: 201). The same phenomenon has been reported in other settings. In Ghana, for example, it has been noted that:

> Despite a range of practices used by tutors, the model of teaching is fundamentally one of transmission. Copying notes and taking exams are central to the learning experience . . . In this context the attempt to introduce child-centred approaches to teaching needs careful consideration.
>
> (Ampiah *et al.* 2000: 1)

The point here is not that traditional value systems which privilege authority figures are obstacles to learner-centred reform. Rather, it is that projects aimed at producing both teacher as effective technician *and* as reflective practitioner have within them an inherent tension. This is well explained in a study conducted in Malawi:

> Current discourse in teacher education in Anglophone countries of the North/West often makes a broad distinction between 'teacher as technician' and 'teacher as reflective practitioner'. The technician is seen as having a restricted role, her job being to deliver the curriculum – which is prescribed at a higher level – as effectively as possible, while the reflective practitioner is expected to play a more extended role, that may include developing the curriculum to suit the context, evaluating and trying to improve her own practice, and mentoring new teachers.
>
> (Stuart and Kunje 2000: 5)

Teacher as technician, or the 'fidelity perspective' of curriculum implementation (Marsh 1993), means that teachers are given explicit instructions about how to go about their practice. The student is thus cast into the role of a passive receiver, and there can be little provision for school contexts in which reflective practice takes place. The fidelity perspective is antithetical to reflection, and reflection and sensitivity to context are essential if pedagogy is to be learner-centred. Without suggesting that there are stages of growth in teacher development, there is reason to suggest that CPD which conflates PRESET and INSET runs the risk of being premised on conflicting basic assumptions. In the African context the tension may be exacerbated by traditional values and historical experience about what it means to learn and to be educated. In the view of Stuart and Kunje (2000: 1):

> There was a clear tension between the 'progressive' aims of MIITEP and the didactic and authoritarian ways in which it was implemented. Some of the reasons include: the lack of basic teaching

materials, especially for science or practical work; the failure to support the tutors; the mismatch between the curriculum and student needs, as well as cultural patterns and expectations about teaching and learning. The aims of training a large number of teachers in the shortest possible time are probably incompatible with the aim of producing and supporting innovative teachers equipped to act as change agents.

Possible explanations of failure

The challenge in understanding the patterns of CPD in Africa is to correctly identify why it is that education provision is actually declining and why CPD programmes so often fail in their implementation. It is here, we suggest, that understanding state formation is crucial. In his classic study of schools in Malawi, Fuller (1991) sets out the complex role of schooling in a 'fragile state', where there are contradictions between modernization and the creation of new elites, and the continuation of tribal or customary forms of social organization which are part of the popular support base of governments. Symbolically, schooling may provide '*signals* of mass opportunity and meritocratic rules of getting ahead' (1991: xvii) without attacking pre-existing economic interests and social organization. 'Whether children are actually learning . . . does not really worry the political actors. The fragile state's primary agenda is to symbolically and visibly penetrate the rural hinterlands and urban shanty-towns' (1991: xvii) while simultaneously protecting its support base in tribal or customary social groups.

Chabal and Daloz (1999) go further than this to suggest that it is possible for a country's education system to decline, for educational development to be insignificant, and at the same time for the members of a large number of (informal) networks to continue to benefit from the failures of the system. Manifestation of this is evident in the high rates of return obtained by elites from limited access to secondary and higher education, particularly in a context of globalization. It may even be true that a country's educational failure is, in this respect at least, more 'profitable' for this group than is 'development' and 'progress'. Certainly, Boyle's (1999) case studies of Kinshasa (Congo), Yaoundé (Cameroon) and Nairobi (Kenya) lead to the conclusion that the collapse of public sector education and the ascendancy of private schooling contribute to shaping the social class character of the civil societies emerging throughout the region.

These studies support our argument that the state in Africa and its relationship to education have historically specific dynamics, and models and expectations of CPD need to be understood in a context which often differs from CPD in states in the West/North. A broad and generalized view of CPD in a range of countries does not readily yield a view of 'best practice'. It is for this reason that we turn to a more selective, contextualized view of 'best practice' in Kenya and South Africa, where we have been actively involved in CDP programmes.[1]

Case studies: Kenya and South Africa

Kenya and South Africa present fascinating contrasts. In African terms, Kenya, having become independent in 1963, has a long history as an independent nation freed of colonial rule. As such, it has had time to settle national priorities and to establish educational policies and practices. In contrast, South Africa, having overthrown apartheid and embraced democracy in 1994, is the continent's most recent 'independent' country, and is still emerging from the phase of policy development. While South Africa is currently reforming in terms of democracy and development, Kenya, despite its advantages, has slipped into stagnant or negative growth, and apparently also into the more pervasive net of corruption. While Kenya has had difficulty in retaining donor commitment, South Africa has been 'inundated' with international aid (Sayed and Jansen 2001: 1). Current annual donor aid to South African education is estimated at R500 million to R1 billion, most of this directed at school reform, including teacher development and whole-school projects (Taylor 2001). The two cases yield insights into the way in which CPD is conceptualized and enacted in very *different* African states. Of the two countries, Kenya is perhaps more representative of sub-Saharan Africa. South Africa is worthy of consideration partly because of its distinctiveness.

Kenya

The context
During the immediate post-independence period after 1963, the expansion of education was a priority for the government of Kenya and indeed there was considerable success up to the mid-1980s, when the gross enrolment ratio reached 102 per cent. As Kenya's economic performance has declined since the mid-1980s, the government has been unable to sustain the promising developments within education of the 1960s and 1970s. Growth within the education sector has ceased, and access to education and retention within the sector has declined in real terms. The situation has been exacerbated by internal inefficiencies throughout the education sector, a lack of strategic planning and a failure on the part of government to prioritize its educational expenditure. While the gross size of the education budget has increased over the last 15 years, the percentage being spent on salaries and administration has increased too, to a level where today over 92 per cent of the education budget is allocated

to salary expenditure. As part of the wider impact of the structural adjustment policies imposed upon Kenya in the latter part of the 1980s, formal cost-sharing was introduced in primary education in 1988. A dramatic decline in the gross enrolment ratio followed, to the position today where it stood at 87 per cent in 2001. Currently there are an estimated 1.8 million eligible primary school children and 1.5 million secondary school children not in school. All the millennium education development goal indicators are in decline, in spite of Kenya's commitment to the Jomtien and Dakar protocols.

CPD in relation to priorities

Developing and implementing a coherent strategic plan for CDP in Kenya has never been a national priority, in spite of a relatively impressive record of short in-service training of teachers at various times. CPD remains a relatively *ad hoc* response to 'events' and, in the terms we have set out above, is instrumentally tied to a model of teacher as technician. The primary consequence of this is that funding for CPD has been erratic and irregular.

Increasing pressure for PRESET militates further against CPD. The Kenyan teacher population stands at around 220,000 teachers, with 65 per cent working in the primary education subsector. Its biggest challenge is HIV/AIDS, with a loss of some 6500 teachers annually. From a formal training perspective, it is clear that teacher training colleges and universities will be unable to cope with this kind of attrition rate over the medium to long term. Already, over 1.3 million college students and schoolchildren in Kenya have lost their parents, with the impact still wider as young children leave school to care for family members.

Although CDP has not been a priority for the government of Kenya, a draft policy framework and strategic plan have recently been prepared as part of an externally funded donor initiative. This will be considered as an example of 'best practice'.

The Schools-based Teacher Development Programme (SbTD)

The SbTD emerged out of UK government support in the education sector to Kenya during the 1990s. Funded by the Department for International Development (DIFD), the Strengthening Primary Education project (SPRED) commenced in 1991. Consistent with Jomtien, SPRED aimed at improved access of all Kenyan children to primary education; and in alignment with human capital theory, at raising the quality of teaching and learning in the key subjects of English, mathematics and science. The strategy was to institutionalize primary level in-service training based in teacher advisory centres (TACs) by upgrading training, resources and administrative support.

Sixty-three new TACs were built and resourced, enabling 1200 trained tutors to support teachers. According to the evaluation report, SPRED was successful in its impact on the professional development of teachers, but unsuccessful in ensuring the institutionalization and operation of TACs and the strengthening of structural links between PRESET and INSET (Cambridge Education Consultants 1997). Failure to institutionalize the project is a familiar theme in the evaluation literature. The weakness of cascade training also emerged as a familiar problem.

Account was taken of SPRED weaknesses in a successor project, SPRED 2. Experience in the field also suggested that INSET in the form of management training for headteachers would support and complement the SPRED project. To this end, the Primary School Management project (PRISM) was initiated. PRISM (1996–2000) was to improve the quality of primary education by increasing the efficiency of primary school management, simultaneously contributing to improved attitudes towards children, and especially girls and children with special needs. Training was underpinned by modules developed by a lead team, and implemented through a 'strengthened' cascade system. From the outset, the project was strongly research driven. Again, evaluation showed that although the project had impacted meaningfully on headteachers and schools, sustainability and institutionalization were not achieved (Barasa *et al.* 2000).

SPRED 3 followed. One of the key components of this programme, which commenced in 1999, was the SbTD, a programme which aimed at developing a national system of school-based teacher development. Key outputs from this programme were the development of a national policy and strategic plan for CDP, and the setting up of appropriate structures and modalities for the delivery of a distance education programme for primary schoolteachers. This programme represents a vindication of donor perseverance as well as attention to research and evaluation accompanying this particular project activity.

A national policy document has been developed, and in line with the strategic plan which has emerged,[2] a national in-service unit has been established within the Ministry of Education, Science and Technology (MoEST). At a strategic level, the MoEST INSET unit has set up a systems framework to deal with CPD which includes: needs analysis; programme design and development; materials development training and support; information flow; teacher support services (recruitment, tutoring, counselling and training support services); quality assurance (monitoring and evaluation); accreditation; and consultancy support.

However, implementation of the programme has been slow. Indeed, it took nearly 18 months for the development team to negotiate the materials printing contracts.[3] In September 2001, the first group of teachers was registered on the programme. The MoEST has developed a phased programme of introduction, and began 2002 operating in three of the nation's 72 districts. An elaborate system of tutor support has been developed based on the teacher advisory centres set up during the course of the SPRED 1 project. Each school has selected three teachers to enrol in the programme. These are lead teachers in English, mathematics and science. In the course of the five-month programme they will create school-based subject teams and will commence mentoring their colleagues. Projections are that within the next two years, some 50,000 primary schoolteachers will have completed the first phase of the programme. Discussions are in progress with the university sector to accredit the learning. Consideration is also being given to linking this training more closely with outside service providers, in particular the universities, thus freeing the MoEST from micro development and management of the process and leaving it free to concentrate on policy, strategic and quality issues.

From informal observation it would appear that what has been developed and initiated is impressive. The preparation for the programme engaged stakeholders in a creative and innovative development process. Schools and teachers have expressed considerable support for the initiative, the INSET unit is operating, the materials have received high praise from international distance education experts, and the monitoring and evaluation procedures being put in place are honouring the need for a bottom-up approach, starting with impact at the teaching and learning end.

Conceptually, the SbTD has received favourable comment. Basing the innovation in the workplace contexts of teachers and using a distance learning mode of delivery, it aims to facilitate in-school impact on teaching and learning. The emphasis of the materials is on reflective practice, and while this is problematic in the context in which many work, the programme will induct teachers into a process of collaborative teaching which facilitates reflection.

The four modules encourage the teachers to focus on their classroom experiences, and to shift their pedagogy from mainly didactic approaches to activity-centred approaches. The provision of teaching and learning materials through the government of Kenya/DFID-funded textbook programme is ensuring that adequate resources are available.

In sum, SbTD appears to be a sophisticated model that embodies the combination of school-based, tutor-supported, distance mode strategies typical of most CPD initiatives in Africa. In addition, it also has the promise and support to move beyond teacher as technician to teacher as reflective practitioner. Two critical questions present themselves, however. First, will the programme succeed in bringing about improved quality of teaching and learning? Second, can the programme be sustained, whether by the MoEST or any other institution, or will it go the way of many development initiatives once external support is removed?

These are questions which confront any development initiative. Clearly, a combination of many factors is necessary to create and sustain an environment for success. Hallack (1998) points to the questionable impact of the SbTD type of programme, arguing that working habits acquired in the early stages of schooling by persons who become teachers – overdependence on memorization, failure to identify symbols and to link them with their concrete manifestations, intellectual passivity and the uncritical acceptance of state-ments as facts – tend to stay with learners to some degree throughout their learning or teaching career. Experience in school reform shows that it is extremely hard to change the core activities of teaching and learning, and particularly to change the culture of teaching towards greater collaborative relationships among students, teachers and other potential partners. Yet, teachers can acquire new ideas, techniques and knowledge, and there is plenty of evidence to show that this happens when information is not only relevant, but also specific enough to be seen to be relevant, and when the transfer of information occurs on an inter- and intrapersonal basis, and when there is sufficient follow-up in the implementation phase. We also know that new ideas, changed practice and enriched knowledge can take root if the organiza-tional framework in which it is being acquired is supportive.

Turning to Kenya specifically, to the broader educational context, and to education development, a stark fact emerges: the process of educational reform in Kenya is, and has been, extremely slow. After the heady immediate post-independence period, and indeed up until the beginning of the 1980s, when impressive gains were made in widening access to education and to providing affordable education of relatively good quality, the situation has deteriorated to a position where access and retention rates are in decline. It is necessary to question, as Bredie and Beeharry (1998) suggest, the policy inten-tion of government, and to find reasons for the gap between rhetoric and practice.

Penny and Ward (2001) argue that what is evident in Kenya is a reluctance to introduce in-depth reforms, weak public administration and institutions and an aversion to the institutionalization of bureaucratic practices. They illustrate, in the case of Kenya, the argument made by Chabal and Daloz that it is possible for an education system to decline, for educational development to be insignificant, and for a number of informal networks to continue to benefit from the failures of the system. In short, the form of the state impacts upon its delivery of CPD, and in this context, the continuing success of SPRED 3 would represent a significant break in pattern.

South Africa

Policy framework
South Africa's transition from apartheid to democracy in 1994 involved mas-sive changes to the education system, some of which could be speedily achieved, others of which have yet to take full form. Under apartheid, provi-sion of education, including teacher education, was racially skewed and highly unequal. Although a strong PRESET/INSET divide was evident, policy on this was largely non-existent or invisible. In the height of struggles against apart-heid education, the chief agent of professional development, the Subject

Advisory Service, was caught up in turmoil and lost legitimacy to the extent that it was no longer able to operate in many schools. The pressure for instrumentalist CPD is clear in post-apartheid South Africa, as in other parts of Africa: current estimates are that of 350,000 teachers in public schools, about 86,000 of which are underqualified (Bot and Schindler 2001). A major nationwide research initiative in 1998 reported poor teacher quality, low morale and poor examination results (see Taylor and Vinjevold 1999).

Restructuring the racially based system proved to be easier than its 'reculturing'; policy formulation simpler than policy implementation; and bringing new staff into existing bureaucracies more straightforward than ensuring the smooth running of the new system. On the one hand, the development of new policies preceded the collapse of apartheid, and an impressive set of policies is now in place. These are widely acknowledged as being 'state of the art' (Sayed and Jansen 2001: 1). Policies are informed by the values within the constitution: liberty, democracy, justice, equality and peace. On the other hand, achieving change through the system has proved difficult. The costs of equity and redress are enormous, and under conditions of neo-liberal globalization, the new government shifted away from its initial redistributive goals towards a form of self-imposed structural adjustment, which entailed curbs on social spending (including spending on education) and tighter accountability measures.

Some of the broad fundamentals for coherent teacher development and CPD have been in place since the early years of the new government. Key policies are:

- A *National Qualifications Framework* (NQF) which is committed to lifelong learning. In this approach, PRESET and INSET are viewed 'as continuous processes' (Department of Education 1995).
- The *Norms and Standards for Educators*, which provides a flexible, generative basis for the construction of qualifications and for the professional development of educators.
- The *Code of Conduct for Educators* which regulates the ethical conduct and professional discipline of all educators registered with the South African Council for Educators (SACE).
- The *Manual for Developmental Appraisal* which sets out appraisal procedures, criteria and instruments for all levels of educators.
- The *Duties and Responsibilities of Educators* which provides job descriptions against which educators may be legally appointed, promoted and appraised.

Education policies have symbolic, material, regulative and procedural functions. In the symbolic function, the 'ideal' educator is described; regulative policies limit the behaviour and actions of groups and individuals; and procedural policies specify who is to take action and through which mechanisms. The policies described above are powerful at the symbolic level. Collectively they present a common and consistent vision of education and the teaching profession. In particular, they are conceptually united by a shared language of teacher roles and competencies, combined with the principles of liberal, democratic education within a culture of human rights (Barasa and Mattson 1998).

In relation to CPD, strengths are evident in the policies: the importance of CPD is affirmed; procedures for effecting CPD reflect democratic and other constitutional principles; and stakeholder involvement ensures the relevance of identified needs. Providers have flexibility in constructing qualifications, and there is provision for quality controls. Funding has been provided for, and teachers are committed to undertake 80 hours of INSET every year.

Nevertheless, the sobering South African situation is that 'The new system exists on paper and in the activities of a broad range of agents, but it has not yet begun to operate' (Parker forthcoming). A number of reasons for this have been suggested. Importantly, Parker argues that there is a proliferation of different players and stakeholder bodies in teacher education, whose roles and responsibilities are not fully clarified, and this has 'undermined the kind of executive decision-making that is necessary for efficient management and implementation'. Another reason is that the restructuring of teacher education as part of higher education is not yet complete, and major policies are not yet in place for funding and the articulation of programmes (Ogude 2001). A trenchant criticism of the policy/practice gap is put forward by Jansen: 'Every single case of education policy-making demonstrates, in different ways, the preoccupation of the state with settling policy struggles in the political domain rather than in the realm of practice' (2001: 272). This criticism that policy has been aimed at achieving political legitimacy and symbolism comes close to Fuller's theory of the importance of 'looking modern' for fragile developing states.

In terms of the different functions of policy, the symbolic certainly has a legitimate place. In the light of the Kenyan experience, however, the key question is whether this symbolism is merely strategic façade. We have seen evidence to suggest that it is not. South Africa does appear very different to Kenya in this respect, as the policy panoply for the regulative and procedural functions of policy are firmly in place. In our view, the fact that the system has not yet come to life is attributable to the complexity of its participatory structures and the proliferation of stakeholder groups, rather than the interests of more or less homogenous dominant power elites. In other words, forms of democratization are slowing progress, rather than domination by traditionally based elites. In the terms of Mamdani's (1996) analysis, the state formations in South Africa and Kenya are differently configured in the three dimensions of deracialization, detribalization/democratization and economic development.

They have different legacies and different distinctive features, and the terrain for CPD is different as well.

That said, the weakness of the South African policy framework for CPD is manifest. The locus of responsibility for CPD has been dispersed vertically downwards to provincial and local levels as well as horizontally across stakeholder interest groups. What conceptual form it might then take, and whether agreement can be reached on implementation, are open questions. There is clearly a risk of nothing materializing at all. Under these circumstances, a potential strength is less readily apparent, and that is the possibilities that the framework is conducive to initiatives being developed outside of the state. An example of this is the emergence of a recently approved national qualification for serving educators, the National Professional Diploma in Education (NPDE), which had its origins in an attempt on the part of a teacher union to assist its underqualified members to obtain accreditation for an INSET programme run through a non-government organization (NGO) (see Allais 2001). However, while the NPDE is exemplary in upholding profession-defined standards and values, these standards and values are instrumentally construed.

Projects

In the interregnum while a comprehensive teacher education policy is awaited, much CPD is being conducted in the form of projects. Given the instrumentalism informing INSET and the amount of donor funding available, the dominance of CPD in project guise is to be expected. We provide two examples of CPD to illustrate practices.

First, the introduction of a new outcomes-based curriculum for schools ('Curriculum 2005') was accompanied by a national in-service programme for teachers. This programme warrants consideration here not necessarily as an example of 'best practice', but because of its sheer scale and importance. It provides an interesting reflection of the problems of mounting an ambitious programme aimed instrumentally at achieving radical transformation in the quickest possible time.

The overall programme consisted of a national pilot project as well as an in-service programme for 300,000 teachers. An NGO was contracted to induct 20 officials from each of the nine provinces into a basic understanding of Curriculum 2005 (C2005); these 'master trainers' would then cascade this knowledge to district officials; finally, district officials would cascade the information to teachers. Policy documents, illustrative learning programmes and learner support materials were distributed as part of the training, and an evaluation and monitoring mechanism were planned.

Pilots were conducted in a number of schools in each province. However, timeframes meant that lessons learnt from the pilots were too late to impact on full-scale implementation. Workshops with teachers were conducted as short, three- to five-day sessions, and in a ministerial review of C2005 provinces and teachers were strongly critical of the timeframe, planning and execution of the implementation (Chisholm 2000: 52). Despite attempts to improve the cascade, the training was widely criticized for doing little more than simply telling teachers about the structure of the new curriculum and familiarizing them with new terminology (for example, teachers become 'educators' and pupils become 'learners').

A finer-grained view of the process is provided by a study of implementation in one provincial region (Potenza and Monyokolo 1999). Teacher development began in 1997, with training commissioned to an NGO. Course materials included effective posters, a facilitator's manual and a workbook for every teacher. Workshop activity involved a curriculum 'learning area' and a packet of potato crisps as a resource. The intention was to show that educators could be innovative and move away from being textbook-bound. However, the effect was to underplay the use of texts – this in a context where teachers often lacked adequate resources. Moreover, the training did not provide an adequate basis for teachers to cascade the ideas to other staff, leading to the predictable problem of 'dilution'. This was exacerbated by lack of ongoing support and development when teachers were back in schools after workshop training. One reason for this was simply the incapacity of departmental officials to service large numbers of schools.

Behind the technical difficulties of the INSET programme lay the heritage of the past. As a result of apartheid education, many teachers had themselves had inferior schooling and basic teacher training. The effects of this are evident in an impact study of the materials distributed to all schools to induct them into new governance and curriculum policies. The study found severe 'dropoff' effects from national to provincial level, from province to district, and from district to schools. More profoundly, teachers 'readily admitted in focus groups that they do not like to read' (Palmer Development Group 1999: vi). Teachers repeatedly asked for practical classroom demonstrations (live or video), actual lesson plans and practical support materials. This finding is congruent with other experiences in INSET. For example, a project aimed at empowering teachers through action research found that teachers were unfamiliar with their role as curriculum developers and actively resisted the role, preferring demonstrations that they could copy (Walker 1994).

When teacher development is aimed instrumentally at hastily achieving a 'new' teacher to enable a new transformatory curriculum in a context in which many teachers have a low base of skills and competencies – and, possibly, different cultural understandings – the way in which teachers appropriate the new paradigm may be antithetical to its premises and aims. Linked to this problem is that sincere commitment to change imperils objective views of real achievement in CPD. Reports or 'evaluations' carried out by education departments, where they exist, are sometimes uncritically at odds with more serious research endeavour. For example, a 97-page publication entitled *Curriculum 2005: The Story of the Grade 1 Pilot Project* is unabashedly celebratory. The fact that it was compiled by the same NGO that conducted the C2005 training suggests the potential hazards of state education departments 'outsourcing' their core responsibilities.

In such a context, challenges to successful CPD clearly go beyond the employment of good models and successful achievement of project inputs. Thus it is encouraging that the Ministerial Review Committee identified the need for a more coherent national strategy for teacher development (Chisholm 2000: 2). Certainly, lessons learnt from the C2005 national in-service programme have the potential to guide future CDP if they are taken on board in future interventions.

The second example is a project that could claim to represent 'best practice': the 'Educator Empowerment and Curriculum Materials Development' project operating in KwaZulu-Natal (Harley 2001). Based on provincial 'ownership' of the project, it was a partnership between the KwaZulu-Natal Department of Education and Culture, a consortium of eight NGOs and a large national school development project.

The project aimed at improving the quality of curriculum practice through increasing the capacity and confidence of educators in using and developing learner support materials (LSMs). In this sense, although 'reflection' was not part of project vocabulary, it was attempting to move teachers beyond the role of teacher as technician. Grades 4 to 9 in 3500 of the poorest schools were targeted, and materials were to be developed in four curriculum areas involving language and the sciences. In Phase 1 of implementation, the trainers were trained and materials developed. Phase 2 was concerned with training through the second tier of the cascade and with the establishment of support networks.

Notable successes were achieved by the two-year project, including the following (Harley 2001):

- its aims were supported and acclaimed by educators and officials in the provincial department;
- it was conceptualized as belonging to the provincial department and it set up partnerships between providers in a way that made good use of available resources and expertise;
- it established appropriate structures, networks and records for efficient administration;
- it achieved significant counterpart contributions to support the project in addition to meeting contractual requirements with respect to inputs;
- it involved educators from the most disadvantaged schools in the production of teachers' guides;

- in a difficult context, it developed and produced a range of quality materials that would become a valuable legacy of the project;
- it was reflective and responded to problems creatively by seeking ways of overcoming difficulties and obstacles;
- it developed an innovative and effective system of distributing materials to schools;
- it instituted measures to counter predictable dilution of the cascade;
- it conducted effective training programmes;
- it succeeded in getting across the idea of resource-based education.

However, successes were at the level of project *inputs* and *favourable perceptions* rather than in terms of *impact*. Gains were fragile, and resided at the level of the individual, not the system. Despite its successes, the project was not ultimately institutionalized by the provincial department which was supposed to 'own' it. Despite exemplary conceptualization and design, there was a major question mark about impact. A profound problem was that teachers focused on LSMs as teaching aids, without providing adequate learning experiences which the materials could support. Unwittingly, the materials were supporting a pedagogy that was itself not adequately promoting conceptual learning and did not take learners beyond their everyday knowledge and understanding.

This is not an unsympathetic view. The new education policies require traditional rural schools to undergo fundamental changes that threaten the foundations on which their cohesion and effectiveness is built, leaving many schools with a profound sense of displacement. Teachers in these schools adopt strategies to engage with a policy system that is not aligned with their personal and professional identities. Mattson and Harley (forthcoming) suggest that teacher education policy and providers reinforce teachers' strategies of mimicry by trying to reform teacher identities in the image of a first world, modern global citizen or 'universal subject' rather than attending to their more pressing and practical needs.

The two examples of CPD in South Africa provided here illustrate the immense task of transforming South African education – including CPD – from its apartheid legacy of profoundly unequal and inadequate provision. This process of transformation requires strong political will as well as capacity building and institutional development in engaging with the smallest units of the system: teachers in their classrooms.

Conclusion

We began this chapter with Mamdani's argument for the specificity of the African experience, as against either absorbing Africa into an existing corpus of theory or viewing it as exceptional and exotic. We have attempted to work against these binaries in providing an account of broad patterns of CPD and specific case study examples of practices in two countries. In relating CPD to broader issues of the state and development in Africa, we hope to contribute other sets of experiences to the corpus of theory on CPD.

More specifically, the experiences of CPD in Kenya and South Africa suggest the importance of state formations and their institutional operations in securing a future for CPD initiatives. Even where there is good framework policy, as in South Africa, limitations in strategic implementation and fiscal capacity may jeopardize CPD programmes. Where a sound policy framework does not exist, as in Kenya, and there is also lack of strategic and fiscal capacity, sustainability of CPD programmes is virtually impossible to achieve. In both cases, donor funding has enabled important CPD initiatives to be started, and the key issue is how these might be institutionalized within the national systems and their local structures. Unless education departments take ownership and responsibility for these CPD programmes and find ways of absorbing and operationalizing them within their own institutions, sustainability will always be at risk. That said, our case studies provide evidence of human agency and a degree of initiative that eschews pessimistic determinism in looking to possible futures for CPD in Africa.

Notes

1   Alan Penny and Ken Harley draw on first-hand experience of CDP in Kenya, and all three authors draw on first-hand experience in South Africa.
2   In spite of external budgetary support for this unit, the policy and strategic plan remains unapproved a year after it was developed.
3   One positive outcome has been a refinement of procurement rules and procedures within the MoEST.

References

Allais, S. (2001) What are learnerships? An overview of learnerships and their benefits, *Open Learning Through Distance Education*, 7(1): 18–19.

Ampiah, J., Fletcher, J., Kutor, N. and Sokpe, B. (2000) Learning to teach in Ghana: an evaluation of curriculum delivery. Discussion paper, Centre for International Education, University of Sussex Institute of Education, http://www.sussex.ac.uk/usie/muster/list.html (accessed 16 Nov 2001).

Barasa, F.S. and Mattson, E. (1998) The roles, regulation and professional development of educators in South Africa: a critical analysis of four policy documents, *Journal of Education*, 23: 41–72.

Barasa, F.S., Harley, K. and Kaabwe, E.S.M. (2000) Primary school management project: an evaluation of the Kenyan Primary School Management project (PRISM), 1995–2000. Unpublished evaluation report produced for DFID.

Bot, M. and Schindler, J. (2001) Macro-indicators 1998: an update, in CEPD *Transformation of the South African schooling system*. Johannesburg: Centre for Education Policy Development, Evaluation and Management.

Boyle, P.M. (1999) *Class Formation and Civil Society: The Politics of Education in Africa*. Aldershot: Ashgate.

Bredie, J.W.B. and Beeharry, G.K. (1998) School enrolment decline in sub-Saharan Africa: beyond the supply constraint. World Bank discussion paper no. 395. Washington, DC: World Bank.

Britzman, D.P. (1991) *Practice Makes Perfect: A Critical Study of Learning to Teach*. Albany, NY: State University of New York Press.

Cambridge Education Consultants (1997) *Strengthening Primary Education in Kenya: An Evaluation of the Strengthening Primary Education (SPRED) Project, Kenya, 1991–1996*. London: Evaluation Department, DFID.

Castells, M. (2000) *The Information Age, Vol III: End of Millennium*. Oxford: Blackwell.

Chabal, P. and Daloz, J.P. (1999) *Africa Works: Disorder as Political Instrument*. Oxford: Indiana University Press.

Chisholm, L. (2000) *A South African Curriculum for the Twenty First Century: Report of the Review Committee on Curriculum 2005*. Pretoria: Ministry of Education.

Day, C. (1995) Leadership and professional development: developing reflective practice, in H. Busher and R. Saran (eds) *Managing Teachers as Professionals in Schools*. London: Kogan Page.

Department of Education (1995) White Paper on education and training (notice 196), *Government Gazette*, 357: 1632.

Dorsey, B.J. (1989) Educational development and reform in Zimbabwe, *Comparative Education Review*, 33(1): 40–58.

Eraut, M. (1987) Inservice teacher education, in M.J. Dunkin (1987) *The International Encyclopaedia of Teaching and Teacher Education*. Oxford: Pergamon.

Farrell, J.P. (1993) *International lessons for school effectiveness: the view from the developing world*, in J.P. Farrell and J.B. Oliveira (eds) *Teachers in Developing Countries: Improving Effectiveness and Managing Costs*. Washington, DC: World Bank, EDI seminar series.

Fullan, M. (1991) *The New Meaning of Educational Change*. New York: Teachers College Press.

Fuller, B. (1991) *Growing-up Modern: The Western State Builds Up Third-world Schools*. New York: Routledge.

Hallack, J. (1998) Education and globalization, *International Institute for Education Planning*, 26: 1–25.

Harber, C. (1989) *Politics in African Education*. London: Macmillan.

Harley, K. (2001) The Zikhulise Educator Empowerment and Curriculum Materials Development Project: summative evaluation of a project of the KwaZulu-Natal

Department of Education and Culture funded by the United States Agency for International Development. Unpublished evaluation report conducted for USAID.

ILO (International Labour Office) (1991) *Teachers in Developing Countries – A Survey of Employment Conditions*. Geneva: International Labour Office.

Kunje, D. and Chimombo, J. (1999) *Malawi: a baseline study of the teacher education system*. Discussion paper, Centre for International Education, University of Sussex Institute of Education, http://www.sussex.ac.uk/usie/muster/list.html (accessed 15 Nov 2001).

Lewin, K.M. (1999) Counting the cost of teacher education: cost and quality issues. Discussion paper, Centre for International Education, University of Sussex Institute of Education, http://www.sussex.ac.uk/usie/muster/list.html (accessed 10 Nov 2001).

Makau, B. and Coombe, C. (1994) *Teacher morale and motivation in sub-Saharan Africa: making practical improvements*. Unpublished document produced for Donors to Africa Working Group on the Teaching Profession.

Mamdani, M. (1996) *Citizen and Subject: Contemporary Africa and the Legacy of Late Colonialism*. Princeton, NJ: Princeton University Press.

Marsh, C.J. (1993) *Key Concepts for Understanding Curriculum*. London: Falmer.

Mattson, L. and Harley, K. (2003) Teacher identity and strategic mimicry in the policy/practice gap, in K. Lewin, M. Samuel and Y. Sayed (eds) *Changing Patterns of Teacher Education in South Africa: Policy, Practice and Prospects*, pp. 284–305. Sandown: Heinemann.

Ogude, N.A. (2001) An assessment of the implications of curriculum and academic programme development on administrative, academic and financial systems of higher education institutions, in M. Breier (ed.) *Curriculum Restructuring in Higher Education in Post-apartheid South Africa*. Bellville: University of the Western Cape.

Parker, B. (forthcoming) Roles and responsibilities, institutional landscapes and curriculum mindscapes: a partial view of teacher education policy in South Africa: 1990 to 2000, in K. Lewin, M. Samuel, and Y. Sayed (eds) *Changing Patterns of Teacher Education in South Africa: Policy, Practice and Prospects*.

Palmer Development Group (1999) Impact assessment and perception audit of national communication directorate materials. Unpublished report produced in association with Resource Development Consultants and the University of Natal.

Penny, A. and Ward, M. (2001) Why do education policies in East Africa fail? What's changing? Unpublished paper presented at the Oxford Conference on International Development in Education, September 2001.

Potenza, E. and Monyokolo, M. (1999) A destination without a map: premature implementation of Curriculum 2005? in J. Jansen and P. Christie (eds) *Changing Curriculum: Studies on Outcomes-based Education in South Africa*. Cape Town: Juta.

Ross, K. and Postlethwaite, T.N. (1992) *Indicators of the Quality of Education: A Summary of a National Study of Primary Schools in Zimbabwe*, research report no. 96. Paris: IIEP.

Sayed, Y. (2001) Continuing professional development and education policy: characteristics, conditions and change. Unpublished discussion paper presented at Putting the Teacher at the Centre Conference, Pretoria, 19–21 October.

Sayed, Y. and Jansen, J.D. (eds) (2001) *Implementing Education Policies*. Cape Town: University of Cape Town.

Stuart, J.S. and Kunje, D. (2000) The Malawi Integrated In-Service Teacher Education Project: an analysis of the curriculum and its delivery in the colleges. Discussion paper, Centre for International Education, University of Sussex Institute of Education, http://www.sussex.ac.uk/usie/muster/list.html (accessed 14 Nov 2001).

Tabulawa, R. (1997) Pedagogical classroom practice and the social context: the case of Botswana, *International Journal of Educational Development*, 17(2): 189–204.

Taylor, N. (2001) How should government, donors, NGOs and teacher education providers relate in promoting school reform? Unpublished paper presented at Putting the Teacher at the Centre Conference, Pretoria, 19–21 October.

Taylor, N. and Vinjevold, P. (eds) (1999) *Getting Learning Right: Report of the President's Education Initiative Research Project*. Johannesburg: Joint Education Trust.

UNAIDS (1999) *AIDS Epidemic Update: December 1999*. Geneva: United Nations.

Walker, M. (1994) Professional development through action research in township primary schools in South Africa, *International Journal of Educational Development*, 14(1): 65–73.

World Bank (2001) *A Chance to Learn: Knowledge and Finance for Education in Sub-Saharan Africa*. Washington: World Bank.

Zeichner, K. (1998) The New Scholarship in Teacher Education, *Educational Researcher*, 28(9): 4–15.

8 Teachers' networks: a new approach to the professional development of teachers in Singapore

David Tripp

Singapore's education system is currently in a period of massive change that began in the mid-1990s when it became clear that a cheap, disciplined and trainable workforce would no longer sustain Singapore's economic growth. It will continue throughout the present decade as the education system develops ways to meet the challenges of globalization, new technology and the knowledge economy. The new direction was first clearly outlined by Singapore's Prime Minister, Goh Chok, in his 1997 address to participants at the Seventh International Conference on Thinking.

Introduction

> The old formulae for success are unlikely to prepare our young for the new circumstances and new problems they will face ... We must ensure that our young can think for themselves, so that the next generation can find their own solutions to whatever problems they can face. Singapore's vision for meeting this challenge for the future is encapsulated in four words: '*Thinking Schools, Learning Nation*'. It is a vision for a total learning environment, including schools, teachers, parents, workers, companies, community organisations and government.
>
> (Goh 1997: 16)

The Prime Minister of Singapore's speech in 1997 marked the start of many initiatives and programmes that the Singapore Ministry of Education has introduced to produce learning outcomes beyond the mastery of content at which the system has hitherto been so successful. Achieving changed learning outcomes requires teacher change, for it is difficult to imagine how teachers who are unable to work in teams would be able to effectively help their students do collaborative project work, or how teachers who do not reflect in order to continuously improve their practice could help students become effective lifelong learners. As the Prime Minister noted, change at both the whole-school and individual levels was necessary:

> Thinking Schools will also redefine the role of teachers. Every school must be a model learning organisation. Teachers and principals will constantly look out for new ideas and practices, and continuously refresh their own knowledge. Teaching will itself be a learning profession, like any other knowledge-based profession of the future.
>
> (Goh 1997: 22)

The focus on the *thinking* teacher is a major shift for Singapore. In the early 1980s, it could be argued, Singapore adopted a more 'teacher-proof curriculum' approach in its attempt to improve the quality of its education. This was necessary at that time, due largely to the relatively small number of graduates in its teaching force, but it is not sufficient to meet the present challenges. Central to the Ministry's initiatives, therefore, is the recognition that in order to achieve the reforms envisaged, its own processes of staff development have also to change. To set up processes that 'value competencies which are built up through experience, practice, sharing and continual learning' (Teo 2001: 10) is a very radical reform in a system in which staff development is still largely a matter of performance appraisal identifying deficits to be remedied through externally provided training.

Equally radical to an essentially hierarchical command system is the requirement that the school have 'an environment that makes ... self-questioning and self-initiated improvement strategies possible' (Singapore Ministry of Education 2000: 9). Unsurprisingly, such changes are uneven and produce a number of contradictions because change processes are located within the current system. So while the Ministry of Education has continued to require staff to attend training courses related to the new initiatives, it has also recognized that:

> teachers will not and cannot be merely told what to do. Subject specialists have tried it . . . Administrators have tried it. Legislators have tried it. Teachers are not assembly line operators, and will not so behave. Further, they have no need, except in rare instances, to fall back on defiance as a way of not heeding. There are a thousand ingenious ways in which commands on what and how to teach can, will, and must be modified or circumvented in the actual moments of teaching.
>
> (Schwab 1983: 242)

In late 1997 the Ministry of Education established the Teachers' Network (TN) in order to develop in Singapore schools what Fullan and Hargreaves (1991) called *'interactive professionalism'* by enabling those teachers and schools ready to benefit from professional development activities by applying leverage on the experiential and tacit knowledge of teachers to move away from the current competencies-based training approach to teacher professional development.

The TN recognized that the 'Thinking Schools, Learning Nation' vision of Singaporeans as effective 'thinkers' and lifelong learners could not be achieved through the learning of new skills or facts alone, but only through changed habits of mind and teachers who could expertly model the desired behaviours. The professional development activities of the TN have therefore sought to cultivate collaborative inquiry to increase teachers' individual capacity to learn, manage knowledge and value diversity, thereby increasing both individual and organizational capacity to manage continuous improvement.

This chapter describes how the TN has begun to do these things, the assumptions behind its strategies and some of its achievements thus far.

Vision and mission

The vision and mission of the TN are stated as follows:

- *Vision:* a fraternity of reflective teachers dedicated to excellent practice through a network of support, professional exchange and learning.
- *Mission:* to serve as a catalyst and support for teacher-initiated development through sharing, collaboration and reflection, leading to self-mastery, excellent practice and fulfilment.

These statements were not given, of course, but inspired by the work of others, principally Peter Senge's notion of the learning organization, which he defines as one 'where people continually expand their capacity to create the results they truly desire. Here new and expansive patterns of thinking are nurtured, where collective aspiration is set free, and where people are continually learning how to learn together' (1990: 1).

The TN was to be a learning organization itself, and, through its professional development activities, to assist schools in becoming learning organizations themselves. In the process of working out how the TN could achieve these outcomes, the ideas and strategies found in the work on learning organizations were distilled into four beliefs that came to form a set of fundamental guiding principles that have continuously informed the ongoing development of the TN and all its activities. These can be summarized as follows:

- *Reflection* is the key to meaningful learning and the generation of new ideas: it transforms teachers' minds and hearts, and engenders growth.
- *Self-mastery* is the key to teachers' personal and professional growth: it enables the development of personal potentials and thus of professional effectiveness.
- *Excellent practice* in teaching is best achieved through the constant collegial examination of pedagogy, the willingness to engage in a variety of improvement strategies and techniques, and the continuous upgrading of knowledge and skills.
- *Fulfilment* is increasing job satisfaction enjoyed by teachers as a result of enhanced competence and confidence.

These beliefs are drawn from and operationalized through the core 'disciplines' of learning organizations. Personal mastery, for instance, is 'the discipline of continually clarifying and deepening our personal vision, of focusing our energies, of developing patience, and of seeing reality objectively' (Senge 1990: 7). Closely related to personal mastery is the discipline of mental models, those 'deeply ingrained assumptions, generalizations, or even pictures or images that influence how we change the world and how we take action' (Senge 1990: 8). One can only be aware of and clarify one's mental model through reflection and dialogue by 'turning the mirror inward; learning to unearth our internal pictures of the world, to bring them to the surface and hold them rigorously to scrutiny. It also includes the ability to carry on "learningful" conversations that balance inquiry and advocacy, where people expose their own thinking effectively and make that thinking open to the influence of others' (Senge 1990: 9).

Systems thinking

One of the problems in fundamental system change is for staff to see innovations as separate fads and wait for them to go away, and here were quite radical innovations in staff development processes underpinned by four different beliefs coming from four different disciplines. Central to Senge's concept of the learning organization is that 'systems thinking is the discipline that integrates the other disciplines, fusing them into a coherent body of theory and practice', and prevents them from 'being separate [and transitory] gimmicks'.[1] These guiding beliefs therefore needed to be taught in ways that would lead to their becoming endemic throughout the whole system, and one part of the answer was to form team learning circles.

Team learning is particularly important for the 'lonely profession'. Teaching in Singapore is generally institutionalized as a private activity between teacher and students, so most teachers work alone in their classrooms and have few opportunities to interact with adults and fellow professionals. This limits the opportunities for them to clarify their assumptions or have support in improving their practice. Team learning does not necessarily result from placing teachers in learning teams, of course; they also need learning processes, and the two key ones taught in the teams are dialogue (a conversation where members suspend assumptions and judgement and 'truly speak and truly listen' to each other) and action research (which is a process for producing incremental improvement of practice).

Knowledge management

Knowledge management is about surfacing, documenting, preserving and sharing the knowledge held by the individual people in an organization. In schools, the majority of knowledge is developed and held by the teachers, and the majority of this is implicit knowledge gained through learning from experience. The management of this knowledge is becoming important because the large number of teachers who were recruited when Singapore introduced universal education in the late 1960s will be retiring over the next few years and taking their knowledge with them. If that knowledge is to be preserved and accessed by others in any way other than through apprenticeship models of induction, it needs to be articulated, archived and disseminated.

Furthermore, there is a strong sense in which teachers are the original knowledge workers because teaching is 'non-routine, ill-structured and creative' (Frenkel *et al.* 1995) involving a number of different kinds of expert professional judgement (Tripp 1993: 140). This being the case, it follows that the management of teachers, especially their professional development, should give them the opportunities and the autonomy to create knowledge, to share their knowledge and be engaged in informal collegial learning.

All the TN activities are based on enabling these processes: dialogue and action research processes in the learning circles enable the interactive surfacing of existing knowledge and experimentation; the teacher-teacher workshops and conferences enable teachers to share their learning with wider audiences; and the TN website is both a repository of teacher knowledge and a means of wider access and dissemination.

Other major influences

Just as the TN's vision and mission statements drew on the work of others, the guiding beliefs of the TN also drew heavily on concepts and approaches from several different fields for their rationale. Constructivism is the major theory behind the TN's activities, the essential point being that learners are not passive recipients of information: they actively evaluate any new information according to their previous experiences, knowledge and beliefs to either expand their previous knowledge or modify its structure. TN activities therefore aim to set up situations that produce learning rather than provide instruction (Angelo 1999: 4). The learning circles are a particularly strong example of one such situation.

A second major source of the rationale for the TN's activities is andragogy, the basic principle of which is that best practices in adult learning will differ from those in children's learning because: differences between children and adults have at least three consequences for learning: 1) Adults have more to contribute to the learning of others; for most kinds of learning, they are themselves a rich resource for learning. 2) Adults have a richer foundation of experience to which to relate new experience and new learnings tend to take on meaning as we are able to relate them to our past experience. 3) Adults have acquired a larger number of fixed habits and patterns of thought and tend to be less open-minded (Knowles 1990: 46–63) The principles of education derived from these characteristics have strongly influenced the design of the TN's learning circles and its teacher-teacher workshops.

Having outlined the educational policies that led to the establishment of the TN and the conceptual underpinning of its development, I now describe some of its programmes and activities, drawing heavily on Tang (2001).

The TN programmes and activities

The conceptual underpinnings outlined above led to the formulation of some key aims for the TN's programmes. TN programmes should:

- recognize the nature and extent of teachers' knowledge, utilizing it to enable teachers to improve their teaching skills through learning from their own and their colleagues' experience;
- use collaborative activities to break down barriers of isolation and allow teachers to support each other in collective problem solving;
- work through and towards building collegial networks, utilizing technology for communication and knowledge management.

These aims have been operationalized through six interrelated programmes:

1   Learning circles
2   Teacher-led workshops
3   The TN conferences

4 Well-being programme
5 TN website
6 Publications

I now describe them in order.

Learning circles

A TN learning circle comprises between four and ten teacher-practitioners who come together with a facilitator to collaboratively identify and solve common problems, challenge assumptions and address real classroom concerns. They are the TN's means of implementing Darling-Hammond's (1998: 8) conclusion that professional development today also means providing occasions for teachers to reflect critically on their practice and to fashion new knowledge and beliefs about content, pedagogy and learners. Learning circles are also the TN's main tool for developing a school's capacity for change through developing more reflective and innovative teachers. Thus they are different from other organizational development processes in Singapore in that they focus on the professional development of the individual teacher, and the participants decide what to work on.

The concept of developing the individual teacher is important: the learning circle process aims to provide teachers with a strategy to, and an experience of, 'repositioning themselves as learners in their own classroom, and to help them start on a journey of knowing who they are' (Tang 2001). It is a major change for many teachers to see themselves as, let alone to find ways of becoming, lifelong learners and producers of knowledge, key players in the creation of the knowledge economy, rather than mere disseminators of the knowledge they have learned.

This is difficult because hitherto we have institutionalized teaching and learning as dichotomous processes. To start teaching is too often to stop learning, and most teachers' lives have gone as follows: first I learned, then I learned to teach, and now and for the rest of my life I will teach so that my pupils will learn what I know; 'Teaching has to become, first and foremost, a learning profession; teachers will have to learn to learn in different ways, and reconstruct themselves as advanced specialist practitioners of learning with their pupils as their apprentices' (Tripp 2002a: 4).

The framework for the learning circle work is a journal, dialogue, and a five-step process referred to as 'action research' – though it is structured more as a problem-solving procedure. The steps are:

1 Identification of problem
2 Planning of improvement
3 Implementaton

4   Observation of results
5   Reflection on the outcomes

Learning circle participants are introduced to processes of dialogue, and the twin concepts of '*co-learner*' and '*critical friend*' are taught in order to create the environment of trust and mutual respect essential to genuine dialogue. *Co-learners* means that everyone, regardless of their professional status and varied experiences, can meet each other on the same platform and recognize each other's expertise. A *critical friend* is seen as:

> a trusted person who asks provocative questions, provides data to be examined through another lens, and offers critique of a person's work as a friend. A critical friend takes the time to fully understand the context of the work presented and the outcomes that the person or group is working toward. The friend is an advocate for the success of that work.
>
> (Costa and Kallick 1993: 49)

A major part of the facilitator's role is to develop participants as co-learners and critical friends, and to see that their interaction is appropriate to these roles.

The purpose of creating a good environment for dialogue is to encourage and enable participants to take risks by surfacing their assumptions, clarifying their mental models, expounding their personal theories, experimenting with new ideas and practices and sharing their successes and problems. These are all essential for learning circles to be an effective strategy for teachers to share their knowledge, skills, expertise – and even more significantly – to identify and articulate their tacit knowledge.

Feedback from teachers involved in TN learning circles suggests that not only do they value the warmth and collegial atmosphere but found the circles to be a powerful approach to learning. For example, in a report on their (1999) learning circle on '*Strategies for narrative writing*', one primary school group wrote of having had:

> a meaningful experience ... The learning circle has also made us more aware of our teaching and why we are doing it. Our dialogues in the learning circle forced us to examine our assumptions that otherwise we may not even have realized we had. The challenge to our assumptions was one of the powerful learnings we had in the circle and it really opened our eyes. We realized that it was our limitations that have kept the pupils from their potential ... It was one of the rare moments in which we were able to share our phobias and insecurities as well as enjoy the camaraderie and sense of affirmation with one

another. The learning circle created a sense of oneness in that we spoke a common language when we spoke of techniques and everyone was eager to try new strategies, and this was the culture that was evolving among teachers in the circle. We were also unconsciously taking responsibility for developing a more specific curriculum that recognized the needs of our cohort and school culture. We took ownership of the curriculum and are now active developers of the curriculum.

Such comments are supported by the average participant approval ratings which, at a >82 per cent average over three years, have been consistently high. In the absence of a comprehensive evaluation, however, there is little of the above kind of evidence showing achievement of a more personal nature, or of longer-term outcomes such as teachers 'repositioning themselves as learners in their own classroom' or starting on 'a journey of knowing who they are'. One of the most obvious ways for teachers to learn is to learn from their pupils, but in a variety of learning circles facilitated by four different professional development officers, I did not observe teachers involving any pupils in their planning activities; and although there were challenges to other participants, these were to their practical suggestions, not to their assumptions, which might have led towards the kind of growth that comes from more personal introspection.

There are several reasons for this. First, the 'action research' is developed by choosing from the problems that the teachers are already engaged with, and as there is no prior reconnaissance or systematic problematization of practice, there is little opportunity to interrogate assumptions and routines. Even after selection of the problem, it is not routine to observe and analyse current practice, and so teachers seek to fix their problem from within the box of their existing 'practical problematic' (Tripp 1993: 16).

Second, the reflection strategy taught did not include any strategies for analysis, and linked to that, although the teachers were supposed to be keeping reflective journals, it seemed that few were, perhaps because nothing was being done with them.

Third, ensuring that the problems are 'authentic, real and specific to the needs or interests of members' is not a straightforward matter. Although facilitators do ensure that learning circles are about the real and specific problems participants face, these are hardly authentic if, as is frequently the case, the problem they choose to work on has been created for them by school or Ministry initiatives that the teachers are required to implement.

Fourth, there is seldom any expert or theoretical input into the discussions of strategies: some teachers do some initial research of their own (such as individual members each finding out about a different one of Gardner's 'intelligences'), but it is more normal for the participants to work out some intervention of their own, and without anything to disrupt their existing views and suggest new approaches, that tends to result in 'more of the same only better'.

Such problems are quite common in this kind of work, of course, and certainly they are not simple: there are dilemmas behind all of them. With regard to the last factor, for instance, many teachers are so used to being expected to implement anything an outside expert suggests that the very presence of someone who is seen to know more than they do about an issue destroys the ethos of a learning circle and undermines other aims.

Two other points have a bearing on this issue. First, all the TN's activities have been designed to build capacities that are not being developed by other means in the current system, and as teachers have plenty of input into their work from others, learning circles concentrate on the core business of encouraging the kind of collegiality that produces teacher-led improvements. In so doing, they give teachers the sense of empowerment that they need to generate innovative practices.

Second, one always has to start with the realities of the current situation, and it is impossible to achieve all the outcomes that one hopes for in the longer run right from the start: it is necessary to prioritize. In order to change their view of themselves and their work, for instance, teachers need to critique their own practice and engage with the research literature on their professional issues – but they have to have the skills and confidence to do so, so it is essential to build those capacities first. If that means keeping to content that is safe and comfortable while one introduces them to the new and often uncomfortable process of collegially critiquing their practices, then that is the place to begin.

These are manifestations of a more general problem with the experience and training of the learning circle facilitators, an issue which will be discussed later in the chapter. Meanwhile, one way of developing authenticity and increasing autonomy of learning circle participation is to encourage individual teachers to pursue their own interests within the common framework of the action research process, rather than to require all teachers in a learning circle to follow the same topic throughout.

Teacher-led workshops

TN workshops are 'by teachers, for teachers'. They have two features which make them unique in, and perhaps to, Singapore. First, they are not plat-forms for experts from outside or above to tell teachers what to do: they are an opportunity for teachers to present their ideas and work to their col-leagues in a non-threatening and collegial atmosphere where everyone is a co-learner and critical friend. This ethos, which is very similar to that of the learning circles, is essential to enabling participants to propose alternative views and possibilities and to challenge and clarify their own and others' suggestions.

To ensure this free exchange of ideas, development of the presenter is a second unique feature of the workshops: each workshop is jointly planned by a TN professional development officer working as a coach and critical friend with every presenter. Presenters first prepare an outline of their workshop, which means that they have to identify, articulate and structure their own knowledge; as most teachers simply teach the set text, this is something they seldom (if ever) do in the normal course of their duties.

Apart from ensuring that this is well done using appropriate professional language, a main concern here is to ensure that everyone, presenter included, will be a co-learner in the workshop. This means training them in facilitation so that they do not present as an expert with all the answers, but share and open for discussion the problems and challenges they face in the classroom, thus creating opportunities for them to learn from the other participants.

Another major concern is to help presenters surface their 'unconscious competence', tacit knowledge and assumptions before each workshop, partly because any increased consciousness of these is significant professional development for the presenter, and also because it is essential if the teacher is to extend their own and the participants' knowledge and practice through the workshop.

Although this method of joint preparation is time consuming and many teachers find it an arduous process, it not only leads to their own professional development, but it also helps them to produce handouts and other materials. Some of these are of sufficient quality to be placed on the TN website, or published and distributed to schools, thus contributing to the knowledge management brief of the TN.

Evaluations of the 186 workshops run in 2002 show that they are well received by participants, mainly because they are introduced to practices that are already working in Singapore schools, and not practices that could work or have worked elsewhere. Almost all teacher-presenters reported that they learned more and grew professionally through conducting their workshops, and for that reason many have volunteered to conduct more workshops on the same or different topics.

The two ideas for improving the workshops have to do with the content in terms of the range of topics, and strengthening the action research processes. Dealing with the topics first, largely because they are by teachers for teachers, they reflect teachers' current interests, and these are almost exclusively skills oriented, so most of the workshops are 'how to' sessions. Most of these, such as 'How to train pupils to answer source-based questions in history' and 'Advanced PowerPoint for Tamil language teachers', are highly specific, and although there are a few on innovative practices, such as the use of drama in science or art in mathematics, most have to do with the implementation of ongoing Ministry initiatives such as problem-based learning, information technology (IT) and creativity.

This is another manifestation of the dilemma of working with the needs and interests that teachers have, as opposed to creating needs and interests that they do not. Again, the latter is done well in other ways in Singapore, and the workshops are the only platform teachers have to discuss their concerns with others, and one has to start somewhere, and progress is being made. It is a significant success, for instance, that in 2002 the workshops on new approaches to the management of pupil behaviour, such as 'Making pupils active partners in their own learning', 'Reducing power struggles', 'Dealing with anger' and 'Communicating effectively with teens', outnumbered currently dominant approaches – for example, workshops that included 'Grouping, classroom layout and discipline', 'Appreciating the importance of school rules' and 'Systematic documentation of discipline records'.

The second idea is to make more explicit links between the workshops and the learning circles, almost all of which are the result of some kind of action inquiry process. An excellent example of how this could be done comes from another state of the Singaporean initiative, the edu.QUEST-SAC project. The project reports are written up by teachers as action learning/action research cycles so that they illustrate the development process used. Many of the TN's workshops could also be structured in the same way to link and further exemplify another fundamental TN process.

Another issue is that the workshops are all single sessions, and it would seem that some sequences of workshops enhance the development process by providing more depth, the opportunity to meet again to discuss results after trying out a new idea, or some linking of sessions into a coherent theme. The TN tried multiple session workshops, but found teachers were unwilling or unable to commit to more than one at a time.[2]

The TN conference

Besides enhancing the self-esteem and public image of teachers by giving them their own professional conference, the main objective of the TN conference is to inform teachers about the macro issues in society that are driving the kinds of change in the education system that they need to implement at the school level. This is teacher education rather than development, for it is important for teachers to see and understand the relationship between education and the other systems in society, and how changes in one system affect education and vice versa; it is a matter of helping them to see both the forest and the trees. For example, the theme for the 2002 conference was 'The classroom of the 21st century: a paradigm shift'; the keynote speakers were all from the private sector and they spoke of the changes in the profile of workers (knowledge and skills) needed by the global knowledge economy.

Informed by the TN's vision of a 'fraternity of reflective teachers', another objective of the conferences is to develop the sense of community among teachers by enabling them to network across schools and learning circles. Besides most of the parallel sessions being presented by teachers, all conferences incorporate discussion forums, conversation sessions, networking boards and other strategies that encourage teachers to establish collegial contacts with each other. Dialogue sessions, led by facilitators, are built into the programme immediately after each keynote address to allow participants to reflect on the key messages and implications, and feed this back to other participants.

Formal evaluation questionnaires of conference participants show high overall satisfaction with the learning and networking experiences, and indicate high levels of confidence and energy among teachers: usually very few can be persuaded to even ask a question in a plenary session, so the number of teachers who were prepared to take the microphone to challenge the speaker's views, assumptions and conclusions was significant.

Well-being programme

The philosophy of this programme is that:

> Traditional professional development agencies tend to ignore the importance of the self in the development of an effective teacher. The Network's well-being programmes aim to complement the other activities by helping teachers work towards self-mastery, in particular to develop their capacity to manage, or better, to lead change, rather than be a victim of it. Central to this process is an individual's ability to recognise that both the construction of and solution to what we perceive as problems, are within ourselves.
>
> (Tang 2001)

This makes sense in that it has long been recognized that we teach who we are, for 'Teaching, like any human activity emerges from one's inwardness, for better or worse' (Palmer 1998: 2), so it is vital that professional development includes programmes that help teachers on their own inward journey to know and accept themselves. The well-being programme therefore 'runs activities that help teachers cope with their emotional, domestic and social demands. Besides a counselling service for teachers, the activities include retreats, workshops on social skills, meditation, physical wellbeing, and being both an effective teacher and mother' (Tang 2001).

Because of its nature it is not possible to comment on the effectiveness of the well-being programme.

The TN website

The TN website was created to help develop independent and self-motivated adult learners, and the home page directs visitors to three main sites. The Forum is a web-based chat room which enables any teacher to engage with others in discussions of professional issues. They need not seek approval to post their views, nor are they censored in any way: the TN merely ensures that no slanderous comments are posted. Teachers' views are also seen as a form of feedback, so they are summarized, collated and sent to a ministerial committee, but in order to keep the discussions open the TN does not allow Ministry staff to post official responses to points brought up by teachers. The Teach and Share site is a repository of successful practices, teaching strategies, lessons plans or notes (even worksheets) which are gathered mainly from the workshops and learning circles, but also from other teachers. This is intended to be 'the first step towards a more comprehensive system for the management of teachers' knowledge' (Tang 2001). The third site provides teachers with links to other useful sites on the internet, including an e-library which gives them free access to more than 10,000 online books, journals and other resources.

Publications

Tang (2001) explains that there are three reasons why the TN regards publishing the works of teachers as a form of professional development:

1   For the authors, putting one's thoughts down on paper is often necessary to clarify and extend one's practice.
2   It makes the knowledge developed by local teachers available to others who can use the ideas and resources to improve their practice.
3   Publication is a high-status activity, and it develops teachers' confidence in the importance and value of their own work.

There are two main categories of publication. The first includes materials contributed by teachers at TN workshops, their learning circle reports and their conference papers, published in house and distributed to all schools. The second category is practice-oriented books written by individuals or groups of teachers; these are printed by publishing houses and sold in bookshops.

Links between activities

One strength of the TN is the consistency that a common vision and a set of beliefs about teachers, teaching and learning provides across the wide variety of different activities that the TN runs. This means that there is a distinctly

'TN' approach in all the different programmes, thus reinforcing and extending participants' experience of collegial professional development, and further developing their skills in it.

A number of specific links between activities are also fostered. As the description of the programmes has already indicated, learning circles share their 'findings' at workshops and conferences, for instance; and conversely, interests generated at workshops can lead to the formation of learning circles, though this has only happened on a few occasions.

Such links could be further developed. Workshop presenters could routinely share their expertise with a learning circle which is working on the same topic. That would both mitigate the problem of lack of expert input into the learning circles, while the teacher to teacher interaction would further build participants' sense of empowerment.

The key characteristic of a network is, of course, the communication links that are established between the participants, and the links that TN has established between its programmes are a form of knowledge management that is entirely appropriate to its development processes.

Though not conceptualized in research terms in the TN rationales, the teacher to teacher links the TN enables are a recognition of the fact that action research is not generalizable through the same processes as traditional experimental research. The nature of action research precludes intentional sampling processes; so instead of extrapolating from a representative sample, for instance, to the whole population, an idea of what is possible is communicated from person to person, often as a principle, so that generalization occurs when what one teacher has made to work in their classroom is also made to work by another teacher in another classroom (Tripp 1991). Institutionalizing effective ways to facilitate this kind of generalization is one of the TN's major achievements.

Teacher involvement in planning and administration

Most of the programmes are organized through committees of teachers for two important reasons. First, in the longer term the Ministry seeks to encourage teachers to rely less on central authority directives for their professional development, and more on their own initiatives, supported by collegial processes. So although it is fully funded and staffed by the Ministry of Education, it is a policy to position the TN as an independent organization, and having teachers on committees that run its programmes strengthens its profile as a learning community, helping to project it as an association of fellow professionals.

Such committee work is another form of professional development because teachers learn from each other in the course of their deliberations. For example, a committee of teachers plans the induction programme for beginning teachers, and in deciding the content of the induction programme the committee members invariably share what they do towards induction in their own schools, and discuss what they think teachers should know and be able to do.

Walking the talk

Tang stresses the importance of TN management applying to its own officers the same concepts and processes used with teachers. Instead of a traditional post-mortem after a TN activity, for instance, staff use a learning process which requires them to surface mental models and examine any unintended consequences of their decisions.

Overall, the TN's organizational structure and operational culture is based on the processes appropriate to the management of knowledge workers earlier described. Similarly, Tang adopted a highly collegial management style which values alternative views and aims for consensual decisions. He has taken seriously the idea that 'The management process is collaborative, not supervisory or controlling', and 'The role of managers in knowledge organisations is not about control, but about guiding and coaching employees, inspiring and motivating them, designing a supportive environment' (Yong Ying-I 2003).

In terms of their own professional development, TN officers meet regularly in the safe environment of their own learning circle to grow in self-mastery and practise the disciplines that the TN advocates. The officers report that it is their own experience of the power of the TN's form of professional and personal growth that has made them passionate about their work, and so more effective in the field. In fact, quite major changes in the behaviour of incoming teachers occur as they become TN officers, and that is also indicative of the efficacy of the TN's forms of professional development.

Challenges

It is essential that the management of teachers and the decision-making process in the school are appropriate, and one of the biggest challenges to this concept of professional development is that the leadership and management culture of most schools is still largely based on industrial, efficiency-driven concepts and processes. The quality and philosophy of school heads is critical because, although the Ministry has invested a considerable amount in moving schools towards becoming learning organizations, and all the TN programmes are informed by learning organizational principles, the number and kind of changes necessary are many and big, as Table 8.1 shows (Tripp forthcoming). Difficulties are further aggravated when the training and development of

Table 8.1 Differences between corporate and learning organizational changes

Traditional corporate change is . . .	Learning organizational change is . . .
Top-down	Bottom-up
Hierarchical	Collegial
Centralized	Localized
Large scale	Small scale
Pre-packaged	Emergent (incrementally developed)
Prescribed in full detail	Agreed framework of common aims
Transmitted to all staff by outside experts	Expert facilitation enabling creation within each team
Uniform across the system	Customized by teams to suit their aims and needs
Compliance required and monitored	Implementation supported and self-evaluation externally evaluated
An occasional special event	An ongoing part of everyday practice

school leaders is separated from the professional development of teachers, as it normally is in Singapore.

A second challenge is that although growth in the number of learning circles was rapid in the first two years, it has levelled out at around 280, involving about 1200 teachers, which is only about 5 per cent of the total teaching force. The problem is a shortage of good facilitators. Learning circles are usually facilitated initially by TN professional development officers; they begin with an initial whole-school training programme on the key processes of reflection, dialogue and action research. They also run a more extended programme to train teachers as learning circle facilitators, and then mentor many of these in the field. These activities take a great deal of time and energy, so growth looks likely to continue to be limited because good facilitation is necessary to adhere to the TN's philosophy and avoid harmful processes such as comfortable collaboration and contrived collegiality (Hargreaves 1994). It is important to remember that 'collaborative cultures are highly sophisticated. They cannot be created overnight. Many forms of collegiality are superficial, partial, and even counterproductive. It is possible to have strong collaborative cultures without strong individual development. We must avoid crushing individuality in the drive to eliminate individualism' (Fullan and Hargreaves 1991: 142).

An apparently obvious answer is for the TN to train enough good facilitators for each school to have at least one, but the skills required for such work are very different from those of a classroom teacher, so a great deal of training and mentoring is necessary. Although there was a demand from schools, Tang (2000) resisted producing a manual that anyone could use with only a few days' training, because he anticipated the emergence of facilitators who did not have a clear understanding of, or a firm commitment to, the TN's ethos and collaborative processes. As he put it, 'The day that Network officers believe that they are fully expert in the learning circle process, or that they have developed a fool-proof manual detailing how to manage all the processes, is the day that they will stop growing and cease to be effective professional developers'.

This is part of a more general problem faced by the TN: its professional development officers are excellent teachers seconded to the TN for only two years. This is a major dilemma that is still being worked through. On the one hand, there are good reasons for this practice: first, it ensures that staff are close to and up to date with teachers' work and school life, and these are important for their credibility with teachers. Second, while at the TN they develop and acquire the kind of skills and experience that are needed in schools, and they take these with them on their return. On the other hand, the work of a TN professional development officer is so different and demanding that they report that it takes about 18 months for them to feel comfortable and become really effective in the role.

The rapid turnover of staff is a persistent and endemic problem for the TN. Apart from coming to understand the TN's philosophy and its implications for their practice, professional development officers have roles to play in almost all of the TN's programmes, and gaining sufficient expertise in these is a difficult task.

Learning circles, for example, are about 'learning by doing, reflecting on the experience, and then generating and sharing new insights and learning with oneself and others' (Wood and McQuarrie 1999: 10), and though that may sound fairly simple, facilitating it is a very complex and demanding matter. TN learning circle facilitators have to play several roles in teaching and modelling the processes. As process facilitators their job is to develop the ability of groups to collaborate and value diversity, balance advocacy, inquiry and decision-making, develop shared understandings, move the group through the action research cycle, and ensure the core disciplines are practised. As critical friends they have to surface and challenge assumptions and beliefs, be a sounding board for new ideas and provide emotional support. As knowledge managers they are supposed to help teachers to explicate their practices and create new knowledge, and then record, publish and disseminate it in various ways.

Underlying all of this is the fact that the kind of teacher professional development designed to occur through the TN's programmes needs quite advanced academic skills and a generally intellectual approach. Good analytic skills are essential for reflection, for instance, and one needs research as well as facilitation skills to help teachers perform good action research. Too few teachers have these skills, and though the TN does have an effective induction programme for new staff, there is insufficient time, training and support for staff to develop the more academic skills necessary to achieve all the desired outcomes of the TN.

Moreover, there are still too few staff to adequately meet all the requests made for the TN's services by schools, let alone the TN's internal development priorities, such as knowledge management. Although all of the TN programmes aim contribute towards this, more could be done towards the surfacing and reporting of teacher knowledge through techniques such as critical incident analysis for the former, and the consistent use of improved IT processes to improve the latter. Handwritten reports filed by author, for instance, prevent many good knowledge management processes, and it is relatively easy to upgrade staff skills and procedures to facilitate reporting and archiving.

Again, there is a shortage of staff in these areas, and training the professional development officers in the kind of advanced techniques for reflection and inductive theorizing that are necessary to facilitate teachers in identifying and articulating their 'theories-in-use' (Argyris and Schon 1974) and tacit knowledge (Polanyi 1964), for instance, would be a very slow and expensive process. Given the core business and limited resources of the TN, the low priority given to managing teachers' experiential knowledge is perhaps appropriate, for it is essentially a research programme which the National Institute of Education is much better equipped to achieve.

Building partnerships to include more outside staff in developing and delivering the TN programmes is one obvious solution: staff of the National Institute of Education could also assist in the delivery of TN programmes on a part-time basis; but the problem is that that though they have the time (for their duty statements include them working in schools), most academics like to 'teach' knowledge and skills to teachers in a fairly formal fashion, for that is what they have been trained and appointed to do. Yet having non-teachers come in to teach teachers is totally antithetical to the whole ethos and specific aims of the TN programmes.

This does not mean that there are no appropriately skilled and intentioned academics, nor that they could not be trained in TN methods. The proposal to coordinate these developments, however, was vigorously opposed by TN staff who have had a long (and unfortunately continuing) experience of academics' lack of collegiality with the teachers with whom they work. As the Ministry is keen to see that its various institutions develop better working partnerships, this situation will change in the near future.

Another way to improve the capacity of the TN and its staff would be for there to be more cross-institutional, part-time appointments. There are some indications that this is already beginning to happen in that both school principals and National Institute of Education academics have expressed interest in spending their sabbaticals working with the TN, and one of the TN professional development officers has now returned to teaching as a 'master teacher'.

This is a promotional category that gives teachers both the platform and the time to work in teacher professional development, and will enable ex-professional development officers to use the expertise developed during their time at the TN to continue to run the TN's activities in their school and regional cluster.

Conclusion

The TN is the result of some senior staff of the Singapore Ministry of Education recognizing that:

- The time-tested approaches that have hitherto delivered such high standards in traditional, examination-oriented learning are much less effective at delivering the radically different learning outcomes needed to create wealth in the highly competitive globalized knowledge economy currently emerging.
- The professional development system can no longer depend solely on a central body of experts to prescribe how best to improve teaching and learning, and train managers and teachers in these methods at the school or classroom levels.
- Teachers, schools and teacher-educators must recognize and tap the experience, wisdom and knowledge of classroom teachers so that they can develop and network ways to meet the changing needs of their students.

Although its teacher-to-teacher links do indeed make it a network, the question is how far the TN has achieved its hope that its model of professional development can result in a *thinking* teacher who not only welcomes change but also has the capacity to lead their own change together with their colleagues.

In the absence of an evaluation, it's not possible to say; and in view of the nature and extent of the changes sought and the continuing development of the TN's programmes, much of the work of the TN is still capacity-building, which means that it is really too early to make that kind of a judgement. In such a case, an action evaluation (Tripp 2002b) is much more appropriate than a conventional one.

Of course, the TN hopes that it will go beyond the 'hows' and seek to understand the 'whys' and the 'whos' in the teaching-learning interaction, but while there is plenty of evidence of the former, for reasons already mentioned the latter is still exceptional. One has to start somewhere, and although Tripp (1993: 22) suggests that a better outcome can be achieved when the 'whys' and 'whos' come before the 'hows' (because the former determine the latter), it can also work well the other way around (see Tripp with Wilson 2002: 126–31 for an example).[3]

It is clear that the ways in which the TN is helping teachers to learn how to solve their problems together and share their solutions, are perhaps more appropriate to the present situation in Singapore. Certainly TN programmes are both useful to teachers and are leading them in the desired direction, for it is clear from teachers' evaluations of the TN's programmes that they are enjoying a kind of professional collegiality that they have not previously experienced, that they are gaining skills and confidence in the processes of working together to improve their teaching, and that they are developing innovative practices.

It is also clear from the foregoing account that the TN has developed a number of innovative practices, among which was the invitation for me to do some evaluative work with them. In doing that, Tang was implementing the Ministry's new approach to ensuring excellence that 'requires the school to question its own current practices and think of more effective and innovative ways of delivering education outcomes' (Ministry of Education 2000: 9). This chapter is the outcome of those processes. There is no doubt that the vision for, and development of, the TN and its programmes is an internationally significant innovation which has begun to provide a new form of professional development for teachers in Singapore. Although it is experimental in many ways, its programmes are soundly based on current knowledge of what works best to assist teachers and schools to meet the challenges that the nation faces at the start of this century.

That does not mean the TN can achieve all of its aims quickly and without difficulty, however, for its programmes are both radical and far-reaching. For instance, the TN aims to develop 'the highest form of professionalism in climates of optimum growth', which is not easy because it requires teachers to render themselves 'vulnerable to critique from both self and others' (Dadds and Hart 2001: 9). That kind of thinking represents a massive cultural change in Singapore which can only be achieved in the longer term, perhaps only over a whole generation of teachers.

Undaunted, however, the TN has set about developing learning strategies and situations most likely to make it happen. With regard to teachers learning techniques for self-critical thinking, for example, a safe, supportive and enabling environment is essential. We know that 'Positive learning capabilities and dispositions develop together most effectively within what can best be described as a learning culture: a milieu which in its very *modus operandi* is designed to encourage both the expression and the development of inquisitive, learning-oriented abilities and attitudes' (Claxton 2000: 21).

This kind of collaborative learning culture is exactly what the TN is producing in and through its programmes. Although this is still very different to the prevailing culture in many schools, the thinking and learning that occurs is changing teachers, and thinking and learning teachers will create thinking schools.

Notes

1 The TN has not yet incorporated Senge's systems thinking processes fully into its activities. For example, teachers are not taught to use the system archetypes in their dialogue or deliberations. But a systems view is particularly important for teachers who can so easily forget that they, their students, schools and all other organizations, are all part of larger systems. Two key principles are used to develop systems thinking in TN activities: one is to foreground the *relationships* or *interdependence* between individual members and subsystems, and between these and the whole organization; the other is *diversity* because it creates the dissonance within the individual that leads to learning.

2 This appears to be a matter of perception, because the National Institute of Education does successfully run four- to eight-session courses for teachers.

3 This is a very complex issue which calls some of our assumptions into question. Nave (in Miech *et al.* 1991: 94), for instance, found that 'three apparently nonreflective teachers . . . changed their practice without becoming more thoughtful'. They denied that they had changed their thinking about their teaching; Nave concluded that 'deeper reflection may not be essential for improved practice' because 'the process of working around an issue of instruction is sufficient to change their practice'.

References

Angelo, T. (1999) Doing academic development as though we valued learning most: transformative guidelines from research and practice. Paper presented at the HERDSA Annual International Conference, Melbourne, 12–15 July.

Argyris, C. and Schon, D. (1974) *Theory in Practice*. San Francisco: Jossey-Bass.

Claxton, G. (2000) Integrity and uncertainty: why young people need doubtful teachers, in C. Watkins, C. Lodge and R. Best (eds) *Tomorrow's Schools: Towards Integrity*. London: Routledge-Falmer.

Costa, A. and Kallick, B. (1993) Through the lens of a critical friend, *Educational Leadership*, 51(2): 49–51.

Dadds, M. and Hart, S. (2001) *Doing Practitioner Research Differently*. London: Routledge/Falmer.

Darling-Hammond, L. (1998) Teacher learning that supports student learning, *Education Leadership*, 55(5): 6–11.

Frenkel, S., Korczynski, M., Donoghue, L. and Shire, K. (1995) Re-constituting work: trends towards knowledge work and info-normative control, *Work, Employment and Society*, 9(4): 773–96.

Fullan, M.G. and Hargreaves, A. (1991) *What's Worth Fighting For? Working Together for Your School*. Andover, MA: Regional Laboratory of the Northeast and Islands.

Goh, Chok Tong (1997) Speech delivered at the opening of the Seventh International Conference on Thinking, Suntec City Convention Centre Ballroom, Singapore, 2 June, http://www1.moe.edu.sg/speeches/1997/020697.htm (accessed 22 April 2003).

Hargreaves, A. (1994) *Changing Teachers, Changing Times*. London: Cassell.

Knowles, M. (1990) *The Adult Learner: A Neglected Species*. Houston, TX: Gulf.

McGregor, D. (1960) *The Human Side of Enterprise*. New York: McGraw-Hill.

Miech, E., Nave, B. and Mosteller, F. (2001) Large-scale professional development for school teachers: cases from Pittsburgh, New York City, and the National School Reform Faculty, in R. Light (ed.) *New Directions for Evaluation*. San Francisco: Jossey-Bass.

Palmer, P. (1998) *The Courage to Teach: Exploring the Inner Landscape of a Teacher's Life*. San Francisco: Jossey-Bass.

Polanyi, M. (1964) *Personal Knowledge*. New York: Doubleday.

Schwab, J.J. (1983) The practical 4: something for curriculum professors to do, *Curriculum Inquiry*, 13(3): 240–65.

Senge, P. (1990) *The Fifth Discipline: The Art and Practice of the Learning Organisation*. New York: Doubleday/Currency.

Singapore Ministry of Education (2000) *The School Excellence Model – A Guide*.

Tang Ning, N. (2001) Address to the Malaysian National Convention for Trainers of English Language Learning and Teaching, Kuala Lumpur, Malaysia, 27–30 August.

Teo Chee Hean (2001) *A high quality teaching force for the future: good teachers, capable leaders, dedicated specialists*. Speech at the Senior Education Officer Promotion Ceremony, http://www1.moe.edu.sg/speeches/2001/sp14042001.htm (accessed 22 April 2003).

Tripp, D. (1993) *Critical Incidents in Teaching: The Development of Professional Judgement*. London: Routledge.

Tripp, D. with Wilson, J. (2001) Critical incidents in action research in education, in S. Sankaran, R. Dick, R. Passfield and P. Swepson (eds) *Effective Change Management Using Action Research and Action Learning: Concepts, Frameworks, Processes and Applications*. Lismore: Southern Cross University Press.

Tripp, D. (2002a) Valuing the teaching profession: purpose, passion and hope. Invited formal response to Margot Cameron-Jones' and Belinda Charles' plenary papers presented at the Singapore National Institute of Education Symposium to mark the opening of the Nanyang Campus, 25 January. Available on VCD from NIE, or in transcript from the author.

Tripp, D. (2002b) A methodological account of a participatory action evaluation process. Paper presented at the Annual conference of the Australian Association for Research in Education, Brisbane, 3 December.

Tripp, D. (forthcoming) Three resources for learning organizational change, *Educational Action Research Journal* (forthcoming).

Wood, F.H. and McQuarrie Jr, F. (1999) On-the-job training, *Journal of Staff Development*, 20(3): 10–13.

Yong Ying-I (2003) *Creating Great Places to Work – Restoring the Spirit*, http://www.gov.sg/mom/newsrm/speech/Speech2002/ms020916.htm (accessed 20 January 2003).

PART 3
CPD for Professional Renewal

9 CPD for professional renewal: moving beyond knowledge for practice

Geert Kelchtermans

Professional development has received considerable attention from educational researchers during the last 15 years. This chapter seeks to summarize some of the key issues in the vast and diverse research literature. Professional development is conceived of as a learning process, resulting from the meaningful interaction between the teacher and their professional context, both in time and space. This interaction eventually leads to changes in a teacher's professional practice as well as in their thinking about that practice. The second part of the chapter reflects on the consequences for the relationship between research and continuing professional development (CPD). Research aims should not be restricted to providing knowledge for the practice of CPD. The promising way ahead lies beyond that, in a much closer intertwining of the agendas of both research and CPD.

Introduction

Professional development (or its variants 'staff development', 'teacher development' or CPD) seems to have become a new 'container concept' in the educational research discourse. The concept has a strong 'face validity'. Almost anyone can imagine something when hearing it. Teachers continue to develop in their job. They keep on 'learning from practice' and become 'more experienced' with every passing year in their careers. The concept calls up something. Apparently it refers to a commonly known phenomenon, with a self-evident meaning. Yet this powerful implicit meaning also constitutes its weakness. From a researcher's point of view, as Evans recently argued, the 'absence of a shared understanding is a problem that manifests itself as: threatened construct validity, difficulties in establishing the parameters of the field of study, and difficulties in identifying the teacher development process'

(2002: 128). Unclear concepts run the risk of eventually losing their distinctive force and becoming meaningless.

In practice the concept of CPD is frequently used, but in very different contexts, referring to different practices and with more or less different meanings. These different meanings often reflect different theoretical approaches and assumptions, which sometimes entail some form of criticism. The literature on staff development and school development, for example, is partly a criticism of the ineffectiveness of more traditional forms of in-service education and training (INSET) (decontextualized, fragmented courses or workshops, focusing on the individual teacher). Little, for example, has strongly argued that 'the training model of teachers' professional development – a model focused primarily on expanding an individual repertoire of well-defined and skilful classroom practice – is not adequate to the ambitious visions of teaching and schooling' (1993: 129), embedded as it is in reform initiatives on student assessment, the promotion of equity in education, the restructuring of schools etc. For these reforms to succeed, more encompassing concepts are needed in which individual CPD and school development intertwine.

It is therefore no surprise that research literature relevant to CPD can be found under very diverse 'key words'. There is of course the literature on teacher education and INSET: the whole range of activities, training programmes or methods used to help teachers develop professionally. Studies on teachers' work lives as well as on their teaching careers also provide important insights. Very close to these studies is the work on school development, forms of staff development and the school as a 'learning organization'. In these studies the emphasis lies on the contextualized character of professional development processes. Quite often the framework for these studies is provided by policy imperatives or theory on educational innovation and school improvement: restructuring schools, innovative teaching practices, determinants of implementation processes etc. School reform implies changes in professional practices, as well as in the knowledge that informs those practices. As such the implementation of educational innovations always demands forms of teacher learning and thus forms of professional development. Several studies also focus on the relationship between the members of the school and external support agencies (for example, school consultants, teacher networks).

Conceptual diffuseness and multiple perspectives make it difficult to draw firm conclusions and develop a solid overarching research-based theory that can be used to construct practices for CPD. Researchers might become frustrated by this. At the same time, however, the conceptual and empirical research shows very clearly that teacher development is a highly complex and multidimensional phenomenon. More specifically, the 'continuing' character of the learning process, as well as its largely idiosyncratic rootedness in people's individual lives, make it particularly challenging to study. One way to deal with this frustrating complexity is to continue to strive for a final, coherent and universal theory, as Evans does. She writes: 'Reflecting contextual and biographical differences, teacher development is, of course, an individualised process . . . Nevertheless, despite this inevitable individualisation, there must exist a teacher development process that is universally applicable when described in terms of the lowest level of decontextualised commonality; it is not the process that is individualised, just the catalyst for it' (2002: 134). A different approach is to try to take the contextual character of CPD seriously and use the findings from research as fragmented pieces of knowledge that can be applied by researchers, CPD providers and teachers to inform and improve their particular practices. In this chapter I will take the latter option.

At this point it is important to stress that CPD may be looked at from at least two general perspectives – or maybe better, two 'research agendas' – that are different, though connected. The first research agenda emphasises the *descriptive* unravelling of the CPD process, both in its form and content. It focuses on the learner's experience and aims to understand its meaning and determinants. The second agenda aims to move beyond description in order to answer the question: how can CPD be organized most effectively? This is the *prescriptive* agenda of the school consultant, the in-service trainer, the induction supervisor . . . of all those people who are concerned with intentionally creating and supporting opportunities for professional learning. Their first interest is not so much a final, encompassing understanding of the phenomenon, but rather lies with the 'pedagogy' for effectively influencing professional development. Although their focus is different, both agendas intertwine and are inevitably present – even if only implicitly – in the justification and ambition of any research attempt on CPD. In this chapter I want to summarize some key lessons from the research on CPD and to reflect on the consequences for the future relationship between research and CPD. My argument is guided by Chris Day's encompassing definition of CPD:

> Professional development consists of all natural learning experiences and those conscious and planned activities which are intended to be of direct or indirect benefit to the individual, group or school and which contribute, through these, to the quality of education in the classroom. It is the process by which, alone and with others, teachers review, renew and extend their commitment as change agents to the moral purposes of teaching; and by which they acquire and develop critically the knowledge, skills and emotional intelligence essential to good professional thinking, planning and practice with children,

young people and colleagues through each phase of their teaching lives.

(Day 1999: 4).

Understanding CPD

The analysis of the relevant research literature on CPD reveals a series of core characteristics that typify the phenomenon. CPD is a *learning process* resulting from *meaningful interaction* with the *context* (both in time and space) and eventually leading to *changes in teachers' professional practice* (actions) and in their *thinking about that practice*.

CPD is a learning process

Professional development implies 'learning' by the teacher. The result of this learning not only becomes visible in changes in one's professional practice (for example, a more effective or differentiated performance), but also in one's thinking about the how and why of that practice. This 'thinking' is reflected in what might be called the teacher's 'personal interpretative framework' (Kelchtermans 1996): the set of cognitions, of mental representations that operates as a lens through which teachers look at their job, give meaning to it and act in it. Elsewhere I have distinguished two important domains in this framework (Kelchtermans 1993). First there is the *professional self*, referring to a teacher's conceptions about themselves as a teacher. These self-representations are of crucial importance to the teacher's job, because teaching involves more than just technical knowledge and skills. Therefore 'it matters to teachers themselves, as well as to their pupils, who and what they are. Their self image is more important to them as practitioners than is the case in occupations where the person can easily be separated from the craft' (Nias 1989: 202–3). This professional self can be described more analytically using five components. *Self-image* is the descriptive component, referring to the way teachers typify themselves as teachers. Closely linked to this is *Self-esteem*, the evaluative component, encompassing a teacher's personal evaluation of themselves as a teacher ('how well am I doing as a teacher?'). Job motivation constitutes the *conative* component and includes the personal motives that make teachers choose their job, stay in it or give it up for another career. A very important component is the normative *task perception*. This involves a teacher's personal answer to the questions What must I do to be a proper teacher? What are the essential tasks I have to perform in order to do well? What do I consider as legitimate duties to perform and what do I refuse to accept as part of 'my job'? Finally there is the prospective component of the *future perspective*: a teacher's more or less articulated expectations about the future development of the job and the way they feel about it. Although intertwined, these five components allow for a more differentiated view of a teacher's self and its development.

The second domain in the personal interpretative framework is the teacher's *subjective theory*, encompassing a teacher's personal system of knowledge and beliefs about teaching (one's answer to the question 'how should I act and why should I act like that?') (see also Clark and Peterson 1986; Day, *et al.* 1993).

These concepts of the teacher's personal interpretative framework are in line with the arguments from the constructivist perspective on (teacher) learning as well as the findings of the so-called 'teacher thinking' research. A core idea of the former is that knowledge (for example as a result of CPD) results from the active interpretation and construction process in which experiences, new knowledge and observations are compared to and analysed against existing mental frames (see, for example, Richardson 1997). The central premise that is exemplified in the numerous teacher thinking studies is that teachers' actions are at least partly guided and influenced by their thinking (Clark and Peterson 1986; Richardson and Placier 2001; Clarke and Hollingsworth 2002). Conceptualizing CPD as a learning process thus necessarily needs to include the close intertwining of both teachers' (more effective) actions in their work and the (increased) validity of the beliefs and knowledge underlying them.

CPD implies interaction with the context

Although CPD refers to a highly individual, almost idiosyncratic learning process, it does not take place in a vacuum. On the contrary, CPD results from the continuous interactions of the individual teacher with their context (and their more or less conscious reflections upon it) (Scribner 1999).[1] This context, however, needs to be understood both in its 'spatial' and its 'temporal' dimensions.

Context in space
In its 'spatial' meaning, context refers to the social, organizational and cultural environment teachers are working in. Just consider the multiple social interactions with colleagues, parents, principals; the shared or contested norms and values, habits and traditions that make up the 'culture' of a particular school; the policy decisions and measures that constitute the political and structural framework schools have to operate in etc. They all make up the context of the particular *working conditions* teachers have to deal with. Research on teachers' work lives has revealed several working conditions that affect (promote or inhibit) teacher development. Reviewing the literature on adult learning, Smylie (1995: 103–4) lists four conditions that may promote learning in the workplace. First, opportunities for individual members of a school to work together and learn from each other should be provided on an ongoing basis.

Second, teachers should be given the chance to work together in groups, as colleagues, in an open atmosphere that allows taken for granted assumptions and beliefs to be communicated and examined. Closely connected is the third condition: the presence of shared power and authority, as well as participatory decision making in the workplace. This implies the acknowledgement that expertise and position or formal status are not necessarily equivalent. Finally, professional learning is also promoted by a certain degree of autonomy and choice for individual members.

Smylie, however, concludes: 'To simply identify workplace conditions conducive to teacher learning is not the same thing as understanding in greater depth the complex, potentially interactive functional relationships of those conditions to learning' (1995: 107). The impact of the working conditions on teachers' learning should not be thought of as a uni-linear process of causal influence, but rather as mediated through interactive processes of interpretation and meaning. Let us illustrate this with the issue of teacher collegiality and collaboration. The quality of the collegial relations among staff members in schools as well as their collaboration are widely acknowledged as very powerful determinants of school development, successful implementation of innovations, job satisfaction etc. Collegiality seems to be the cure for all 'diseases' in schools. However, autonomy (teachers working on their own) and collegiality (different forms of collaborative work) can both affect teacher development in positive and negative ways (Little 1990; Hargreaves 1993). Clement and Vandenberghe (2000) found that collaboration in itself is not the most promising path in terms of professional development, but that rather a positive balancing of collegial collaborative work on the one hand and individual, autonomous work on the other works far better. This balance, however, will have to take different forms in different schools and for different teachers. Avila de Lima (2001) found that some interpersonal ties in schools limited or destroyed teachers' opportunities for professional development and growth. Friendship, for example, reduced access to alternative perspectives on how to meet students' needs and did not address improper professional conduct. Recently, Achinstein supported this conclusion in her research on the role of conflict in collegial communities. Her findings show that close collegial communities in schools can block opportunities for growth and development if they exclude the issue of conflict. Conflict, she argues, is central to community. Communities of colleagues are arenas of dissent, diversity and discussion. It is in how teachers manage conflicts, whether they suppress or embrace their differences, that the community's potential for professional development and organizational learning is determined (Achinstein 2002). So the factual presence of colleagues in a school staff, being one of the most self-evident working conditions in the teacher job, turns out to have a complex impact on CPD, mediated through processes of meaning construction. The same holds for other working conditions.

To complicate things even further, the example of collegiality and collaboration already shows that the interpretative processes of meaning construction are not neutral, but always entail (even if often implicitly) issues of value choices. It is never only a matter of technical effectiveness and efficiency. Teaching and teacher development can't escape an inherent moral dimension (see, for example, Goodlad *et al.* 1990; Jackson *et al.* 1993; Hargreaves 1995; Kelchtermans 1996). In making a choice among different action alternatives, teachers not only use technical criteria, but also a moral idea of what is 'best' for the students. In any case their 'technical' decisions have 'moral' consequences, in terms of the degree to which they do or don't do justice to the educational needs of students. However, 'doing justice', or more generally the issue of what constitutes 'good teaching', is a matter of debate and discussion. Even among colleagues from the same school, there may exist great differences in what they see as good teaching, as well as what working conditions are desirable or necessary to perform this good teaching. As such, these desired working conditions become issues of professional interest, because teachers will strive to establish those working conditions, safeguard them when they are threatened or restore them when they are lost. In other words, on the basis of their interpretative evaluation of the working conditions, teachers will engage in micro-political action (Kelchtermans and Ballet 2002). Research on the micro-politics of the school has started to disentangle the relationship between working conditions and professional development, showing how the ongoing processes of negotiation, of power and influence, and the explicit and implicit attempts to control the working conditions actually determine whether and in what way teachers can develop professionally (see, for example, Smylie 1992 on teacher leaders; Blase and Anderson 1995 on educational leadership; Achinstein 2002 on teacher communities; Kelchtermans and Ballet 2002 on beginning teachers and so on). The teacher job is thus characterized by a continuous process of negotiation (explicit or implicit) about values, norms and goals, or put more generally, about what constitutes good education/schooling. The moral and political aspects of teaching are closely connected. The result of that interaction will in part determine why and under what conditions particular opportunities for professional development can effectively be taken up by teachers and turned into real learning experiences (Clement and Vandenberghe 2000).

However, when addressing the issue of professional development, one should not narrow the relevant moral and political context to that of the school and its micro-politics. Teachers also work in a particular macro-political context of government policies. Research on the intensification of the teacher job, for example, clearly shows how life and work in schools is more and more looked at and evaluated from instrumentalist, economic criteria that deeply affect teacher identities, educational goals and practices (for example, Apple and Jungck 1996; Vandenberghe and Huberman 1999; Troman 2000; Gitlin

2001). Others have argued that this educational policy environment exemplifies how 'performativity' has become the overall frame of reference for policy makers. Borrowing from the work of Lyotard, these authors mean by performativity an 'obsession with efficiency and effectiveness', with standards and tests, with general accountability procedures and even comparative rankings of schools in terms of quality (for example, Blake *et al.* 1998, 2000). This particular policy environment deeply affects teachers' professional identities, as well as the goals, content and form of their professional learning (Sachs 2000, 2001; Troman 2000; Woods and Jeffrey 2002).

Context in time

The contextualized nature of teachers' work and professional development should not only be understood in spatial, but also in temporal, terms. People have a biography, they live their lives between birth and death. As such their life history – or more specifically their career – constitutes the temporal context in which CPD takes place. Teacher learning at a certain moment in time can only be properly understood against the background of earlier experiences on the one hand and in terms of the teacher's expectations about the future on the other. Past, future and present together constitute the inevitable 'situatedness in time', that characterizes teachers' work.

Several studies on teachers' careers illustrate how professional development focuses on different issues and 'development tasks' in different stages of a career (see, for example, Ball and Goodson 1985; Sikes *et al.* 1985; Huberman *et al.* 1993; Richardson and Placier 2001: 910 ff.). Special attention has been given to the beginning of the teaching career, since this so-called 'induction period' is a time of intensive professional learning, both in terms of pedagogical didactical skills and in terms of professional identity development (see, for example, Sikes *et al.* 1985; Bullough *et al.* 1992; Rust 1994; Tickle 1994).

Rather than linking professional development to a system of career stages, a large number of authors choose a narrative-biographical approach. Their research focuses on the narrative accounts by which teachers make sense of their experiences during their career: 'This work is centred on the practical understandings that teachers develop as they enter into and begin to teach and on the ways in which beginning and/or experienced teachers come to frame their understandings within their life stories or life experiences' (Carter and Doyle 1996: 129). In other words, what I called the personal interpretative framework (professional self and subjective educational theory) results from this 'framing' (Kelchtermans 1993).

In narrative-biographical studies, 'career' is no longer conceived of as a chronological line of events (facts), but rather as a meaningful narrative construct.[2] Through retrospective reflection, teachers construct their career experiences into a meaningful story and as such they continuously build and rebuild their identities as teachers, as well as their subjective theories about teaching. It is not so much the formal biography that is of interest, but rather the 'career story' as constructed by the teachers.

These studies show that in teachers' career stories certain events function as 'turning points'. They constitute a problem or question normal, routine behaviour. Teachers feel forced to react by reassessing certain ideas or opinions, by changing elements of their professional behaviour etc. These so-called *critical incidents* appear to be powerful triggers of professional learning, because they 'touch' a teacher's professional self, bring it up for discussion and result in the refining of their subjective educational theory (Clement and Vandenberghe 2000: 93). However, critical incidents are mostly only recognized as such in retrospect: in looking back, teachers identify certain events and experiences (e.g. professional development activities) as having had a profound influence on both their thoughts and professional actions (Sikes *et al.* 1985; Kelchtermans 1993; Woods 1993). Their influence needs to be understood from their situatedness in the temporal context. One cannot meaningfully, for example, identify and isolate these incidents from their biographical context in order to predict their impact.

The approach to CPD from the biographical perspective aims at understanding why particular learning processes, insights and understandings occur or become at all possible, because the learning has to be situated in the person's own biography. The relationship between past experiences and actual professional development is not to be understood in terms of historical causality (facts producing particular learning outcomes), but rather in terms of an (auto)biographical narrative account in which the person reconstructs experiences into a meaningful story. Goodson, however, has rightly argued that 'life stories' (as narrative constructions by the teachers of their professional actions and development) ought to be embedded (by researchers) in their wider sociohistorical contexts, resulting in the construction of 'life histories' (Goodson 1992). As such, the biographical approach to CPD brings together the relevant context, both in its spatial and temporal dimensions.

Individual and organizational development

So the interactionist character of CPD implies that teachers are influenced in their professional development by the particularities of the context, both in time and space. This influence, however, is not a deterministic relationship, but rather a two-way 'dialogue' through which teachers make sense of their experiences and act accordingly, even if this dialogue is partly determined by structural conditions.

This image of 'dialogue' can also be taken further to think about the relationship between individual and organizational development. After reading the preceding paragraphs, it should be no surprise that this relationship is a complex issue as well (Richardson and Placier 2001: 922). The development of the school as an organization implies changes in the structural and cultural characteristics that constitute the working conditions for teachers. These working conditions do 'condition' or 'mediate' individual teachers' professional learning and growth (McLaughlin and Yee, 1988). Scribner stresses the 'nestedness' of teacher work contexts and the influence of these contexts on professional learning. In his model, professional development is influenced by work context, by learning activities and by motivators. He argues for the importance of the different intrinsic and extrinsic factors that motivate teachers to engage in learning activities, but concludes: 'In spite of factors that motivated teachers to learn, facets of work context acted as filters privileging some learning activities while limiting others' (Scribner 1999: 259). Kelchtermans and Vandenberghe (1998) found that teachers' decisions to participate in professional development activities are often determined by a balancing of costs and benefits. The benefits always have to do with personal interests and with the potential the professional development has to eventually improve pupils' learning in the classroom. There are, however, different possible costs, apart from the financial ones. Very important is what we called 'social-organisational costs'. This refers to the quality of collegial relations in the school. For example: participating in a workshop or training might imply that colleagues have to take over one's pupils and thus get a heavier workload. If this possibly has a negative effect on good collegial relations, teachers may decide not to take the course because the risk of losing good relations with one's colleagues is too high a price to pay. And 'participation in professional development remains primarily the decision of individual teachers', as Desimone *et al.* (2002: 105) recently concluded. In the same longitudinal study, they further found that much of the variation in professional development and teaching practice is between individual teachers within schools, rather than between schools (p. 105). This implies that the goals or needs for development at the level of the organization are often different from those of individual teachers.

Yet, in its turn, the professional development of individual teachers may affect the actual organization, change particular conditions at the level of the organization and thus effectively contribute to school development. In his plea for a new professionalism, David Hargreaves identifies two core conditions: 'To improve schools, one must be prepared to invest in professional development; to improve teachers, their professional development must be set within the context of institutional development' (1994: 436). Day takes up and broadens this idea by acknowledging that the content and goals of relevant professional development concern the school and the teacher, but the latter both as a human being and a professional. He argues that the planning of personal professional development and organizational development need to go hand in hand. Records of that planning:

> should enable a balance of learning and development opportunities which at any given time might be focused predominantly upon

personal need (of the teacher as human being), and long-term professional need (of the teacher as a member of a learner community of
professionals), as well as practitioner need and the needs of a particular school.

(Day 1999: 112)

Identifying and evaluating CPD

Two intertwined and important issues still need to be discussed: the criteria
for CPD and its evaluation.

Criteria for CPD

There is lots of 'learning' or 'development' going on in teachers' day-to-day
practice, but how do we distinguish what is to be considered as CPD? Phrased
this way, the question of the criteria addresses the concern with the distinctive
description and identification of CPD as a phenomenon. This essentialist concern, however, ignores the fundamental normative and political question of
what constitutes good CPD and who is to define it. Different types of answer
have been given to this question. Clement and Vandenberghe (2000), for
example, identified three core themes in professional development: an
increased sense of control (feeling capable of doing the job properly); a degree
of flexibility (feeling able to successfully deal with new demands or tasks in the
job); and increased capacity for accountability (being more able to provide
educational justification for one's actual practice). These core themes can be
used as formal indicators of professional learning. These authors stress the
importance of personal relevance in self-reports by teachers on their learning,
thus avoiding any normative stance about the content of CPD. The criterion
for relevance is placed with the teachers.

Hargreaves (1995) takes a different approach, emphasizing the content of
teaching and thus of teacher development. He argues that a proper concept of
teacher development should take into account four closely interwoven dimensions: technical, moral, political and emotional. If one wants to do justice to
the full richness of the teacher job, professional development should not only
be conceived of in terms the technical issues of the acquisition of knowledge
and skills. Since teaching is a job in which one takes up responsibility for other
people, there is an inherent moral dimension to it. Caring and doing justice to
the needs of the learners for which one is responsible inevitably demands
judgements and decisions with moral consequences:

> Attending to the moral dimensions of teaching usually involves dis-
> tinguishing between better and worse courses of action, rather than
> right and wrong ones. There are no clear rules of thumb, no useful
> universal principles for deciding what to do . . . [The teachers] must

> live their moral lives in the swamp . . . especially when moral certain-
> ties grounded in tradition or science are collapsing and people must
> rely on their own reflective resources as a basis for moral judgment.
>
> (Hargreaves 1995: 15)

Since there is no evident agreement on what counts as 'best' for the students or even on what constitutes good teaching, when making such judgements teachers cannot rely on a clear set of rules and norms. That's why the
task perception, the personal normative programme a teacher is working by,
constitutes a crucial aspect of the their self (Kelchtermans 1996). This moral
dimension further implies the need for personal commitment and therefore
the impossibility of emotional indifference in the teacher job. Emotions play a
central role in teaching (Hargreaves 1995, 1998). In her introduction to a special issue of the *Cambridge Journal of Education* on the emotions involved in
teaching, Nias (1996: 293) writes that:

> this special issue takes the view that as an occupation teaching is
> highly charged with feeling, aroused by and directed towards not just
> people but also values and ideals. It points to the increasingly political
> nature of teachers' emotional responses to their workplace condi-
> tions. It suggests that behind practitioners' affective reactions to both
> their work and the settings in which it takes place lies their close
> personal identification with their profession. Yet, it also argues that
> identification is not enough; teachers grow and develop only when
> they also 'face themselves'.

Nias joins Hargreaves' claim that the different dimensions in teaching and
teacher development should be seen as closely intertwined. I also recall that in
his definition of CPD, Day also explicitly mentions the 'emotional intelligence' and the 'moral commitment' (1999: 4).

Acknowledging the width in teacher development, the distinction of the
four dimensions may operate as a tool to evaluate the comprehensiveness of
CPD programmes. Hargreaves' contribution to the issue of criteria lies in this
argument for sufficient width in the content of CPD in order to avoid one-
sidedness.

However important it is to listen to teachers' self-reports on the personal
relevance of CPD and to acknowledge the multidimensionality in the teaching
job, the reflection on criteria inevitably brings one to the awareness that in
actual policy, educational thinking and (more specifically) in CPD activities,
very different opinions about teaching as a profession are being acted out.
A critical analysis of the policy discourse brought Sachs (2000, 2001) to the
conclusion that the dominant discourse reflects a strong managerialist thinking that leads to what she calls an 'entrepreneurial' concept of teacher identity:

teachers are supposed to be efficient, effective and accountable providers of the desired educational services and products. These outputs have to show quality and meet the demands of the clients (consumers). Procedures for quality control and evaluation by the government must guarantee effective performance and product quality. Teachers are thus supposed to be the skilled executors of actions and plans that have been developed elsewhere. In this view the professional identity of teachers is 'individualistic, competitive, controlling and regulative, and externally defined' (Sachs 2001: 157). The managerialist view of professionalism is thus perfectly in line with the performativity view (see above). Very different and even contrary to the managerial discourse, Sachs argues, stands the idea of democratic professionalism, which demands an activist professional identity among teachers, in which collaborative cultures are an integral part of teachers' work practices. Sachs (2000: 87) defines a set of key principles that:

> provide the strategic and conceptual scaffolding through which an activist teacher professionalism can be created and sustained. They include: inclusiveness rather than exclusiveness . . . collective and collaborative action; effective communication of aims, expectations etc.; recognition of the expertise of all parties involved; creating an environment of trust and mutual respect; being responsive and responsible; acting with passion; experiencing pleasure and fun.

As Sachs' analysis shows, different and competing concepts of professionalism are structuring policy and educational discourses. Dealing with the issue of 'professionalism' in CPD inevitably implies taking a stance towards different sets of values and norms.

Evaluating CPD

Directly linked to the criteria for CPD is the issue of evaluation. The question of the effects of CPD is closely linked to the different goals of the enterprise, but the ultimate goal remains the improvement of students' learning opportunities. Some researchers have tried to evaluate the direct effects of CPD on improvements in teaching or on student outcomes through empirical research. Garet *et al.* (2001) analysed the impact of what they call the structural features (the form, the duration and the degree of collective participation) and the 'core features' (content focus, opportunities for active learning, aiming at increased coherence in teachers' thoughts and actions on the one hand and externally imposed standards and norms for assessment on the other) of professional development. Working with a national probability sample of 1027 mathematics and science teachers in the USA, they conclude that the three core features of professional development have significant positive effects on teachers' self-reported increases in knowledge and skills, and changes in classroom practice. It is through these core features that the identified structural features significantly affect teacher learning. With their quantitative study these authors confirm important findings in more qualitative studies, focusing on describing and understanding best practice. A recent longitudinal study by the same group of researchers largely confirmed their findings (Desimone *et al.* 2002).

Guskey's book, *Evaluating Professional Development*, provides an encompassing framework to deal with the evaluation issue, looking for the effects and effectiveness of activities aimed at enhancing the professional knowledge and skills of educators, so that they might, in turn, improve the learning of students. Guskey treats professional development as a 'systemic process that considers change over an extended period of time and takes into account all levels of the organization' (Guskey 2000: 20). He argues that the quality of professional development is influenced by the content, the process and the context. They determine the effects on the knowledge and practice of all participants in the school (teachers, administrators, parents etc.). In order to evaluate this complex process properly, he argues, one should collect data on five 'critical levels of professional development evaluation', namely on the participants' reactions, on the participants' learning, on the support by the organization and changes in the organization's support, on the participants' use of new knowledge and skills, and, finally, on the student learning outcomes (2000: 82 ff.). This evaluation procedure allows not only a deepening of one's understanding of the (determinants of) the effects of CPD, but also allows one to learn from this and improve future CPD practices.

This brings us to the second part of the chapter, in which we address more explicitly the relationship between research and the practice of CPD.

The relationship between research and CPD

Researchers' decisions on how to study CPD are not merely technical. A self-critical reflection on the assumptions underlying their actual practices is necessary to avoid the risk of actually contributing to a project of 'professionalism' that one might disagree with. The kind of knowledge that we generate in research, as well as the form and content our actual CPD practices take, determine to what kind of professionalism for teachers we are in fact contributing (Goodson 2000: 14).

Knowledge-for-practice

Most research on CPD results in what Cochran-Smith and Lytle (1999) have called 'knowledge-for-practice'. The research findings can be used as guidelines to design CPD activities, to anticipate problems that are likely to occur, or to take into account the specificities of a particular situation. As such the studies reflect the descriptive and prescriptive agenda aiming at both analytically unravelling the CPD process and developing a knowledge base to provide effective CPD.

Because of the dynamic and contextualized character of CPD, most research extended the original interest in the determinants of professional learning to the mediating factors in the process. In their overview of the research on the acquisition of professional knowledge by experienced teachers, Wilson and Berne (1999) emphasize the social and interactive character of effective CPD. They conclude that three types of situation in which participants get 'opportunities to talk' entail a strong potential for professional learning: talking about subject matter, about pupils and learning, and about teaching. This 'talking' turned the participants into a community of learners that redefined their practice. Teacher learning 'ought not to be bound and delivered but rather activated' (Wilson and Berne 1999: 194). This is not so easy since 'participation' is the only thing one can successfully determine, as opposed to the character or even the content of what is eventually learned. Or to put it another way: one can lead a horse to the water, but one can't make it drink. What teachers come to know as a result of the learning depends, in part, on what the project leaders and participants negotiate. This is called the 'agenda-setting dilemma': through negotiation, CPD providers always have to bridge the gap between their own goals and those of the participants. These differences in goals make it difficult to achieve a level of critical learning in which participants act as critical colleagues who discuss and challenge their knowledge. The researchers found that many participants in CPD activities are not willing to question their beliefs and ideas, let alone replace them with others (Wilson and Berne 1999). It is clear that exchanging the traditional workshop format for other activities does not guarantee that the desired learning takes place.

The same holds for the findings from the research on working conditions that possibly contribute to professional development. Although these findings may be used as guidelines in designing and implementing activities for CPD, there is no guarantee of success. The 'application' of these findings in design processes will always have to go hand in hand with a careful 'intake' of the participants, taking into account their learning agendas and motivations for participation, anticipating possible difficulties for the participants in putting their new knowledge and understanding into practice, as well as forms of follow-up support when the participants actually start putting into practice what they have learned.

It is clear that even the research based 'knowledge-for-practice' cannot be applied in a 'cook book'-like way. 'Recipes' with guaranteed success, when literally applied, simply don't exist in education, for one can never escape the particularities of the context. The relationship between instructive research outcomes and the actual practice of professional development will always be one of mediation in which the creative, designing, CPD provider translates this knowledge into particular practices. This translation is a necessary, but never a sufficient, condition for effective CPD practice. It takes into account the particularities of context and content, the agendas of the participants, the larger political context, possible normative issues and reflections about the desirability of the 'content', etc. For that reason, research on CPD should take into account the reflective, thoughtful decisions and actions of professional development providers as they are doing their job. Their 'knowledge-in-practice' seems of crucial importance to enhance our understanding of professional development, yet so far few studies have explicitly addressed the actual knowledge-in-practice of CPD-providers.

Beyond the traditional relationship between research and CPD

Cochran-Smith and Lytle (1999) have convincingly argued that not only 'knowledge-for-practice' and 'knowledge-in-practice' are important, but that research should also aim at 'knowledge-of-practice'. This, however, demands a fundamental change in the relationship between research and practice. The traditional position of the researcher as outsider, who studies the object of research in a detached way, has to be given up and exchanged for forms of collaborative work by teachers, trainers and researchers in both the practice of CPD and the research of that practice.

This idea seems to have been taken up in the fast growing literature on professional learning communities. These studies have revealed a great deal about the organizational conditions that must be developed to support and sustain teacher learning over time. The potential for professional learning of these networks and learning communities largely depends on the acknowledgement that two types of knowledge have to inform the practice: 'Keeping a balance between inside knowledge (the experiential knowledge of teachers) and outside knowledge (knowledge created by research and conceptualization) is a hallmark of successful collaboratives' (Lieberman 2000: 223). Thus one finds a strong advocacy among those authors for different forms of 'action research' in which teachers (in collaboration with external researchers) participate in the generation of professional knowledge.

Recently, King made a strong case, arguing that 'although teachers can engage in careful individual inquiry about their practice, inquiry as a collaborative activity among teachers at a school is what contributes to professional community' (2002: 244). Individual inquiry or inquiry by subgroups may even cause fragmentation of the community, he found. His study further shows how supportive organizational structures and specific forms of leadership can contribute to successful collaborative inquiry, without, however, guaranteeing success. The effectiveness of action research by teachers depends to a great extent on particular conditions of available time, the quality of professional relationships and leadership, as Christenson *et al.* (2002) have shown.

Professional learning communities seem to be a promising field for further research on CPD that takes into account the local context, the needs of participants and – in and by itself- the actual empowerment of teachers as they become co-researchers of their own practice. The latter point is stressed by Cochran-Smith and Lytle (1999: 289) in their plea for 'inquiry as a stance' as a constitutive basis for genuine professional development:

> Fundamental to this notion is the idea that the work of inquiry communities is both social and political; that is, it involves making problematic the current arrangements of schooling; the ways knowledge is constructed, evaluated, and used; and teachers' individual and collective roles in bringing about change.

Their concept explicitly takes up the political dimension in professional development, and in particular the fundamental question of to what form of professionalism CPD is actually contributing. Learning communities as a format for CPD don't provide any guarantee that the professional learning will critically question the wider political issue of who defines what counts as valid goals, meaningful practices and professional identities. By not taking this critical attitude the literature on learning communities may in fact provide the perfect working format to strengthen the impact of the managerialist concept of professionalism: teachers learning collaboratively how to implement more effectively the goals and practices that have been defined by others. Sachs' concept of the activist professional is in line with the 'inquiry as a stance', as she states that 'democratic schools and an activist identity are concerned to reduce or eliminate exploitation, inequality and oppression. Accordingly the development of this identity is deeply rooted in principles of equity and social justice' (2001: 157). She argues for two interconnected strategies. First, teachers and teacher communities should acknowledge the importance of self-narratives and their relation to social, political and professional agendas. Second, the activist identity is developed in communities of practice that are not self-contained entities, but develop in larger contexts (historical, social, cultural, institutional) with specific reference to resources and constraints. Their development requires sustained engagement and the negotiation of shared meanings (2001: 158). This brings her very close to Goodson's argument that the study of teachers' life and work should 'develop structural insights which locate the teacher's life within the deeply structured and embedded environment of schooling . . . This provides a prime "trading point" for teachers as researchers (insiders) and the external researchers (outsiders)' (Goodson 2000: 20).

Looking ahead

To sum up, future research on CPD cannot escape answering the question of what kind of teacher professionalism it actually wants to contribute to. 'Activist identity' and 'inquiry as a stance' are powerful concepts, showing a promising way ahead, beyond the traditional relation of research and CPD practice. In that perspective, genuine *professional* development becomes possible, allowing for professional learning, the generation of relevant knowledge and its application in practices that do justice to the educational needs of all learners – pupils, students and teachers. Only then does CPD become a:

> process by which, alone and with others, teachers review, renew and extend their commitment as change agents to the moral purposes of teaching; and by which they acquire and develop critically the knowledge, skills and emotional intelligence essential to good professional thinking, planning and practice with children, young people and colleagues through each phase of their teaching lives.
>
> (Day 1999: 4)

Notes

1 The strong impact of working conditions on teachers' development is also (negatively) supported by research on teacher stress and burnout, that may be considered as the opposites of professional development (Vandenberghe and Huberman 1999).

2 For overviews of the narrative approach in research on teachers and teacher development, see Casey (1995); Carter and Doyle (1996) and Gudmundsdottir (2001). There also exists a strong German line of biographical research on teachers and teaching, which intensively addresses the epistemological and theoretical grounds of this work (see, for example, Krüger and Marotzki 1996).

References

Achinstein, B. (2002) *Community, Diversity, and Conflict Among Schoolteachers: The Ties that Blind.* New York: Teachers College Press.

Apple, M.W. and Jungck, S. (1996) You don't have to be a teacher to teach this unit: teaching, technology and control in the classroom, in A. Hargreaves, and M.G. Fullan (eds) *Understanding Teacher Development*, pp. 20–42. London: Cassell.

Avila de Lima, J. (2001) Forgetting about friendship: using conflict in teacher communities as a catalyst for school change, *Journal of Educational Change*, 2: 97–122.

Ball, S. and Goodson, I. (eds) (1985) *Teachers' Lives and Careers*. London: Falmer Press.

Blake, N., Smeyers, P., Smith, R. and Standish, P. (1998) *Thinking Again: Education After Postmodernism*. London: Bergin & Garvey.

Blake, N., Smeyers, P., Smith, R. and Standish, P. (2000) *Education in an Age of Nihilism*. London: Routledge-Falmer.

Blase, J. and Anderson, G. (1995) *The Micro-politics of Educational Leadership: From Control to Empowerment*. New York: Teachers College Press.

Bullough, R., Knowles, J. and Crow, N. (1992) *Emerging as a Teacher*. London: Routledge.

Carter, K. and Doyle, W. (1996) Personal narrative and life history in learning to teach, in J. Sikula, T.J. Buttery and E. Guyton (eds) *Handbook of Research on Teacher Education*, 2nd edn, pp. 120–42. New York: Macmillan.

Casey, K. (1995) The new narrative research in education, *Review of Research in Education*, 21: 211–53.

Christenson, M., Slutsky, R., Bendau, S., Covert, J., Dyer, J., Risko, G. and Johnston, M. (2002) The rocky road of teachers becoming action researchers, *Teaching and Teacher Education*, 18: 259–72.

Clark, C. and Peterson, P. (1986) Teachers' thought processes, in M.C. Wittrock (ed.) *Handbook of Research on Teaching*, 3rd edn, pp. 255–96. New York: Macmillan.

Clarke, D. and Hollingsworth, H. (2002) Elaborating a model of teacher professional growth, *Teaching and Teacher Education*, 18: 947–67.

Clement, M. and Vandenberghe, R. (2000) Teachers' professional development: a solitary or collegial (ad)venture? *Teaching and Teacher Education*, 16: 81–101.

Cochran-Smith, M. and Lytle, S.L. (1999) Relationships of knowledge and practice: teacher learning in communities, *Review of Research in Education*, 24: 249–305.

Day, C. (1999) *Developing Teachers: The Challenges of Lifelong Learning*. London: Falmer.

Day, C., Calderhead, J. and Denicolo, P. (eds) (1993) *Research on Teacher Thinking: Towards Understanding Professional Development*. London: Falmer.

Desimone, L., Porter, A., Garet, M., Yoon, K.S. and Birman, B. (2002) Effects of professional development on teachers' instruction: results from a three-year longitudinal study, *Educational Evaluation and Policy Analysis*, 24(2): 81–112.

Evans, L. (2002) What is teacher development? *Oxford Review of Education*, 28(1): 123–37.

Garet, M.S., Porter, A.C., Desimone, L., Birman, B.F. and Suk Yoon, K. (2001) What makes professional development effective? Results from a national sample of teachers, *American Educational Research Journal*, 38(4): 915–45.

Gitlin, A. (2001) Bounding teacher decision making: the threat of intensification, *Educational Policy*, 15(2): 227–57.

Goodlad, J., Soder, R. and Sirotnik, K. (eds) (1990) *The Moral Dimension of Teaching.* San Francisco: Jossey-Bass.

Goodson, I. (ed.) (1992) *Studying Teachers' Lives.* London: Routledge.

Goodson, I. (2000) Professional knowledge and the teacher's life and work, in C. Day (ed.) *The Life and Work of Teachers: International Perspectives in Changing Times,* pp. 13–25. London: Falmer Press.

Gudmundsdottir, S. (2001) Narrative research on school practice, in V. Richardson (ed.) *Handbook of Research on Teaching,* 4th edn, pp. 226–40. Washington: AERA.

Guskey, T. (2000) *Evaluating Professional Development.* Thousand Oaks, CA: Corwin Press.

Hargreaves, A. (1993) Individualism and individuality: reinterpreting the teacher culture, *International Journal of Educational Research,* 19(3): 227–46.

Hargreaves, A. (1995) Development and desire: a postmodern perspective, in T.R. Guskey and M. Huberman (eds) *Professional Development in Education: New Paradigms and Perspectives,* pp. 9–34. New York: Teachers College Press.

Hargreaves, A. (1998) The emotional practice of teaching, *Teaching and Teacher Education,* 14(8): 835–54.

Hargreaves, D. (1994) The new professionalism: the synthesis of professional and institutional development, *Teaching and Teacher Education,* 10(4): 423–38.

Huberman, M., Grounauer, M. and Marti, J. (1993) *The Lives of Teachers.* London: Cassell.

Jackson, P.W., Boostrom, R.E. and Hansen, D.T. (1993) *The Moral Lives of Schools.* San Francisco: Jossey-Bass.

Kelchtermans, G. (1993) Getting the story, understanding the lives: from career stories to teachers' professional development, *Teaching and Teacher Education,* 9(5/6): 443–56.

Kelchtermans, G. (1996) Teacher vulnerability: understanding its moral and political roots, *Cambridge Journal of Education,* 26(3): 307–23.

Kelchtermans, G. and Ballet, K. (2002) The micro-politics of teacher induction: a narrative-biographical study on teacher socialisation, *Teaching and Teacher Education,* 18(1): 105–20.

Kelchtermans, G. and Vandenberghe, R. (1998) *Internal use of external control and support for quality improvement.* Paper presented at the Annual Meeting of the American Educational Research Association, San Diego (ERIC-document ED 425 495/EA 029271).

King, M.B. (2002) Professional development to promote schoolwide inquiry, *Teaching and Teacher Education,* 18: 243–57.

Krüger, H.-H. and Marotzki, W. (eds)(1996) *Erziehungswissenschaftliche Biographieforschung* [*Biographical Research in Education*]. Opladen: Leske & Budrich.

Lieberman, A. (2000) Networks as learning communities: shaping the future of teacher development. *Journal of Teacher Education,* 51(3): 221–27.

Little, J.W. (1990) The persistence of privacy: autonomy and initiative in teachers' professional relations, *Teachers College Record,* 91(4): 509–36.

Little, J.W. (1993) Teachers' professional development in a climate of educational reform, *Educational Evaluation and Policy Analysis*, 15(2): 129–51.

McLaughlin, M.W. and Yee, S. (1988) School as a place to have a career, in A. Lieberman (ed.) *Building a Professional Culture in Schools*, pp. 23–44. New York: Teachers College Press.

Nias, J. (1989) *Primary Teachers Talking: A Study of Teaching as Work*. London: Routledge.

Nias, J. (1996) Thinking about feeling: the emotions in teaching, *Cambridge Journal of Education*, 26(3): 293–306.

Richardson, V. (ed.) (1997) *Constructivist Teacher Education: Building a World of New Understandings*. London: Falmer.

Richardson, V. and Placier, P. (2001) Teacher change, in V. Richardson (ed.) *Handbook of Research on Teaching*, 4th edn, pp. 905–47. Washington: American Educational Research Association.

Rust, F. (1994) The first year of teaching: it's not what they expected, *Teaching and Teacher Education*, 10(2): 205–17.

Sachs, J. (2000) The activist professional, *Journal of Educational Change*, 1(1): 77–95.

Sachs, J. (2001) Teacher professional identity: competing discourses, competing outcomes, *Journal of Educational Policy*, 16(2): 149–61.

Scribner, J.P. (1999) Professional development: untangling the influence of work context on teacher learning, *Educational Administration Quarterly*, 35(2): 238–66.

Sikes, P., Measor, L. and Woods, P. (1985) *Teacher Careers: Crises and Continuities*. London: Falmer Press.

Smylie, M. (1992) Teachers' reports of their interaction with teacher leaders concerning classroom instruction, *The Elementary School Journal*, 93: 85–98.

Smylie, M. (1995) Teacher learning in the workplace: implications for school reform, in T. Guskey and M. Huberman (eds) *Professional Development in Education: New Paradigms and Practices*, pp. 92–113. London: Teachers College Press.

Tickle, L. (1994) *The Induction of New Teachers: Reflective Professional Practice*. London: Cassell.

Troman, G. (2000) Teacher stress in the low-trust society, *British Journal of Sociology of Education*, 21(3): 331–53.

Vandenberghe, R. and Huberman, M. (1999) *Understanding and Preventing Teacher Burnout: A Sourcebook of International Research and Practice*. Cambridge: Cambridge University Press.

Wilson, S.M. and Berne, J. (1999) Teacher learning and the acquisition of professional knowledge: an examination of research on contemporary professional development, *Review of Research in Education*, 24: 173–209.

Woods, P. (1993) *Critical Events in Teaching and Learning*. London: Falmer Press.

Woods, P. and Jeffrey, B. (2002) The reconstruction of primary teachers' identities, *British Journal of Sociology of Education*, 23(1): 89–106.

10 Critical practitioner inquiry: towards responsible professional communities of practice

Susan Groundwater-Smith and Marion Dadds

This chapter argues for the development and authentic improvement of schools to be based upon systematic practitioner inquiry undertaken as a collegial activity embedded within the culture of the school. The chapter traces the various iterations of practitioner inquiry in Australia and the United Kingdom and acknowledges, in particular, the work of Lawrence Stenhouse, which continues to underpin many of the tenets of school-based research. Attention is paid to the challenges of identifying, gathering, interpreting and acting upon evidence that has been collected in valid and ethical ways and two case studies are presented to illuminate the issues. The authors outline the risks and tensions associated with practitioner inquiry, but argue that the benefits far outweigh the costs.

Introduction

Changing what happens in schools is serious and difficult work. In spite of burgeoning information and communication technologies, of changing views of how learning occurs and of new and different forms of curriculum and assessment, there remains a fundamental persistence in what happens in schools and classrooms. This is particularly so in the secondary sector with the domination of content matter organized into discipline-based key learning areas with few opportunities for cross-curriculum linkages or team teaching. Even in primary schools, with their greater flexibility in terms of organizing the curriculum and classroom arrangements, teacher directed learning remains the dominant mode.

When, over the past century, there has been so much educational research which could point to different practices, why is it that certain regimes remain so entrenched? We would argue that it may well be that practitioners in our schools, in fact, have a healthy distrust of much academic research, which fails to account for the finely nuanced differences between schools.

Practitioner researchers in schools can, and do, write of places in which they live out their daily professional lives. However, is it possible that they can change the operation of the school itself through their research? Our argument, in this chapter, is that for practitioner research, or what we refer to as 'practitioner inquiry', to have an impact beyond the immediate classroom, it needs to be embedded in the overall school culture. For schools to change, it is not only important that there is local knowledge about practices, but it is also critical that there is a widespread culture within the school itself which will act upon that knowledge in planned and coherent ways.

The argument is developed by the following: first, we examine the nature of practitioner research in the field of education. Second, we explore the intersecting notions of the knowledge-building school and evidence-based practice. Third, we recognize the emerging partnership arrangements which can support schools wishing to work in this way, and we shall provide case studies from both British and Australian contexts. Finally, we indicate that for schools to have a commitment to practitioner inquiry they need to be adequately resourced and supported within long-term time frameworks.

Our discussion, throughout, will assume an inclusive model of professional learning in which practitioners engage as members of a community of practice (Wenger 1998). Communities of practice are characterized by Wenger as the natural social structures for the ownership of knowledge, as a living part of the practice of their members. He sees insight, understanding and knowledge about practice arising from complex and nuanced processes of social interaction. Practice itself is understood as a learning process. Furthermore, we argue that for the learning to be well founded it requires an orientation to critical inquiry, based upon carefully and systematically collected evidence.

In our conclusion we turn to the increasing trend to subject schools and the professionals who work within them to the strictures of the 'audit society'. We make the case that when teachers are well informed, through evidence-based practice, grounded in their own research, then they are well positioned to make the important practical and moral judgements required for schools to be both effective and socially just institutions.

Practitioner inquiry in the field of education

It is not our intention here to undertake a sweep of the practitioner inquiry landscape. This had already been most ably undertaken by scholars who have been active in the field of action research in education for many years. John

Elliott (1991), for example, has written extensively regarding the practice of teacher inquiry in curriculum reform and as an outcome of undertaking post-graduate award-bearing courses in higher education (Elliott and Sarland 1996). General histories of action research have also been written (for example, McKernan 1991; Noffke and Stephenson 1995). Critical discussions have been published (Carr and Kemmis 1986; Altrichter *et al.* 1993; Cochran-Smith and Lytle 1993, 1999) and whole journals, such as *Educational Action Research* have been devoted to documenting action research studies and related issues. Rather, we are concerned to outline those matters which lead us to the view that practitioner inquiry, if it is to effect real change in schools, cannot rest with isolated individuals within the school.

It is not by chance that we have moved the language for this discussion from 'action research' to practitioner inquiry. While the former term has been the more widely used it now presents us with some problems. Action research has become as much an implementation tool for large educational bureaucracies and employing authorities as it has been a process of investigation which is emancipatory in nature (McDonald 2000). The problem is that often the questions being addressed are not those of the practitioners, but those of the agencies providing the funds. So while we maintain the earlier sentiments of action research, we prefer the portmanteau term of 'practitioner inquiry' which clearly places the research in the hands of those engaged in the educational enterprise as equal partners.

Words and terms are slippery things, no matter how hard we try to pin them to the board. Just as the transmutation of 'action research' into 'practitioner inquiry' creates problems for us, so too does the shift from 'research' into 'inquiry' if it denotes a lowering of the status of the activity. In adopting the latter term, we take the position that inquiry is a form of research and may from time to time use the words interchangeably. Our understanding of the relationship between the two and the implications for what happens in schools owes a great deal to the work of Lawrence Stenhouse.

Our debt to Lawrence Stenhouse

Lawrence Stenhouse, the founder of the Centre for Applied Research in Education at the University of East Anglia, is one who struggled long and hard with the question of 'what counts as research?' Stenhouse's minimal definition of research is that it is systematic self-critical inquiry, based upon a stable and deep curiosity (1981). He has also written of research as 'systematic inquiry made public' (1979). Stenhouse argues that curiosity is wonderfully dangerous because it leads to social change. It proposes heresy and threatens faith in those embedded and enduring practices which conspire to keep schools so little changed. It is for this reason that the Stenhousian position accords so well with notions of evidence-based practice, which we discuss at a later point in the chapter, and where we make the case that evidence itself is never unproblematic and can also be 'wonderfully dangerous'.

Stenhouse reminds us that the researcher is never free of his or her values. He places a greater emphasis upon *interests* and the ways in which researcher interests can be made transparent, thus making the researcher accountable for them. Indeed, a little later in this chapter we shall turn to the interests of the students and teachers as researchers in schools. The researcher is interested in the phenomenon being examined, not only in terms of curiosity, but also in terms of perceived advantages and disadvantages which may arise from the work. Similarly, the school as an institution has interests in the inquiry and its outcomes. For Stenhouse, research work is moral work. No one can claim theoretical innocence. We would also extend this argument to claim that schools themselves need to be seen as moral institutions with a concern for ethicality, equity, social justice and transparency.

It is transparency which particularly lies behind the concern with publication of forms of inquiry. Practitioner inquiry which remains private cannot be scrutinized and thus made available for criticism and debate. Unfortunately, in the case of traditional educational research, much which is made public is not made available, in the sense that typical academic publications do not regard practitioners in the field as their principal audience. Research journals rarely find their way into the professional libraries of those in schools.

Stenhouse (1981: 17) suggests that 'perhaps too much research is published to the world, too little to the village'. For him, the local collegial group, dedicated to action, is the first audience for practitioner inquiry. For us, this is the school, or a collective of schools or school-university partnerships as knowledge-building organizations. Often individual studies, undertaken as projects in government programmes, or as part of award-bearing courses at universities, are not made available to the whole school community and become the 'secret business' of the elect few, though there are documented exceptions (see Dadds 1995).

We recognize, as Kemmis does in the fifth Lawrence Stenhouse Memorial Lecture conducted by the British Educational Research Association (1995), that substantial changes have taken place in social theory and education studies since Stenhouse's death in 1982. Kemmis makes more problematic Stenhouse's understanding of research as a public activity. He argues that the mediation of theory and practice is a public process which takes place within the *politics* of debate among real groups, in real time, and that there is a struggle for meaning and action. Reform, led by practitioner inquiry, is far more difficult than Stenhouse proposed. It is this geopolitical nature of the work to which we shall return at the conclusion to this chapter. But we also recognize, in the section which follows, that state politics play their inescapable part.

Just as we make the case that schools as institutions are very particular contexts, we also argue that there are national variations which need to be accounted for. Practitioner inquiry, often characterized as 'action research', looks rather different in Europe, the USA, Canada or South Africa, and so too does its manifestation in Australia and England. As two researchers who have facilitated practitioner inquiry in these two countries we shall look to them as specific contexts to illustrate our arguments. But first we will discuss issues associated with our assumptions, values and beliefs in relation to practitioner inquiry in school settings.

Practitioner inquiry in schools: values and beliefs

Schools are clearly places for learning: teachers' learning about their students; students' learning about themselves; students' learning about habits of mind and the established curriculum; all learning about learning itself. Schools are places for adults and young people, all acting as knowledge workers. Most importantly, at the heart of the matter lies the educational interests and needs of the students. It is our belief that these educational interests are paramount. In this sense our orientation to practitioner inquiry is implicitly and explicitly ideological (Lather 1986). This does not mean that all players in the field agree consistently about what the needs and interests of young people are; rather it means that there is a common orientation towards the children's educational experiences and learning as the end point of the inquiry. In this sense the students are the consequential stakeholders in the business of practitioner inquiry in schools.

As we have observed, schools are places for adult learning also. In aspiring to a methodology for practice that enhances young people's educational lives we also want to place value on the lives of the adults in that workplace. The work that we shall report makes explicit the connection between the development and well-being of the children and that of their teachers and other educators. Stenhouse's classic insight that there is no curriculum development without teacher development (1976) continues to inform our practice where we aspire to a research approach which is also a developmental methodology. A methodology that values children and gives scant regard to their teachers stands little chance of success. If the young people in schools are to benefit from practitioner inquiry, ways must be sought to be respectful of the needs of their teachers, as partners, leaders and creators of educational knowledge. We believe that society cannot care well for children by abusing and disregarding their teachers.

Practitioner inquiry is usually facilitated research in that in most instances it is supported by partners from universities (Groundwater-Smith 1998). The role of the academic researcher is to work *with* teachers, rather than *on* teachers. In the projects which are reported below the aspiration has been to work within a tradition that develops 'practice-sensitive researchers at the university and research-sensitive practitioners at the school site' (Gifford 1986: 77). The teachers' insider resources are invaluable for thinking beyond the surface meaning of data; for drawing upon insider knowledge of the children and the school; for offering a more detailed insight into the context of the inquiry. The teachers' subjective, insider perspectives add to the strength and validity of the inquiry.

While we are mindful of the difficulties and complexities that are involved in becoming a practitioner researcher it is also important to develop an awareness that the very skills of teaching and the skills of research are highly commensurable (Conner 1994; Dadds 1995). Teachers, as researchers, are well able to identify good questions about children's learning. Furthermore, in carrying an inquiry forward they may already be skilled at interviewing and listening; observing, analysing and evaluating children at work and their work outputs; and working collaboratively with each other. They are also well able to read the practical possibilities which may arise from their findings and consider ways in which to reconceptualize practice in the light of deliberative inquiry.

It is also important to recognize that university researchers in faculties of education are teachers, and they too have and require multiple skills. University practice is also professional practice. So, we include ourselves within the collective term 'practitioner inquirers'. This chapter is not addressed exclusively to those working in schools. It equally applies to universities as learning institutions in the fullest sense of the phrase.

Finally, in this brief discussion of the underlying values and beliefs informing the work of the authors of this chapter, we would indicate that we acknowledge and respect the intellectual potential of practitioner inquiry to contribute to educational theory building. By engaging in careful, critical and systematic study of their work, teachers as researchers are an important resource for the development of educational theory whether they are teachers within schools or universities. This is well illustrated by such practitioners as Schratz and Walker (1995) where they draw upon their teaching about research as a form of research in its own right.

Practitioner inquiry in the Australian context

Before discussing practitioner inquiry in Australia it is important to understand something of the broader educational picture in that country. School education is principally the responsibility of the states and territories, each of which has its own department of education. The federal government has oversight of tertiary education and also conducts, from time to time, national programmes in areas such as literacy, numeracy, information technology and government priorities. In this case, funds are distributed to the states with some specific indications of how they might be spent. However, the programmes in their detail will ultimately vary from state to state and territory to territory depending upon local legislation.

A further distinctive feature of school education is the extent to which the non-government sector is operative. While some 70 per cent of the nation's children attend state schools the remainder go to either Catholic parochial schools, which are themselves organized into a system, or to independent schools which operate autonomously. Schools in the non-government sector receive funding from the federal government.

Clearly there are variations in the ways in which school education is organized. Nonetheless, we can find some common features; practitioner inquiry in the Australian educational context is one which has been explicitly concerned with both constructing professional self-understanding and engaging in educational reform.

Since the mid-1970s and in a similar manner to that reported in England (Elliott and Sarland 1995) many individual practitioners have conducted action research projects, usually within the structure of a higher degree framework. While such projects led to a degree of self-understanding and enlightenment generally they were directed to change in individual classroom practice rather than change in the whole school. This tradition has extended to initial teacher education, with many programmes now having internships, within which students are required to conduct modest action research inquiries, as much to learn the skills of investigation as to address the problematics of practice.

A more collegial form of action inquiry emerged during the halcyon days of the Disadvantaged Schools programme (a national federally funded equity programme), when schools identified features of teaching and learning which were of concern when addressing the needs of students who were educationally disadvantaged by way of poverty, ethnicity and/or Aboriginality. The schools designed projects to address these needs. A condition of funding was that school-based projects should be managed by a representative committee and evaluated. Thus the action research spiral was enacted – observe, gather evidence, reflect, act, observe – within an environment which was collegial and free of the constraints of status and power. This programme in this form no longer exists.

However, during the early 1990s developments in practitioner inquiry in Australia were established, through two related national programmes. The National Schools Network (NSN) and the Innovative Links between Schools and Universities for Teacher Professional Development programme were both developed as explicit programmes of school reform led by systematic inquiry (Groundwater-Smith 1998).

In the case of the NSN, schools addressed a common question, 'What is it about the ways in which teachers' work is organized that gets in the way of student learning?' It is important to recognize that this question was not one developed by schools' authorities alone, but by a coalition of employing authorities in both government and non-government sectors and teachers' unions as well as parent organizations. At the local level, schools could address this question by looking at such issues as timetable arrangements, school and classroom organization, or matters such as the role of stakeholders in school-based decision making.

In the case of *Innovative Links*, schools identified their own questions and worked with university partners to investigate their issues. They also formed roundtables where they worked with several other schools, finding common ground in the research and reform processes. Many projects arising from these programmes have been reported at research conferences over the past decade.

In both of these programmes school- and university-based practitioners worked in teams to create professional knowledge about practice and to use that knowledge to improve, and even redesign, practice. The tradition was a Stenhousian and Deweyan one; in the first instance because research was seen as systematic inquiry made public and in the second because the practitioners were seen as learners in a community of practice with a responsibility to work through the interaction between theory and practice. In effect, the practitioners became critical readers of the text of practice.

Collecting and analysing data has been seen as a central problematic in practitioner inquiry; so too is collecting and analysing theory. It is not seen as sufficient to give an account of a phenomenon, but to construct an accounting for the phenomenon, as a preliminary to engaging in action and reform. For example, in *Innovative Links*, a responsibility of the academic associate was to support the schools in their critical reading of the relevant research literature.

Now, at the beginning of a new millennium, another form of practitioner inquiry is emerging in school education in Australia. This is what may be described as evidence-based practice where schools work on the identification, collection and interpretation of evidence as the basis for improving teaching and learning for both students and their teachers across the school community. In these cases practitioner inquiry forms the foundation for ongoing teacher professional development and school improvement within the overall school culture. We believe that this trend is not merely more of the same, but an innovation of a different order. Before examining these challenges it is important to know something of practitioner inquiry in the United Kingdom.

Practitioner inquiry in the United Kingdom

While it is clear from our discussion of the work of Lawrence Stenhouse that although practitioner inquiry is strongly rooted in the education tradition of the United Kingdom, events in recent decades have greatly changed the educational landscape and thus the ways in which practitioner inquiry can be enacted. During four terms of conservative rule a range of policies and practices, which impacted upon every facet of educational life, were introduced into Britain. In spite of a change of government, there is little evidence that the strength and direction of these changes has abated.

Following the Thatcher government's election manifesto of 1987, the Education Act of 1988 introduced major changes in the management, status and content of the state schools attended by most of the nation's children. For many, these 'reforms' have impacted adversely upon teachers' capacities to engage in practitioner inquiry as a means of exercising informed professional judgement. McDonald (2000) outlined the main features of the changes in terms of devolved financial management, a detailed and compulsory national curriculum, national testing with associated target setting, placing schools into a market environment and publicly shaming and humiliating schools that are perceived to have failed. While we shall return to the issues of compliance and professional accountability at the end of this chapter, we are more concerned here to argue that the context for practitioner inquiry in British schools has potentially been one which faces serious and destabilizing constraints. For not only are schools subject to inspection and control, but increasingly the teacher education curriculum itself and the management practices of faculties of education within universities are also scrutinized by an authoritarian inspectorial or quality control system. Benevolent and sustaining partnerships between schools and universities to support practitioner inquiry are becoming increasingly difficult to maintain unless they are directly aligned with government intentions and government policies.

The notion of knowledge production being pursued for the good of the profession is being replaced by knowledge production for policy solutions. As Atkinson (2000: 318) notes, 'increasing central control over education policy and practice has put the autonomy of educational research into question'. These comments followed the release of the Tooley and Darby report (1998) which criticized the relevance and quality of educational research which was characterized as unduly qualitative, critical and feminist.

Paradoxically, the work of the Teacher Training Agency (TTA) has encouraged the notion of teaching as a research-based profession and the development of school-university consortia as a means of examining those classroom practices which relate to national priorities. In addition, the Department for Education and Skills (DfES) has made grants available for teachers to pursue individual, or collective, teacher research projects under the Best Practice scholarship awards scheme. While there is some flexibility in these schemes for teacher researchers to define their own areas of interest, there is also strong encouragement for projects to be located within national development priorities, as defined collectively by government and consultant teacher researcher groups. However, there seems to be little overt emphasis in either of these schemes for whole schools to examine critically their sociocultural practices and the effects of these upon student learning, and wider systems or government policies, as in the Australian initiatives mentioned.

The research-based initiatives of the recently established National College for School Leadership (NCSL) (www.ncsl.org.uk) might begin to make a difference, however, to whole school practitioner research development. Emphasis is being placed on the collective development, at school level, of professional knowledge about teaching, learning, curriculum and leadership. Through its new 'Networked Learning Communities' initiative, the NCSL is seeking to underpin the validity of the notion of the knowledge creating school, acknowledging its potential for making a wider contribution to knowledge transference within, and across, systems.

Against this background of difficulties and new opportunities, commitment to practitioner research has been sustained in both school and academic communities in the United Kingdom and whole-school approaches to the development of practical theories about learning are progressing.

Knowledge-building schools and evidence-based practice

So how do schools, as learning organizations, work to build and act upon knowledge of their practices? Clearly the task is one which requires not only considerable skills, but a will and determination.

As indicated at the Third International Practitioner Research Conference (Goodwin and Groundwater-Smith 2000: 1):

> Inserting practitioner research into school culture is no easy matter. We are not speaking here of an individualistic enterprise where one or two teachers in a school have sought to investigate and change some aspect of practice; but rather, where research is an undertaking embedded into the school's corporate being.

Recently, in Sydney, New South Wales, teachers from seven schools, four from the government sector and three independent schools, sat together and discussed the possible formation of a coalition of knowledge-building schools. They saw themselves contributing to the ongoing improvement of the work of their schools through the systematic and public collection and discussion of evidence regarding teaching and learning within the lived life of the school. They had a view that evidence was best considered in a forensic rather than adversarial environment; that is to say, that it should be constructed and examined in ways which illuminate understanding rather than as a means of proving a particular case.

The participants in the discussion saw themselves as:

- developing and enhancing the notion of evidence-based practice;
- developing an interactive community of practice using appropriate technologies;
- making a contribution to a broader professional knowledge base with respect to educational practice;
- building research capability within their own and each other's schools by engaging both teachers and students in the research processes; and
- sharing methodologies which are appropriate to practitioner inquiry as a means of transforming teacher professional learning.

The embryonic coalition believed that by embedding inquiry practices into the daily work of the schools it would be possible to evolve an authentic workplace learning culture. They recognized that professional learning is not an exclusively individualistic enterprise but that learning and growth can take place at the organizational or corporate level. What is of particular note is that the coalition did not form in response to external initiatives such as a funded programme or university partnership, but because the schools themselves had an expressed desire to work in a particular way. Having said that, it was also critical that the Centre for Practitioner Research, situated at the University of Sydney, was able to (and wanted to) support the coalition and provide it with some sort of institutional base.

The notion of schools as knowledge creating organizations has been strongly argued for by Hargreaves (1999a, 1999b), and this idea is informing the coalition as well as the Networked Learning Communities initiative of the National College for School Leadership in the United Kingdom.

Considering schools as knowledge creating organizations, rather than knowledge consuming organizations, grows from contemporary discourses which acknowledge and respect the work of practitioners in various enterprises, be they automobile manufacturers, hospitals, retailers or schools. Advocates perceive that given the appropriate conditions much can be learned through gathering, interpreting and acting upon local evidence.

In considering the necessary factors for the knowledge creating school Hargreaves (1999b: 126–7) believes it is likely to be one in which the following conditions, *inter alia*, prevail:

- a culture of, and an enthusiasm for, continual improvement;
- a strong awareness of the external environment;
- high sensitivity to the preferences of key stakeholders;
- coherent, but flexible planning;
- recognition of expert knowledge held by teachers;
- professional knowledge creation as a whole-school process;
- a readiness to innovate, treating mistakes as opportunities for learning.

Clearly, central to the development of the knowledge-building school is the notion of evidence and its relation to practice.

Evidence-based practice and the knowledge-building school

How then do we best understand the notion of evidence-based practice and the ways in which it contributes to the knowledge-building school and practitioner inquiry? Davies (1999) suggests that evidence-based practice in education operates at two levels. The first is to utilize evidence from worldwide research and literature on education; the second is to establish sound evidence, by systematically collecting information about particular phenomena. A school which wishes to use evidence in order to improve practice needs to do both.

A further issue raised by Davies is to query not only what counts as evidence, but also to consider the question of evidence about 'what'? One might be interested, for example, in considering the consequences which result from changing a specific assessment practice. Or, a school might want to investigate the kinds of meanings students and their teachers and parents attach to the concept of what constitutes good learning. In either case they will need to ask themselves, 'what counts as valid evidence in relation to the question being posed?' We would argue that the evidence must be commensurable with that question.

In line with this thinking, Hargreaves (1999a) has suggested that evidence-based practice is an important term for us to consider when wishing to move towards school improvement and teachers developing a soundly informed knowledge base. Indeed, as we have indicated, he goes further, in a second article (1999b) to propose that schools should use evidence in order to become knowledge creating organizations.

Hargreaves has not been without his critics. Elliott (1999a) believes that the knowledge formation of which Hargreaves writes is founded on a positivistic view of evidence in that his accounts of useful and worthwhile educational research are based upon a 'quasi-causal mechanism' (p. 7). Elliott goes on to argue that Hargreaves has given a questionable status to what may be called 'indubitable knowledge'; that is, knowledge which may not be challenged. Nonetheless, he concedes that the concept of evidence as the basis for practice is a worthwhile ambition, if the effect is seen as producing evidence that is *actionable* by teachers.

Elliott's very real concerns (1999b) regarding the directions which evidence-based practice may take are based upon his questioning of a medical model where evidence is narrowly constituted and positivistically derived. He reminds us that we need to be guarded in adopting a model where the question of 'what makes research educational?' may not be addressed.

Atkinson (2000) also challenges Hargreaves' views, arguing that he decontextualizes and depoliticizes issues around power and knowledge, effects and consequences. We would argue that while Hargreaves' intentions may be more aligned with supporting government policy, his identification of the conditions for schools as knowledge-building organizations is a worthwhile and helpful scaffold upon which practitioner inquiry may be constructed.

Earlier we made the claim that the nature of evidence itself must be considered in relation to practitioner inquiry. We can think of the purposes for gathering evidence in two ways. The first is to use the evidence in adverserial settings where it is utilized to prove a case. Those seeking for that elusive, indeed we would argue impossible, goal of 'best practice' would wish to prove that one method is unarguably better than another. Thus, in medicine, using randomized control trials, there are those that seek the 'best treatment' irrespective of the multitude of variables within any medical condition. Similarly, education has been beset by the 'best practice' holy grail; as if it is possible to identify one best way, for example, to teach reading, or for leaders to organize teachers' professional development.

The second purpose for gathering evidence is to conceive of it within a discourse of forensic science, where the investigator is seeking above all else to understand a particular phenomenon. Knowledge-building schools clearly wish to achieve a deep understanding of that which happens within them: teaching and learning; managing human and material resources; communication and participation; and so on. Of course, this does not mean that practitioner inquiry should not concern itself with the quality of evidence, but rather the purposes to which that evidence is to be put. Norris and Robinson (2001) quite properly point out that a distinction should be made between weak and strong evidence.

Evidence gathered by practitioner inquirers needs to stand a number of tests:

- *Is it ethical?* This test requires that the evidence is collected with informed consent from all participants in the research enterprise. Thus it does not set out to deceive or to coerce. Furthermore, there is a determination to minimize harm or damage. Of course, it is not possible to claim that *no* harm will be done simply because there may be unanticipated and harmful consequences.
- *Has it been triangulated?* The gathering of evidence from only one source (e.g. a survey) may produce a distorted picture of the phenomenon. It is essential that several data sources are explored and the subsequent results examined and explained.
- *Has it been intersubjectively verified?* The interpretation of evidence cannot rest only upon one investigator; it is important that it is explored from a number of angles, by a variety of stakeholders.

As well as these basic tests we would also add some further desiderata. We would argue that for the quality of the evidence to meet such standards the inquiry should be allowed sufficient *time*. A criticism of practitioner research undertaken within the context of a project is that the time frames lead to a 'speeded up' game of inquiry and action (Heatley and Stronach 2000: 415). Too often the school-based practitioners are meeting the needs and deadlines of funding agencies who want to advise policy makers working within highly constrained time frames. Also, as Ponte (2002), working in a Dutch context, points out, teachers need quite a long and continuous period of time to master practitioner inquiry. Not only does it involve them in developing a new skills base, but also in the formation of new and different attitudes to research. This cannot occur overnight.

We would also argue for the involvement, where appropriate and possible, of the consequential stakeholders; that is, the students themselves. As we shall demonstrate in our case studies, 'student voice' is not only a matter of inclusion in terms of students as subjects of the inquiry, but also a matter of students being active and participative in the research processes themselves.

Finally, we would see it as important that results from practitioner inquiry are widely disseminated and discussed, thus adding to the greater pool of professional knowledge. In the cases which we discuss below there has been an emphasis upon presenting reports within the given schools and writing for conferences and journals. It will be noticed that many presentations are co-authored, giving school-based practitioner researchers opportunities to write for a wider audience.

Case studies in evidence-based practice

Here we present two case studies, one located in Sydney, the other a research project funded by the University of Cambridge Institute of Education, 'Curriculum Organization, Practice and Children's Learning (COPS) in the Primary School' conducted in England, which elaborate the possibilities of evidence-based practice for teacher professional development and educational change.

Independent Girls School

Independent Girls School (IGS) (a pseudonym) is a large denominational comprehensive girls' school (K-12) situated in metropolitan Sydney and is a member of the earlier mentioned Coalition of Knowledge-Building Schools. IGS has been established in its current site for over a hundred years. It is well respected in the Sydney community for its progressive orientation, particularly with regard to technology innovation. During 1997–98 the school took part in a national project (Cuttance 1999). In response to a public advertisement it undertook to evaluate aspects of its technology innovation and provide a report which would later be available for analysis and synthesis by the overall project.

During the conduct of its evaluation the school engaged the assistance of an academic associate who would advise on research methods, design and implementation strategies. Many of the debates between the practitioner researchers, the academic associate and the project's managers revolved not only around the nature of the evidence being collected but also around the validity of a study which itself sought to decontextualize the school's findings in order to develop rubrics of 'best practice'. These debates were rigorous and often quite fiery. The association with the visiting academic was seen by the school's principal and the director of teaching and learning to have sufficient merit to establish a longer-term affiliation in the agreed form of a researcher in residence whose initial term in office was to be three years. Clearly, then, the appointment was designed to embed school-based inquiry into the norms and values of the school and the professional development of its teachers. Also it was clear that debate, critique and high levels of participation were to be encouraged.

The school-based research, led by the researcher in residence, was to be advised by a committee comprising the school principal, the chaplain (who had a particular responsibility to oversee ethics considerations), two parents (one from the junior school and one from the senior school) six students, the director of teaching and learning, the head of the junior school and the researcher in residence herself. It is important to note that this structural support was designed after many discussions regarding the range and purpose of the practitioner inquiry with which the school would engage.

IGS now has a five-year history of developing evidence-based practice. A number of papers and journal articles have outlined the work of the school and its orientation to school-based research (among them are Goodwin and Groundwater-Smith 2000; Groundwater-Smith 2000; Groundwater-Smith and Hunter 2000; Groundwater-Smith 2001a, 2001b; Groundwater-Smith and Mockler 2001; Corrigan and Groundwater-Smith 2002; Groundwater-Smith and Hayes 2001). Over 20 projects have been completed, reported and acted upon. A sample of projects from 2001 is detailed below.

In the junior school (kindergarten to Year 5) a major project has been an investigation of 'What makes a good school?' Senior school students were trained as focus group leaders. Working in teams of three with randomly sampled groups of junior school pupils a series of questions regarding the children's perceptions of what makes a school a good school were put. In asking the first question the corollary was also examined; that is, those things which prevented the school being a good school in students' terms. While there was a strong affirmation of the school's encouragement of student learning, major issues arose around concerns about bullying and teachers' reward systems.

Across the senior school the researcher in residence acted as a critical friend to the director of studies who managed a series of commissions of inquiry focusing upon assessment and reporting within faculty frameworks to examine the following three questions:

- What do we believe we currently do when we 'mark' students' work?
- How do we provide feedback?
- How can we consider new ways of assessing and reporting upon student work?

Each term concluded with a mini-conference across faculties. Thus directly or indirectly all members of the senior school staff were involved in a form of practitioner inquiry.

The 'Learning to Lead in Year 8' project was concerned with three things:

- learning through leadership;
- learning about leadership;
- learning leadership.

The purpose of the project was to develop generative student leadership that would enhance the IGS middle school as a community of learners who feel safe, valued and respected. Through investigation with students, their teachers and their parents, practitioner researchers worked to identify the qualities of a good student leader in the context of the Years 6–8 in middle school. Following consultation with the research committee a written questionnaire was developed and undertaken by all Year 8 students. It was designed to be interesting and amusing to undertake. A student representative group was formed to discuss findings and an electronic chat room was established to allow further inputs from Year 8 students and their parents. This phase of the project concluded with a student forum to which parents were invited. The forum presented results and invited discussion regarding a 2002 training programme which would be formatively evaluated after one year of its operation.

Finally, in 2001, a photographic project was undertaken which gave a group of students an opportunity to document their responses to a new middle school arrangement. Photographs were presented in poster form and were discussed at the beginning of the school year in 2002.

Clearly practitioner inquiry has become a substantial enterprise at the school which is admittedly an economically privileged one. However, the enterprise has not been without concerns, risks and tensions. We shall examine these after further considering our second case.

COPS: struggles for curriculum control

The second project which we wish to discuss is the UK COPS programme. Three university researchers worked with a group of teacher researchers in three primary schools to research dimensions of the schools' different forms of curriculum organization and children's experiences of learning. There was a group of researchers in each primary school and one in the university. The teachers were considered to be novice inquirers to be supported by more experienced researchers. The project was seen to be multi-purpose and designed to be of benefit to the participants as well as developing educational knowledge for wider dissemination.

The approach to the inquiry emerged in practice by working pragmatically through the challenges and opportunities which partnership between schools and university presented. It was 'invention-in-action'.

What was agreed was that the children's interests were central. In doing so there was a shared ideological belief that all participants would show high levels of concern for the children's educational interests throughout the project. The teachers, acting as practitioner researchers, saw themselves as 'child-centred' despite what they saw as the hostile political climate in which they had worked in recent years, emphasizing education for the economy. Some, for example, expressed frustrations about an imposed curriculum which their experience showed to be incompatible with the needs of many of their children. Evidence from their COPS research supported their case, although it was also true to say that many of the children were learning well within the imposed statutory curriculum framework, and this their teachers welcomed.

We wrote earlier in this chapter of teachers' pedagogical skills being commensurable with practitioner inquiry skills and that teacher insider knowledge can often illuminate an otherwise confusing picture. One example illustrates this.

One morning the university researcher, working with the given school, arrived to find teachers doing what they called 'warm up exercises' in data gathering and analysis, to be greeted by a degree of excitement and debate. They had been talking with some children about their experiences during an Office for Standards in Education (Ofsted) inspection, asking questions of the children's learning in some of the Ofsted observed lessons. One pupil, Miranda, spoke in some detail of her learning during history. What puzzled the teachers was the child's consistent use of the present tense to describe the actions and thoughts of the Greek sculptor who was the focus of the lesson and was involved in building the Parthenon. Why was Miranda using the present tense to talk about her history lesson? Together, the university researcher and the teachers offered some possible explanations. The first came from one of her previous teachers who declared that Miranda had always been an unusual child so that this 'peculiarity' in her thinking was nothing exceptional. Someone else wondered whether or not the child was sufficiently aware yet that history is about the past, not the present. A third explanation, building on this, posed the possibility of developmental differences in children's history learning. At what point does the child begin to grasp a more realistic sense of time past? Was Miranda at an earlier stage of development where the stories of history are a more compelling influence on learning than abstract time concepts? This third hypothesis opened up new thinking for Miranda's class teacher, Mary, who began to realize that she had taught this lesson through story and drama; an approach which involved present tense thinking and present tense language. She told how she had set up imaginary scenes in the lesson of the quarry from where the Parthenon material was being dug. In role, Mary had acted as an overseer of the quarry, taking the children around, explaining what was happening. She made reference to the sculptor, who was carving his own image on his shield – an illegal act. The sculptor was worrying about getting himself into trouble, which he eventually would at some point in the future. Mary used the language of 'here is', 'he is', 'he will'. This was the language of the present and the future. Little wonder that Miranda had recalled her experience from the drama in these time perspectives. Mary's explanation had been informed by her recall and revisualization of the lesson. This information gave us the clue we needed; that the teacher's own language may well have conveyed a sense of time which was contrary to that which history demanded. Miranda had been unable to disassociate the teacher's language of the present and future from a historical concept of time.

It was clear that this theory building could not have occurred without Mary's accessible, insider memory of the lesson. Certainly, an outsider who did not have access to this kind of teacher insight, nor to the teacher's own explanation of her research data, might have settled for a different and, possibly, less valid explanation.

The point of this extended anecdote is to illuminate the ways in which facilitated practitioner inquiry can open up new possibilities for teacher professional learning and for academic learning. The teachers felt that they came to their understanding of the nature of children's learning through experienced inquiry and not from reading or hearing of the 'grand theory' which is claimed to be such an important resource for professional practice.

The COPS project provided many instances of this kind and led participants to raise important questions about the ways in which the statutory national curriculum was currently being conceptualized and enacted. It also cut across the notions that teachers had of themselves as practitioner inquirers. Some teachers were sceptical at the beginning about their capacity to do research despite the protestations of the university researchers to the contrary. The two years of the project led them to a have a greater confidence in their knowledge of research processes and their skills in carrying them forward.

Some teachers were also sceptical as their work progressed that the qualitative, small-scale nature of their studies could be characterized as 'research'. Their concepts of research were often limited to the scientific, quantitative model. The notion of systematic inquiry which was also reflective, interpretative and inclusive of qualitative data caused some anxiety. Some teachers expected quick and fast statistical analysis attached to readily implemented solutions. They found, on the contrary, that inquiry can raise more problems than it solves; but that it offered new ways of seeing and understanding teaching and learning.

In addition, teachers found themselves struggling with a research process which was cumulative and grounded. Questions changed as data sets emerged. Many had been exposed to the notion of research as hypothesis testing, where the hypothesis itself was fixed. They came to accept the legitimacy of emergent and shifting research designs as inquiry pursued new insights into practice.

Finally, research as a collaborative and collegial exercise, directed to whole-school development, rather than direct improvement in individual classroom practice, is difficult to sustain in an environment which emphasizes the latter. As we have indicated, practitioner inquiry embedded in whole-school development has its own associated concerns, risks and tensions. In this particular school, however, practices were developed to ensure wider dissemination and use of the research project, both in the school community and beyond. The headteacher, for example, positively encouraged the research team to present their work to other school colleagues and to look for opportunities for the new knowledge about children and learning to inform school development plans. The dissemination sessions triggered wider professional debate and analysis in the school, leading to some other teachers and assistants examining aspects of their own provision for children. In addition, the research was shared and discussed with school governors and parents. There was also dissemination and knowledge transference across the three schools in the project and to others beyond via conferences and in-service courses at the university. We do not know, however, what the longer-term impact of these processes has been on other teachers and schools. This is, in general, a greatly under-researched area.

Concerns, risks and tensions in practitioner inquiry in the context of the knowledge-building school

An important issue is that associated with the relationships which arise from the ways in which the inquiry may be facilitated. From the first of the cases quoted, that of the IGS where practitioner inquiry was facilitated by a 'researcher in residence', it may be inferred that the researcher in residence occupies a position that is both inside the school and outside it as well. This is the fifth year of her association with the school and like any frequent visitor she is relatively well known. However, she is not physically located in the school, she does not have an office or any executive powers. She is university based, but in an honorary position. Certainly this positioning means that she has relative autonomy in both the school and university setting, but then again, she does not have responsibility for carrying out actions which may result from the inquiry.

When a whole school uncovers, in those publicly accountable ways, as outlined in this chapter, practices which may be highly problematic, it is not possible to disguise them or walk away from them. The very act of gathering the evidence and developing publicly accessible reports means that expectations are raised that issues will be addressed and concerns dealt with.

Kemmis (2000) speaks of connecting the 'lifeworlds of educational research'. Academic researchers and practitioner researchers operate in different realms with different mores and rewards. Nonetheless, the problems and processes on one side are interconnected with problems and processes on the other. Real dialogue between the two, acting as 'education citizens' in possession of practical professional knowledge, not merely as experts in their fields, can contribute to a more inclusive critique of educational practices as well as informed, well judged actions.

But the tension is not only that which may exist between the facilitator of practitioner inquiry and those within the school itself. It will also exist within the school as a complex, social environment. Kemmis and Wilkinson (1998) write of participatory action research, or what we refer to as practitioner inquiry, as having six characteristics: social; participatory; collaborative; emancipatory; critical; and recursive. In recognizing the inherently social nature of the work, Kemmis and Wilkinson draw attention to the relationship which exists between the individual and the social – the individual is inscribed in the social, inhabits and is habituated by the social (Bourdieu in Robbins 1991). Neither operates apart from the other. In a knowledge-building school it is not possible for teachers to escape to their individual classrooms. They are members of a community of practice.

As we suggested earlier in this chapter, practitioner inquiry is often seen to be individualistic, even private. The researcher is seen to be working and thinking alone, rather than in a community of practice where critique and argument can occur. Anderson and Kerr (1999: 12) have suggested that: 'The insider status of the researcher, the centrality of the action, the requirements of spiralling self-reflection on actions, and the intimate dialectical relationship of research to practice, all make practitioner research alien (and often suspect)'. Coffield (1996: 3) has similarly identified a 'heavy concentration on the role of individuals' as being 'the weakest aspect of both British and European policies in education, related research, training and employment'.

By way of contrast, the work with which IGS and the COPS project have been engaged is dialogic in nature. The premise is that the identification of the problem to be addressed, the collection and interpretation of evidence and the design of action must occur in a context which allows a diversity of views to emerge and an authentic debate to occur, as was the case with Miranda's story. Here we draw upon the arguments of Guba and Lincoln (1994) who have evolved a constructivist version of inquiry in the provision of social services such as education. They argue that 'realities' are mentally constructed, socially and experientially based, local and specific in nature. At the same time they acknowledge that elements are shared among individuals and even across groups, but often in tacit and unproblematized forms. Constructions are not more or less 'true', in any absolute sense, but are more or less *informed*. They recognize that there is a complicated set of linkages between the inquirer and the object of the inquiry and that in order to evolve a shared or consensual construction an ongoing dialogue must be maintained.

These cases raise questions about the ways in which professional knowledge is constructed and understood in schools. As Fishman and McCarthy (2000: 16) observe, Stenhouse believed that teachers need to become 'outsiders to their own research'. They need not only to collect data but also to interpret it critically. This is no easy matter, particularly when given practices have become reified and are thus seen as unchallengeable.

We would argue that caution needs to be exercised when engaged in practitioner inquiry that the celebratory does not transcend the critical. While it is quite defensible to celebrate achievements, this should not be at the expense of developing critical, even emancipatory insights. A knowledge-building school will not only be developing knowledge about sound and justifiable practices, but will have to confront and deal with some which are contentious and problematic. It is a risky business indeed.

Perhaps some of the greatest risks come not from within the schools themselves but from the changing external educational environment where trust in the professionalism of teachers and their capacity to make sound and ethical educational judgements has been brought into question through the adoption of an audit mentality.

Conclusion

We believe that practitioner inquiry, in and of itself, is in good shape. What is less evident is the will to adopt such inquiry within the notion of the knowledge-building school with all of the attributes spelled out earlier in this chapter. As MacDonald (2000) and Atkinson (2000) have noted there is a strong tendency for the processes of practitioner inquiry, or 'action research' as many know it, to be appropriated for the purposes of policy implementation, as a powerful tool supporting faithful adherence to government directives. In effect, it may become a leading strategy which meets the needs of the audit society to control public policy and restrict professional judgement.

The increasing trend to an audit society is an international phenomenon. Governments throughout the world are holding those responsible for the delivery of services, be they care for the aged, the maintenance of justice or the provision of education, to be accountable in ways which eschew professional judgement. Public sector reforms and the ensuing policies in the United Kingdom, the USA and Australia and elsewhere have led to the development of the audit society and audit cultures (Power 1999; Strathern 2000). In implementing these public sector reforms the major concern has been with issues of public accountability by making practices and processes more transparent as well as efficient, effective and economic. The audit society uses its resources to achieve predetermined outcomes which themselves are measurable. Not surprisingly there is little room for negotiation or professional judgement. As the audit requirements are intensified and articulated, less trust is invested in the moral competence of the practitioner to respond to the needs of those they serve. In effect, and in relation to education, as Elliott (2001) has observed, there is a bureaucratic rather than a professional domination of expertise and practice.

Of course, in public sector management it is essential that there are mechanisms for monitoring the effectiveness of the given enterprise, given that levels of investment run to billions. It is expected of those implementing the programmes that they can account for the ways in which they have managed their resources and produced their outcomes. But when does reasonable accountability become onerous audit?

When teachers are well informed, through evidence-based practice, grounded in their own research, then they are well positioned to make the important practical and moral judgements required for schools to be both effective and socially just institutions. They become what Sachs (2000, 2002) calls 'activist professionals'. In addition, there is evidence that practitioner researchers in schools are capturing a new sense of responsible professional autonomy when they engage in self-directed practitioner research against the disempowering backdrop of the audit society (Dadds and Kynch 2001). Such empowerment is not, however, without its tensions, especially when critical practitioner research uncovers dilemmas between the imposed, dominant government agenda and the perceived needs of the learners. At such points, teachers may come face to face with the limits of their own power to influence the imposed systems in directions that accord fully with their values (Dadds *et al.* 2002).

We would argue that the situated professional knowledge created by teachers as a result of sustained and well-supported inquiry is a form of accountability which transcends the narrow performance measures so beloved by bureaucrats. It is authentic accountability which sees as its stakeholders those most affected by educational practices: students, parents, teachers and the broader community. Improving schools is about making them just and humane sites for learning for all. It is far more than the bottom line on a budget statement.

References

Adler, P. and Adler, P. (1998) Observational techniques, in N. Denzin and Y. Lincoln (eds) *Collecting and Interpreting Qualitative Materials*. Thousand Oaks, CA: Sage.

Altrichter, H., Posch, P. and Somekh, B. (1993) *Teachers Investigate their Work*. London: Routledge.

Anderson, G. and Kerr, K. (1999) The new paradigm wars: is there room for rigorous practitioner knowledge in schools and universities? *Educational Researcher*, 28(5): 12–21.

Atkinson, E. (2000) In defence of ideas, or why 'what works' is not enough, *British Journal of Sociology*, 21(3): 318–30.

Carr, W. and Kemmis, S. (1986) *Becoming Critical: Education, Knowledge and Action Research*. London: Falmer Press.

Cochrane-Smith, M. and Lytle, S. (1993) *Inside/Outside: Teacher Research and Knowledge*. New York: Teachers College Press.

Cochrane-Smith, M. and Lytle, S. (1999) Relationships of knowledge and practice: teacher learning in communities, in A. Iran-Nejad and C. Pearson (eds) *Review of Research in Education*, 24(2): 251–307.

Coffield, F. (1996) A tale of three little pigs: building the learning society with straw. Paper presented to the annual conference of European Educational Research Association (EERA), Seville, Spain, 28 September.

Conner, C. (1994) Higher degrees that serve the school or institution, in H. Bradly, C. Conner and G. Southworth (eds) *Developing Teachers, Developing Schools*. London: Fulton.

Corrigan, G. and Groundwater-Smith, S. (2002) What learners think is fair and valid assessment. Paper presented to the *'Challenging Futures' conference: 'Changing Agendas in Teacher Education'*, University of New England, Armidale, 3–7 February.

Cuttance, P. (1999) Report upon the Innovation and Best Practice project. Symposium presented at the annual conference of the Australian Association for Research in Education, Melbourne, December.

Dadds, M. (1995) *Passionate Enquiry and School Development: A Story about Teacher Action Research*. London: Falmer Press.

Dadds, M. and Kynch C. (2001) Lighting the fire of practitioner research. Paper presented to the British Educational Research Association annual conference, University of Leeds.

Dadds, M., Easton C. and Simco N. (2002) *Learning About Children's Perceptions of Statutory Assessment tests (SATs) through Partnership Research*. Lancaster: St Martin's Research Publications.

Davies, P. (1999) What is evidence based education? *The British Journal of Education Studies*, 47(2): 108–21.

Elliott, J. (1991) *Action Research for Educational Change*. Milton Keynes: Open University Press.

Elliott, J. (1999a) Evidence-based practice, action research and the professional development of teachers, *Goldsmith Journal of Education*, 2(1): 2–19.

Elliott, J. (1999b) What future for educational research without an educational theory? Paper presented to the British Educational Research Association annual conference, Brighton, September.

Elliott, J. (2001) How performance audit prevents teachers from evaluating their teaching. Keynote address presented to the International Study Association for Teachers and Teaching (ISATT) 10th biennial conference, University of Algarve, Faro, Portugal, 21–5 September.

Elliott, J. and Sarland, C. (1995) A study of 'teachers as researchers' in the context of award-bearing courses and research degrees, *British Educational Research Journal*, 21: 371–86.

Fishman, S. and McCarthy, L. (2000) *Unplayed Tapes: A Personal History of Collaborative Research*. New York: Teachers College Press.

Gifford, B. (1986) The evolution of the school-university partnership for educational renewal, *Education and Urban Society*, 19(1): 19–26.

Goodwin, N. and Groundwater-Smith, S. (2000) Beyond the individual: corporate professional learning in schools. Paper presented to the 3rd International Practitioner Research Conference, University of Innsbruck, 26–8 September.

Groundwater-Smith, S. (1998) Putting teacher professional judgement to work, *Educational Action Research*, 6(1): 21–37.

Groundwater-Smith, S. (2000) Evidence-based practice: towards whole school improvement. Paper Presented to the annual conference of the Australian Association for Research in Education, Sydney, 4–7 December.

Groundwater-Smith, S. (2001a) Building research capability to inform practice. Paper presented to the ISATT 2001 conference, Faro, Portugal, September.

Groundwater-Smith, S. (2001b) Supporting and sustaining the knowledge-building school. Paper presented to the European Educational Research Association annual conference, Lille, France, 5–8 September.

Groundwater-Smith, S. and Hayes, M. (2001) Transforming assessment, transforming professional learning. Paper presented at the annual conference of the Australian Association for Research in Education, Notre Dame University, Fremantle, 1–5 December.

Groundwater-Smith, S. and Hunter, J. (2000) Whole school inquiry: evidence-based practice, *Journal of In-Service Education*, 26(3): 583–600.

Groundwater-Smith, S. and Mockler, N. (2001) The knowledge-building school: from the outside in, from the inside out. Paper presented to the 3rd CERG conference, University of Technology, Sydney, Kuring-gai Campus, 16–17 February.

Grundy, S. (1995) *Action Research as Professional Development*, Occasional Paper No. 1. Murdoch: Innovative Links Project.

Guba, E. and Lincoln, Y. (1994) Competing paradigms in qualitative research, in N. Denzin and Y. Lincoln (eds) *Handbook of Qualitative Research*, pp. 105–17. Thousand Oaks, CA: Sage.

Hargreaves, D. (1999a) Revitalising educational research: lessons from the past and proposals for the future, *The Cambridge Journal of Education*, 29(2): 242–60.

Hargreaves, D. (1999b) The knowledge creating school, *British Journal of Education Studies*, 47: 122–44.

Heatley, G. and Stronach, I. (2000) Plotting effective narrative writing with 10-year-old children: an action research study, *Educational Action Research*, 8(3): 403–17.

Kemmis, S. (1995) Some ambiguities in Stenhouse's notion of 'the teacher as researcher': towards a new resolution, In J. Rudduck (ed.) *An Education that Empowers*, pp. 73–112. Clevedon, OH: Multilingual Matters.

Kemmis, S. (2000) Educational research and evaluation: opening communicative space. The 2000 Radford Memorial Lecture presented at the annual conference of the Australian Association for Research in Education, Sydney.

Kemmis, S. and Wilkinson, M. (1998) Participatory action research and the study of practice, in B. Atweh, S. Kemmis and P. Weeks (eds) *Action Research in Practice: Partnerships for Social Justice in Education*, pp. 21–36. London: Routledge.

Lather, P. (1986) Research as praxis, *Harvard Educational Review*, 56(3): 257–77.

McDonald, B. (2000) How education became nobody's business, in H. Altrichter and J. Elliott (eds) *Images of Educational Change*, pp. 20–36. Buckingham: Open University Press.

McKernan, J. (1991) *Curriculum Action Research*. London: Kogan Page.

Noffke, S. and Stephenson, R. (eds) (1995) *Educational Action Research: Becoming Practically Critical*. New York: Teachers College Press.

Norris, N. and Robinson, J. (2001) Generalisation: the linchpin of evidence-based practice? *Educational Action Research*, 9(2): 303–10.

Ponte, P. (2002) Action research by teachers: performance and facilitation in theory and practice. Doctoral thesis.

Power, M. (1999) *The Audit Society: Rituals of Verification*. Oxford: Oxford University Press.

Robbins, D. (1991) *The Work of Pierre Bourdieu*. Milton Keynes: Open University Press.

Rudduck, J. and Hopkins, D. (eds) (1985) *Research as the Basis for Teaching: Readings from the Work of Lawrence Stenhouse*. Portsmouth, NH: Heinemann.

Sachs, J. (2000) The activist professional, *The Journal of Educational Change*, 1(1): 77–95.

Sachs, J. (2001) Teacher professional identity: competing discourses, competing outcomes, *Journal of Education Policy*, 16(2): 149–61.

Sachs, J. (2002) *The Activist Teaching Profession*. Buckingham: Open University Press.

Schratz, M. and Walker, R. (1995) *Research as Social Change*. London: Routledge.

Shore, C. and Wright, S. (2000) Coercive accountability, in M. Strathern (ed.) *Audit Cultures*. London: Routledge.

Stenhouse, L. (1979) Research as a basis for teaching (inaugural lecture, UEA), in L. Stenhouse (1983) *Authority, Education and Emancipation*. London: Heinemann.

Stenhouse, L. (1981) What counts as research? *British Journal of Educational Studies*, 29(2), reprinted in J. Rudduck and D. Hopkins (eds) (1985) *Research as a Basis for Teaching: Readings from the Work of Lawrence Stenhouse*. London: Heinemann.

Strathern, M. (ed.) (2000) *Audit Cultures*. London: Routledge.

Thesen, J. and Kuzel, A. (1999) Participatory inquiry, in B. Crabtree and W. Miller (eds) *Doing Qualitative Research*, 2nd edn, pp. 269–92. Thousand Oaks, CA: Sage.

Tooley, J. and Darby (1998) *Educational Research, a Review: A Survey of Published Educational Research*. London: Ofsted.

Wenger, E. (1998) *Communities of Practice: Learning Meaning and Identity*. New York: Cambridge University Press.

11 Using research to improve practice: the notion of evidence-based practice

John Elliott

The author begins by examining the role of government agencies in promoting the idea of teaching as an evidence-based profession within the UK and the rather different 'trajectories of meaning' that have become associated with the idea. In doing so he identifies their implications for the role of teachers and their relationship to the 'knowledge' generated from educational research. He argues that the discourse surrounding 'evidence-based practice' raises fundamental issues concerning the relationship of teachers to research evidence. The author explores these issues in relation to his involvement with the work of the Norwich Area Schools Consortium (NASC). The Consortium was funded by the Teacher Training Agency (TTA) in England and Wales for the purpose of recasting the relationship between teaching and educational research. In focusing on engaging teachers in and with research into the pedagogical dimensions of 'disaffection from learning', they were challenged to deepen their understanding of a complex phenomenon which they encountered in their classrooms on a daily basis. The author argues that what counts as credible and relevant evidence about teaching and learning is ultimately defined by the teachers who engage with research, and not by the genre in which the research is carried out. He also makes out a case for engaging teachers in research as a condition of them being in a position to use research. In conclusion he draws a distinction between policies based on a standards-driven model of educational change and those based on a pedagogically-driven model.

Introduction

Within the UK the TTA (Teacher Training Agency, a government body) played a major role, during the final years of the twentieth century, in constructing a new discourse about the professional development of teachers. Central to this discourse is the idea of *teaching as an evidence-based profession*. In this respect the TTA initiated schemes to provide grants to teachers for carrying out small-scale research projects, and disseminated the findings of selected research studies they undertook for masters degrees and PhDs. It established a National Teachers Panel to represent the voice of teachers as users of educational research. From 1997 the TTA funded four pilot research consortia to promote teachers' engagement with research in Leeds, Manchester, Newcastle and Norwich. The consortia consisted of partnerships between schools, local education authorities (LEAs) and higher education institutions. The broad focus of each consortium was on pedagogical practice in classrooms, and the strategic goal that underpinned this focus was that of raising the educational achievements of students.

From the TTA's perspective (see TTA 1998) too little educational research in the recent past had focused on teaching and learning in schools, or involved teachers in utilizing and disseminating its findings. It argued that educational research 'has avoided this and tackled less challenging aspects of the educational system'. The TTA was quite explicit about its aspiration to exercise more influence over the funding of educational research, and to ensure that it became focused on pedagogy. It claimed to have influenced the deployment of substantial Higher Education Funding Council (HEFC) funds to establish the 'Teaching and Learning' research initiative (see TTA 1998) under the administration of the Economic and Social Research Council (ESRC). Indeed, the National Teachers Panel became involved in reviewing, on behalf of the 'users' of research, proposals to the ESRC Teaching and Learning programme from university-based researchers.

More recently the task of reshaping educational research to provide a basis for the development of teaching as an evidence-based practice has been taken up directly by the Department for Education and Skills (DfES), following the publication of the Hillier Report (Hillier *et al.* 1998) into the state of educational research within the UK. The crisis in the UK surrounding teacher recruitment and supply also led to the DfES asking the TTA to focus on this as its core business, while the department took more responsibility for steering initiatives linked to the continuing professional development (CPD) of teachers. The Teacher Research Grant scheme has been recreated as the DfES Best Practice Scholarships, and the research consortia laid the foundations for the Networked Learning Communities initiative that is being administered through the National College for School Leadership (NCSL).

There are two broad interpretations of UK government initiatives to promote teaching as an evidence-based profession. One interpretation (I shall refer to the other later in this introductory section) is that they are simply trying to ensure that educational research produces findings that are relevant and useful to teachers in their efforts to improve classroom practice. This, of course, implies greater regulatory control over how educational knowledge is constructed and used, but control that can be justified in terms of constructing a knowledge base to empower teachers as professionals. Such an interpretation has been widely espoused within the TTA and the DfES, and will be endorsed by many teachers who dismiss educational research as high on theory and low on practicality.

Indeed, many academic educational researchers in the UK, Europe and the USA over the past 30 years, including this author, have expressed concern about the fact that teachers rarely use the findings of research *on* education to inform their practice. We tended to argue that in order to engage teachers *with* research it was necessary to engage them *in* a form of research that addressed and sought to ameliorate the practical problems they experienced in their particular contexts of action (see e.g. Stenhouse 1975, 1979; Elliott 1978, 1991; Carr and Kemmis 1986). It was out of this internal critique of the credibility and relevance of much educational research for teachers that the practitioner action research movement emerged, with its emphasis on teachers as active participants working alongside academic researchers to actively construct useful knowledge (see, for example, Elliott and Adelman 1974; Elliott and Mac-Donald 1975; Elliott 1976; Ebbutt and Elliott 1985; Hustler *et al.* 1986; Sanger 1989; Hollingsworth and Sockett 1994; O'Hanlon 1996, 2002; Altrichter 1997; Hollingsworth 1997; Somekh 2000; Day *et al.* 2002; Elliott and Zamorski 2002). Such collaboration implied that teachers not only engaged in the activities of gathering, analysing and interpreting evidence but had a voice in what counted as credible and relevant evidence to gather in the first place.

However, in recent years some educational researchers in the UK, notably David Hargreaves (1996, 1997, 1999) and David Reynolds (1998), have argued for a reshaping of educational research to provide more useful and relevant evidence to teachers in a form that neither presumes that teachers need to do research in order to use it, or that what counts as relevant and useful evidence is sufficiently contestable for teachers to have a say about. For these academics the problem of developing teaching as an evidence-based practice is one of reshaping educational research to produce the right kind of knowledge, and then ensuring that it is easily accessible to teachers.

For Hargreaves, priority should be given in educational research to the production of evidence that yields actionable knowledge of 'what works', which he defines in a purely instrumental sense. He argues that: 'research should provide decisive and conclusive evidence that if teachers do X rather than Y in their professional practice, there will be a significant and enduring improvement in outcome' (1997: 412). Such evidence will largely be couched in terms of statistical probabilities gathered through experimental trials.

The discourse of evidence-based practice promoted by various government initiatives is often perceived to stem from rationales for a reinstatement of a quantitative paradigm of educational research provided by David Hargreaves and David Reynolds at their annual lectures to the TTA in 1996 and 1998 respectively, rather than from rationales for teachers' engagement *in* research provided by Stenhouse (1975, 1979) and other like-minded academics in the field of education. Hargreaves is one of the main architects of the government sponsored National Educational Research Forum established after the publication of the Hillier Report. Also, the establishment at the Institute of Education in the University of London of a national coordinating centre for the production of systematic reviews of educational research (the EPPI Centre) to facilitate evidence-based policy and practice is likely to reinforce the future dominance of quantitative experimental studies of the kind advocated by Hargreaves and Reynolds (see A. Oakley 2000, 2001; Hammersley 2001).

In spite of the role of academics like Hargreaves and Reynolds in shaping the terms of the discourse of evidence-based practice, two rather different 'trajectories of meaning' are circulating in the UK policy context. One implies that, in order to use research, teachers need to be engaged *in* researching their own practices within their particular action contexts. This does not mean that the only useful research evidence for teachers is that which they generate. It does, however, imply that in order to make good use of evidence it must be deemed credible to teachers as a basis for researching their own situated practices. It further implies that such credibility will depend on the extent to which teachers are able to exercise a significant measure of control over methodology through their active participation in designing educational research projects and programmes (for example, in relation to what is to count as useful and relevant evidence about their practices).

The other, more dominant 'trajectory of meaning' at the present time does not imply that teachers as a profession should be actively engaged in research at the level of their own classrooms and schools. However, it does sanction the idea of more 'user' involvement in the design of 'practically relevant' research projects and programmes, although this appears to fall short of giving teachers a significant voice on questions of research methodology.

Hargreaves' definition of what counts as relevant and useful evidence for teachers appears to positively feed a second broad interpretation of government initiatives as an attempt to co-opt teachers into a strictly instrumental view of practically relevant educational knowledge, and thereby disconnect it from fundamental questions about the ends of education in the wider society (see Elliott 2001; Elliott and Doherty 2001).

This second interpretation will tend to be associated with academic critiques of Hargreaves' account of evidence-based practice (for example, Hammersley 1997; Lomax 1999; Elliott and Doherty 2001; Elliott 2002).

It would be a mistake, however, to view government policy initiatives as unambiguously reflecting one 'trajectory of meaning' for evidence-based practice to the exclusion of the other. Although the policy discourse tends to be dominated by the framing provided by academic consultants like Hargreaves and Reynolds, the policy initiatives in practice embody conflictual tendencies at the heart of which stand the issues surrounding teachers' engagement with research, as outlined above.

The DfES Best Practice Scholarships endorse teachers' engagement in researching their own practices while, at the same time, appearing to require a measure of compliance to a procedural framework that makes presumptions about what constitutes relevant and useful evidence (for example, in terms of the significance of standardized measures of learning outcomes). The TTA Research Consortium initiative in practice embodied a tension between the two trajectories of meaning referred to. This created space for lively debates about the conceptualization of the process of engaging teachers with research evidence. The issues have now been inherited by the Networked Learning Communities initiative.

It could be argued that the conflicting 'trajectories of meaning' embedded in the implementation of policies to effect evidence-based teaching have very different sources, such that the 'dominant' trajectory stems from the policy context and its counter-oppositional position from the contexts of implementation: the collaborating school and higher education systems. In the experience of this author, as the coordinator of one of the former TTA consortia, this is an oversimplified explanation. The two 'trajectories of meaning' at tension with each other appeared to be constructed and sustained through networks of affiliation that cut across so-called 'interest groups': schoolteachers, LEA officials, higher education based researchers and government officials (see Elliott 1999). How then do we best understand the practical intentions which underpin policy initiatives to promote evidence-based practice?

- As an attempt to empower teachers by giving them more access to relevant and useful evidence about their practices, and by implication to limit the epistemic control exercised by much higher education based educational research.
- As an attempt to disempower teachers by controlling their thinking about what is to count as relevant and useful evidence, and thereby restricting their access to knowledge of a particular kind; namely, to knowledge that is instrumentally useful as a basis for driving up externally defined standards.

This author is of the view that these initiatives embody both intentions and are sustained at tension with each other through their respective interpersonal networks of affiliation that cut across 'interest groups' (see Brennan and Noffke 2000). This is not to deny that one intentionality dominates the policy context but, as policy interacts with practice, spaces are opened up in both the policy and implementation contexts for the other intentionality to gain a measure of leverage, and thereby render the discourse of evidence-based practice inherently unstable.

It was the spaces created by the tension within the discourse itself that enabled the TTA research consortia to explore the issues surrounding the problem of engaging teachers with research. What follows is an examination of these issues in the context of the NASC.

Engaging teachers *in* and *with* research: the experience of NASC

Teachers researching the issue: what counts as credible evidence?

The overall focus of the NASC was on the 'pedagogical dimensions of student disaffection from learning'. This focus shaped the kind of evidence that was considered to be relevant – namely, evidence about the relationship between disaffection as a phenomenon that teachers encountered in their classrooms on a daily basis and the pedagogical strategies they employed. Moreover, following discussions with headteachers before the research got underway 'disaffection' was broadly defined as 'disengagement from learning' to include the 'quietly disaffected' in addition to students who manifested their disaffection more obviously through disrupting lessons and truanting.

This broad definition raised issues early on in the project about what counted as evidence of disaffection from learning and the validity of teachers' inferences from patterns of student behaviour in classroom settings. If disaffection is to be entertained as a possible outcome of the operation of pedagogical factors, or even a partial one inasmuch as other factors are also implicated, then what evidence can be trusted as a basis for identifying it? Can it be operationally defined in terms of an agreed set of behavioural indicators? What about the quietly disaffected whose condition is not obvious to their teachers, and who in behavioural terms appear to be playing the learning game? On what reliable evidential basis can one identify such students?

Given this context, some of the Phase 1 research projects initiated by teachers within their schools addressed these methodological issues quite explicitly. Those engaged in such projects were sometimes reluctant to regard them as anything more than exploratory investigations, or even to call them 'research'. They tended to use different approaches to exploring the question 'What counts as credible evidence?' Four examples will be provided below (for detailed accounts of some of the NASC research studies see Elliott and Zamorski 2002).

Example 1

Staff in one school embarked on a piece of survey research in an attempt to discover an agreed set of behavioural indicators as a basis for selecting a research sample of disengaged students (see Gutteridge 2002). They discovered a lack of any high level of agreement on the majority of the indicators listed in the questionnaire and concluded that disengagement from learning manifested itself behaviourally in different ways for different students and was bound strongly to particular curriculum and teaching contexts. Interestingly this project was initiated at a meeting when a teacher circulated a list of personal behavioural indicators he tacitly employed to intuitively identify a disaffected student. The list generated considerable discussion in which other teachers produced counter instances and conflicting behavioural evidence. As a result the teacher, who was the overall coordinator for research in the school, circulated his list to all members of staff, asking them to reflect about the behavioural indicators they tacitly employed and to add any not included on his list. The final list was then used as a basis for constructing the questionnaire.

Example 2

In another school, teachers embarked on a study of students they called RHINOs (Really Here In Name Only) based on an intuitive belief that significant numbers of underachieving students were quietly coasting through lessons, 'invisible' to their teachers (see A. Oakley 2002). In undertaking this study, they soon encountered the problem of what counted as credible or trustworthy evidence for identifying these 'quietly disaffected' students. They discovered, from interviewing teachers, that annual assessments of students' achievements in relation to estimates of their potential were unreliable as a basis for identifying underachievement and possible RHINOs. The teachers concluded that a combination of observational evidence, which focused on the classroom behaviour of particular individual students, combined with in-depth follow-up interviews with them, generated the credible evidence for identifying RHINOs. They also concluded, on the basis of their observations and interviews, that the existence of RHINOs appeared to be linked to poor learning environments in particular classroom settings. This study tended to confirm the intuitive beliefs which it was set up to test, and had school-wide implications for identifying underachievers and improving the quality of learning environments in classrooms.

Evidence and intuition

Both the above examples illustrate a form of hypothesis testing which originates from teachers reflecting about the evidential basis of their intuitive judgements, and then seeking to test their judgements against systematically gathered evidence. In this context, evidence is perceived to be credible by teachers if it informs and educates, rather than simply displaces, their intuitions.

This does not imply that evidence only becomes credible if it confirms teachers' intuitive beliefs (prejudices). The outcomes can be counter-intuitive as the following example demonstrates.

Example 3

Modern foreign language (MFL) teachers in one school were experiencing significant numbers of disruptive students in their lessons and frequent absenteeism from them. They believed that the major cause of their problem lay in parental attitudes to the value of learning MFLs. Disaffection from their lessons was a parentally condoned phenomenon. The teachers decided on reflection to turn their intuitive belief into a research hypothesis and test it through a survey of parental attitudes to MFLs. The outcome of the research was counter-intuitive. The majority of the parents surveyed expressed a positive attitude to their children learning MFLs. As a result the teachers began to focus their attention on factors operating inside their classrooms.

The proposition that teachers do not have to have their beliefs confirmed in order to find research evidence credible is highly consistent with Kennedy's (1999) US study of the ways teachers evaluate different kinds of research evidence. When presented with examples of different genres of research 'only a small fraction of teachers said that either of these studies was persuasive because their own experiences reinforced the study's findings'. Kennedy discovered that most of the research that teachers found persuasive and relevant to their practice also provoked new thinking on their part.

The role of teachers in determining what counts as evidence about their practices

Kennedy's study is also relevant to the issue, long debated within the educational research community, about whether teachers need to do research in order to meaningfully engage with it. The study appears to confirm the view that teachers can meaningfully engage with research without necessarily having to do research, as some methodologists have tended to argue. An initial reading would suggest that teachers' engagement *in* research is not a necessary condition for evidence to become credible in their eyes, although it may be the case that in certain contexts teachers are more likely to find evidence credible if they are involved in its generation. Such involvement can range from fully participative studies, such as those cited in the above examples, through collaborative research between outsider researchers and teachers, to 'outsider research' that consults teachers at particular points. Research projects in the NASC varied in these respects.

The following is an example of research led by an outsider (see Doherty and Elliott 1999; Doherty 2001, 2002) but which engaged teachers in the process at particular points. It is cited at this point to further illuminate the relationship between teachers' intuitive beliefs and their perceptions of what constitutes 'credible evidence'. It suggests that for teachers to find externally generated evidence credible and trustworthy they may need a context which enables them to examine it in the light of their own reflections about the evidential basis of their intuitive judgements.

Example 4

Such a context was provided in one school where all the staff met for half a day to consider questionnaire evidence of students' classroom and school experiences. Three groups of students had collaborated with a University of East Anglia researcher in designing this questionnaire. The researcher invited the teachers to discuss and challenge *'the main findings'* contained in three summary reports in the light of their own experience. In responding, teachers drew on the evidential basis of their own intuitive judgements and rendered them increasingly explicit, as well as recalling research they were familiar with that either confirmed or challenged the findings reported. By the end of the meeting, staff had collectively assembled clusters of evidence around the main findings from the questionnaire which generated further questions to be addressed and hypotheses to be tested through research in the school and its classrooms. In retrospect the researcher used the phrase 'data poles' to describe the function the reports of the questionnaire findings he introduced into the meeting unintentionally served. In doing so he found himself drawing an analogy with the functions of 'poles' in directing the flow of radioactivity in a nuclear reactor. By the end of the meeting his reports had become somewhat dispensable, he argued, because in the process the teachers provisionalized and problematized the evidence they contained in the light of their experience and other research evidence they were aware of. In this way the evidence contained in the reports was incorporated into a 'wider evidence framework' constructed through the discussion, and now owned collectively by the staff as a common stock of professional knowledge.

Evidence only appeared to become credible to the teachers cited in the example above through contexts of reflection that enabled them to claim ownership over it, in the sense of making it part of the 'frame of reference' they employed in their everyday professional judgements. If this point is generalizable beyond the school depicted above then it suggests that, in teachers' encounters with evidence, there may need to be 'an examination of the implications of evidence for action in an open and equal forum, as a precursor to the collection of evidence or accompanying the suggestion of changes in practice based upon it' (Doherty and Elliott 1999: 5). Such a forum would not simply provide a context for disseminating research findings to a passive audience. It would be integral to a research process that actively engages teachers in knowledge creation. Through it teachers are enabled to define what counts as credible and useful/relevant evidence rather than having it defined for them.

Kennedy's interview study may also be understood on a 'second reading' as providing a context in which teachers do not simply engage with evidence but, in doing so, become engaged in researching their own practice. She presents her findings as if their validity is independent of the context she creates for teachers to engage with the research they are asked to read. However, she claims that teachers' judgements that a particular piece of research is plausible and relevant do not mirror qualities that are inherent in the study itself. Rather, they are the outcome of an inquiry the teachers undertake into the connection between the evidence presented and their own teaching practices. In this sense teachers' engagement with research does indeed depend on them researching their practice, at least in a minimal sense. It is not a matter of teachers straightforwardly *applying* the findings from other people's research to their own practices. This would presume that the credibility and usefulness of such findings had been independently established prior to teachers engaging with them. One wonders how many of Kennedy's teachers would have come to value some of the studies they read if she had not provided a context that enabled them to use them as a resource for inquiring into their own practices.

The discussion of the possible implications of the example of outsider-led research described above suggests that the distinction between engaging teachers *with* and *in* research may pose a false dichotomy. Its usefulness presumes a context in which universities have traditionally exercised hierarchical and bureaucratic control over what is to count as knowledge about educational practice in schools. As Hollingsworth and Sockett (1994: ch.1) summarize this legacy, 'Scientific conclusions are discovered by university researchers, tested in the Heraclitan fire of the refereed journal, and handed down to efficient classroom technicians'. It is only in a context where teachers are being expected to passively implement the findings of outsider research that the contrast between engaging teachers *in* and *with* research has much point.

Since the TTA's initiative in establishing four research consortia can be interpreted as an attempt to reconstitute the relationship between universities and schools in a form that gives teachers greater control over what is to count as knowledge about their practices, then the example of outsider-led research in the NASC, cited above, may itself constitute some evidence of its effectiveness in this respect (as also would the Phase 2 cross-school research on 'rewards and sanctions' and 'classroom management', since it was in many respects led by researchers based at the University of East Anglia). However, as described earlier, the idea of evidence-based practice that underpins the rationale for the TTA consortia itself became the subject of debate within the educational research community (see Hargreaves 1996, 1997; Hammersley 1997; Reynolds 1998; Elliott 1999, 2001; Elliott and Doherty 2001). One strand of this debate has been the issue of whether the idea is being used to legitimate the erosion rather than the strengthening of teachers' judgements as a basis for action in classrooms. In this context there may still be some point in drawing a distinction between teachers' engagement *in* and *with* research if there is a continuing tendency to interpret the latter as a passive stance to evidence.

Evidence, context, and the complexity of teaching

Although the student questionnaire, referred to earlier, was constructed by the students themselves with the support of an external researcher, this also involve detailed discussions with key members of staff in the school to ensure that teachers' concerns were also being addressed. Much of the evidence generated by educational research is ignored because it fails to match teachers' concerns. Again Kennedy's (1999) study is illuminating in this respect. She found that what makes evidence credible or plausible to teachers is that it helps them to make sense of the complex triangular relationship between teaching, learning and subject matter in their classrooms. Different genres of research – experiments, surveys, case studies and narratives – can be of equal value if they help teachers deepen their understanding of the complexity of this relationship. If they fail to address this concern, teachers find little value in them, regardless of genre. The studies which teachers found to be of little value 'each addressed only one or another corner of the triangle connecting teachers, subject matter, and learners'. The provision of student performance data was not viewed by teachers as particularly useful. They found it difficult to interpret 'without more knowledge of what these students' teachers were doing'.

This may explain why teachers involved in the NASC displayed less interest in externally generated data sets that focused exclusively on student performance. They found it difficult to use this data to make sense of the complexities of life in their classrooms. Giving teachers more control over the design of research generally and the questions it asks may increase the possibility that the complexity of teaching and learning as they experience it is addressed. This is very well exemplified by Zamorski and Haydn (2002) in their account of teachers' participation in the design of the NASC's cross-school 'classroom management' research at the beginning of Phase 2 of the programme.

In the course of their Phase 1 investigations, many teachers became more aware of disaffection as a context bound phenomenon which manifested itself in particular learning environments rather than others. They also became more aware of the variety of ways in which different students manifested their disaffection behaviourally in the same learning environment:

> I find every student is so different, and what one person is manifesting can be a very obvious thing, just an attitude where they are not going to work . . . with other students it can be so different . . . even as simple as trying to get you into conversation about something completely outside the subject and in that sense trying to distract you from teaching them because they are trying to avoid work.
>
> (Teacher researcher)

The Phase 1 projects, and the reports on them, revealed the value teachers perceived in gathering evidence of students' perceptions and interpretations of life in classrooms, either through interviews or questionnaire surveys or both. Observational evidence was also important but, alone, was generally not regarded as sufficient. Participating teachers tended to attribute great importance to understanding the reasons why individual students became disaffected from learning in particular lessons. When asked what kind of evidence they found useful the following responses were not untypical:

> Listening to them telling us why they are disaffected if we could do that. Finding the reasons why they are disaffected.

> . . . talking to children. The amount of insight we got . . . in half an hour . . . You would think 'Well, this person is underachieving, why? They were shy initially, but once you hit upon the key issue . . . The key issues were different for everyone . . . we got loads and loads of stuff . . . lesson observations have been good but all that has been able to confirm is 'Yes, this is a (quietly) disaffected child and they behave in this way'. The patterns in which they behave are quite similar . . . The reasons behind the behaviours are all unique. That's what you need to know. You can identify the fact that that child is underachieving but [need] to find out why.

> I have been happy with what I have done because the part of research that I was involved in was with one of my Year 10 English groups and it has improved my rapport with them, it has improved my understanding of them. I think it has made them feel valued and I think it will probably lead to an improvement in their grades. But I think that's a side thing. I think that has come out of talking to them. I think it's like any good teacher. If we had more time to talk to pupils we would get better results and because we allocate a time to talk to them because of the research I think that is paying off. In terms of ideas about RHINOs I think it does raise issues . . . it has made me look a bit more at what is happening.

Some teachers, including the last one quoted, were ambiguous about whether the evidence elicited by talking to individual children and the insights they gained as a result constituted proper research. They saw such evidence-gathering activity as an integral component of 'good teaching' rather than something that was confined to a separate activity called research, with its own distinctive aims and purposes. It is interesting that the last teacher quoted saw the value of the insights he gained and their pay-off for his teaching as spin-offs from the research rather than part of its central purpose. The reason for this appears to lie in the belief that proper research should yield generalizable findings about the relationship between teaching and learning that have clear practical implications. While the teacher in question valued the insights he personally gained from talking to individual children, he was less certain that he had produced any useful 'research outcomes': 'I'm a bit afraid of generalizing . . . I would generalize about boys being more likely to be RHINOs and teachers being wary of confrontation and therefore enabling this to go on . . . I wouldn't say that arising out of the research I had thought "Gosh, if I did this, this would be better".'

However, in talking to individual students and asking them why they experienced disaffection in particular learning environments, other teachers began to question the value of research aimed at discovering pedagogical solutions that could be generalized to populations of students:

> . . . the other thing I did was talk to pupils in general about their learning and I think what I found was . . . they are all individually very different . . . it's very easy to come up with general strategies . . . we are sort of throwing strategies at whole-class situations or whole-school situations whereas what we really should be looking at is smaller events and individual pupils . . . there's never a dialogue about learning or teaching or why they don't learn.

From this perspective, credible research evidence emerged from the detailed study of particular cases. Given sufficient time, the tension between the two perspectives on what counted as credible research evidence might have been resolved within the consortium. Signs of a move in this direction were present at Phase 2 in the work of the 'classroom management' group (see Zamorski and Haydn 2002) as it designed a qualitative study to run in parallel with a cross-school survey of student perceptions of teachers and teaching. Whereas the survey offered the group a prospect of generalization through aggregating data across classroom, subject and school contexts, the qualitative study offered them a prospect of generalization through the comparison of individual cases of disaffection. By designing an interview study that would enable them to compare and contrast the experiences of individual disaffected students in relation to their different classroom, subject and school contexts, the group acknowledged the possibility of accumulating evidence from particular cases as a different basis for generalization to that provided by the survey. It is unfortunate that the period of the NASC funding terminated and we were unable to establish a context in which the relative value of the two sets of findings could be fully discussed with teachers throughout the consortium. It may well have gone a long way to resolving the tension between the two perspectives on credible research evidence that emerged in the course of the programme.

Teachers who talked to students in order to discover why they were disaffected in particular learning environments became increasingly reluctant to view the relationship between pedagogy and 'disaffection' as a straightforward linear one between cause and effect. The relationship came to be viewed as a very context-bound and complex affair. Pedagogy was viewed as only one category of factors configuring with others to shape learning environments. For example, the following were considered to be significant components of these configurations: personality characteristics; the climate of expectations in the home and the community as well as the school generally; peer relationships and cultures outside lessons; gender differences:

> . . . because I'm a mathematician I expected to see certain patterns that you would say 'Oh, yes. I can understand why that happens'. It has given certain patterns but not the ones I was expecting. So in that sense [the research] has actually opened up the way I see the exclusion room . . . the students are being a problem not for obvious reasons . . . There's more to it than the person who's teaching them or the subject they are doing. It seemed to be a lot wider than that.

> . . . it depends where the survey starts and finishes. One of the things we might argue for this school is that our parents are not largely very ambitious for the children . . . So I think in a sense some of the disengagement of the kids is a social thing, I would argue a lot of it is social. But we are not actually doing research on that.

Some teachers, like the above, came to feel that exploring the relationship between pedagogy and disaffection should not restrict the evidence gathered to pedagogical factors. They did not imply that as pedagogues they were powerless to effect changes in their students' levels of engagement and motivation; only that in order to do so they needed to understand how the pedagogical factors interacted with other factors to shape these levels. This emerged as an issue for teachers in a policy context where they felt that they alone were being held to account for the educational destinies of their students, and that the influence of wider social factors on students' attainment levels was being played down. Perhaps many teachers engaged in the NASC had always intuitively experienced the relationship between teaching and learning as a complex affair, as Kennedy's study would suggest. In which case, the interview evidence made teachers more consciously aware of this complexity, and gave them the confidence to articulate what they already knew and to resist a policy-driven discourse that oversimplified the relationship. At this point it should be pointed out that, although some teachers may have initially feared that the TTA would reinforce such a discourse, their fears diminished in the course of time, particularly during Phase 2 when the particular TTA link officer for the NASC in post at that time reassured teachers that they were not expected to assume a straightforward linear relationship.

The status of evidence that raises more questions than answers

An increasingly conscious awareness of the complexity and context-bound nature of the phenomenon they were investigating made busy teachers anxious about drawing valid conclusions from the evidence they had gathered. They experienced a tension between the process they were engaged in and the expectation that *'proper research'* yielded clear and firm conclusions. The origins of this expectation are a matter for speculation, but it appeared to stem from a dominant conception of science embedded in our culture and transmitted through the educational system, including higher education. Given this expectation about what 'proper research' entails, the problem for the NASC teachers was that the evidence they gathered kept raising more questions than answers. A number of Phase 1 reports failed to generate 'findings' within the time set for their submission (summer 1999) but pointed to an ongoing process of question-posing. As one teacher commented: 'Certainly I would like to see people encouraged to carry it on because I think from what I have read most people would say they had made a start but they hadn't actually finished. Everything you do raises more questions'.

In fact a number of teachers began to value this kind of inquiry for its own sake as a process of continuous reflection on their practice. Engagement in such 'reflective inquiry' became a source of professional satisfaction for these teachers, in as much as it moved them beyond a narrowly instrumentalist and reactive view of their practice.

The perception that 'proper research', regardless of its scale, produced evidence to support the drawing of firm conclusions was sometimes seen to be reinforced by remarks made by some senior staff and colleagues in their schools, or by academics or TTA consultants. For example:

> The great difficulty is . . . feeling secure that you have the evidence to support what you believe to be happening, to be able to demonstrate to others that it is . . . rigorous research . . . I am not even bothered with rigour to be truthful . . . the fact of the matter is that [the project] has involved inquiry, it has involved an assessment of the evidence and people have written up, albeit tentatively, what their findings have been. Some smart academic may say well that is rubbish isn't it? . . . that they have done the same thing and much better. My answer to that is 'So what?' I think process is arguably more important than the product and I think we should not underestimate the value of the process.
>
> (Headteacher)

The headteacher here appears to be saying that engaging teachers in a dynamic process of evidence gathering which promotes reflection about teaching is more valuable than being able to produce an end product in the form of a set of validated findings. If the evidence teachers gather in the process provokes thinking about their practice, then that is sufficient. Another headteacher came to a similar conclusion when he explained how long it had taken him to see the potential of the NASC for achieving a cultural change in the way all his teachers think about their practice. He no longer saw teachers' engagement in the process of research as something the value of which simply depended on being able to demonstrate the validity of its findings to others not so engaged. This last headteacher subsequently began to explore ways of engaging all his staff in exploratory research within their classrooms. Strategies in this respect are still evolving in the school nearly a year after the consortium funding from the TTA ceased.

Experience within the NASC suggests that the adoption of a whole-school approach to engaging teachers in the kind of reflective question-posing inquiry referred to above presented practical problems for some school managers. These are somewhat different from the problems posed by a 'research and disseminate' approach that attempts to engage all teachers with research evidence generated within the school by either outsider researchers or a small group of staff, or a mixture of both. It appears to be more difficult for a large number of teachers in a school, compared with a small group, to sustain engagement in a process that involves time-consuming observations and interviews with students in their own and each other's classrooms. Academic staff of the university were available to assist teachers with this kind of data-gathering, and a small number of teachers made use of this support. Given the fact that the Office for Standards in Education (Ofsted) inspections coincided with the NASC programme in a number of schools, there was an understandable reluctance on the part of many teachers to open their classrooms to even more external observation, even from their peers. Some headteachers and senior staff confronted realities in their staffrooms and their school that made a 'research and disseminate' approach attractive, inasmuch as it avoided pressurizing staff to commit time to a process that risked any further lowering of confidence and morale while, at the same time, providing opportunities for all staff to reflect about evidence and its implications for their practice. Although the majority of the NASC schools adopted this approach to engaging teachers with research, at least three schools also evolved strategies for fostering among their staff a research stance that was integral to their teaching.

Ideographic and nomothetic conceptions of credible evidence

In the context of school-based research into student disaffection, many of the NASC teachers were concerned that evidence was credible to their professional colleagues within and beyond their school. 'Disaffection' was viewed as a problem all teachers had to handle on a daily basis. Most of those engaged in Phase 1 projects felt an obligation to report their work to other teachers within their school, and across the consortium as a whole.

A tension emerged between ideographic and nomothetic conceptions of credible and useful evidence. The former conception attributes value to the study of particular cases while the latter attributes value to the study of populations. Evidence gathered from the ideographic study of particular cases had obvious value for those engaged with the case, but for them its value to others was less obvious. On the other hand, evidence gathered for the purpose of generalizing to populations appeared to many teachers to possess plausibility and relevance to others. Some of the Phase 1 projects largely adopted a case study approach to evidence gathering, while others veered towards aggregating data based on questionnaires and structured interview surveys. Some attempted a mixed mode approach with a view to creating fruitful links between the two kinds of evidence.

The reader may feel that a false dichotomy emerged in the context of the NASC. If this is so, it is a dichotomy that is well explored and represented in the methodological literature of the social sciences. In the NASC context it constituted a creative tension that enabled many teachers to explore and discuss possibly fruitful links between the two kinds of evidence, as happened in the 'classroom management project'.

Interestingly, the Phase 1 research report that appears to have had the greatest impact to date on teachers across the consortium was unambiguously ideographic; namely, the case studies of RHINOs (see J. Oakley 2002). It even influenced the successful submission of a research proposal to the ESRC on the 'invisible child' in the mathematics classroom. This might be viewed as quite consistent with the claims of certain case study methodologists (see, for example, Stake 1995) that ideographic accounts are 'naturalistically generalizable' in the sense that it is the readers who do the generalizing, by discovering similarities between the case(s) depicted and those they have direct experience of.

Cross-school research and the drift in favour of nomothetic methods

Phase 2 of the NASC programme involved a shift away from the Phase 1 projects, generated by individual and small groups of teachers within their schools, towards a small number of cross-school projects on topics which emerged from the sharing of ideas and issues across the Phase 1 projects. Each cross-school project was collaboratively planned by teachers and academic staff members at the University of East Anglia. Interestingly, the two largest cross-school projects tended to prioritize the gathering and statistical analysis of questionnaire data about teachers' and students' perceptions of events and situations, although in some schools this data was supplemented by case data gathered through classroom observation and interviewing.

The teachers involved in the Phase 2 projects were not primarily concerned with the credibility of their evidence to academic researchers as such, but they did see the latter as an important source of technical expertise to draw on in the production of 'credible' survey evidence. They felt that to make evidence credible to teachers across the consortium, it should consist of aggregated data capable of yielding generalisable findings.

The majority of teachers involved in the cross-school Phase 2 projects were happy to be engaged in research with respect to defining both the research agenda – the questions to be addressed – and the kind of evidence worth gathering. They were more hesitant when it came to claiming ownership over the processes of gathering and analysing evidence, and expected much of this to be carried out by the 'experts' from the university. One academic research mentor related the following episode: 'One afternoon when we were trying to get the cross-school projects in place, I felt that in the last half an hour, some of the teachers were looking to me to just do a questionnaire and give it to them. In the end we worked it out together over about three meetings and a pilot, and I'm sure that this was a much better approach'.

The reason for this dependence may appear to be obvious. Teachers did not see themselves as possessing the necessary technical skills and did not connect them with the skills of the good teacher. These perspectives, however, stemmed from what has now become a dominant view about the nature of 'credible research evidence'. Nomothetic survey evidence is presumed to be more credible to colleagues across the consortium as a whole, because it promises to yield tidier and more generalizable findings than ideographic case study evidence. This preference in the context of across-school research for gathering quantifiable evidence about teachers' and students' perceptions of life in classrooms resulted in a greater dependency on the academic staff of the university than was apparent with many of the Phase 1 case study projects initiated in particular schools. It may have also been reinforced by teachers' experience of the time-consuming nature of qualitative case study research, and their anxiety and doubt about the adequacy of their evidence as a basis for producing firm and clear conclusions.

The knowledge and skills involved in designing surveys and analysing survey data were not perceived by teachers initially to be an integral part of their role. Whereas a number of the participating teachers in Phase 1 did perceive the knowledge and skills involved in gathering and analysing ideographic evidence as integral to being a good teacher, they were hesitant about regarding such activities as 'proper research'.

The view of the relationship between teaching and research that tended to shape the cross-school research was reinforced by professional norms which worked against teachers collaborating to gather qualitative data about particular cases of teaching and learning – for example, by observing each other's lessons and interviewing the students involved about their interpretations of events. Teachers displayed, with some exceptions, a reluctance to embark on data-gathering activities in each other's classrooms. They feared that their colleagues would experience such activities as intrusions into their professional domain, particularly in a climate where they carry overtones of inspection and performance appraisal and threaten to drain trust out of professional relationships.

The development of a proposed code of practice for collaborative classroom research, aimed at maintaining trust, was not generally sufficient to overcome this fear. Ideographic research methods involve more than technical expertise. They involve the exercise of very high levels of interpersonal skill and ethical competence in face-to-face situations. Many teachers not only lacked confidence in relation to this personal dimension of qualitative research, but needed to be convinced that the time invested in developing the necessary research skills would have sufficient pay-off for their own teaching, given what is demanded of them. For example, the teachers engaged in the Phase 1 projects did not make full use of the funds available to buy themselves out of teaching duties for periods to engage in peer observation activities. This was because they feared that reduced continuity of contact might jeopardize the exam and test results of their students, for which they would be held accountable.

Given the above constraints on the use of case study research methods by teachers, it should not surprise us to find some teacher researchers preferring survey methods as their primary means for generating 'credible research evidence', in spite of the attempts of University-based coordinators and mentors during both phases of the programme to get teachers to appreciate the relative strengths and limitations of each approach. Many teachers did develop some appreciation of these. Nevertheless, in the circumstances depicted above and given the pressures of time that mounted during Phase 2, the use of surveys appeared to offer teachers the prospect of producing a set of reasonably tidy and useful findings, even if the evidence provided only partial insights into how and why particular students became disaffected in their particular learning environments.

The retreat from qualitative methods at Phase 2 may well prove to be only a temporary stage in teachers learning to do research. The time and trouble involved in doing qualitative research, and concerns about generalizability, may only provide a partial explanation for a shift towards survey-based research. There were, for example, signs at Phase 2 of some teachers beginning to broaden their research expertise to include quantitative methods and becoming more independent of the university team in this respect. They developed skills with the help of university mentors in working the Statistical Package for Social Sciences (SPSS) computerized data analysis package.

At some future stage of the consortium, if it proves sustainable in some form, many teachers might well develop a deeper understanding of the pros and cons of different approaches to research. This began to be evident, as indicated earlier, in the work of the group of teachers involved in the cross-school 'classroom management' project. The university-based project coordinator and its mentor were able to demonstrate to the teachers involved the potential in using the analysis of qualitative data as a basis for questionnaire design. The group then struggled to accommodate the insights they had gained into the complexity of teaching from the qualitative analysis into the framing of the questions for the survey. They then went on to help with the design of a parallel qualitative study, subsequently carried out by the project coordinator, to complement the survey evidence. It was unfortunate that there was not sufficient time for the teachers to become involved in the production of a synthesis analysis of the two data sets.

Beyond the battle between paradigms

In spite of the tensions and issues noted above, a very noticeable feature of the NASC project has been the developing confidence of teachers in handling different kinds of research evidence. Initially, teachers were tentative, even defensive, about their ability to go 'beyond the known'. Later, they became more at ease, and developed a much broader view about what research was, and what it was for. This was arguably an outcome of the rich mixture of the personnel involved in the NASC: professional researchers (some with international reputations), teacher-educators who were comparatively new to educational research, full-time doctoral students and teachers with varying degrees of research experience. This involvement of people with several different layers and levels of research expertise helped to broaden and question views of what constituted credible and relevant evidence, and what research was for.

Teachers in the NASC did not only find evidence about their own practices and classroom situations credible and relevant. Both case study evidence gathered in others' classrooms and decontextualized survey evidence became credible and relevant, albeit for different reasons, inasmuch as both provoked thought about the complexities of teaching and learning in their own classrooms. This supports Kennedy's finding that research evidence of very different kinds, whether case studies or surveys or even experimental studies, can provoke such thinking. This is because teachers are able to forge analogies between such studies and their own practices.

What counts as credible and relevant evidence is ultimately defined by the teachers who engage with research and not by the genre in which the research is carried out. Although the distinctive features of each genre may appeal to different ways of knowing and understanding teaching and learning

situations, Kennedy found that teachers do not attribute monolithic importance to any one set of characteristics. This was confirmed by our experience, in
the context of the NASC, of engaging teachers *in* and *with* research. It is an
experience that offers a challenge to both quantitative and qualitative educational researchers who presume that what constitutes 'useful' evidence can
be defined independently of teachers.

Learning how to handle the complexity of 'life in classrooms' as a focus for the CPD of teachers: implications for educational research and policy

Standards-driven educational reform over the past decade and a half in the UK
has encouraged teachers to view pedagogy as the construction of *rationally* or
logically ordered learning environments. Such reform has shaped pedagogy in
terms of learning requirements that stem from 'social and economic needs' as
these are defined by policy makers, and are cast in the form of standardized
and measurable intended learning outcomes (see Hinchliffe 2001: 31).
Standards-driven reform has also shaped educational research as a source of
means-end rules (encapsulated in a particular concept of 'evidence') for
rationally ordering the learning environment to produce such outcomes. It
involves the construction of a clockwork world characterized by repetition and
predictability. The learning environment is viewed as a closed and linear system governed by the laws of cause and effect. Such a system leaves little space
for the 'personal', for the cultivation of the individual learner as a unique
centre of consciousness with a distinctive point of view, endowed with particular talents and abilities, and possessing particular characteristics. Seen in this
light it is not surprising to find that current pedagogical practice in schools
tends to neglect the complexity of classroom life, and fails to meet the needs of
individual learners. The counterproductive side-effect of a pedagogy shaped by
standards-driven educational reform is widespread disaffection from learning.
The experience of the NASC project suggests that many teachers understand
this, implicitly if not explicitly.

What is required as a future focus for the professional development of
teachers in the UK, and other countries that have embraced a similar reform
ideology, is a shift in the policy context towards providing better support for
teachers to develop their pedagogical practice in a form that acknowledges the
complexity of teaching and learning. I have argued elsewhere that such a
development will involve the creation of more *aesthetically ordered* learning
environments that accommodate the diverse needs of individual learners and
the personal dimension of learning in specific classroom situations (see Elliott
2003). Such environments are dynamic, complex systems characterized by a
large measure of unpredictability with respect to learning outcomes, a high

degree of conscious self-monitoring on the part of the teacher and learners and spaces for conversation and dialogue about the process of teaching and learning. Their creation is a matter of *personal artistry* on the part of teachers, rather than the application of a uniform control technology of teaching derived from the research findings of 'teacher effectiveness' research.

If one views *educational* change in terms of an intelligent response to the pedagogical problems and challenges that confront teachers in handling the complexity of life in their classrooms, then one might describe it as *pedagogically-driven educational reform*. This view of educational reform stands in marked contrast to the *standards-driven reform* movement that has tended to shape pedagogy in educational institutions according to a change agenda which ignores this complexity and views the ideal learning environment as a simple, stable, linear system that behaves in quite predictable ways.

Pedagogically-driven reform depends upon the capacity of teachers to progressively deepen their understanding of the complex situations they face in attempting to create high quality learning environments that meet the diverse learning needs of their learners. Such *situational understanding* is developed not so much in advance of their practical interventions but in conjunction with them. Understanding informs action and action informs understanding. This is the process by which teachers develop their practical knowledge of how to create aesthetically ordered learning environments, and is often depicted as a form of action research in which 'action' is an integral part of the research and 'research' an integral part of the action. As indicated earlier, such a process provides a context for utilizing research 'evidence' generated outside the particular action situation.

As a mode of knowledge construction and utilization in a pedagogical context, action research cannot be dissociated from the creative activity of constructing an educationally worthwhile learning environment for learners. It will, therefore, mirror the form of such activity and can be depicted as an aesthetically organized construction of practical/educational knowledge, in which the teacher selects, assembles and synthesizes a diversity of inquiry devices (together with different kinds of externally generated evidence) in terms of his or her judgements about their appropriateness to the pedagogical situation.

Action research is often accused of not being 'proper research' because the model of research is drawn from the natural sciences and its search for the logical or rational order of things. The assumption underlying this model is that there exists a set of transcendental methodological principles for organizing the construction of knowledge in the form of a uniform corpus of methods and procedures. In other words, the form in which knowledge is constructed must mirror the rational order that is presumed to exist in the world. This model of research separates 'science' and 'artistry'. It leaves little room for the idea of a practical educational science as a form of disciplined inquiry that supports the artistry of teachers as they attempt to construct *aesthetically ordered* learning environments in their classrooms and schools. What disciplines educational action research is not the use of a fixed corpus of methods and procedures, or the use of a cumulative body of evidence generated outside the particular pedagogical context, but the need to get a clearer understanding of the complexities of a teaching situation in order to create more meaningful learning environments for students.

If learning how to handle the complexity of teaching and learning is to become the focus for the CPD of teachers it implies a radical rethinking of the relationship between pedagogy, research and educational policy. This chapter has hopefully contributed to rethinking the triangle, particularly with respect to the relation between pedagogy and research. With respect to policy, it implies a shift away from a standards-driven and socially engineered model of change towards supporting a pedagogically-driven model that gives space for teachers to exercise artistry in their teaching. This will involve recasting National Curriculum frameworks in forms that permit teachers to respond more flexibly to the diversity and complexity of the learning needs that exist in their classrooms. Such recasting will imply more focus on the process of teaching and learning, and take the form of frameworks couched in terms of principles and criteria rather than specific learning outcomes. Their main purpose will be to guide rather than prescribe the development of school-based programmes. There are signs that this is happening in the UK, particularly with respect to the post-14 curriculum.

A shift of emphasis in the model of change-shaping policy will also involve developing an integrated model of *professional accountability* and *development*. Such a model will place a higher trust in teachers with less emphasis on the production of standardized and measurable learning outcomes and more emphasis on the responsibility of teachers to construct learning environments that challenge, engage and motivate all pupils. Such an emphasis would require teachers to elicit feedback from their peers and their students on a continuous basis, and to regularly produce reflective reviews of their attempts to improve the quality of teaching and learning in their classrooms. These would function as a contribution to the development of pedagogical scholarship within the teaching profession. The establishment of government sponsorship and funding for teachers wishing to research and report their attempts at pedagogical innovation in the form of the Best Practice Scholarships, and for pedagogically focused 'learning networks' that extend across clusters of schools, may be viewed as moves in the direction of an integrated high-trust model of professional accountability and development.

In the UK we appear to be witnessing a parting of the ways between academic educational research funded through the ESRC and action research-based professional development funded increasingly through government agencies. Although the former prioritizes a focus on pedagogy through the

ESRC's Teaching and Learning initiative, it tends to be shaped by the methodologies of the behavioural sciences and to emphasize the use of experimental trials and quantitative methodologies (although not exclusively). The ESRC initiative places great stress on disseminating its findings to potential 'user groups', including the teaching profession. Support for action research-based professional development in schools was once the exclusive province of higher education institutions through funded research and development projects and part-time postgraduate provision. This is decreasingly the case. Action research, and with it CPD provision for teachers, appears to have been 'colonialized' by government agencies who now directly fund teachers, schools and school networks, and then leave it to them to decide the terms and conditions of academic support. Academics, who as teacher-educators, worked collaboratively with teachers to understand the complexities of life in their particular classrooms, have become increasingly marginalized in the educational research community. It is a community shaped by a national research assessment exercise that significantly rewards those who achieve recognition and receive funding from the ESRC. The academics referred to may no longer feel at home in an academy governed by quality assurance mechanisms that divorce teacher education from educational research.

The education policy context currently shaping both the professional development of teachers and educational research appears to have entered a schizoid phase in the UK. On the one hand the policies currently shaping educational research in the academy appear to be reinforcing an idea of 'evidence-based' teaching that supports standards-driven change in classrooms. On the other hand the policies currently shaping the professional development of teachers appear to be reinforcing a rather different idea of 'evidence-based' teaching that supports pedagogically-driven change. The question is whether such change is sustainable in a situation where the theoretical and methodological resources once provided by education departments in the academy are in a state of decline.

References

Altrichter, H. (1997) Practitioners, higher education and government initiatives in the development of action research: the case of Austria, in S. Hollingsworth (ed.) *International Action Research: A Casebook for Educational Reform*, ch. 3. London: Falmer Press.

Brennan, M. and Noffke, S. (2000) Social change and the individual: changing patterns of community and the challenge of schooling, in H. Altrichter and P. Posch (eds) *Images of Educational Change*, ch. 5. Buckingham: Open University Press.

Carr, W. and Kemmis, S. (1986) *Becoming Critical: Education, Knowledge and Action Research*. Lewes: Falmer Press.

Ebbutt, D. and Elliott, J. (eds) (1985) *Issues in Teaching for Understanding*. London: Longman/Schools Curriculum Development Committee.

Day, C., Elliott, J., Somekh, B. and Winter, R. (eds) (2002) *Theory and Practice in Action Research*. Oxford: Symposium Books.

Doherty, P. (2001) The curriculum dimensions of student disaffection: a single site case study. Unpublished PhD thesis, University of East Anglia.

Doherty, P. (2002) Engaging pupils in researching disaffection within a school, in J. Elliott and B. Zamorski (eds) (2002) *Teachers Research Disaffection*, special issue of *Pedagogy, Culture and Schooling* devoted to collaborative research within the Norwich Area Consortium.

Doherty, P. and Elliott, J. (1999) Engaging teachers in and with research: the relationship between evidence, context and use. Presentation to the annual conference of the British Educational Research Association (BERA), University of Sussex, Brighton.

Elliott, J. (1976) Developing hypotheses about classrooms for teachers' practical constructs: an account of the work of the Ford Teaching Project, *Interchange*, 7(2): 2–22.

Elliott, J. (1978) What is action research in Schools? *Journal of Curriculum Studies*, 10(4): 355–7.

Elliott, J. (1991) *Action Research for Educational Change*. Buckingham: Open University Press.

Elliott, J. (1999) Evidence-based practice, action research and the professional development of teachers, *Goldsmiths Journal of Education*, 2(1): 1–19.

Elliott, J. (2001) Making evidence-based practice educational, *British Educational Research Journal*, 27(5): 555–74.

Elliott, J. (2003) Re-thinking pedagogy as the aesthetic ordering of learning experiences, invited paper for the annual conference of the Philosophy of Education Society (UK), New College, Oxford, April.

Elliott, J. and Adelman, C. (eds) (1974) *Ford Teaching Project Reports and Documents*. Norwich: CARE, University of East Anglia.

Elliott, J. and Doherty, P. (2001) Restructuring educational research for the 'Third Way', in M. Fielding (ed.) *Taking Education Really Seriously: Four Years' Hard Labour*, ch. 16. London: Routledge-Falmer.

Elliott, J. and MacDonald, B. (eds) (1975) *People in Classrooms*. Norwich: CARE Occasional Publications No. 2, University of East Anglia.

Elliott, J. and Zamorski, B. (eds) (2002) *Teachers' Research Disaffection*, special issue of *Pedagogy, Culture and Schooling* devoted to collaborative research within the Norwich Area Consortium.

Gutteridge, D. (2002) Identifying the disaffected, in J. Elliott and B. Zamorski (eds) *Teachers Research Disaffection*, special issue of *Pedagogy, Culture and Schooling* devoted to collaborative research within the Norwich Area Consortium.

Hammersley, M. (1997) Educational research and teaching: a response to David Hargreaves' TTA lecture, *British Educational Research Journal*, 23(1): 141–61.

Hammersley, M. (2001) On 'systematic reviews' of research literatures: a 'narrative' response to Evans and Benfield, *British Educational Research Journal*, 27(5): 543–54.

Hargreaves, D. (1996) *Teaching as a Research-based Profession: Possibilities and Prospects*. London: TTA.

Hargreaves, D. (1997) In defence of research for evidence-based teaching: a rejoinder to Martyn Hammersley, *British Educational Research Journal*, 23(4): 405–19.

Hargreaves, D. (1999) Revitalising educational research: lessons from the past and proposals for the future, *Cambridge Journal of Education*, 29(2): 239–49.

Hillier, J., Pearson, R., Anderson, A. and Tampkin, P. (1998) *Excellence in Research on Schools*, research report 74. London: Department for Education and Employment.

Hinchliffe, G. (2001) Education or pedagogy?, *Journal of Philosophy of Education*, 35(1).

Hollingsworth, S. (ed.) (1997) *International Action Research: A Casebook for Educational Reform*. London: Falmer Press.

Hollingsworth, S. and Sockett, H. (eds) (1994) *Teacher Research and Educational Reform: Ninety-third Yearbook of the National Society for the Study of Education*. Chicago: University of Chicago Press.

Hustler, D., Cassidy, T. and Cuff, T. (eds) (1986) *Action Research in Classrooms and Schools*. Boston, MA: Allen & Unwin.

Kennedy, M. (1999) A test of some common contentions about educational research, *American Educational Research Journal*, 36(3): 511–41.

Lomax, P. (1999) Working together for educative community through research, *Research Intelligence*, 68.

O'Hanlon, C. (ed.) (1996) *Professional Development through Action Research in Educational Settings*. London: Falmer Press.

O'Hanlon, C. (2002) Reflection and action in research: is there a moral responsibility to act?, in C. Day, J. Elliott, B. Somekh and R. Winter (eds) (2002) *Theory and Practice in Action Research*, pp. 111–21. Oxford: Symposium Books.

Oakley, A. (2000) *Experiments in Knowing: Gender and Methods in the Social Sciences*. Cambridge: Polity Press.

Oakley, A. (2001) Making evidence-based practice educational, *British Educational Research Journal*, 27(5): 575–6.

Oakley, J. (2002) RHINOS – a tale of collaboration between teachers within a school to identify the passively disaffected, in J. Elliott and B. Zamorski (eds) (2002) *Teachers Research Disaffection*, special issue of *Pedagogy, Culture and Schooling* devoted to collaborative research within the Norwich Area Consortium.

Reynolds, D. (1998) *Teacher Effectiveness*, TTA Corporate Plan launch 1998–2001. London: TTA.

Sanger, J. (ed.) (1989) *The Teaching, Handling Information and Learning Project*, Library and Information research report no. 67. London: British Library.

Somekh, B. (2000) Changing conceptions of action research, in H. Altrichter and J. Elliott (eds) *Images of Educational Change*, ch. 9. Buckingham: Open University Press.

Stake, R.E. (1995) *The Art of Case Study Research*. London: Sage.

Stenhouse, L. (1975) *An Introduction to Curriculum Research and Development*. London: Heinemann.

Stenhouse, L. (1979) Using research means doing research, in H. Dahl, A. Lysne and P. Rand (eds) *Spotlight on Educational Problems*. Oslo: University of Oslo Press.

TTA (Teacher Training Agency) (1998) *Promoting Teaching as a Research and Evidence-Based Profession*, Corporate Plan launch 1998–2001. London: TTA.

Zamorski, B. and Haydn, T. (2002) Exploring the relationship between classroom management and pupil disaffection: an account of across-school collaborative research, in J. Elliott, and B. Zamorski (eds) (2002) *Teachers Research Disaffection*, special issue of *Pedagogy, Culture and Schooling* devoted to collaborative research within the Norwich Area Consortium.

12 Evaluating CPD: an overview

Daniel Muijs, Christopher Day, Alma Harris and Geoff Lindsay

The international research literature has consistently shown that professional development is an essential component of successful school development and teacher growth, well-being and success (Hargreaves 1994; Day 1999). It has confirmed that where teachers are able to reflect, access new ideas, experiment and share experiences within school cultures in which leaders encourage appropriate levels of challenge and support, there is greater potential for school and classroom improvement. Improving schools invest in the development of their staff and create opportunities for teachers to collaborate and to share best practice (McLaughlin and Talbert 2001). Evidence also suggests that attention to teacher learning can impact directly and indirectly upon improvements in student attitudes to learning, teaching processes and achievement. Where teachers have clear professional identities, have intrinsic as well as extrinsic rewards for their work, they are more satisfied and expand and develop their own teaching repertoires. In relation to their moral and instrumental purposes, it is more likely that they will provide sustained commitment and an increased range of learning opportunities for students (Joyce *et al.* 1998). In short, the research literature demonstrates that continuing professional development (CPD) can have a positive, direct impact on curriculum and pedagogy, as well as on teachers' sense of efficacy and their relationships with students (Talbert and McLaughlin 1994).

Introduction

CPD is increasingly seen as a key part of the career development of all professionals. It is a shared responsibility with employers because it serves the interests of both, though not necessarily simultaneously. The concept is often left ill-defined, however, being in many cases conflated with the related concepts of in-service training and on the job learning. Both are more limited than CPD, as CPD can encompass a wide variety of approaches and teaching and learning styles in a variety of settings (inside or outside of the workplace). It is distinguishable from the broader concept of lifelong learning, which can include all sorts of learning. It is seen primarily as being related to people's professional identities and roles, and the goals of the organization they are working for (Galloway 2000).

In this chapter we use Day's (1999) definition of CPD. While many others have been formulated over the years, they tend to focus upon the different kinds of activities needed to maintain or enhance, 'knowledge, expertise and competence', (Hoyle 1980; Joyce and Showers 1980; Madden and Mitchell 1993). In contrast Day's definition focuses upon teachers' learning within their broader change purposes, highlighting the complexities of these. It thus provides an extended conceptual framework within which to consider models for evaluating CPD:

> Professional development consists of all natural learning experiences and those conscious and planned activities which are intended to be of direct or indirect benefit to the individual, group or school, which contribute, through these, to the quality of education in the classroom. It is the process by which, alone and with others, teachers review, renew and extend their commitment as change agents to the moral purposes of teaching; and by which they acquire and develop critically the knowledge, skills and emotional intelligence essential to good professional thinking, planning and practice with children, young people and colleagues throughout each phase of their teaching lives.
>
> (Day 1999: 4)

It is clear from this definition that any evaluation of CPD must take account of its indirect and direct impact upon different stakeholders, of its effects not only upon knowledge and skills but also upon commitment and moral purposes, and upon the thinking and planning as well as the actions of teachers, taking account of their life and career phases and the contexts in which they work. However, the research evidence about evaluation practices in relation to CPD shows that:

- it rarely focuses upon longer term or indirect benefits;
- it rarely differentiates between different kinds of benefits in relation to different purposes in the definition (i.e. moral purposes, relevance to phase of development, change, thinking, emotional intelligence);
- it is often based upon individual self-report which relates to the quality and relevance of the experience and not its outcomes;
- it usually occurs summatively, after the learning experience, rather than formatively, so that it can be used to enhance that experience;

- it rarely attempts to chart benefits to the school or department (possibly because these are often not explicitly contained within its purposes).

It is clear that evaluation practice is most useful when it explores the interrelationship between the impact on teacher, school and pupil. This interrelationship is complex but it is important to recognize that the outcomes of CPD are not solely confined to the individual. Evaluation processes should be sophisticated enough to track multiple changes and different levels of impact in relation to the orientation of CPD.

Whatever the learning model and context, the purposes, processes and outcomes of CPD are problematic because of the dynamic interaction with teachers' own implicit and explicit, conscious and unconscious learning and development needs, which themselves are always 'filtered' by personal, school and environmental factors. In other words, what is learnt from a learning activity or experience may be different from that which is intended to be learnt. For this reason, we prefer to characterize different CPD activities or 'orientations' (see Figure 12.1).

For example, CPD may be primarily oriented towards school needs (school focused), pupil needs (pupil focused), policy implementation needs (policy focused), teacher needs (teacher focused) but have explicit (and sometimes

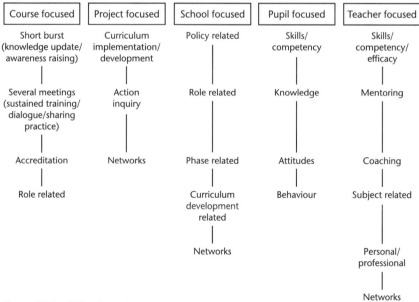

Figure 12.1   CPD orientations

unpredictable) secondary orientations. A focus on one does not preclude learning which relates to others. In practice, most evaluative strategies used to gauge the impact of CPD are frequently low level and do not take into account the different purposes, outcomes and levels of impact associated with various forms of CPD.

A further aspect of purpose concerns the use of CPD as part of a formal accreditation process. Many professions, whether regulated by statute or through a professional society, now require individual professionals to demonstrate that they are maintaining, at least, and preferably developing, their competence. The requirement for evidence of CPD is increasingly being specified. For example, the newly instituted Health Professions Council, as the regulatory body, plans to institute requirements for CPD at the level of individual registrants from 2006 (Health Professions Council 2003). Many professional bodies have also set up systems of monitoring (e.g. the British Psychological Society in 2002). Statutory regulation of the teaching profession has only recently been instituted, through the General Teaching Council. Although there is currently no specific requirement for teachers to provide evidence of maintaining and developing their competence, but evidence from other professions suggests this is likely to occur in the near future.

The importance of formal professional regulation of CPD lies in the requirement for evidence of having undertaken CPD and more importantly, of the individual professional's competence having been maintained/improved. In this case, the evaluation of CPD takes on greater importance. For example, adjudication of complaints about individuals' competence may require evidence of the effectiveness of CPD undertaken.

Lieberman (1996: 187) provides a classified list of practices that encourage development which 'moves teachers beyond simply hearing about new ideas or frameworks for understanding teaching practice'. Usefully, she identifies three settings in which such practices occur:

1 Direct teaching (e.g. conferences, courses, workshops, consultations).
2 Learning in school (e.g. peer coaching, critical friendships, mentoring action research, task-related planning teams).
3 Learning out of school (e.g. networked learning communities, visits to other schools, subject/phase networks, school-university partnerships).

Most CPD models and practices emphasize formal CPD programmes and activities. However, Knight (2002) argues that current learning theories pointing to the situated nature of learning suggest that this emphasis on formally delivered CPD may need to be adjusted to allow more scope for, and set more value on, informal on the job learning, the importance of which is not currently recognized. More departmentally or subject-based CPD (in which teachers choose new pedagogical techniques to put into practice and present to each other, talk about a teaching topic and see what ideas exist in the group about it, and audit who does what and when) is posited as an alternative by Knight (2002). In this way departments or subject areas can become locations where teachers build a shared repertory of practice, drawing on the implicit and explicit knowledge and skills already existing in the group. These kinds of non-formal learning which emphasize the need to build on teachers' practical knowledge will require internally and externally applied forms of evaluation.

Evaluation models, therefore, must take account of the settings in which CPD occurs. Models for the effective evaluation of CPD (that is, that which will further benefit planning, models, strategies, outputs and outcomes) also need to be designed so that they will be able to relate to different:

- purposes (e.g. maintenance, improvement, change);
- locations (e.g. on/off site);
- impact of learning models used (e.g. didactic, collaborative);
- outcomes (e.g. direct/indirect benefits for school, department, teacher, classroom, pupil).

One way of framing evaluation in terms of the orientations of CPD and possible benefits to the organization and/or individual teacher is provided by Day (1999) (see Figure 12.2), although it does not deal with the difficult (and possibly intractable) relationship between teacher learning and pupil learning and achievement.

Effective CPD

A key factor in ensuring effective CPD is matching appropriate professional development provision to particular professional needs. This 'fit' between the developmental needs of the teacher and the selected activity is critically important in ensuring that there is a positive impact at the school and class-room level (Hopkins and Harris 2001). Where staff development opportunities are poorly conceptualized, insensitive to the concerns of individual participants and make little effort to relate learning experiences to workplace conditions, they make little impact upon teachers or their pupils (Day 1999). Although there have been claims that CPD needs to be linked to both individual and organizational goals if both individual and organizational change are to be achieved (Jones and Fear 1994), from the perspective of our definition of CPD, it is clear that there will be regular occasions during the life cycle of organizations and at particular times of national reform when these needs will predominate, and times in individual teachers' career development

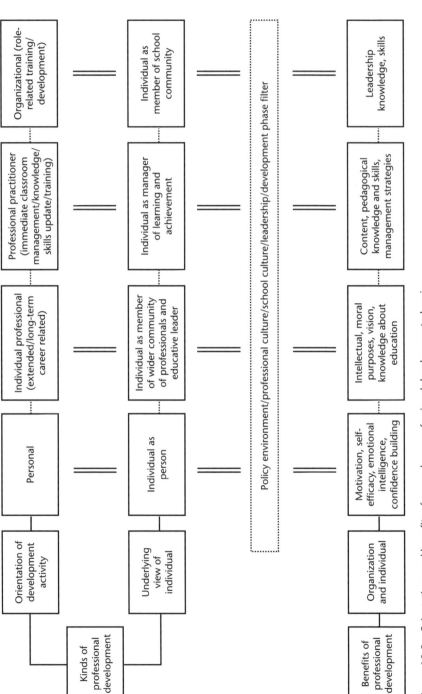

Figure 12.2 Orientations and benefits of career-long professional development planning

when their needs must prevail. Needs assessment at both these levels is necessary (Day 1991). It is plausible that if only individual goals are considered there is a risk that CPD may not result in school improvement, and may run counter to organizational philosophies and objectives; or, if organizational goals totally dominate, then teachers can become frustrated and less motivated to put CPD into practice (Edmonds and Lee 2001). However, this suggests that schools are as yet far from becoming the learning communities which research shows provide the most effective learning and achievement for all.

Guskey (1994), reviewing research on professional development, highlights the following key considerations in planning effective CPD:

1   Change is both an individual and organizational process. CPD needs to focus on the classroom level, but also needs to ensure that school culture and structures support the CPD effort.
2   Plan large-scale change, but do so incrementally to minimize chances of failure.
3   Work in teams to help alleviate the fear of change, but make sure that the teams are not too large, as the risk exists that too much time is wasted on meetings rather than action.
4   Include procedures for feedback on results, especially information that the new method seems to be working, as change in affective attitudes often follows changes in outcomes, that in turn follow from changes in behaviour.
5   Provide continuing follow-up, support and pressure, especially during the early phases of implementation when most problems will be encountered. It takes significant on the job practice and support if new practice is to become habitual.
6   Integrate programmes with existing initiatives, to avoid innovation overload.

As Guskey points out, however, effectiveness of professional development is context-specific and over time there is a need for an optimal mix of CPD experiences which take into account teachers' life stage and career development, along with school-identified needs (Day 1991).

Evaluating CPD: limitations and levels

Evaluation is as basic to professional development as it is to education. Unfortunately, as is so often the case in education, systematic evaluations of professional development programs are rarely undertaken ... Millions of dollars have been provided in the name of faculty professional development, but the quality of these programs goes virtually unchallenged.

(Clare 1976: 1)

As the above quote illustrates, most current evaluation of CPD falls short in a number of ways and areas. Guskey (2000: 8–10) suggests that these limitations can be summarized as follows:

1   Most 'evaluation' consists merely of summarizing the activities undertaken as part of the professional development programme: what courses were attended, how many credits accrued etc. This clearly gives no indication of the effectiveness of the activities undertaken, making this form of data collection inadequate as a means of looking at the effects of CPD.

2   Where some evaluation does exist, this usually takes the form of participant satisfaction questionnaires. Obviously, this allows one to gauge whether participants consider the event to have been enjoyable and successful, but does not engage with issues such as gains in knowledge or changes in practice expected from professional development, and certainly does not evaluate whether there have been changes in student outcomes.

3   Evaluations are also typically brief, one-off events, often undertaken post hoc. As most meaningful change will tend to be long term, and many professional development activities will take place over a longer period of time, evaluation efforts need to reflect this and likewise take place over time. Evaluation will also need to be built in, to run alongside professional development activities.

A recent study of CPD activity in England (Edmonds and Lee 2001) similarly found that in most cases evaluation took the form of a feedback sheet that was completed by teachers, and which included questions on delivery, content, whether they felt the course had met its objectives, and in some cases whether it was cost-effective and was likely to impact on teaching and learning. Other forms of follow-up were unusual, with actual effects on teaching and learning hardly ever being studied, and long-term monitoring of impact usually not present. Teachers reported that they thought CPD improved teaching and learning, but were unable to provide hard evidence of its impact.

This lack of attention to the evaluation of CPD is by no means limited to the education sector. Other professions, that likewise attach a lot of importance to CPD and training, show similar concerns for the lack of evidence collected on the outcomes of CPD. One example is dentistry, where in a recent article Grace (2001) expressed concern about the lack of evaluation of the impact or outcomes of training. In addition, it is important to recognize the different levels at which the potential impact of CPD can be gauged. Guskey's (2000) model offers a particularly helpful way of thinking about gauging impact at different levels, and may be related directly to different orientations and intended outcomes.

Level 1: participants' reactions

Currently this is the most common and easily collectable form of evaluative evidence. However, in many ways it is also the least informative, as participants' reactions to the CPD tend to be impressionistic and highly subjective. Questions addressed at Level 1 will include whether the participants enjoyed the event and thought it was useful, whether it addressed their needs, was well-presented and well-organized, and so on. Three main types of question can be answered using this approach: content questions (e.g. were issues addressed relevant, was the material pitched at an appropriate level), process questions (e.g. was the session leader well prepared, were the materials suitable) and context questions (e.g. was the room the right size or temperature) (Guskey 2000). As can be seen from these questions, while they address possible prerequisites of professional development that can facilitate CPD leading to change, they do not themselves measure or guarantee this.

Level 2: participants' learning from CPD

Level 2 in Guskey's framework comprises participants' learning from CPD. There are several types of learning (cognitive, affective or behavioural) that can result from CPD. Harland and Kinder (1997) provide a more detailed description of outcomes at this level, distinguishing informational outcomes; new awareness, knowledge and skills as cognitive outcomes and value congruence outcomes; and motivational and attitudinal outcomes as affective outcomes. Knight (2002) distinguishes two main types of knowledge: procedural/ practical knowledge (lower-level skills) and declarative/propositional knowledge (higher-order knowledge, including knowledge of facts, abstract knowledge of principles and abstract knowledge of ideas). These different types of knowledge are acquired and modified in different ways, thus probably requiring different methods of evaluation. As well as specific knowledge and skills and affective outcomes, CPD may result in a renewed commitment of teachers as change agents, and in renewed or extended moral purpose. These outcomes are crucial to teacher effectiveness, and need to be taken into account at this level of evaluation.

Level 3: organizational support and change

Guskey's third level of evaluation concerns organizational support and change. It is clear from the research on school improvement and the growing body of literature on change that CPD programmes are unlikely to have a lasting effect without organizational support. A supportive school ethos and an expectation that all teachers will engage in CPD have been found to be important factors in securing change as a result of CPD (Edmonds and Lee 2001). CPD activities have been found to transfer more easily into changed behaviours and teaching practices if there is a good fit with individuals' professional and personal values, and if professional development approaches already exist in the organization (Knight 2002). As well as being important in leading to the success of CPD programmes, organizational change can often be a prime goal of such programmes. Therefore, organizational-level outcomes and support are important parts of CPD evaluation, since they have an impact upon motivation on the one hand and sustainability of change on the other. Issues such as alignment of the programme to organizational policies, organizational support for the programme (especially from leadership), organizational resources provided to the programme (including, crucially, time), organizational barriers to the successful completion of the programme and general organizational effectiveness and culture (see school effectiveness literature) are all important aspects in this regard (Guskey 2000).

Level 4: participants' use of new knowledge and skills

When a CPD programme is directly intended to change practice, it is essential to evaluate whether participants are actually using the new knowledge and skills acquired. Evaluation of this level will have to take place after a reasonable time, which will depend on the complexity of the knowledge or skills to be acquired and the amount of time participants have had to develop and practise these skills (Guskey 2000; Grace 2001). It is also important to take into account the fact that there are phases that most learners go through before implementation and levels of use of a particular learned skill. These are described by Hall and Hord (1987) as non-use, orientation (information seeking), preparation, mechanical use of the skill (day to day), routine use of the skill (establishes pattern of use), refinement (varies use depending on context), integration (coordinates use with colleagues to gain greater impact) and renewal (re-evaluates quality of use and modifies to increase impact). Not all learners will reach all levels of use. Crucial in evaluating use is determining exactly what counts as what level of use, and how this will be measured. Well defined critical indicators are needed (e.g. 'asks pupils to explain their answers throughout the lesson'). Once critical indicators have been defined, ways must be found of measuring them. Level of use will have to be defined differently depending on goals, and can range from simple use or non-use distinctions to more subtle gradations of use (e.g. non-use, novice use, expert use). Critical indicators turn concepts into practically measurable variables.

Level 5: student outcomes

The fifth level identified by Guskey is the one least likely to be measured in evaluations at present, but also the one that is most important because it assesses the impact on student learning. Student learning can be defined and measured in a number of ways. A first distinction is between cognitive outcomes, such as mathematical attainment, and non-cognitive outcomes, such as attitudes to school. Both require different methods to determine programme effects (Guskey 2000).

The most common form of measuring cognitive outcomes is through testing. Standardized and non-standardized testing forms a key part of the educational system, and is usually considered to provide the most reliable measure of cognitive outcomes (Muijs and Reynolds 2000). As well as cognitive outcomes, non-cognitive outcomes can often be the goal of interventions. CPD can aim to change teaching in ways that improve pupils' enjoyment of the subject, attitudes to school or self-esteem. Many different non-cognitive outcomes exist, and consequently there are many different ways of measuring such outcomes. Psychometrically valid, externally developed scales exist for most affective outcomes (for example, Harter's Self-Perception Profile for Children and Marsh's Self-Description Questionnaire for measuring pupil self-concept). Qualitative measures can also be gathered, such as interviews with pupils, which may be most useful with younger children, with whom standardized instruments often appear unreliable (Muijs forthcoming).

Guskey suggests that when designing CPD evaluations one should work backwards, starting with Level 5, both in planning the CPD activity and its evaluation. This ensures that the final goal of improving pupil outcomes is central to the process.

While Guskey suggests five levels of evaluation, starting with participants reactions, following both Stake (1967) and Stufflebeum (1983), we would add an antecedent level, focusing on the prior conditions of the evaluation. These would include motivations behind and reasons for the professional development programme/activity, why the particular programme was chosen, or why it was developed in a particular way, policy backgrounds and other factors affecting the choice and development of the programme.

Lacking in all the models mentioned above, and in almost all evaluations, is the issue of the cost-effectiveness of CPD. As Benfield *et al.* (2001) rightly point out in the context of medical practice, CPD should not be undertaken if the costs to the system outweigh the benefits. Also, if other ways of raising the performance teachers and students are more cost-effective, doubts would have to be raised over the validity of conducting CPD. It would also be useful to know the cost-effectiveness of different modes of CPD. Currently we know little.

Evaluating CPD: possibilities and practicalities

It is clear that there are a wide variety of levels at which CPD can be evaluated, and that because of the influences upon, and the complexities and unpredictabilities of, learning, change and development, the most useful evaluations will need to combine methods, marrying the rigour of quantitative measures to the deeper formative information provided by qualitative methods – a process sometimes known as 'holistic' evaluation (Clare 1976). Especially where CPD programmes are complex and multi-faceted, this needs to be reflected in evaluation strategies, with methods appropriate for each component (Schwartz *et al.* 1977). In addition, any evaluation design needs to take careful account of the important relationship between purposes and outcomes in order for evaluation processes to be meaningful.

Effective evaluation of CPD will usually need to serve two main purposes: summative evaluation (does the programme/activity improve outcomes?) and formative assessment (how can the programme/activity be improved?). These two goals can best be served by collecting data in different ways. Test scores, for example, are often used summatively, while interview and survey data can be used to guide formative evaluation (Scannell 1996). In order to be authentic (i.e. take account of the different levels identified by Guskey and minimize bias) data needs to be collected from a variety of stakeholders rather than just one group, and a variety of research methods need to be used (Smith 2002).

Evaluation can be carried out either entirely in-house or with the help of external experts. When in-house evaluation is carried out, evaluation capacity must exist, and where necessary be developed through professional development (Trevisan 2002). When external evaluation is preferred, it is important to ensure that participants contribute to evaluation design and activities, as use of evaluation results has often been found to be patchy where this is not the case (Torres and Preskill 2002). Furthermore, it has been found that where participants themselves are not involved in developing evaluation, they are less likely to take account of evaluation information to change their practice (Gordan 1997).

For evaluation to be most effective in contributing to learning through CPD, feedback should be provided to participants wherever possible (Schwartz *et al.* 1977). Providing continuous feedback that is useful to programme developers is also one way of reducing 'excessive evaluation anxiety', which has been found to be a problem in many evaluations. Characterized by conflict with evaluators, refusal to cooperate, stalling and resistance and trying to hide programme weaknesses, evaluation anxiety often results from negative past experience of evaluation, high personal stakes in the innovation and fear of negative consequences. Evaluation anxiety is strongest where the evaluation is conducted by external agents or senior management. As well as providing continuous feedback, evaluation anxiety can be reduced by stressing positive as well as negative outcomes, involving stakeholders in the evaluation, clearly explaining the purpose of the evaluation and discussing prior experiences of evaluation with stakeholders (Donaldson *et al.* 2002).

Evaluation at its best will provide not just an overview of whether CPD itself has been successful, but will also have strong positive learning benefits to teachers in the school (Knight 2002). It is important, however, to remember that CPD evaluation should not become too burdensome a procedure on schools and teachers involved in the process. Good evaluation should be built in from the outset of the professional development programme or activity, and not added on at the end (Guskey 2002).

Final comment

One of the most striking findings from the growing school improvement research base is that improving schools are marked by a constant interchange of professional dialogue at both a formal and informal level. Similarly, schools that are improving invest in professional development and are able to engage staff in various forms of professional learning. It has been argued that creating a collaborative professional learning environment for teachers is the 'single most important factor' for successful school improvement and 'the first order of business' for those seeking to enhance the effectiveness of teaching and learning (Eastwood and Louis 1992: 215). Consequently, it would seem imperative that schools adopt evaluative approaches to CPD that not only accurately gauge learning outcomes at organizational, teacher and student level but that also accurately assess professional learning needs. At present, such evaluation mechanisms do not appear to be in place with respect to most CPD, evaluation usually being limited to simple satisfaction checklists. It would appear from this review that evaluative practices need to be much more sophisticated and fine-grained to capture the complexity of organizational and individual change whether evolutionary, incremented or transformational. A range of evaluative approaches are needed that match Guskey's (2000) five levels and have the potential to give meaningful formative and summative feedback to schools and teachers. These need to be adapted to the aims and goals of CPD. Without such evaluative approaches, gauging the relative effectiveness of different forms of CPD will remain elusive, and by implication investment in forms of CPD that have little or no impact on the teacher and learner will remain a real possibility.

Table 12.1 A framework for evaluation

Purposes focus	Participant satisfaction	Change in participant views/attitudes	Improve participant knowledge/skills	Change participant behaviour	Organizational change	Student outcome
Course focused	Satisfaction questionnaires at end of or during course Participant interviews at end of or during course Learning logs during course	Participant questionnaires at start and end of course or later Participant interviews at start and end of course or later Learning logs during course	Participant questionnaires at start and end of course or later Participant interviews at start and end of course or later Learning logs during course Tests at end of course (and start)	Participant questionnaires following course (at remove) Participant interviews following course (at remove) Logs or journals following course (at remove) Interviews with students following course (at remove) Direct observation following course (at remove)	Participant questionnaires following course (at remove) Questionnaires to other stakeholders (management, students) Participant interviews following course (at remove) Interviews with other stakeholders (peers, management, students) Collection of documentary evidence (minutes, planning documents etc.)	Tests (state-mandated, standardised or specific) Alternative forms of assessment (portfolios, performance etc.) Interview with learners Non-cognitive outcome measures (self-esteem scales, attitude scales etc.)

Project focused	Ongoing questionnaires during project	Ongoing learner questionnaires	Ongoing learner questionnaires	Ongoing learner questionnaires	Direct observation following course (at remove)	Tests (state-mandated, standardised or specific)
	Ongoing participant interviews during project	Ongoing learner interviews	Ongoing learner interviews	Ongoing learner interviews	Ongoing questionnaires	Alternative forms of assessment (portfolios, performance etc.)
	Reflective learning logs and journals during project	Reflective learning logs during project	Reflective learning logs during course	Reflective logs or journals	Questionnaires to other stakeholders (management, students)	Interviews with learners
				Interviews with students	Ongoing learner interviews	Non-cognitive outcome measures (self-esteem scales, attitude scales etc.)
				Direct observation	Interviews with other stakeholders (peers, management, students)	
					Collection of documentary evidence (minutes, planning documents etc.)	

Continued

Table 12.1 Continued

Purposes focus	Participant satisfaction	Change in participant views/attitudes	Improve participant knowledge/skills	Change participant behaviour	Organizational change	Student outcomes
School focused	Questionnaires, either ongoing or at start/end of activity depending on nature of CPD (e.g. sabbaticals or networks)	Questionnaires, either ongoing or at start/end of activity depending on nature of CPD (e.g. sabbaticals or networks)	Questionnaires, either ongoing or at start/end of activity depending on nature of CPD (e.g. sabbaticals or networks)	Questionnaires, either ongoing or at start/end of activity depending on nature of CPD (e.g. sabbaticals or networks)	Ongoing questionnaires	Tests (state-mandated, standardised or specific)
					Questionnaires to other stakeholders (management, students) Ongoing learner interviews	Alternative forms of assessment (portfolios, performance etc.)

Teacher focused						
Satisfaction questionnaires Participant interviews Learning logs	Interviews either ongoing or at start/end of activity depending on nature of CPD Reflective learning logs and journals	Interviews either ongoing or at start/end of activity depending on nature of CPD Reflective learning logs and journals Tests where suitable Teacher questionnaires Teacher interviews Learning logs	Interviews either ongoing or at start/end of activity depending on nature of CPD Reflective learning logs and journals Interviews with students Direct observation	Interviews with other stakeholders (peers, management, students) Collection of documentary evidence (minutes, planning documents etc.)	Interviews with learners Non-cognitive outcome measures (self-esteem scales, attitude scales etc.)

A possible framework that would allow educators to select a suitable evaluation mechanism for CPD experiences or events is shown in Table 12.1. This framework recognizes that CPD can have numerous outcomes, can operate at different levels (often simultaneously), and that different methods (both qualitative and quantitative) are suitable for this purpose.

Acknowledgement

We are grateful to the DfES in England for allowing us to draw upon some of the work we are currently undertaking as part of a DfES funded project ('Evaluating the Impact of CPD').

References

Benfield, C.R., Morris, Z.S., Bullock, A.D. and Frame, J.W. (2001) The benefits and costs of continuing professional development (CPD) for general dental practice: a discussion, *European Journal of Dental Education*, 5: 47–52.

Clare, R. (1976) Evaluation: the misunderstood, maligned, misconstrued, misused and missing component of professional development. Paper presented at the POD Network Faculty Development Conference, Airlie, Virginia, October.

Day, C. (1991) Quality assurance and professional development, *British Journal of In-Service Education*, 17(3): 189–95.

Day, C. (1999) *Developing Teachers: The Challenges of Lifelong Learning*. London: Falmer Press.

Donaldson, S.I., Gooler. L.E. and Scriven, M. (2002) Strategies for managing evaluation anxiety: toward a psychology of program evaluation, *The American Journal of Evaluation*, 23(3): 261–73.

Eastwood, K.W. and Louis, K.S. (1992) Restructuring that lasts: managing the performance dip, *Journal of School Leadership*, 2(2): 212–24.

Edmonds, S. and Lee, B. (2001) Teacher feelings about continuing professional development, *Education Journal*, 61, 28–9.

Galloway, S. (2000) Issues and challenges in continuing professional development, in S. Galloway (ed.) *Continuous Professional Development: Looking Ahead*. Proceedings of a symposium by the Centre on Skills, Knowledge and Organizational Performance, Oxford, May.

Gordan, M. (1997) Cutting the Gordian knot: a two-part approach to the evaluation and professional development of residents, *Academic Medicine*, 72(10): 876–80.

Grace, M. (2001) Evaluating the training, *British Dental Journal*, 191(5): 229–50.

Guskey, T.R. (1994) Professional development in education: in search of the optimal mix. Paper presented at the annual meeting of the American Educational Research Association, New Orleans.

Guskey, T.R. (2000) *Evaluating Professional Development*. Thousand Oaks, CA: Corwin Press.

Guskey, T.R. (2002) Does it make a difference? Evaluating professional development, *Educational Leadership*, 59(6): 45–51.

Hall, G.E. and Hord, S.M. (1987) *Change in Schools: Facilitating the Process*. Albany, NY: SUNY Press.

Hargreaves, A. (1994) *Changing Teachers: Changing Times*. London: Cassell.

Harland, J. and Kinder, K. (1997) Teacher continuing professional development: framing a model of outcomes, *British Journal of In-service Education*, 23(1): 71–84.

Health Professions Council (2003) *Key Decisions: HPC Consultation 2002*. London: Health Professions Council.

Hopkins, D. and Harris, A. (2001) *Creating the Conditions for Teaching and Learning: A Handbook of Staff Development Activities*. London: David Fulton.

Hoyle, E. (1980) Professional development of teachers, in E. Hoyle and J. Megarry (eds) *World Year Book of Education*. New York: Nichols Publishing.

Jones, N. and Fear, N. (1994) Continuing professional development: perspectives from human resource professionals, *Personnel Review*, 23(8): 49–60.

Joyce, B. and Showers, B. (1980) Improving inservice training: the messages of research, *Educational Leadership*, 37(5): 379–85.

Joyce, B., Calhoun, E. and Hopkins, D. (1998) *Models of Teaching: Tools For Learning*. Buckingham: Open University Press.

Knight, P. (2002) A systemic approach to professional development: learning as practice, *Teaching and Teacher Education*, 18(3): 229–41.

Lieberman, A. (1996) Creating intentional learning communities, *Educational Leadership*, 54(3): 51–5.

Madden, C.A. and Mitchell, V.A. (1993) *Professions, Standards and Competence: A Survey of Continuing Education for the Professions*. Bristol: University of Bristol.

McLaughlin, M. and Talbert, J. (2001) *Professional Communities and the Work of High School Teaching*. Chicago: University of Chicago Press.

Muijs, R.D. (forthcoming) Measuring teacher effectiveness, in D. Hopkins and D. Reynolds (eds) *The Learning Level*. London: Routledge-Falmer.

Muijs, R.D. and Reynolds, D. (2000) *Effective Teaching: Evidence and Practice*. London: Paul Chapman.

Scannell, D.P. (1996) Evaluating professional development schools: the challenge of an imperative, *Contemporary Education*, 67(4): 241–3.

Schwartz, H., Lichon, D., James, K., Melniz, C. and Olson, G. (1977) The use of multiple research methodologies to evaluate an inservice curriculum. Paper presented at the annual meeting of the American Educational Research Association, New York.

Smith, C.L. (2002) Using continuous system level assessment to build school capacity, *The American Journal of Evaluation*, 23(3): 307–19.

Stake, R.E. (1967) The countenance of educational evaluation, *Teachers College Record*, 68(7): 523–40.

Stufflebeum, D.L. (1983) The CIPP model for program evaluation, in G.F. Madaus, M.S. Scriven and D.L. Stufflebeum (eds) *Evaluation Models: Viewpoints on Educational and Human Services Evaluation*. Boston, MA: Kluwer-Nijhoff.

Talbert, J. and McLaughlin, M. (1994) Teacher professionalism in local school contexts, *American Journal of Education*, 102(2): 123–53.

Torres, R.T. and Preskill, H. (2002) Evaluation and organizational learning: past, present and future, *The American Journal of Evaluation*, 23(3): 387–95.

Trevisan, M.S. (2002) Evaluation capacity in K-12 school counseling programs, *The American Journal of Evaluation*, 23(3): 291–305.

Index

Page numbers in *italic* refer to tables, those in **bold** denote main discussion. *n* indicates a chapter note.

THE ACTIVIST TEACHING PROFESSION

Judyth Sachs

This is a thoughtful, provocative and important book. Clear, concise, articulate and pulling no punches, Judyth Sachs maps out an agenda for a new 'transformative professionalism' which celebrates the complexities of teacher identities and work, and acknowledges the tensions between standards of accountability and autonomy. She argues persuasively for a reorientation of policy from managerial to a democratic and radical reconceptualisation of teacher education programmes and notions of teacher professionalism. Her text, richly supported by case studies of practice, will appeal to teachers and teacher educators worldwide who are committed to principles of active participation, trust and community.

Professor Chris W. Day, University of Nottingham

- What forms of professionalism are shaping the teaching profession?
- How can the concept of teacher professionalism be revitalized so that it is relevant to the needs and aspirations of teachers working in increasingly difficult and constantly changing work environments?

The Activist Teaching Profession examines the issue of teacher professionalism as a social and political strategy to enhance the status and activities of the teaching profession. The book is contextualized within current debates, both government policy and scholarly, about teacher professionalism. Evidence to support the development of alternative forms of teacher professionalism utilizing new structural arrangements with various stakeholders through collaboration and cooperation, is represented using examples from Australia and elsewhere. Teacher inquiry is presented as an initiative whereby teacher professionalism can be developed. A strategy for re-establishing the moral and intellectual leadership of the teaching profession along activist lines is developed in the last section of the book. Issues surrounding teacher professional identity are examined in the light of the discourses that are shaping teacher professionalism. Rethinking professional identity provides a basis for developing new forms of teacher professionalism. The Activist Teaching Profession is both a wake up call and a call to action for teachers and the community alike.

Contents

Series editor's preface – Teacher professionalism in transition – Rethinking the practice of teacher professionalism – The politics of professionalism – Preparing activist teacher professionals – Teacher research for professional renewal – Professional in practice – New professional identities for new times – The activist teacher professional – References – Index.

192pp   0 335 20818 5 (Paperback)   0 335 20819 3 (Hardback)